rds & Commons.

BRITISH PRIME MINISTERS
OF THE NINETEENTH CENTURY
POLICIES AND SPEECHES

CANNING

*

WELLINGTON

*

PEEL

*

PALMERSTON

*

DISRAELI

*

GLADSTONE

*

SALISBURY

BRITISH PRIME MINISTERS
OF THE
NINETEENTH CENTURY

Policies and Speeches

By

JOSEPH HENDERSHOT PARK

NEW YORK UNIVERSITY PRESS
WASHINGTON SQUARE · NEW YORK

GEOFFREY CUMBERLEGE · OXFORD UNIVERSITY PRESS
LONDON

Printed in the United States of America

To My Wife

LAURA MARGARET WOOD PARK

8007

For out of olde feldis, as men saith,
    Cometh this newe corn fro yere to yere:
And out of olde bokis, in good faith,
    Cometh this newe science that men lere.

Preface

STUDENTS who are imbued with the idea of obtaining happiness and progress for humanity by governmental activity need to beware lest they too easily fall prey to dogmas. The judgments of one generation are apt to give way to the judgments of another: individuals who learn by rote and accept without question the conclusions of any so-called school of thought will hardly give great assistance to the solution of the difficulties that beset society. Rather are they more likely to be helpful with suggestions if they have carefully examined the teachings, the experiments, and the experiences of leaders who have faced a wide variety of problems. Specifically, it is much less useful to know what Gladstone's views were on a particular subject than to know the reasons that led him to those views. And the best way to learn those reasons is to let Gladstone speak for himself.

Selections which appear in these pages have been made with the thought that they express ideas general enough in their implications to be of interest even to the present, that they are related to historical developments which history volumes still emphasize, and that without serious cutting they represent rather completely the sentiments of the speakers and therefore convey to the reader the impression of the personality behind the speech in a way that shorter sections bearing upon a greater variety of topics would fail to do. Many of the speeches can be obtained elsewhere only with considerable effort. The writer feels justified, therefore, in presenting them in what he deems to be convenient form and with an introduction which, he hopes, may give the proper setting. He has felt that it is inadvisable to substitute consistency in spelling, capitalization, and punctuation for older usages which by the very lack of uniformity may appear to befit the speakers, the times, and the subjects of discussion.

The writer thanks two friends of long standing for performing the task of reading the manuscript and offering comments and suggestions concerning it: Dr. Theodore Francis Jones, professor of history at New York University, and Dr. Arnold J. Zurcher, professor of political science and head of the Institute of Public Affairs and Regional Studies of New York University.

Table of Contents

Chapter I

THE HERITAGE

Chapter I

THE HERITAGE

Society of the days of the Industrial Revolution and the French Revolution questioned, like society of succeeding days, whether its institutional developments were abreast of the social, political, and economic demands of the time. The resultant controversy was, indeed, so far from being either insignificant or limited in its inferences on government in general and the English constitution in particular that English statesmen of the nineteenth century were greatly affected. One school of thought had emphasized the necessity of accepting the solutions of the past as applicable to existing queries on social organizations; another had stressed the desirability of applying abstract reasoning to these problems.

Edmund Burke (1729-1797), because of his consummate ability as champion of the more conservative attitude, has usually been allowed to speak for those who subscribed to the first thesis.[1] He believed that the English constitution had come by historic evolution best to care for the interests and wants of the governed. He looked upon the opponents to this constitution, who, trusting in the magic power of human reason, cried out for change, as "little, shriveled, meager, hopping, loud and troublesome insects of the hour"—"half a dozen grasshoppers under a fern" making the field ring with their importunate clink. He gave oft-quoted advice to its critics, entreating them to "study it until you know how to admire it, and if you cannot know and admire, rather believe that you are dull than that the rest of the world has been imposed upon." Reformers of the constitution, he feared, would become its destroyers. Therefore, he was not favorably inclined to radical Parliamentary re-

[1] For a recent presentation of selected writings and speeches of Burke, see Ross J. S. Hoffman and Paul Levack, *Burke's Politics* (New York: Alfred A. Knopf, Inc., 1949).

form and, late in his career, was even unwilling to support measures that had been proposed for promoting religious toleration through repeal of the Test and Corporation Acts. But, on the other hand, he opposed increased authority for the king and his court. If he objected to a government by all, he was not less hostile to a government by a very small clique. The struggle of the American colonies seemed to him justifiable, accordingly, in so far as it represented a proper resistance to oppression of such a clique rather than a result of radical philosophic speculation. A use of force to subject an English people overseas would, he feared, prove fatal to English liberties elsewhere throughout the world. Like a true eighteenth-century Whig he felt that a public-spirited minority could best care for the nation's needs.

Naturally an anniversary celebration of the Glorious Revolution, which upheld French desire and interpretation of liberty, aroused Burke's anger. And in *The Reflections on the Revolution in France,* published in 1790, he clearly stated his case: Experience and not a priori reasoning had produced the British Government. The pre-eminence of property rights and a religious establishment in it prevented destructive change. The French for their part would do well to build upon their own past instead of accepting a "shameless and fearless" democracy.

The effects of the *Reflections* were tremendous: It became the embodiment and justification of conservative opinion. The King himself said that it was "a good book, a very good book; every gentleman ought to read it." It led to a break between Burke and his colleague, Fox, a leader of the Whigs and an adherent of French experiments in government. Followers of Burke acting with the Tories caused the Whigs, organized in opposition, to appear as a small faction. And it gave to the Radicals an object of attack and therefore, perhaps, acted as a unifying force for a cause it was seeking to destroy.

The radical creed of the period was expressed in the writings of Tom Paine, Mary Wollstonecraft, and in a less popular way by the works of James Mackintosh and William Godwin. Paine, hardly as fundamentally radical or as able a logician as Mary Wollstonecraft, became by the sharpness and brilliance of his attack upon Burke's thesis the symbol of the radical movement. He was a leader who seemingly represents the fulfillment of Schiller's ideal: "The pause, the central point of

thousand thousands." His *Rights of Man* stated in clear terms
the theories of political rights held by the French Revolutionists.
This pamphlet may be looked upon, indeed, as the manifesto
of the contemporary English radical societies. Questioning the
right of any generation to bind its successors and ridiculing the
vanity and presumption of governing beyond the grave as
the most insolent of all tyranny, it declared for freedom from the
burdens of the moldy past. Paine's fame was furthered by his
own activity in the affairs of both the American and the French
Revolutions. His adherents were not unwilling to improve the
national anthem by a variation of its usual phrases:

> God save great Thomas Paine,
> His "Rights of Man" proclaim
> From pole to pole.

His opponents, on the other hand, burned him in effigy frequently enough so that the event was a common sight;[2] they
wore "Tom Paine shoe nails" that they might trample him under
foot, and they purchased the famous "Tom Paine pitcher"
whereon was inscribed immediately under a serpent which possessed Paine's head the legend:

> Observe the wicked and malicious man,
> Projecting all the mischief that he can.

Several weeks earlier than the appearance of the first part of
The Rights of Man, Mary Wollstonecraft had published *A Vindication of the Rights of Men*. Disdaining Burke but following
Rousseau, she wrote that the birthright of man "is such a degree
of liberty, civil and religious, as is compatible with the liberty of
the other individuals whom he is united with in a social compact."[3] Beyond the inalienable right of liberty he possesses certain other natural rights including that of self-improvement.
Such rights, she explained, could not be exercised under an
existing English Government, the practices of which were established not on reason but on the weakness or power of the ruling
princes. "The liberty of the honest mechanic—his all—is often

[2] Cf. Walter Phelps Hall, *British Radicalism, 1791-1797* (New York:
Columbia University and Longmans, Green and Company, 1914).

[3] Mary Wollstonecraft, *Vindication of the Rights of Men* (London, 1790),
p. 7.

sacrificed to secure the property of the rich." The House of Commons as the organ of government which administered this system she considered to be corrupt and undignified. And not only would she give more opportunity to the poor, redistribute property on a more equitable basis, and reduce the authority of the monarch but she would reform the whole Parliamentary electoral process. So long as the House of Commons continued to be that dead weight of benumbing opulence "where the sheep obsequiously pursue their steps with all the undeviating sagacity of instinct," what right had Burke to deride the philosophy or activity of a French national assembly? Nurture, not nature, is, for her, the determining factor toward progress. Environment may transform the individual. This theme was developed even more pronouncedly in *A Vindication of the Rights of Woman* than in *A Vindication of the Rights of Men*.

Of other writers who adhered to radicalism, James Mackintosh is noteworthy for an apt expression of his ideas and William Godwin for the intricate philosophy of his *Political Justice,* which dogmatically visioned the perfectibility of the race and the gradual approach of a millennium, provided men were guided by principles of pure reason and freed from the incubus of existing institutions. Perhaps the increase of scientific knowledge and the progress in mechanisms in the latter part of the eighteenth century gave promise for future improvements sufficient to cause Godwin's theories a hearing among the intellectual class.

But the man who represented the government of the day chose to follow the teachings of Burke. Pitt the Younger (1759-1806) was selected, when he was twenty-four years of age, to be George III's First Minister. A worthy son of the great Whig leader, "the immortal Chatham," he was instilled with regard for the constitutional practices which, obtaining after the Glorious Revolution, emphasized Parliamentary supremacy while preserving an important place for the king in the scheme of government as well as for the idea that effective guidance of a Cabinet emanated from a brilliant leadership. Pitt won fame, in his early career, by his support of economic reform and by his interest in Parliamentary reform and such a liberal movement as the abolition of the slave trade: believing that the Prime Minister should be the person at the head of finances and finding at hand both confusion and abuses in financial affairs, he endeavored by various means to bring order out of chaos, to improve revenue, and to limit the use of royal patronage. On the question of Parliamentary reform he declared it to be his intention for 1785 to "exert his whole power and credit as a man, and as a minister, honestly and boldly, to carry such a meliorated system of representation" as might place the constitution on a footing of permanent security. As for the abolition of the slave trade, he promised his friend, William Wilberforce, to give the matter constant attention and to omit no practicable means to forward it.

But the turn of events and the burden of responsibilities so far bent Pitt toward the conservative policies of George III that it may be questioned whether the King, experienced and opinionated in politics, did not himself exert influence, before the days of the French Revolution, upon the mind and movement of the Minister who was more than twenty years his junior.[4] In time Pitt became the opponent of Parliamentary reform, strengthened conservative tendencies of the day by elevating many a squire to membership in the House of Lords, and, even if he did not give up until the early years of the new century a temperate proclivity for religious toleration, dreaded more and more the possible effects of the French Revolution upon English subjects and, with the support of the English public, suppressed associations which were proposing what he deemed radical changes in the constitution. No one can doubt that England was hard pressed in the war with France that began in 1793 and ended only with Waterloo; but many critics have questioned whether suppression was the best method of treating disaffection engendered by warfare and its concomitants and whether Pitt did justice to his own feelings when his conduct apparently inspired his successors, even in a period of peace, to follow his example in dealing with social disorder. In any case English Prime Ministers whose words are recorded herein were wont to refer at one time or another in their careers either with approval or disapproval to the phrase of Burke and the activity of Pitt.

[4] Donald Grove Barnes, *George III and William Pitt* (Stanford University: Stanford University Press, 1939), *passim*.

Chapter II

CANNING

Chapter II

CANNING

G EORGE CANNING (1770-1827), forsaking political leanings of boyhood days, avowed the wisdom which the teachings of Burke and Pitt displayed. In the grave of the latter his political allegiance had been buried, said he in 1812;[1] on the death of the former in 1797 he wrote, "There is but one event, but that is an event for the world—Burke is dead."[2] A quarter of a century later he still looked upon Burke as the manual of his politics[3] and history as the key to politics.

As, in far realms, where eastern kings are laid,
In pomp of death, beneath the cypress shade,
The perfumed lamp with unextinguished light
Flames through the vault and cheers the gloom of night:
So, mighty Burke in thy sepulchral urn,
  To fancy's view the lamp of truth shall burn.
Thither late times shall turn their reverent eyes,
Led by thy light, and by thy wisdom wise.[4]

Canning's defense of the constitution and his hostility to the radicalism of the French Revolution clearly appears in a Parliamentary speech of 1810 (page 15). By this time he had already held office both under Pitt and under the Duke of Portland, in whose administration he had presided (1807-1809) over the Foreign Office during a critical period of the war. Well known is his support of the campaign against Napoleon in Spain and his responsibility for the capture of the Danish fleet when England and Denmark were not at war. Hostility to his colleague, Lord Castlereagh, because of the latter's conduct of the war,

---

[1] *Dictionary of National Biography.*
[2] *Ibid.*
[3] Harold Temperley, *The Foreign Policy of Canning* (London: George Bell and Sons, Ltd., 1925), p. 35.
[4] From "New Morality," appearing in 1798.

11

led to a duel in 1809; and immediately thereafter Canning resigned his place, not to return to political office until 1816 and even then in the subordinate capacity of President of the (India) Board of Control. As a member of the Cabinet he supported the policy of repression the government applied to a people restless and turbulent owing to the economic disabilities under which they labored after 1815. He and his colleagues might better have attacked, it has frequently been suggested, the fundamental causes of the distress by legislative activity than have given themselves over to the passage of the famous Six Acts of 1819 [5] by which the rights of English subjects were much curtailed in a time of peace. The best explanation of his conduct is given in "Vindication of Governmental Policies" (page 21).

Canning's popularity grew when he resigned in 1820 rather than become involved in the famous official action against Queen Caroline. But the espousal of a popular cause did not lead him to accept any radical theory of Parliamentary reform. His attitude on this question is stated with finality in "Parliamentary Reform—Repeal of the Test Act" (page 43). In 1822 he accepted the seals of the Foreign Office at a time that was propitious for the activity of a skillful diplomat. Whether or not his blocking of Continental intervention in American affairs gave the opportunity for Secretary John Quincy Adams to play upon principles formulated by Canning even more cleverly than the Foreign Minister himself, it is agreed both by his contemporaries and by modern historians that in the most famous of all his speeches he vindicated his policy (cf. "Address on the King's Message Respecting Portugal," page 30). His interest in the struggle of the Greeks for independence, like his interest in the freedom of the Spanish from French coercion, played to popular enthusiasm. His course of action kept the reactionary party from complete triumph in Portugal. Moreover, his experience, his talents, and his popularity were influential in causing him to be chosen by King George IV as Prime Minister (April

[5] These were the Training Prevention Bill to keep the populace from drilling, the Misdemeanors Bill making treason trials quick and easy, the Seizure of Arms Bill increasing the authority of magistrates, a measure dealing with libels, the Seditious Meetings Prevention Bill, and the Newspaper Stamp Duties Bill.

1827) upon Lord Liverpool's retirement. Canning's ministry was short, lasting until his death in August 1827; but during this period he spoke brilliantly upon Catholic emancipation (page 38) and made clear his ideas on the question of repeal of the Test and Corporation Acts (page 43) and on a current economic problem (page 46).

Although fame from oratorical abilities came, especially for the first half of the nineteenth century, from the delivery of speeches in Parliament, Canning himself made use of both the platform (cf. "Vindication of Governmental Policies," page 21) and the press. Moreover, his own literary productions so far showed the mark of genius that it may be asked whether, had he chosen to expend his energies in this rather than in the political field, his name would not have become connotative of the highest literary attainments. As regards his effectiveness as a speaker, there seems to have been a divergence of opinion. Lord Brougham, himself a great orator of the day, declared that "his declamation, though often powerful, always beautifully ornate, never deficient in admirable diction, was certainly not of the very highest class. It wanted depth; it came from the mouth, not from the heart; and it tickled or even filled the ear rather than penetrated the bosom of the listener. The orator never seemed to forget himself and be absorbed by his theme; he was not carried away by his passions, and he carried not his audience along with him. An actor stood before us, a first-rate one no doubt, but still an actor; and we never forgot that it was a representation we were witnessing, not a real scene." [6] However as Canning's biographer [7] points out, these opinions are probably at variance with the impressions of the very great majority of those who listened to Canning. And he adds, "If ever an orator carried his audience with him, it was Mr. Canning in his celebrated reply on the Portuguese question. Never was an assembly of men warmed into a higher pitch of enthusiasm than were the members of the House of Commons when they broke up on that memorable night. He positively electrified his audience when he uttered those striking words, 'I called the

[6] Henry, Lord Brougham, *Historical Sketches of Statesmen Who Flourished in the Time of George III* (Philadelphia, 1839), II, 98.

[7] Augustus Granville Stapleton, *George Canning and His Times* (London, 1859), chap. iii.

New World into existence to redress the balance of the Old.'
The whole House was moved as if an electric shock had passed
through them; then all rose for a moment to look at him. This
effect I witnessed from under the gallery." Wilberforce thought
that he surpassed Pitt and Fox, though he acknowledged that
the lash of his wit and satire "would have fetched the hide off
a rhinoceros." And Byron called him

> Our last, our best, our only orator.

1. Defense of the Constitution

Parliamentary reform had become a vexatious problem to Pitt the Younger during the latter part of the eighteenth century. Indeed, circumstances transformed him from exponent to opponent of the proposition: in the decade of the nineties Pitt appeared to glory in attacks upon the endeavors of Charles Grey to get Parliamentary sanction for reform. These attacks emphasized arguments such as Burke used. After Pitt's death, Mr. T. Brand, inspired by the Radical, Francis Burdett, rose on May 21, 1810, to submit to the consideration of the House of Commons a motion respecting Parliamentary reform, of which he had given previous notice, declaring that a moderate reform was necessary to preserve the confidence of the people in a system of government where the existing anomalies permitted great power to proprietors of decaying and rotten boroughs and no representation at all to many opulent and populous places. He proposed the appointment of a committee to inquire into the state of the representation and to suggest what remedies might be applied to any evils that existed. During the ensuing debate Canning gave his speech on the defense of the constitution. It is to be found in Cobbett's Parliamentary Debates (XVII, 155-61).

The speech itself may appear to lack eloquence because it has been reported in the third person but it does retain, presumably, Canning's force of argument. It may be pointed out that there were frequent controversies at this period over the phraseology of a public speaker—with one editor insisting in the case of Canning's speech on Portugal that the alterations were of style and language rather than of sentiment and the shorthand writing of a reporter efficient "to the utmost degree of perfection of which it is susceptible."

Mr. *Canning* conceived the question proposed by the motion to be plainly this, whether that House should declare itself inadequate to the performance of its functions—whether it should abdicate its authority? The House would, he hoped, pause before it decided in the affirmative upon such a serious subject. To what consequences such a decision must lead, 'through what variety of untried being,' it was likely to take both the House and the country, he thought it unnecessary to describe. And for what purpose was such a dangerous experiment recommended—to conciliate truly not the sober reflecting part of the people, because he did not believe any thing of this nature was requisite to their satisfaction; no; but, a particular class, whose study it was to create agitation and make a noise about reform. For that class he could never hesitate to express his confirmed disdain. They were not deserving of any favour from that House, because for that House or the constitution they felt no solicitude. If such persons could attain their object, they would constitute such a system of popular delegation, as could not exist as a co-ordinate authority in the constitution of England. There could be no question that there existed such a party in the country, who pretended a zeal for reform but in reality sought anarchy, and, as the best mode of accomplishing their object, reviled and distrusted that House, the object of whose views was not its improvement, but its destruction: a vain, contemptible, degraded crew, who magnified themselves into the nation, and diminished the nation into a faction; who declared their own infallibility, and depreciated the judgment of all others; a body who were too weak to be respected—too despicable to be feared. But even this wretched body, though they demanded reform, declared that the reform proposed, would not prove sufficient. No, they would have the House of Commons omnipotent; they would have it every thing; all other establishments nothing; they would make it, like the rod of the prophet, swallow up all around it.

An honourable gentleman who had spoken early in the debate, (Mr. D. Giddy) had ably and satisfactorily shewn the incompatibility of any co-ordinate powers in the other branches of the legislature, with the existence of a House of Commons, such as the wildness of the democratic theory supposes—an assembly, which should be in itself the full, complete, immediate, and adequate representation and concentration of the will, the wishes and the interests of the whole nation. This is not the nature, it is not the just theory of a British House of Commons: nor is the argument of the honourable gentleman (Mr. D. Giddy) that such a House of Commons, if it existed, would draw to itself all the power of the state, the exaggeration of an enemy of reform. Friends of reform in former instances have delivered the same opinion. And one of the ablest men that ever professed the creed of parliamentary reform—a man who professed it honestly and without participating in the views and principles of the reformers of the present day—a man too honest and too enlightened, not to have changed in some degree the opinions of his youth, after the experience of the last 15 years, (he meant Sir James Mackintosh, of whom he spoke with the sincerest sentiments of esteem and friendship). Sir James Mackintosh,[8] in his most eloquent publication in defence of the early parts of the French Revolution, in discussing the question of parliamentary reform, had stated distinctly his opinion, that such would be the power and preponderance of a reformed House of Commons, that the powers of the Lords and of the Crown would be but "as dust in the balance against it." That Sir James Mackintosh now or ever seriously wished for such a reform, he (Mr. Can-

[8] See reference in chap. i. Sir James was knighted in 1803.

ning) did not believe. In him this declamation was nothing else but the ebullition of a young and ardent mind, enamoured of the fair form of ideal liberty, and of the theories, the fallaciousness of which, and the danger of which he had not then had occasion to appreciate. But what he declaimed in the sport and exuberance of a classical imagination there are those, who would now reduce to sober and fatal practice; for he had no doubt that such was the general opinion and calculation of those who now so clamourously called for reform out of doors. Therefore he would resist them, because he saw no good that could result from conceding to them, while there was too much reason to apprehend great evil. To explain the grounds of that apprehension, to shew the effects of any attempt at the practical application of theoretic notions of democratic reform, he need only refer to the cases, already quoted in support of the other side of the argument, of America and France—to illustrate the circumstance of the former his honourable friend (Mr. S. Bourne) had already quoted the authority of a writer, who, on his arrival from that country about ten years ago, was industrious in proclaiming the baneful effects of a democracy, although of late years, still more industrious in supporting those who looked for what this writer called reform.

For his own part, he would freely own, that indulging, as he did, every desire for the dignity of that House, and cherishing every rational hope for the prosperity of the people, he could never consent so to raise them above their natural level as that every other constituted establishment of the state should be "but as dust in the balance." No; he would never conciliate the reformers at such a price; and, at any expense short of that, he did not think they were to be conciliated.

The case of France, he would contend, afforded an equally strong ground of objection to the description of reform sought by designing persons out of doors, as that of America. For what, he would ask, had been the case actually in France? The reformed legislative assembly absolutely set out with the principles of revolution; but even if they had not done so; if their ideas had been purely patriotic, they were, in the wild frenzy of fantastic reformation, so strangely constituted, that it was impossible they could move in a natural orbit; it was impossible they should not run into an irregular and eccentric course, whirling every surrounding object into their dangerous deviation. Would the House follow that rash and awful example? Would they go wavering and perplexed to a Committee, without any adequate means to attain their object, or even without any adequate object to attain—without one fixed idea, except the wise notion that whatever is, is wrong, and the sober expectation that, by some lucky expedient, the right may be hit upon! There was, however, one principle to which those reformers pretended, and which of late, they appeared unusually eager to profess—a veneration for the throne itself, and an high respect for the individual by whom it was filled. But, unfortunately, that House well knew such language had not even the merit of originality. By such pretences it was, the unhappy Louis had been deceived. By such men it was he had been deluded into the notion that he had an interest separate from his people, and a place in the hearts of those who flattered that they might betray him. He hoped sincerely there was not a man in that House, who was not eager to ward off the melancholy omen. Why (said Mr. Canning) why should we embark upon this dangerous voyage? Why should we trust ourselves to this unknown ocean? We have heard that the ancient empires of the earth have been uprooted; that the most solid monarchies have been crushed; that oligarchies the best established have been destroyed, and that England alone stands erect among the ruins! And why have we so stood? because, say the reformers, we have been radically corrupt. Sir, I will not bow to the whimsical deduction; I will rather deduce from some wise distinction the source of our prosperity. Like the nations which have fallen, we have a monarchy. Like the nations which have fallen, we have an aristocracy; but unlike every one of those nations, we possess—an House of Commons! This is our proud distinction; this is the sole palladium of our salvation; and this we are now called upon to regenerate, by the mad cry of unmeaning reformation!

But, (say the discontented) the House of Commons, constituted as it now is, has hurried the nation into extravagant expenditure, and unnecessary wars. It is not the fact. There has not been a war during a century, which was not in its commencement strictly popular. The people it was who goaded the government and the House to hostility—the people it was who forced and goaded even the pacific sir Robert Walpole into the declaration of war. The people it was who at first urged the American war, and at last decried it when it became unfortunate; the people it was who encouraged the war with France, which saved this country from all the miseries entailed on that. What a pity then it was, that the House and the country at large did not become converts to the opinions of the honourable gentleman and the few by whom he was supported in opposition to that war! What a pity they were not dipped in the well of his political sagacity, that they might meet, rebaptised, all the inevitable mischievous consequences which must have followed. After having thus gone through the history of ages, the friends of reform scrutinized the present times, and passed their unqualified censure on every vote of that House, and on every member with whom they were dissatisfied. All with whom they were not pleased, had, it seemed some sinister motive. Now, even allowing this to be the case; even allowing that some extra considerations did enter into the minds of each unpopular representative, how would the reformers remedy it? Would they banish human nature from their reformed House of Commons? No, but they would banish the boroughs. Now, if they would only take the trouble to examine borough members' votes, they would find that just as many voted on the popular as on the unpopular side of the question, so they would neither lose nor gain by their reform. They might in this way alternately subtract from each side, till they had eradicated all. Decimation would be mercy compared to this plan of reform; and, indeed, whether one considered its motive or its consequences, its justice would appear exactly to correspond with its policy.

The accusations of the reformers against that House were exactly those which could be made justly against themselves, for there never yet was a state democratic and powerful, which had not a tendency to war. The compliances which they sought from the House it was impossible they ever could obtain. The House of Commons owed to the people, a manly but not a servile obedience; they should be respectful, but not enslaved; they should not watch the eye, nor bend to the nod, nor crouch to the unspoken will of the multitude, but proceed in the plain path of undeviating independence; they should act to the people as representatives, just as they should act toward their Creator as men, virtuously but freely, founding their hopes of retribution on their consciousness of honesty. He was as ready as the honourable gentleman to lament, that more liberal and solid provisions had not been made for securing the liberty of the subject, at the period of the restoration; but this made directly against the right honourable gentleman's own arguments, for Charles the second was restored chiefly by the spirit and strong impulse of the people. Let it be recollected too that it was the extent of the popular influence, which at the restoration prevented the arrangement of those provisions for the security of popular freedom, which an honourable gentleman, repeating an observation in the celebrated tract of his deceased friend (Mr. Fox,) had expressed his regret did not take place. A just sympathy with the people, and a reasonable attention to their desires, was no doubt, the duty and must ever be the inclination of that House. The people, unquestionably, could reason fairly when they had time; but as, notoriously, their first impulse was feeling, he did not think it would be politic, or for the interest of the country, to have that House quite subject to popular control.

Every class of the people he must contend was fully represented in that House, and its general conduct since the revolution, excepting the septennial act [9] of the whigs, tended to ameliorate the country. Therefore he saw no necessity for the proposed reform. As to the argument of that necessity which had been drawn from particular votes, he asked what assurance could be offered that similar votes would not take place even after the desired reform? He believed that, while human nature was unchanged, no change in the constitution of that House could guard against some improper decisions; and he could not discern, 'mid all the perils of surrounding nations, a nobler security to English independence than the established House of Commons. Should he then ungratefully now forget those benefits? Should he impoliticly fling aside all hope of future advantage, and trust to the conflicting wisdoms of a reforming committee to strike out some new and speculative system? He saw no necessity for the experiment; the House of Commons was all that the honestly patriotic could desire it. What question but here met a discussion? What grievance but here met its remedy? What man in the land so poor but here had his advocate? The experiment of reform had been tried in France and failed. They had it before their eyes. No honest visionary in this country should now be so blinded as to seek here, in the hope of benefit, what the corrupt men there sought to cover their ambition. If they did, some more cunning and ambitious visionary would take advantage of the tumult to place himself on the throne. They would soon see popular commotion end in military despotism, and find philosophical disquisitions superseded by practical oppression. "I cannot consent (said Mr. Canning) to hazard this. If I am obliged to choose between the capricious chances of an undefined committee and the ancient edifice which has so long upheld our rights, shielded our dignity, and secured our interests, I shall not hesitate—'Stet fortuna domus.'—Let the venerable fabric, which has sheltered us for so many ages, and stood unshaken through so many storms, still remain unimpaired and holy; sacred from the rash frenzy of that ignorant innovator who would tear it down, careless and incapable of any substitution."

[9] The act of 1716.

2. Vindication of Governmental Policies

This speech was delivered on March 18, 1820, at a public dinner at Liverpool in honor of Canning's re-election. It is noteworthy, as has been mentioned, for its defense of the government's repressive policies—policies which were the aftermath of the disturbances, the unrest, the agitation, and the violence following the hoped-for but unattained "peace without parallel." It may be found conveniently in Robert Walsh's Select Speeches of the Right Honourable George Canning (Philadelphia, 1844).

Short as the interval is since I last met you in this place on a similar occasion, the events which have filled up that interval have not been unimportant. The great moral disease which we then talked of as gaining ground on the community has, since that period, arrived at its most extravagant height; and, since that period, also, remedies have been applied to it, if not of permanent cure, at least of temporary mitigation.

Gentlemen, with respect to those remedies—I mean with respect to the transactions of the last short session of Parliament previous to the dissolution—I feel that it is my duty, as your representative, to render to you some account of the part which I took in that assembly to which you sent me; I feel it my duty also, as a member of the Government by which those measures were advised. Upon occasions of such trying exigency as those which we have lately experienced, I hold it to be of the very essence of our free and popular Constitution, that an unreserved interchange of sentiment should take place between the representative and his constituents; and if it accidentally happens, that he who addresses you as your representative, stands also in the situation of a responsible adviser of the Crown, I recognize in that more rare occurrence a not less striking or less valuable peculiarity of that Constitution under which we have the happiness to live,—by which a Minister of the Crown is brought into contact with the great body of the community; and the service of the King is shown to be a part of the service of the people.

Gentlemen, it has been one advantage of the transactions of the last session of Parliament, that while they were addressed to meet the evils which had grown out of charges heaped upon the House of Commons, they have also, in a great measure, falsified the charges themselves.

I would appeal to the recollection of every man who now hears me, —of any, the most careless estimator of public sentiment, or the most indifferent spectator of public events, whether any country, in any two epochs, however distant, of its history, ever presented such a

21

contrast with itself as this country in November, 1819, and this country in February, 1820? [10] Do I exaggerate when I say, that there was not a man of property who did not tremble for his possessions?—that there was not a man of retired and peaceable habits who did not tremble for the tranquillity and security of his home?—that there was not a man of orderly and religious principles who did not fear that those principles were about to be cut from under the feet of succeeding generations? Was there any man who did not apprehend the Crown to be in danger? Was there any man, attached to the other branches of the Constitution, who did not contemplate with anxiety and dismay the rapid, and, apparently, irresistible diffusion of doctrines hostile to the very existence of Parliament as at present constituted, and calculated to excite, not hatred and contempt merely, but open and audacious force, especially against the House of Commons?—What is, in these respects, the situation of the country now? Is there a man of property who does not feel the tenure by which he holds his possessions to have been strengthened? Is there a man of peace who does not feel his domestic tranquillity to have been secured? Is there a man of moral and religious principles who does not look forward with better hope to see his children educated in those principles?—who does not hail, with renewed confidence, the revival and re-establishment of that moral and religious sense which had been attempted to be obliterated from the hearts of mankind?

Well, gentlemen, and what has intervened between the two periods? A calling of that degraded Parliament; a meeting of that scoffed at and derided House of Commons; a concurrence of those three branches of an imperfect Constitution, not one of which, if we are to believe the radical reformers, lived in the hearts, or swayed the feelings, or commanded the respect of the nation; but which, despised as they were while in a state of separation and inaction, did, by a co-operation of four short weeks, restore order, confidence, a reverence for the laws, and a just sense of their own legitimate authority.

Another event, indeed, has intervened, in itself of a most painful nature, but powerful in aiding and confirming the impressions which the assembling and proceedings of Parliament were calculated to produce. I mean the loss which the nation has sustained by the death of a Sovereign,[11] with whose person all that is venerable in monarchy has been identified in the eyes of successive generations of his subjects; a Sovereign whose goodness, whose years, whose sorrows and sufferings, must have softened the hearts of the most

[10] Cf. n. 5 in chap. i on the Six Acts.
[11] George III died on January 29, 1820, after a long period of mental disorder and physical weaknesses.

ferocious enemies of kingly power; whose active virtues, and the memory of whose virtues, when it pleased Divine Providence that they should be active no more, have been the guide and guardian of his people through many a weary and many a stormy pilgrimage; scarce less a guide, and quite as much a guardian, in the cloud of his evening darkness, as in the brightness of his meridian day.

That such a loss, and the recollections and reflections naturally arising from it, must have had a tendency to revive and refresh the attachment to monarchy, and to root that attachment deeper in the hearts of the people, might easily be shown by reasoning; but a feeling, truer than all reasoning, anticipates the result, and renders the process of argument unnecessary. So far, therefore, has this great calamity brought with it its own compensation, and conspired to the restoration of peace throughout the country with the measures adopted by Parliament.

And, gentlemen, what was the character of those measures?— The best eulogy of them I take to be this: it may be said of them, as has been said of some of the most consummate productions of literary art, that, though no man beforehand had exactly anticipated the scope and the details of them, no man, when they were laid before him, did not feel that they were precisely such as he would himself have suggested. So faithfully adapted to the case which they were framed to meet, so correctly adjusted to the degree and nature of the mischief they were intended to control, that, while we all feel they have done their work, I think none will say there has been any thing in them of excess of supererogation.

We were loudly assured by the reformers, that the test, through-out the country, by which those who were ambitious of seats in the new Parliament would be tried, was to be—whether they had supported those measures. I have inquired, with as much diligence as was compatible with my duties here, after the proceedings of other elections; and, I protest I know no place yet, besides the hustings of Westminster and Southwark, at which that menaced test has been put to any candidates. To me, indeed, it was not put as a test, but objected as a charge. You know how that charge was answered: and the result is to me a majority of 1,300 out of 2,000 voters upon the poll.

But, gentlemen, though this question has not, as was threatened— been the watchword of popular elections, every other effort has, nevertheless, been industriously employed to persuade the people, that their liberties have been essentially abridged by the regulation of popular meetings. Against that one of the measures passed by Parliament, it is that the attacks of the radical reformers have been particularly directed. Gentlemen, the first answer to this averment is, that the act leaves untouched all the constitutional modes of assembly which have been known to the nation since it became free. We are fond of dating our freedom from the Revolution. I should be glad to know in what period, since the Revolution (up to a very late period indeed, which I will specify)—in what period of those reigns growing out of the Revolution—I mean, of the first reigns of the House of Brunswick—did it enter into the head of man, that such meetings could be holden, or that the legislature would tolerate the holding of such meetings, as disgraced this kingdom for some months previous to the last session of Parliament? When, therefore, it is asserted, that such meetings were never before suppressed, the simple answer is—they were never before systematically attempted to be holden.

I verily believe, the first meeting of the kind that was ever attempted and tolerated (I know of none anterior to it) was that called by Lord George Gordon, in St. George's fields, in the year 1780, which led to the demolition of chapels and dwelling-houses, the breaking of prisons, and the conflagration of London. Was England never free till 1780? Did British liberty spring to light from the ashes of the metropolis? What! was there no freedom in the reign of George the Second? None in that of George the First? None in the reign of Queen Anne or of King William? Beyond the Revolution I will not go. But I have always heard, that British liberty was established long before the commencement of the late reign; nay, that in the late reign (according to popular politicians) it rather sunk and retrograded: and yet never till that reign was such an abuse of popular meetings dreamt of, much less erected into a right, not to be questioned by magistrates, and not to be controlled by Parliament.

Do I deny, then, the general right of the people to meet, to petition, or to deliberate upon their grievances? God forbid. But social right is not a simple, abstract, positive, unqualified term. Rights are, in the same individual, to be compared with his duties; and rights in one person are to be balanced with the rights of others. Let us take this right of meeting in its most extended construction and most absolute sense. The persons who called the meeting at Manchester tell you, that they had a right to collect together countless multitudes to discuss the question of parliamentary reform: to collect them when they would and where they would, without consent of magistrates, or concurrence of inhabitants, or reference to the comfort or convenience of the neighbourhood. May not the peaceable, the industrious inhabitant of Manchester say, on the other hand, "I have a right to quiet in my house; I have a right to carry on my manufactory, on which not my existence only and that of my children, but that of my workmen and their numerous families depends. I have a right to be protected, not against violence and plunder only, against fire and sword, but against the terror of these calamities, and against the risk of these inflictions; against the intimidation or seduction of my workmen; or against the distraction of that attention and the interruption of that industry, without which neither they nor I can gain our livelihood. I call upon the laws to afford me that protection; and, if the laws in this country cannot afford it, I and my manufacturers must emigrate to some country where they can." Here is a conflict of rights, between which what is the decision? Which of the two claims is to give away? Can any reasonable being doubt? Can any honest man hesitate? Let private justice or public expediency decide, and can the decision by possibility be other, than that the peaceable and industrious shall be protected—the turbulent and mischievous put down?

But what similarity is there between tumults such as these, and an orderly meeting, recognized by the law for all legitimate purposes of discussion or petition? God forbid, that there should not be modes of assembly by which every class of this great nation may be brought together to deliberate on any matters connected with their interest and their freedom. It is, however, an inversion of the natural order of things, it is a disturbance of the settled course of society, to represent discussion as every thing, and the ordinary occupations of life as nothing. To protect the peaceable in their ordinary occupations, is as much the province of the laws, as to provide opportunities of discussion for every purpose to which it is necessary and properly applicable. The laws do both; but it is no part of the contrivance of the laws, that immense multitudes should wantonly be brought together, month after month, and day after day, in places where the very bringing together of a multitude is of itself the source of terror and of danger.

It is no part of the provision of the laws, nor is it in the spirit of them, that such multitudes should be brought together at the will of unauthorized and irresponsible individuals, changing the scene of meeting as may suit their caprice or convenience, and fixing it where they have neither property, nor domicil, nor connexion. The spirit of the law goes directly the other way. It is, if I may so express myself, eminently a spirit of corporation. Counties, parishes, townships, guilds, professions, trades, and callings, form so many local and political subdivisions, into which the people of England are distributed by the law: and the pervading principle of the whole is that of vicinage or neighbourhood; by which each man is held to act under the view of his neighbours; to lend his aid to them, to borrow theirs; to share their councils, their duties, and their burdens; and to bear with them his share of responsibility for the act of any of the members of the community of which he forms a part.

Observe, I am not speaking here of the reviled and discredited statute law only, but of that venerable common law to which our reformers are so fond of appealing on all occasions, against the statute law by which it is modified, explained, or enforced. Guided by the spirit of the one, no less than by the letter of the other, what man is there in this country who cannot point to the portion of society to which he belongs? If injury is sustained, upon whom is the injured person expressly entitled to come for redress? Upon the hundred, or the division in which he has sustained the injury. On what principle? On the principle, that as the individual is amenable to the division of the community to which he specially belongs, so neighbours are answerable for each other. Just laws, to be sure, and admirable equity, if a stranger is to collect a mob which is to set half Manchester on fire; and the burnt half is to come upon the other half for indemnity, while the stranger goes off, unquestioned, to excite the like tumult and produce the like danger elsewhere!

That such was the nature, such the tendency, nay, that such, in all human probability, might have been the result, of meetings like that of the 16th of August,[12] who can deny? Who that weighs all the particulars of that day, comparing them with the rumours and the threats that preceded it, will dispute that such might have been the result of that very meeting, if that meeting, so very legally assembled, had not, by the happy decision of the magistrates, been so very illegally dispersed?

It is, therefore, not in consonance, but in contradiction to the spirit of the law, that such meetings have been holden. The law prescribes a corporate character. The callers of these meetings have always studiously avoided it. No summons of freeholders—none of freemen —none of the inhabitants of particular places or parishes—no acknowledgment of local or political classification. Just so at the beginning of the French Revolution: the first work of the reformers was to loosen every established political relation, every legal holding of man to man; to destroy every corporation, to dissolve every subsisting class of society, and to reduce the nation into individuals, in order, afterwards, to congregate them into mobs.

Let no person, therefore, run away with the notion, that these things were done without design. To bring together the inhabitants of a particular division, or men sharing a common franchise, is to bring together an assembly, of which the component parts act with some respect and awe of each other. Ancient habits, which the re-

---

[12] The meeting at Manchester which led to the so-called Peterloo massacre.

formers would call prejudices; preconceived attachments, which they would call corruption; that mutual respect which makes the eye of a neighbour a security for each man's good conduct, but which the reformers would stigmatize as a confederacy among the few for dominion over their fellows; all these things make men difficult to be moved, on the sudden, to any extravagant, and violent enterprize. But bring together a multitude of individuals, having no permanent relation to each other—no common tie, but what arises from their concurrence as members of that meeting, a tie dissolved as soon as the meeting is at an end; in such an aggregation of individuals there is no such mutual respect, no such check upon the proceedings of each man from the awe of his neighbour's disapprobation; and, if ever a multitudinous assembly can be wrought up to purposes of mischief, it will be an assembly so composed.

How monstrous is it to confound such meetings with the genuine and recognized modes of collecting the sense of the English people. Was it by meetings such as these that the Revolution was brought about, that grand event, to which our antagonists are so fond of referring? Was it by meetings [13] in St. George's-fields? in Spa-fields? in Smithfields? Was it by untold multitudes collected in a village in the north? No! It was by the meeting of corporations, in their corporate capacity;—by the assembly of recognized bodies of the state; by the interchange of opinions among portions of the community known to each other, and capable of estimating each other's views and characters. Do we want a more striking mode of remedying grievances than this? Do we require a more animating example? And did it remain for the reformers of the present day to strike out the course by which alone Great Britain could make and keep herself free?

Gentlemen, all power is, or ought to be, accomplished by responsibility. Tyranny is irresponsible power. This definition is equally true, whether the power be lodged in one or many;—whether in a despot, exempted by the form of government from the control of the law; or in a mob, whose numbers put them beyond the reach of the law. Idle, therefore, and absurd, to talk of freedom where a mob domineers! Idle, therefore, and absurd, to talk of liberty, when you hold your property, perhaps your life, not indeed, at the nod of a despot, but at the will of an inflamed, and infuriated populace! If, therefore, during the reign of terror at Manchester, or at Spa-fields, there were persons in this country who had a right to complain of tyranny, it was they who loved the Constitution, who loved the monarchy, but who dared not utter their opinions or their wishes

[13] Meetings at which there were aspects of rioting.

until their houses were barricaded, and their children sent to a place of safety. That was tryanny! and, so far as the mobs were under control of a leader, that was despotism! It was against that tyranny, it was against that despotism, that Parliament at length raised its arm.

All power, I say, is vicious that is not accompanied by proportionate responsibility. Personal responsibility prevents the abuse of individual power: responsibility of character is the security of men whose existence is permanent and defined. But strip such bodies of these qualities, you degrade them into multitudes, and then what security have you against any thing that they may do or resolve, knowing that, from the moment at which the meeting is at an end, there is no human being responsible for their proceedings? The meeting at Manchester, the meeting at Birmingham, the meeting at Spa-fields or Smithfields, what pledge could they give to the nation of the soundness or sincerity of their designs? The local character of Manchester, the local character of Birmingham, was not pledged to any of the proceedings to which their names were appended. A certain number of ambulatory tribunes of the people, self-elected to that high function, assumed the name and authority of whatever place they thought proper to select for a place of meeting; their rostrum was pitched, sometimes here, sometimes there, according to the fancy of the mob, or the patience of the magistrates; but the proposition and the proposer were in all places nearly alike; and when, by a sort of political ventriloquism, the same voice [14] had been made to issue from half a dozen different corners of the country, it was impudently assumed to be a concord of sweet sounds, composing the united voice of the people of England!

Now, gentlemen, let us estimate the mighty mischief that has been done to liberty by putting down meetings such as I have described. Let us ask, what lawful authority has been curtailed; let us ask, what respectable community has been defrauded of its franchise; let us ask, what municipal institutions have been violated by a law which fixes the migratory complaint to the spot whence it professes to originate, and desires to hear of the grievance from those by whom that grievance is felt;—which leaves to Manchester, as Manchester, to Birmingham, as Birmingham, to London, as London, all the free scope of utterance which they have at all times enjoyed for making known their wants, their feelings, their wishes, their remonstrances;—which leaves to each of these divisions its separate authority—to the union of all or of many of them the aggregate authority of such a consent and co-operation; but which denies to any itinerant hawker of grievances the power of stamping their

[14] Presumably that of Orator Hunt and his associates.

names upon his wares; of pretending, because he may raise an outcry *at* Manchester or *at* Birmingham, that he therefore speaks the sense of the town which he disquiets and endangers; or, still more pre- posterously, that because he has disquieted and endangered half a dozen neighbourhoods in their turn, he is, therefore, the organ of them all, and, through them, of the whole British people.

Such are the stupid fallacies which the law of the last session has extinguished and such are the object and effect of the measures which British liberty is not to survive.

To remedy the dreadful wound thus inflicted upon British liberty, —to restore to the people what the people have not lost—to give a new impulse to that spirit of freedom which nothing has been done to embarrass or restrain, we are invited to alter the constitution of that assembly through which the people share in the legislature; in short, to make a radical reform in the House of Commons.[15]

[15] The remaining portion of the speech deals largely with Parliamentary reform.

3. Address on the King's Message Respecting Portugal

Canning echoed, in a Parliamentary speech, the sentiments of the King's message (December 12, 1826) which expressed determination to leave "no effort unexhausted to awaken the Spanish Government to the dangerous consequences" of aggression against England's ally, Portugal. He explained that national honor would permit no compromise on certain obligations such as were involved in the alliance with Portugal, an alliance renewed in the Treaty of Vienna of 1815 but resting on the Treaty of 1661 which gave Charles II a wife and dowry and a task of defending Portugal by land and sea, even as England itself, and also on a treaty of alliance of 1703, contemporaneous with the Methuen Treaty which regulated the commercial relations of the two countries. Furthermore he felt that an obligation now existed to render assistance to Portugal—in other words, that the casus foederis *had arisen. Bands of Portuguese rebels, armed and trained in Spain, had carried terror to their own country. He called, therefore, for a vote for the defense of Portugal. But he met with some opposing arguments from members of the House and with an amendment, moved by Mr. Hume, "that the House be called over this day week." Canning's reply, which contains his celebrated reference to the New World, is given in the following extract. It may be found in Walsh's* Selected Speeches of the Right Honourable George Canning *and in* HANSARD's The Parliamentary Debates *(XVI [N.S.], 390-98).*

I rise, Sir, for the purpose of making a few observations, not so much in answer to any general arguments, as in reply to two or three particular objections which have been urged against the Address which I have had the honour to propose to the House.

In the first place, I frankly admit to my honourable friend (Mr. Bankes,) the member for Dorsetshire, that I have understated the case against Spain—I have done so designed—I warned the House that I would do so—because I wished no further to impeach the conduct of Spain, than was necessary for establishing the *casus foederis* on behalf of Portugal. To have gone further—to have made a full statement of the case against Spain—would have been to preclude the very object which I have in view; that of enabling Spain to preserve peace without dishonour.

The honourable gentleman (Mr. Bright) who spoke last, indeed, in his extreme love for peace, proposes expedients which, as it appears to me, would render war inevitable. He would avoid interference at this moment, when Spain may be yet hesitating as to the course which she shall adopt; and the language which he would hold to Spain is, in effect, this—"You have not yet done enough to implicate British faith, and to provoke British honour. You have not done enough, in merely enabling Portuguese rebels to invade Portugal, and to carry destruction into her cities; you have not done enough in combing knots of traitors, whom, after the most solemn engagements to disarm and to disperse them, you carefully reassembled, and equipped and sent back with Spanish arms, to be plunged into kindred Portuguese bosoms. I will not stir for all these things. Pledged though I am by the most solemn obligations of treaty to resent attack upon Portugal as injurious to England, I love too dearly the peace of Europe to be goaded into activity by such trifles as these. No. But give us a good declaration of war, and then I'll come and fight you with all my heart."—This is the honourable gentleman's contrivance for keeping peace. The more clumsy contrivance of His Majesty's Government is this:—"We have seen enough to show to the world that Spain authorized, if she did not instigate, the invasion of Portugal"; and we say to Spain, "Beware, we will avenge the cause of our ally, if you break out into declared war; but, in the mean time, we will take effectual care to frustrate your concealed hostilities." I appeal to my honourable friend, the member for Dorsetshire, whether he does not prefer this course of His Majesty's Government, the object of which is to nip growing hostilities in the ear, to that of the gallant and chivalrous member for Bristol, who would let aggressions ripen into full maturity, in order that they may then be mowed down with the scythe of a magnificent war.

My honourable friend (Mr. Bankes) will now see why it is that no papers have been laid before the House. The facts which call for our interference in behalf of Portugal, are notorious as the noonday sun. That interference is our whole present object. To prove more than is sufficient for that object, by papers laid upon the table of this House, would have been to preclude Spain from that *locus penitentiae* which we are above all things desirous to preserve to her. It is difficult, perhaps, with the full knowledge which the Government must in such cases possess, to judge what exact portion of that knowledge should be meted out for our present purpose, without hazarding an exposure which might carry us too far. I know not how far I have succeeded in this respect; but I can assure the House that if the time should unfortunately arrive when a further exposition shall become necessary, it will be found, that it was not for want of evidence that my statement of this day has been defective.

An amendment has been proposed, purporting a delay of a week, but in effect, intended to produce a total abandonment of the object of the Address; and that amendment has been justified by a reference to the conduct of the Government, and to the language used by me in this House, between three or four years ago. It is stated, and truly, that I did not then deny that cause for war had been given by France in the invasion of Spain, if we had then thought fit to enter into war on that account.[16] But it seems to be forgotten that there is one main difference between that case and the present— which difference, however, is essential and all sufficient. We were then *free* to go to war, if we pleased, on grounds of political expediency. But we were not then *bound* to interfere, on behalf of Spain, as we now are bound to interfere on behalf of Portugal, by the obligations of treaty. War might then have been our free choice, if we had deemed it politic: interference on behalf of Portugal is now our duty, unless we are prepared to abandon the principles of national faith and national honour.

It is a singular confusion of intellect which confounds two cases so precisely dissimilar. Far from objecting to the reference 1823, I refer to that same occasion to show the consistency of the conduct of myself and my colleagues. We were then accused of truckling to France, from a pusillanimous dread of war. We pleaded guilty to the charge of wishing to avoid war. We described its inexpediency, its inconveniences, and its dangers—(dangers, especially of the same sort with those which I have hinted at to-day:) but we declared, that, although we could not overlook those dangers, those inconveniences and that inexpediency, in a case in which remote interest and doubtful policy were alone assigned as motives for war, we would cheerfully affront them all, in a case—if it should arrive— where national faith or national honour were concerned. Well, then, a case *has* now arisen, of which the essence is faith—of which the character is honour. And when we call upon the Parliament, not for offensive war—which was proposed to us in 1823—but for defensive armament, we are referred to our abstinence in 1823, as disqualifying us for exertion at the present moment: and are told, that because we did not attack France on that occasion, we must not defend Portugal on this. I, Sir, like the proposers of the amendment, place the two cases of 1823 and 1826, side by side, and deduce from them, when taken together, the exposition and justification of our general policy. I appeal from the warlike preparations of to-day,

---

[16] A Spanish situation troubled European statesmen from 1820 on. Spanish revolutionists had forced reforms which caused French reactionaries to wish for intervention. Moreover, this French group feared the effect of the Portuguese King's action in granting a liberal constitution upon his return from a fourteen-year sojourn in Brazil. The Congress of Verona (1822) permitted French intervention of Spain, but Canning, who had opposed such procedure, finally decided on the policy which he herein mentions. He did help to thwart any attempt to conquer the Spanish colonies.

to the forbearance of 1823, in proof of the pacific character of our counsels; I appeal from the imputed tameness of 1823, to the Message of to-night, in illustration of the nature of those motives, by which a Government, generally pacific, may nevertheless be justly roused into action.

Having thus disposed of the objections to the Address, I come next to the suggestions of some who profess themselves friendly to the purpose of it, but who would carry that purpose into effect by means which I certainly cannot approve. It has been suggested, Sir, that we should at once ship off the Spanish refugees now in this country, for Spain; and that we should, by the repeal of the Foreign Enlistment Act, let loose into the contest all the ardent and irregular spirits of this country. Sir, this is the very suggestion which I have anticipated with apprehension, in any war in which this country might be engaged, in the present unquiet state of the minds of men in Europe. These are the expedients, the tremendous character of which I ventured to adumbrate rather than to describe, in the speech with which I prefaced the present motion. Such expedients I disclaim. I dread and deprecate the employment of them. So far, indeed, as Spain herself is concerned, the employment of such means would be strictly, I might say, epigrammatically just. The Foreign Enlistment Act was passed in the year 1819, if not at the direct request, for the especial benefit of Spain. What right, then, would Spain have to complain if we should repeal it now, for the especial benefit of Portugal?

The Spanish refugees have been harboured in this country, it is true; but on condition of abstaining from hostile expeditions against Spain; and more than once, when such expeditions have been planned, the British Government has interfered to suppress them. How is this tenderness for Spain rewarded? Spain not only harbours, and fosters, and sustains, but arms, equips, and marshals the traitorous refugees of Portugal, and pours them by thousands into the bosom of Great Britain's nearest ally. So far, then, as Spain is concerned, the advice of those who would send forth against Spain such dreadful elements of strife and destruction, is, as I have admitted, not unjust. But I repeat, again and again, that I disclaim all such expedients; and that I dread especially a war with Spain, because it is the war of all others in which, by the example and practice of Spain herself, such expedients are most likely to be adopted. Let us avoid that war if we can—that is, if Spain will permit us to do so. But in any case, let us endeavour to strip any war—if war we must have—of that formidable and disastrous character which the honourable and learned gentleman (Mr. Brougham) has so eloquently described; and which I was happy to hear him concur with me in deprecating, as the most fatal evil by which the world could be afflicted.

Sir, there is another suggestion with which I cannot agree, although brought forward by two honourable members (Sir R. Wilson and Mr. Baring,) who have, in the most handsome manner, stated their reasons for approving of the line of conduct now pursued by His Majesty's Government. Those honourable members insist that the French army in Spain has been, if not the cause, the encouragement of the late attack by Spain against Portugal; that His Majesty's Government were highly culpable in allowing that army to enter Spain; that its stay there is highly injurious to British interests and honour; and that we ought instantly to call upon France to withdraw it.

There are, Sir, so many considerations connected with these propositions, that were I to enter into them all, they would carry me far beyond what is either necessary or expedient to be stated on the present occasion. Enough, perhaps, it is for me to say, that I do not see how the withdrawing of the French troops from Spain, could effect our present purpose. I believe, Sir, that the French army in Spain is now a protection to that very party which it was originally called in to put down. Were the French army suddenly removed at this precise moment, I verily believe that the immediate effect of that removal would be, to give full scope to the unbridled rage of a fanatical faction, before which, in the whirlwind of intestine strife, the party least in numbers would be swept away.

So much for the *immediate* effect of the demand which it is proposed to us to make, if that demand were instantly successful. But when, with reference to the larger question of a military occupation of Spain by France, it is averred, that by that occupation the relative situation of Great Britain and France is altered; that France is thereby exalted and Great Britain lowered, in the eyes of Europe;— I must beg leave to say, that I dissent from that averment. The House knows—the country knows—that when the French army was on the point of entering Spain, His Majesty's Government did all in their power to prevent it; that we resisted it by all means, short of war. I have just now stated some of the reasons why we did not think the entry of that army into Spain, a sufficient ground for war; but there was in addition to those which I have stated, this peculiar reason,—that whatever effect a war, commenced upon the mere ground of the entry of a French army into Spain, might have, it probably would not have had the effect of getting that army out of Spain. In a war against France at that time, as at any other, you might, perhaps, have acquired military glory; you might, perhaps, have extended your colonial possessions; you might even have achieved, at a great cost of blood and treasure, an honourable peace; but as to getting the French out of Spain, *that* would have been the one object which you, almost certainly, would not have accomplished. How seldom, in the whole history of the wars of Europe, has any war between two great Powers ended, in the obtaining of the exact, the identical object, for which the war was begun.

Besides, Sir, I confess I think, that the effects of the French occupation of Spain have been infinitely exaggerated.

I do not blame those exaggerations; because I am aware that they are to be attributed to the recollections of some of the best times of our history; that they are the echoes of sentiments, which in the days of William and of Anne, animated the debates and dictated the votes of the British Parliament. No peace was in those days thought safe for this country while the crown of Spain continued on the head of a Bourbon. But were not the apprehensions of those days greatly overstated?—Has the power of Spain swallowed up the power of maritime England?—Or does England still remain, after the lapse of more than a century, during which the crown of Spain has been worn by a Bourbon,—niched in a nook of that same Spain—Gibraltar; an occupation which was contemporaneous with the apprehensions that I have described, and which has happily survived them?

Again, Sir—is the Spain of the present day the Spain of which the statesmen of the times of William and Anne were so much afraid? Is it indeed the nation whose puissance was expected to shake England from her sphere? No, Sir, it was quite another Spain—it was the Spain, within the limits of whose empire the sun never set— it was the Spain *"with the Indies"* that excited the jealousies and alarmed the imaginations of our ancestors.

But then, Sir, the balance of power!—The entry of the French army into Spain disturbed that balance, and we ought to have gone to war to restore it! I have already said, that when the French army entered Spain, we might, if we chose, have resisted or resented that measure by war. But were there no other means than war for restoring the balance of power?—Is the balance of power a fixed and unalterable standard? Or is it not a standard perpetually varying, as civilization advances, and as new nations spring up, and take their place among established political communities? The balance of power a century and a half ago was to be adjusted between France and Spain, the Netherlands, Austria, and England. Some years afterwards, Russia assumed her high station in European politics. Some years after that again, Prussia became not only a substantive, but a preponderating monarchy.—Thus, while the balance of power continued in principle the same, the means of adjusting it became more varied and enlarged. They became enlarged, in proportion to the increased number of considerable states—in proportion, I may say, to the number of weights which might be shifted into the one or other scale. To look to the policy of Europe, in the times of William and Anne, for the purpose of regulating the balance of power in Europe at the present day, is to disregard the progress of events, and to confuse dates and facts which throw a reciprocal light upon each other.

It would be disingenuous, indeed, not to admit that the entry of the French army into Spain was in a certain sense, a disparagement—an affront to the pride—a blow to the feelings of England:— and it can hardly be supposed that the Government did not sympathize, on that occasion, with the feelings of the people. But I deny that, questionable or censurable as the act might be, it was one which necessarily called for our direct and hostile opposition. Was nothing then to be done?—Was there no other mode of resistance, than by a direct attack upon France—or by a war to be undertaken on the soil of Spain? What, if the possession of Spain might be rendered harmless in rival hands—harmless as regarded us—and valueless to the possessors? Might not compensation for disparagement be obtained, and the policy of our ancestors vindicated, by means better adapted to the present time? If France occupied Spain, was it necessary, in order to avoid the consequences of that occupation—that we should blockade Cadiz? No. I looked another way— I sought materials of compensation in another hemisphere. Contemplating Spain, such as our ancestors had known her, I resolved that if France had Spain, it should not be Spain *"with the Indies."* I called the New World into existence, to redress the balance of the Old.

It is thus, Sir, that I answer the accusation brought against His Majesty's Government, of having allowed the French army to usurp and to retain the occupation of Spain. That occupation, I am quite confident, is an unpaid and unredeemed burden to France. It is a burden of which, I verily believe, France would be glad to rid herself. But they know little of the feelings of the French Government, and of the spirit of the French nation, who do not know, that, worthless or burdensome as that occupation may be, the way to rivet her in it would be, by angry or intemperate representations, to make the continuance of that occupation a point of honour.

I believe, Sir, there is no other subject upon which I need enter into defence or explanation. The support which the address has received, from all parties in the House, has been such as would make it both unseemly and ungrateful in me to trespass unnecessarily upon their patience. In conclusion, Sir, I shall only once more declare, that the object of the Address, which I propose to you, is not war:—its object is to take the last chance of peace. If you do not go forth, on this occasion, to the aid of Portugal, Portugal will be trampled down, to your irretrievable disgrace:—and then will come war in the train of national degradation. If, under the circumstances like these, you wait till Spain has matured her secret machinations into open hostility, you will in a little while have the sort of war required by the pacificators:—and who shall say where that war shall end?

4. The Catholic Question

Canning rose for the first time as First Lord of the Treasury and Chancellor of the Exchequer (May 1, 1827) after Peel had explained that his own opposition to Roman Catholic concessions made office under the new Premier impossible for him. Canning, saying that he refused to participate in an anti-Catholic administration, gave data on the Catholic question before taking up the question of its existing status. Catholics lived under disabilities, both political and penal, from laws that had been passed from time to time since the sixteenth century. Penal laws came eventually to be largely unenforced, but restrictions on political activities still remained. Pitt the Younger had hoped to give Catholic emancipation but George III interfered. Canning believed that Pitt's opinion on the subject had remained unchanged during his lifetime, and he professed to be his proud heir. Canning's complete speech may be found in R. Therry's The Speeches of the Right Honourable George Canning ([London, 1828], Vol. VI), or in Hansard (XVII [N.S.], 428-41).

But to come to the present condition of that Question, I say again, it remains in this Government, in the state it was truly described to be in by Lord Castlereagh in 1812, and precisely as it has been since repeatedly described by myself; in short, as it was described to be in 1825, in a debate which took place in the month of March upon the state of Ireland; and in the very last debate in the last session of Parliament, in the same year, upon Catholic emancipation. On that occasion I used these words: "I hold myself as perfectly free as any other member of this House, to pronounce an opinion upon this as a great national question, and as such, to give it my support, reserving only to myself the right of selecting the time when I am to give this support, and the manner in which it is to be afforded, according to my judgment of the degree of success which is likely to attend such an exertion." These were the words I used then, and my opinions are not in the slightest degree varied at the present moment. Such was the footing upon which this question stood when I was the colleague of my right honourable friend; and such *is* the footing on which it stands now. Let it be observed, therefore, by those with whom I have formerly acted, and from whose objections on this occasion I do not shrink, however the acknowledgment I have made may be attempted to be converted into matter of opposition, that, with those who form the present Cabinet, and some of whom formed part of the last, the Catholic Question now stands on the same ground as it stood on under Lord Liverpool's Government; —that is, it is a question which each member of the Government is at liberty, if he pleases, to bring forward in the Cabinet, or to propound to Parliament; but if any member of the Government shall so bring it forward in either House of Parliament, he is bound distinctly to state that he does so in his individual capacity only, and not as pledging his colleagues to his own opinions on the subject. This, Sir, is the position of the Catholic Question now; it is the same in which it was placed in the year 1812; it is the same in which it has now stood for fifteen years successively. That it should remain in this state is a fact which I know has been much objected to by many; but, if I consider the state of the country at large—the inclination of men's minds upon this matter in England as well as in Ireland—and the infinite difficulties which surround the attempt at present to alter that state—in my judgment, and in my conscience I believe it to be the only footing upon which it can be at present left; unless the views of partizans are to be consulted, the accomplishment of whose wishes on the one hand, or whose attempt to stifle free and growing opinions on the other, would, in the result, lead to a convulsion, in one part or other, of the United Kingdom. Now, Sir, I am not prepared for convulsion, in either. I would not raise hopes which I do not see any immediate means of realising. In making this observation, I am not speaking of the moral accomplishment of those hopes, but of exciting expectations without having good grounds to anticipate their immediate or speedy fulfilment. I remember too well, and but a short memory indeed is required for that purpose, how much has been uttered in the way of complaint in debates of this House upon the Catholic Question, about things being said and done that had raised expectations in Ireland [17] which ought not, it has been observed, to have been excited, unless the authorities from whom those acts and declarations emanated were prepared to follow them up.

Now, Sir, it is precisely because of my not being at present prepared to follow them up, that I will not raise such expectations. Much and cordially as I agree with those who view the measure itself of emancipation, as calculated to tranquillize Ireland, I yet estimate very highly the degree of passive resistance to it, which exists in this country. I would not act against the feelings any more than I would against the interests of England. But if, looking to the character and extent of that resistance, I am asked whether I despair of the ultimate success of the question, I answer, that I do not despair that the good sense of the English people, by candid discussion, and repeated consideration of it, will ultimately concede the question. I say, I think, Sir, the time will come, when well-meaning

[17] Pitt, perhaps unwittingly, had led proponents of Catholic emancipation to look forward to adequate legislation for that purpose.

and conscientious, and even intelligent people, now among the most strenuous and most honest opponents of the great measure, will look back with a degree of surprise, and almost incredulity, at the opposition which they have, up to this time, manifested to it. But, though I think this, I am not prepared to run counter, in the mean time, to English feelings. A single week of peace in England, is worth a much larger portion of time devoted to the accomplishment of a great, but yet, partly, a theoretical, good, in another portion of the empire. Though I thus confidently expect the dawn, I am by no means prepared to hasten it; though I know the present darkness upon this subject—for darkness I must consider it—will be succeeded by a great illumination in the minds of men, I am disposed to watch patiently the progress of that enlightenment. This result, I heartily hope, but I will not endeavour to anticipate it by any attempt to force the judgments of the community.

I hope I have now, Sir, given the honourable gentlemen every satisfactory explanation upon the topics which have been this night referred to.

So far as I am aware, I have kept nothing back; but when I am taunted by questions such as that which some honourable gentlemen have put to me, whether I do not know that in the very *penetralia* of the royal breast there exist feelings repugnant to the Catholic claims, I reply, that I would venerate in that most illustrious individual, as I did in his royal father, the repugnant feelings which actuate him on this question. I would hurt no feelings, as I have already said, of that nature. But if I am asked by that honourable gentleman, whether I think the Coronation Oath is any obstacle in the way of concession on the part of the Crown, I answer, No. No more did Lord Liverpool—no more did my right honourable friend himself (Mr. Peel); and if the time shall ever come when it may be necessary to argue this question, I shall derive my best argument, for the view I take of that point, from the opinions which have already been addressed to Parliament upon the subject by those great authorities. Let not, then, the people of England take up the notion, that, by the carrying of the Catholic Question, the peace of their country would be endangered. The time has passed when those pernicious influences, which have been so much adverted to, could be any longer exercised by the Catholic Church, with any effect upon its peace or its welfare. But do the honourable gentlemen, who so much deprecate all discussion of this question imagine that discussion can be avoided? Do they suppose that if we will not consider it, it is a question which will sleep? Or do they believe, that if it should sleep, it will be awakened by any other than a dreadful and deplorable emergency? No, Sir, we must look it in the face. We must not turn from it. But, though I believe that it is a question which has gained strength from the change which has taken place in the Government—(a change, God knows! not of my seeking, but arising out of the King's determination)—though I concur with those who imagine that it is a cause which has acquired additional power—I would not force it by pressing it upon Parliament now any more than I did when I formed, with my right honourable friend near me, one of the Government of Lord Liverpool.

I am not conscious that I have omitted to reply to any of the matters which have been suggested to me; but if I have, I shall be sincerely obliged to any querist who will remind me, be he who he may, of any such omissions.

I trust I have succeeded in showing that I am, where I have the honour to be, not by my own solicitation, but by the pleasure of my Sovereign. I had previously recommended the formation of an Administration, from which I should have been excluded. That plan was rejected by those whom it embraced, and another proposed in its stead, to which I could not have acceded, without, at the same time, recording my acknowledgment that the opinions of my past political life, upon one of the most important of all the questions which I have ever been called on to consider, furnished a justifiable ground of exclusion from the highest office in the Government. I will conclude, by repeating one or two remarks which I remember to have made to the House in 1822. I was then appointed to a post, which I owed not to the favour of His Majesty's Government, but to the commands of His Majesty himself: a post, fraught with wealth, distinction, and honour.[18] From this post I was recalled immediately after my nomination to it, contrary to my own feelings and wishes, to hold office in this country. I made the sacrifice—(to a poor man, be it permitted me to say, no indifferent or trivial one), —without hesitation, and—so help me God—without any stipulations. But if, Sir, when that proposal to take office was made to me, it had been accompanied—(as in fairness it should have been, if I was to be ousted on account of the opinions that have since been excepted against me)—with this sort of intimation from the Ministers who recalled me:—"Though we call you into the Government, because your services are necessary to us, yet remember, that if, by any unfortunate chance, the highest situation in that Government should become vacant, and should in all other respects be eligible for a person holding your situation in Parliament and in the councils of the country—remember, that because you support the Catholic claims you are to waive all pretensions to it." If their proposal, I say, had

[18] The governor-generalship of India.

been accompanied with such an intimation, I would, with the same disdain and indignation with which I have more recently rejected their offer to serve under a Protestant Premier (using the term Protestant in the familiar sense only in which we are accustomed to use it in discussions of this kind), have rejected that proposal, containing, as it would have done, a condition which I should have regarded as the badge of my helotism, and as the indelible disgrace of my political existence.

5. Parliamentary Reform—Repeal of the Test Act

Mr. Canning gave the following reply to critics who asserted that he refused to answer questions concerning the principles and formation of his administration. The speech is inserted not only because it portrays early nineteenth-century Parliamentary procedure but also be-cause it gives evidence of Canning's reliance upon a utilitarian philosophy rather than the concepts of the French school. It may be found in Therry's The Speeches of the Right Honourable George Canning (Vol. VI) or in HANSARD *(XVII [N.S.], 539-41 [May 3, 1827]).*

MR. CANNING then rose, and said:—I hope that the House will permit me to say a very few words in reply to the very didactic speech of the honourable baronet [19] who has just favoured the House with his opinions, and in explanation of my observation upon a former occasion. The speech of the honourable baronet refers principally to the reception which I have given to a question addressed to me in the commencement of this debate. I do not object to that question itself upon any considerations connected with its object; but I must take leave to say that I have never known, in the whole of my parliamentary experience, those rules which courtesy points out, and which convenience sanctions, to have been violated to so great a degree by any member of this House, as in that instance. Upon the understanding that the answer is to be a mere matter of courtesy, it sometimes does happen that a member, without any previous notice, asks leave to put a brief question to the Minister, upon a subject of pressing importance. Such I have (speaking from my own recollection and experience) always understood to be the course; but I never, I repeat, recollect any instance of a question without notice being accompanied by a speech such as we have this night heard from the honourable member opposite (Mr. Dawson). This was my impression, and I have since consulted others, who declare it to be theirs also, and pronounced to be a correct one. That any honourable member, under the pretence of asking a question, should seize the opportunity of introducing a motion, and that motion too thrust forward in the middle of another motion of great and paramount importance,—the business of the evening,—and the discussion upon which the House was most anxiously awaiting, is, however, I repeat, a circumstance altogether unprecedented in the annals of Parliament. To that question thus put to me, and under these circumstances, I applied my observation, when I said the attempt was only calculated to excite disgust. There is a consequence, too, resulting from it which the honourable gentleman does not forsee;

[19] Sir E. Knatchbull.

and that is, that no Minister, if such a course be pursued, will feel himself bound to answer questions at all, of which ample and regular notice is not given. The honourable member made it a matter of complaint against me, and alleged it as a reason for his conduct, that I was not in my place at the time he expected, and when he wished his question to be answered. But did not the honourable gentlemen recollect it was usual, in such cases, to have the courtesy to give some notice of a member's intention? If he had given me the slightest intimation that he intended to put any question to me, it certainly would have brought me down instantly to give a reply; but, even then, I might have felt not a little surprised at the course pursued by the honourable member—a course so absurd and so inconvenient that any one must see it could not for a moment be tolerated. I rejoice, Sir, however, that the standard of opposition is at length unfurled in this House. Such an act is, to me, worth a thousand professions of qualified neutrality. In whatever mind the feeling of opposition lurks, let it come boldly forth, and boldly will I meet it. There have been one or two questions put to me— I trust the House will extend its indulgence to me, while I briefly answer them. I am asked what I mean to do on the subject of parliamentary reform? Why, I say—to oppose it—to oppose it to the end of my life in this House, as hitherto I have done. I am asked what I intend to do respecting the repeal of the Test [20] and Corporation Acts? My answer is—to oppose it too. It has happened by some accident that the Test Act is one of the few subjects upon which it has never yet been my lot to pronounce an opinion fully in this House; but I have an opinion upon it, and I do not hesitate to declare it. I think that the exertions of the Legislature ought to be directed to the redress of practical and not theoretical grievances. I think that any meddling with the Test Act—of which the alleged grievances are comparatively theoretical [21]—might tend to prejudice that great question (the Catholic Question), which is attended with real practical and pressing grievances to those whom the present laws relating to it affect, and the success of which I have most truly at heart. I will, therefore, oppose the repeal. I hope I have spoken out. I hope I have made myself clearly understood. As to the charge brought against me by the honourable baronet (Sir E. Knatchbull), that the Government, when called upon to give an answer upon the

[20] According to the Test Act (1673) holders of military and civil office were obliged to receive the sacrament according to the Church of England and declare by oath their disbelief in transubstantiation. The Corporation Act (1661) provided a religious test for holders of office in a corporate town.

[21] Dissenters were annually forgiven for breaking the law by the passage of an indemnity act.

subject of its composition and its policy, left the answer to those who had no apparent interest in the question, or connection with it. Sir, I deny the charge. I say, without hesitation, that the accusation is untrue. I did not shrink from the question. The question to which the honourable baronet adverted was not addressed to me. I never have shrunk—I never will shrink—from explanation or defence, whether the charge preferred against me, be conveyed in the avowed hostility of the open and manly foe, or in the less dangerous insinuation of the disavowed opponent.

6. The Corn Trade

Mr. Canning found himself, during the debate on the Corn Amendment Bill, opposed to members who desired to go back toward the principle of higher protection for grain. High protection had been assured, both for security reasons and for the benefit of the agricultural class, by the arrangement in 1815 which fixed 80s. as the price at which import of wheat was to become duty-free. By a statute of 1822 the figure was changed to 70s. In neither case did the plan function well, and Canning, working in conjunction with the famous economist, William Huskisson, got through the House of Commons in 1827 the principle of the sliding scale whereby imports might come in on the basis of a 20s. duty when the price had fallen to 60s., the duty to fall as prices rose and vice versa. Wellington caused the Lords to accept an amendment that wrecked the principle, and Canning, in order to care for an immediate emergency, proposed to admit wheat now in warehouses in the country or which had been shipped from Canada, according to the terms of the plan which the House of Commons had recently accepted. Both Houses eventually agreed. Canning, himself, like Pitt the Younger, possessed proclivities toward theories of free trade. The following speech may be found in Therry's The Speeches of the Right Honourable George Canning (Vol. VI) or in HANSARD (XVII [N.S.], 1337-38 [June 18, 1827]).

MR. CANNING rose to reply:—I shall trespass on the indulgence of the House for a very few minutes, in reply to the only objection I have heard advanced to the Resolution which I have had the honour of proposing. My answer to the only objection I can recollect will be brief—but I beg to begin by replying to a question which has been put to me by an honourable gentleman opposite. He asks me whether I do not think it right to protect the agricultural interest? I do consider that the agricultural interest ought to be protected, aye, and protected too as a primary interest of the country. Such is the bounden duty of this House. But I also consider, that the course of legislation, pursued for some years past, has not been to promote the permanent interest of the agriculturists. The mistaken views that had obtained, and the erroneous notions that were acted upon, in the period that I allude to, are in no instance more flagrant —not that I mean to cast blame on those who committed these mistakes, and it was by accident that I did not participate in the acts which led to them—but the erroneous notions that they had acted upon, appear, in no instance, more flagrant than in the operation of the Acts of 1815 and 1822. Can any man look to the consequences of these bills, and say, they have not been most grievous to the agricultural interest? I must also say, that I consider the bill now before the House of Lords, calculated, had they been pleased to adopt it, to afford more secure protection to that interest, than any other measure whatever that has hitherto been proposed, professing to have that object in view. I consider that it was calculated to produce that which, of all effects, I should consider most desirable, not highness nor lowness, but steadiness of price. I consider that it was calculated to guard against those ruinous fluctuations which, ever since the bill of 1815, have pressed with alternate but equal violence on, as they are called, the two conflicting interests, which, I say, are not conflicting, but consentient interests—fluctuations which, in times of plenty, caused alarm; and in times of scarcity, aggravated the miseries of famine. The adoption of the bill in the House of Lords would have gone a greater way to curb those evils and prevent their recurrence, than any measure, which, in my memory, or in that of all those with whom I have conversed on the subject, has yet been presented to the consideration of Parliament. It was upon that ground, and not from any undue partiality for a particular plan, that I originally gave my concurrence to the bill that passed this House. And I beg to inform the House, that, unless I find reason to alter my present opinion, it is something very like that bill which will receive my support.

The principle of the measure that will receive my support, is one which, rendering the Corn Trade, instead of a series of successive speculations and experiments, instead of being mutually ruinous to the home trader, as well as to the foreign trader or importer, will make it mutually a matter of convenience—will make it, in short, a trade which would assist, and be beneficial to both, and, at the same time, be conformable to the interests of the country at large. Such are the grounds on which I shall approve a bill, and such ought to be the grounds, and those only, on which Parliament should grant its sanction to any measure whatever connected with the trade in corn. . . . . .

Chapter III

WELLINGTON

Chapter III

WELLINGTON

STRIKING, indeed, is the contrast between Canning and the Duke of Wellington (1769-1852) who, five months after the former's death, formed a ministry. Both were members of the Tory party, but they were far apart in ideas of both foreign and domestic policy. Wellington opposed Canning's solution of Spanish-American difficulties and, himself a defender of the landed interests, was none too friendly to the commercial class which was destined to reap so rich an ingathering from Canning's activity. If Canning felt at times the need of support from important elements of the country and the press, the Duke, in contrast, was suspicious of popular movements, cared little for public opinion, hated news writers, and thought that newspapers were "absolutely incapable of understanding, much less of stating the truth on any subject." Unlike Canning, he supported George against Caroline. He was against Catholic emancipation which Canning favored; but they both agreed in their opposition to Parliamentary reform.

Wellington's ideas, moreover, are of peculiar interest because in the perplexities of the early nineteenth century he revealed much of the feeling of an eighteenth-century aristocrat:[1] character molded by tradition was a test of men for him rather than training based upon the individual's abilities and aptitude. The French Revolution and its theories, says a recent biographer,[2] lay like a shadow across him, a warning never to be forgotten.

Mention of Wellington's activity prior to 1815 is hardly necessary. The man who in 1809 was made Viscount Wellington of Talavera and in 1814 first Duke of Wellington was born as

[1] Sir Herbert Maxwell, *The Life of Wellington* (Boston: Little, Brown and Company, 1899), II, 141.
[2] Oliver Brett, *Wellington* (London: William Heinemann, Ltd., 1928), p. 292.

Arthur Wellesley, fourth son of Garrett Wellesley, first Earl of Mornington. Never very clever at school, he was commissioned in the Army and gained much valuable military and some political experience in India. His return to England in 1805 led first to the appointment as Chief Secretary of Ireland and later to the conduct of the campaign in the Iberian Peninsula against Napoleonic forces. The victory at Waterloo naturally made him the hero of the day. But the long experience in warfare had taught him to give commands and to accept the burden of responsibility without consultation with others, and when a desire to remain active drew him to the fields of diplomacy and politics he possessed neither the training nor the tact nor perhaps the abilities for tasks which were thrust upon him.[3] In English domestic affairs he was lacking in fundamental knowledge of political and social questions, and he was destined to find both Cabinet and nation unlike an army in their hesitancy to obey orders.

Wellington remained away from home most of the time from 1815 to 1818 in order to deal with questions concerning the occupation of France. From 1818 to his death in 1852 he was an active figure in domestic affairs and his political influence was evidenced by the fact that he was largely responsible for the appointment of Canning to the Foreign Office in 1822. He was destined, however, to experience a growing distrust of the latter's policy, and finally he became so bitter that, when Canning assumed Liverpool's place, Wellington resigned from the Cabinet and from the leadership of the Army.

But he himself was leader of the government in January 1828 and immediately found disturbing problems confronting his administration. Within a month he was working on the repeal of the Test and Corporation Acts. Wellington's reasons for action are given in "Corporation and Test Acts Repeal Bill" (page 55). Lord Eldon and others of the old Tory group were displeased by the course of events. But if this Tory group was aroused at the repeal of Test and Corporation Acts, it became sullen and sour at Catholic emancipation. The Duke in spite of a statement of intentions to the contrary[4] gave way before pressure. For his

[3] Cf. Richard Aldington, *Wellington* (London: William Heinemann, Ltd., 1946), p. 253.
[4] Cf. Hansard, XIX (N.S.), 167.

explanations, see "Catholic Emancipation," page 58. A further consideration of his attitude toward religious questions may be found in "Additional Problems in Church and State Relationships" (page 71). Wellington's administration was plagued much by the economic distress of the nation that had continued from the Panic of 1825. That the Duke himself had clear vision on the situation may be gleaned from "The State of the Country" (page 77). But the hindrance to his continuation in office and the opportunity for a Whig revival of power were presented in the question of Parliamentary reform. His own famous speech on November 2, 1830, expressed his opinions so clearly that it is sometimes said to have precipitated immediately the struggle on the question (cf. "Parliamentary Reform," page 82). The Radical *Examiner*, mindful alike of the impressions caused by his surrender on two political questions and of another momentous problem on the horizon, needed but a revised nursery rhyme to sum up the situation:

> Heigh diddle diddle,
> The Duke is the riddle;
>   The cow has le'pt over the moon.
> The cunning dogs laugh to see such fine sport,
> And the Whigs fall a licking the spoon.

Wellington continued to oppose change even after his administration was ended both in the days of Chartism (page 84) and during a period of enthusiasm for Owenite socialism (page 86).

At the expiration of the Whig administration, Wellington again held position in 1834, first taking general charge of the government until Peel found it possible to get home from Rome and later becoming Foreign Secretary. After 1835, however, he held no important office though the Conservatives deemed it necessary to leave him in the Cabinet without office and the Whigs, especially under Melbourne, found it convenient to rely upon his moderation, when he was in opposition, as an antidote to radicalism. His death in 1852 was accompanied by tangible evidence of the respect and esteem in which he was held by his countrymen; the outward symbol of the popular sentiment which has impressed later generations, however, has not been so much the watchful gaze of the million and half who looked upon the funeral procession but rather the tribute which an outstanding poet of the age paid in one of the greatest of odes:

> O friends, our chief state-oracle is mute!
> Mourn for the man of long-enduring blood,
> The statesman-warrior, moderate, resolute,
> Whole in himself, a common good.
> Mourn for the man of amplest influence,
> Yet clearest of ambitious crime,
> Our greatest yet with least pretence,
> Great in council and great in war,
> Foremost captain of his time,
> Rich in saving common-sense,
> And, as the greatest only are,
> In his simplicity sublime.

As a speaker Wellington was far from brilliant. His articulation was indistinct, his diction bleak; he made no pretensions to eloquence. But he had clear understanding and, as Greville said, "a bold, manly and high tone, not like a practised debater, but a man with a vigorous mind and determined character. What he says is much to the point; no nonsense or verbiage; he says strongly and simply what he has to say." To Disraeli's thinking he possessed "a gruff, husky sort of a downright Montaigneish naïveté about him which is quaint, unusual, and tells." He did not lack ability to persuade, and, if, as is sometimes said, he explained the Battle of Waterloo so well that George IV was ever after able to imagine himself an actual spectator of the event, perhaps, upon occasion, the Duke could make use of histrionicism.

1. Corporation and Test Acts Repeal Bill

The following speech, express-ing very briefly but clearly Wel-lington's reasons for advocating a change in laws that dealt with church and state relationships, was given in the House of Lords on April 17, 1828. It can be found in HANSARD *(XVIII [N.S.], 1502-5). Additional data on the subject of religious disabilities can be found in Canning's speeches, "The Cath-olic Question" (page 38) and "Par-liamentary Reform—Repeal of the Test Act" (page 43), in chapter 2.*

The Duke of Wellington said:—I did not mean to trouble your lord-ships with my opinions on the present measure in this stage of the proceedings, and I should have reserved what I intended to offer for a future opportunity, had it not been for the statements of my noble and learned friend,[5] relative to the line of conduct adopted by gov-ernment, when the present bill was first brought forward in the other House. It is certainly true, that my right honourable friends in the other House did oppose the bill when it was first introduced to their notice: and the principle on which they opposed it was, that although they did not approve entirely of the existing law on the subject, they had found it to conduce so much to the advantage of Church and State, without impairing the religious peace of the country—a peace which has been enjoyed by this country in a greater degree than by any other—that they conceived we might risk the loss of our present ad-vantages, if the system under which those advantages had been at-tained and preserved should be inconsiderately abrogated. That principle it was on which they opposed the bill in the first instance. Afterwards, however, on finding that a large majority of the House of Commons agreed to the bill, and that many who opposed it, opposed it on grounds not applicable to the measure now before your lord-ships, my right honourable friends adopted the measure with an amendment, which, in their opinion, afforded ample security to the Church, at the same time that the bill itself as modified, appeared to be calculated, so far from impairing, to improve the religious peace which this country has so long enjoyed. On that principle it was, that the measure, which had been originally opposed by my right honourable friends connected with government in the other House, afterwards received their concurrence and support.

I fully agree with my noble friend, that the security of the Church of England, and the union existing between it and the State, depend neither on the law about to be repealed by the pres-ent bill, nor upon the provisions of this measure itself. That union

[5] Lord Eldon.

and security, which we must all desire to see continued, depend upon the oath taken by his majesty, to which we are all, in our respective stations, parties, and not only on that oath, but on the act of Settlement, and the different acts of union from time to time agreed to; all of which provide for the intimate and inseparable union of Church and State, and for the security of both.

The question we have to consider is, what security does the existing system of laws as they now stand, afford the Church Establishment. My lords, I am very dubious as to the amount of security afforded through the means of a system of exclusion from office, to be carried into effect by a law which it is necessary to suspend by an annual act, that admits every man into office whom it was the intention of the original framers of that law to exclude. It is perfectly true, it was not the intention of those who brought in that Suspension-law originally, that Dissenters from the Church of England should be permitted to enter into corporations under its provisions. The law was intended to relieve those whom time or circumstances had rendered unable to qualify themselves according to the system which government devised. It has also been said, that the Dissenters availed themselves of the relaxation of the law for the purpose of getting into corporations; and this the law allowed.

What security then, I ask, my lords, is to be found in the existing system? So far from Dissenters being excluded by the Corporation and Test acts from all corporations—so far is this from being the fact—that some corporations are absolutely and entirely in the possession of Dissenters. Can you suppose, my lords, that the repeal of laws so inoperative as these can afford any serious obstacle to the perfect security of the Church, and the permanent union of that establishment with the State? The fact is, that the existing laws have not only failed completely in answering their intended purpose, but are anomalous and absurd—anomalous in their origin, absurd in their operation. If a man were asked the question, on his election to any corporate office, whether he had received the Sacrament of the Church of England, and he said "No," then he lost every vote that had been tendered on his behalf, and there was an end of his election; but if, on the contrary, by accident or design he got in without the question relative to the Sacrament being put to him, then the votes tendered for him were held good, and his election valid; so that no power could remove him from the office which he held. I ask my noble and learned friend, is there any security in that? My noble and learned friend says, that the original intention of the framers of these acts was, that the Sacrament should not be taken by Dissenters; but the law requires that a man, on entering into any corporation, shall receive the Sacrament without regard to his religious belief. Thus, my lords, an individual whose object it is to get into a particular office, may feel disposed, naturally enough, to take the Sacrament before his election, merely as a matter of form, and thus a sacred rite of our Church is prostituted to a shameful and scandalous purpose.

I confess, my lords, I should have opposed this bill if I thought it calculated to weaken the securities at present enjoyed by the Church. I consider the opposition offered in the first instance, by my right honourable friends in the other House of Parliament, as arising out of a desire to preserve the religious peace of the country, at the same time that they secured the integrity of the Establishment. My right honourable friends at first contemplated the existing system as having given religious peace to this country for forty years. I repeat that, during forty years, that peace has never been disturbed, nor the question which is now before your lordships agitated. But, my lords, the subject of security and of religious peace was fully discussed in the other House, through which the bill before your lordships was carried by a large majority, and it now comes before your lordships and is opposed by a small minority here. Under these circumstances, I conceive that the present measure comes before you with no trifling recommendations. You have had petitions from many parishes in this kingdom, and from various societies of professing Christians, all tending to show that religious rancour and animosity can alone be generated by a perseverance in the present system, and that their contraries may be expected to arise out of a departure from it. To these sentiments I think it is our duty to consent, taking the chance for religious peace which the majority of the House of Commons consider as likely to arise, and to be continued, out of the present measure, conjoined with some degree of security—perhaps all the security necessary—offered to the Church. I, therefore, think it advisable to entertain the proposition submitted to you by the noble lord. By agreeing to it, you will attain the advantages to which I have alluded, at the same time, that you will ensure a security fully equivalent to the security, if security I may call it, which your lordships are about to repeal, by agreeing to the bill now before you.

2. Catholic Emancipation

This speech can be found in HANSARD *(XXI [N.S.], 41-58). It was delivered on behalf of the second reading of the Roman Catholic Relief Bill (April 2, 1829).*

Further background will be found in the comments on Canning's speech, "The Catholic Question," in chapter 2 of this book (page 38).

The Duke of Wellington rose and addressed their lordships as follows:—It is now my duty to move your lordships to read this bill a second time, and to explain to your lordships the grounds on which I recommend this measure to your lordships' attention. I may be under the necessity of requesting a larger portion of your time and attention, upon this occasion, than I have hitherto been in the habit of doing; but I assure you, my lords, that it is not my intention to take up one instant of your time with respect to myself, or my own conduct in this transaction, any further than to express my regret, that I should differ in opinion on this subject from so many of those for whom I entertain the highest respect and regard. I must, however, state, that I consider the part which I have taken upon this subject as the performance of a public duty, absolutely incumbent upon me; and I will say, that no private regard, no respect for the opinion of any noble lord, could induce me to depart from the course which I have considered it my duty to adopt. I must likewise say this—that, comparing my own opinions with that of others, upon this subject, I have, during the period I have been in office, had opportunities of forming a judgment upon this subject, which others have not possessed; and they will admit, that I should not have given the opinion I have given, if I was not intimately and firmly persuaded that that opinion was a just one.

My lords, the point which I shall first bring under your lordships' consideration is the state of Ireland. I know that, by some, it has been considered that the state of Ireland has nothing to do with this question—that it is a subject which ought to be left entirely out of our consideration. My lords, they tell us, that Ireland has been disturbed for the last thirty years—that it is a disturbance we have been accustomed to—and that therefore it does not at all alter the circumstances of the case, as they have hitherto appeared to this House. My lords, it is perfectly true that Ireland has been disturbed during the long period I have stated; but within the last year or two political circumstances have, in no small degree, occasioned that agitation. Besides that, my lords, I must say,—although I have no positive legal proof of the fact,—I have every reason to believe, that there has been a considerable organization of the people, for the purposes of mischief. My lords, this organization is, it appears to me, to be proved, not only by the declarations of those who formed and who arranged it, but likewise by the effects which it has produced in the election of churchwardens throughout the country—in the circumstances attending the election for the county of Clare [6]—in the circumstances that preceded and followed that election—in the proceedings of the gentleman who went at the head of a body of men to the north of Ireland—in the simultaneous proceedings of various bodies of men in the south of Ireland, in Templemore, Killenaule, Cahir, Clonmel, and other places—in the proceedings of another gentleman in the king's county; [7] and in the recall of the former gentleman from the north of Ireland by the Roman Catholic Association. In all these circumstances it is quite obvious to me, that there was an organization and direction of the people, proceeding from some superior authority; and this organization has certainly produced a state of society in Ireland which we have not heretofore witnessed, and an aggravation of all the evils which had before afflicted that unfortunate country.

My lords, late in the year a considerable town was attacked in the middle of the night by a body of people who came from the neighbouring mountains—the town of Augher. They attacked it with arms, and were driven from it with arms by the inhabitants of the town. This is a state of things which I feel your lordships will admit ought not to exist in a civilized country. Later in the year still, a similar event occurred in Charleville; and, in the course of last autumn, the Roman Catholic Association deliberated upon the propriety of adopting, and the means of adopting, the measure of ceasing all dealings between Roman Catholics and Protestants. Is it possible to believe that supposing these dealings had ceased—supposing this measure had been carried into execution—as I firmly believe it was in the power of those who deliberated upon it to carry it into execution—is it possible to believe, that those who could thus cease these dealings would not likewise have ceased to carry into execution the contracts into which they had entered? Will any man say, that people in this situation are verging towards that state, in which it would be impossible to expect from them that they would be able to perform the duties of jurymen, or to administer justice between man and man, for the protection of the lives and

[6] The famous election in which Daniel O'Connell who had founded the Catholic Association ran against the popular Protestant landowner, Vesey Fitzgerald, who had been asked to assume government office. O'Connell, though disqualified from taking a seat in Parliament, won in the race to the dismay of the Duke.

[7] This county received its name in the reign of Mary.

properties of his majesty's subjects? My lords, this is the state of society to which I have wished to draw your attention, and for which it is necessary that parliament should provide a remedy.

Before I proceed to consider what those remedies should be, I wish just to show your lordships what is the effect of this state of society upon the king's prerogative. My lords, his majesty could not create a peer; and the reason he could not create a peer was this— his majesty's servants could not venture to recommend to him to incur the risks of an election in another part of the country, and the risks which might have attended any accident at that election, which might have occasioned the shedding of blood. Such a disaster must have been productive of an immediate civil war in the country; but not only was that the case, my lords, but I confess that I had the strongest objection to give another triumph to the Roman Catholic Association. Then we are asked "why do you not carry the law into execution?" Why, my lords, in all that I have stated hitherto there was no resistance to the law. The magistrates were terrified, and did nothing; the troops did not happen immediately to be upon the spot, and there was no resistance. There were no troops, except in the case of the procession that went to the north of Ireland. I believe there was no instance of any opposition to the king's troops, and there was no instance in which the law could be carried into execution. When we hear noble lords reproaching the government for not carrying into execution the law in Ireland, as it was carried into execution in England, the observation shows that they do not understand the state of things in Ireland. The truth of the matter is, that in England, when the law was carried into execution, in the year 1819, a large body of persons assembled for an illegal purpose; they resisted the order of the magistrates to disperse, and having resisted that order, the magistrates ordered the troops to disperse them; [8] but in this case there were no circumstances of the same kind: no order was given to disperse; no order could be given to disperse—because no magistrates were present; and, if they had been present, there were no troops to disperse them. The truth is, the state of society was such as rendered these events possible every hour; and it was impossible that the magistrates could be at every spot, and at all times, to put an end to these outrages, which really are a disgrace to the country in which they exist. But, my lords, neither the law nor the means in the possession of government enable government to put an end to these things. It was necessary, therefore, to come to parliament.

[8] Reference to Peterloo in chapter 2, "Vindication of Governmental Policies" (page 21).

Now, let us see what chance there was of providing a remedy for this state of things by coming to parliament. My lords, we all recollect perfectly well, that the opinion of the majority in another place is, that the remedy for this state of things in Ireland is a repeal of the disabilities affecting his majesty's Roman Catholic subjects. We might, to be sure, have come and asked parliament to enable us to put down the Roman Catholic Association; but what chance had we of prevailing upon parliament to pass such a bill as that, without being prepared to come forward and state that we were ready to consider the whole condition of Ireland, with a view to apply a remedy to that which parliament had stated to be the cause of the disease. Suppose that parliament had given us the bill to put down the Roman Catholic Association, would such a law as that which has passed this year be a remedy for the state of things which I have already described to your lordships as existing in Ireland? Would it, I ask, do any one thing towards putting down the mischiefs which are the consequences of that organization? Would it do any thing towards giving you the means of getting a better state of things in Ireland, without some further measure to be adopted?

But, my lords, it is said, "if that will not do, let us proceed to blows." What, I suppose, is meant by "proceeding to blows" is coming to civil war. Now, I believe that every government must be prepared to carry into execution the laws of the country by the force placed at its disposition—by the military force, in case that should be necessary; and above all things, to oppose resistance to the law, in case the disaffected or the ill-disposed are inclined to resist the authority or sentence of the law; but as I have already stated to your lordships, there was no resistance of the law;—nay, more, I will go further, and say, I am positively certain, that this state of things existing in Ireland for the last year and a half, bordering upon civil war—being attended by nearly all the evils of civil war—might have continued a considerable time longer, to the great injury and disgrace of the country, and those who managed the state, if they would have taken care to prevent that resistance which might have ended in that state of things being put down. They know as well as I do they are not strong enough to wrestle with the king's government, backed by the law; they know perfectly well they would have been the first victims of that resistance; but knowing this, and knowing, as I do, that they are sensible, able men, and perfectly aware of the materials upon which they have to work, I have not the smallest doubt that the state of things which I have stated to your lordships would have continued for years, and that you would never have had an opportunity of putting it down in the manner some noble lords imagine.

But, my lords, even if I had been certain of possessing such means of putting it down, I should certainly have considered it my duty to avoid resorting to those means. I am one of those who have probably passed a longer period of my life engaged in war than most men, and principally, I may say, in civil war; and I must say this— that if I could avoid, by any sacrifice whatever, even one month of civil war in the country to which I am attached, I would sacrifice my life in order to do it (cheers). I say that there is nothing which destroys property and prosperity, and demoralizes character, to the degree that civil war does: by it the hand of man is raised against his neighbour, against his brother, and against his father; the servant betrays his master, and the whole scene ends in confusion and devastation. Yet, my lords, this is the resource to which we must have looked—these are the means to which we must have applied, in order to have put an end to this state of things, if we had not made the option of bringing forward the measures, for which I hold myself responsible.

But let us look a little further, my lords. If civil war is so bad, when it is occasioned by resistance to the government—if it is so bad in the case I have stated, and so much to be avoided—how much more is it to be avoided when we have to arm the people, in order that we may conquer one part of them by exciting the other part against them? My lords, I am sure there is not a man who hears me, whose blood would not shudder at such a proposition, if it were made to him; and yet that is the recourse to which we should be pushed at last, by continuing the course we have been adopting for the last few years.

However, I entreat your lordships not only to look at it in this view, but likewise to revert a little to what passed on a former similar occasion. My lords I am old enough to remember the rebellion of 1798. I was not employed in Ireland at the time, I was employed in another part of the dominions; but, my lords, if I am not mistaken, the parliament of Ireland at that time went up to the lord lieutenant with a unanimous address, (I believe they walked up in a body) beseeching his excellency to take every means to put down that unnatural rebellion, and promising their full support in order to carry that measure into execution. The lord lieutenant did take those measures, and did succeed in putting down that rebellion. Well, my lords, what happened in the very next session? The government proposed to put an end to the Irish parliament, and to form a legislative union between the two kingdoms, for the principal purpose of proposing this very measure (cheers); and in point of fact, the very first measure that was proposed after this legislative union—after those successful endeavours to put down this rebellion —was the very measure with which I am now about to trouble your lordships.

Why, then, I ask, is it possible noble lords can believe that, supposing there was such a contest as that which I have anticipated— is it possible noble lords can believe that such a contest could be carried on, much less brought to a conclusion, without the measure which I now propose being insisted on by one at least, if not both Houses of parliament? I am certain, my lords, when your lordships look at the division of opinion which prevails in both Houses of parliament upon this question,—when you look at the division of opinion which prevails in every family in this country and in Ireland, from the most eminent in station down to the lowest,—when you look at the division of opinion which prevails amongst even the Protestants in Ireland—when your lordships look at these circumstances, I am sure you will perceive the vast difference there would be between a contest carried on now, and that which was carried on at a former period.

My lords, I beg your lordships to recollect that, upon a recent occasion, there was a Protestant Declaration of the sentiments of Ireland. As I said before, the parliament of Ireland, in the year 1798, with the exception of one or two persons, were unanimous; and, on a recent occasion, there were seven marquises, twenty-seven earls, a vast number of peers of other ranks, and not less than two thousand Protestant gentlemen of property in the country, who signed the Declaration, stating the absolute necessity of making these concessions. Under these circumstances it is, that this contest would have been carried on—circumstances totally different from those which existed at that period I before alluded to. But, is it possible to believe that parliament would allow such a contest to go on? Is it possible to believe that parliament, having this state of things before them—that this House, seeing what the opinion of the other House of parliament is—seeing what the opinion of the large number of Protestants in Ireland is—seeing what the opinion of nearly every statesman, for the last forty years, has been on this question—would continue to oppose itself to measures brought forward for its settlement? It appears to me absolutely impossible that we could have gone on longer, without increasing difficulties being brought on the country.

But it is very desirable that your lordships should look a little to what benefit is to be derived, to any one class in the state, by continuing the disabilities, and only taking those coercive measures which will have all the evils which I have stated. We are told, that the benefit will be to preserve the principles of the constitution of 1688—that the measures of 1688 permanently excluded Roman Catholics from parliament—and that they being so permanently excluded from parliament, it is necessary to have recourse to all those evils, in order to keep up that permanent exclusion. Now, I wish very much that the noble lords would take upon themselves the trouble I have taken to see how the matter stands as to the permanent exclusion of Roman Catholics from parliament. My lords, in the Bill of Rights, there are some things permanently enacted, which I sincerely hope will be permanent;—those are, the liberties of the people; the security for Protestantism of the person on the throne of these kingdoms, and that he shall not be married to a papist. Then there is an Oath of Allegiance and Supremacy to be taken by all those of whom that Oath of Allegiance is required, which is also permanent; but there is no Declaration against Transubstantiation. There is also an Oath of Allegiance, different from that which is required to be taken by a member of parliament. I beg your lordships will observe that, although this Oath of Allegiance was declared to be permanent, it was altered in the reign of William and Mary. This shows what that permanent act was. Then, with respect to the oaths to be taken by members of parliament, I beg your lordships to observe, that these oaths, the Declaration against Transubstantiation, and the sacrifice of the mass, are not in the act of William 3rd but in the act of 30th Charles 2nd. During the reign of Charles 2nd, there were certain oaths imposed, first on Dissenters from the Church of England, by the 13th and 14th Charles 2nd, and to exclude Roman Catholics, by the 25th, and 30th Charles 2nd. At the period of the Revolution, when king William came, he thought proper to extend the basis of his government, and he repealed the oaths affecting the Dissenters from the Church of England, imposed by the 13th and 14th Charles 2nd, and likewise that affirmative part of the Oath of Supremacy, which Dissenters from the Church of England could not take. This is the history of the alteration of these oaths by William 3rd, from the time of Charles 2nd. But, my lords, the remainder of the oath could be taken by Dissenters, but could not be taken by Roman Catholics. The danger, with respect to Roman Catholics, had originated in the time of Charles 2nd, and these oaths still existed in the time of William 3rd; but the oath was altered, because one of the great principles of the Revolution was, to limit the exclusion from the benefits of the constitution as far as it was possible. Therefore we have the great principle of the Revolution, as well as the principle I before stated, which consisted of the Bill of Rights and liberties of the subject. Now, the noble lords state, that what they call the principles of 1688—that is to say, these oaths excluding Roman Catholics—are equally permanent with the Bill of Rights, by which the Protestantism of the Crown is secured. If noble lords will do me the favour to look at the words of the act—I have it ready—they will find that the difference between the two things is just the difference between that which is permanent and that which is not. The Bill of Rights declares that the Protestantism of the Crown shall last for ever—that the liberties of the people shall be secured for ever; but it is remarkable, that as to these oaths which were enacted on the same occasion, not one word is said about their lasting forever, or as to how long they should last.

Well, then, my lords, what follows? The next act we have is the Act of Union with Scotland; and what does that act say?—Why, that the oaths to be taken by the members of parliament are to be laid down by the 1st of William and Mary until parliament shall otherwise direct. This is what is called a "permanent act of parliament—a permanent provision, for all future periods, to exclude Catholics from seats in parliament!" My lords, I beg to observe, that if the act which excludes Roman Catholics from seats in parliament is permanent, there is another clause (I believe the 10th of chap. 8, 1st of William and Mary) which requires officers of the army and navy to take these very oaths, previous to their acceptance of their commissions. Now, if the act made in the first year of William and Mary, which excludes Roman Catholics from parliament, is permanent, I should like to ask noble lords why the clause in that act is not equally permanent? I should like to ask the noble and learned lord on the cross-bench to answer that question. If the oaths were permanent in the one case they were equally so in the other; and yet the noble and learned lord consented to the bill of 1817, which repealed oaths required to be taken by officers of the army and navy. . . . . .

Then, if this principle of exclusion—if this principle of the constitution of 1688, as it is called—be not permanent, if it be recognized to be not permanent, not only by the Act of Union with Scotland (in which it is said, that the exclusive oath shall continue until parliament otherwise provide), but also by the later act of Union with Ireland, I would ask your lordships, whether you are not at liberty now to consider the expediency of doing away with it altogether, in order to relieve the country from the inconveniences to which I have already adverted? I would ask your lordships, whether you are not called upon to review the state of the representation of Ireland—whether you are not called upon to see, whether, even supposing that that principle were a permanent one, it be fit that parliament should remain as it has remained for some time, groaning under a popish influence exercised by the priests over the elections in Ireland. I would ask your lordships, I repeat, whether it be not right to make an arrangement, which has for its object, not only the settlement of this question, but at the same time to relieve the country from the inconveniences which I have mentioned. I have already stated the manner in which the organization I have already alluded to works upon all the great interests of the country; but I wish your lordships particularly to attend to the manner in which it works upon the church itself. That part of the Church of England which exists in Ireland is in a very peculiar situation: it is the church of the minority of the people. At the same time, I believe, that a more exemplary, a more pious, and a more learned body of men, than the members of that church do not exist. The clergy of that church certainly enjoy and deserve the affections of those whom they were sent to instruct, to the same degree as their brethren in England enjoy the affections of the people of this country; and I have no doubt that they would, if necessary, shed the last drop of their blood in defence of the doctrines and discipline of their church. But violence, I apprehend, is likely to affect the interests of that church; and I would put it to the House, whether that church can be better protected from violence by a government united in itself, united with parliament, and united in sentiment with the great body of the people—or by a government disunited in opinion, disunited from parliament, and by the two Houses of parliament disunited. I am certain that no man can look at the situation of Ireland, without seeing that the interest of the church, as well as the interest of every class of persons under government, is involved in such a settlement of this question as will bring with it strength to the government, and strength to every department of the state.

Having now, my lords, gone through the general principles which have induced me to consider it desirable to bring forward this measure, I will trouble your lordships for a short time longer, whilst I explain generally the provisions of the bill before the House.

My lords; the bill is in itself very simple. It concedes to the Roman Catholics the power of holding every office in the state, excepting a few connected with the administration of the affairs of the church; and it also concedes to them the power of becoming members of parliament. I believe it goes further, with respect to the concession of offices, than any former measure which has been introduced into the other House of parliament. . . . . . I have . . . . considered it my duty, in making this act of concession, to make it as large as any reasonable man could expect it to be; seeing clearly, that any thing which remained behind would only give ground for fresh demands, and being convinced, that the settlement of this question would tend to the security of the state, and to the peace and prosperity of the country.

I have already stated to your lordships my opinion respecting the expediency of granting seats in parliament to Roman Catholics; and I do not conceive that the concession of seats in parliament can, in any manner, affect any question relative to the Church of England. In the first place, I beg your lordships to recollect that at the time those acts, to which I have before alluded—the one passed in the 30th of Charles 2nd, and the other at the period of the Revolution —were enacted, it was not the church that was in danger—it was the state. It was the state that was in danger—and from what? It was not because the safety of the church was threatened. No! but it was because the sovereign on the throne was suspected of popery, and because the successor to the throne was actually a papist. Those laws were adopted, because of the existence of a danger which threatened the state, and not of one which threatened the church. On the contrary, at that period, danger to the church was apprehended, not from the Roman Catholics, but from the Dissenters from the Church of England. I would ask of your lordships, all of whom have read the history of those times, whether any danger to the church was apprehended from the Roman Catholics? No! Danger to the church was apprehended from the Dissenters, who had become powerful by the privileges granted to them, under the act of parliament passed at the period of the Revolution. I think, therefore, that it is not necessary for me to enter into any justification of myself for having adopted this measure, on account of any danger which might be apprehended from it to the church. Roman Catholics will come into parliament by this bill, as they went into parliament previous to the act of the 30th of Charles 2nd. They sat in parliament up to that period, and were not obliged to take the Oath of Supremacy. By this bill they will be required to take the Oath of Allegiance, in which a great part of the Oath of Supremacy is included; namely, that part which refers to the jurisdiction of foreign potentates; and I must say, that if the church be in danger, it is better secured by this bill than by the 30th of Charles 2nd, which has continued in force up to the present moment; though the object for which that act was recognized at the period of the Revolution; namely, to keep out the House of Stuart from the throne—has long since ceased to exist by the extinction of that family.

It is the opinion of nearly every considerable man in the country, that the time is now arrived for repealing those laws. Circumstances have been gradually moving to their repeal, ever since the extinction of the House of Stuart; and at last the period is come, when it is quite clear that that repeal cannot with safety be any longer delayed.

But I know that there are many in your lordships' House, and many in the country, who think—and I admit that formerly I was of the same opinion—that the state ought to have some security for the church, against the proceedings of the Roman Catholic clergy, besides the oaths imposed by the act of parliament I have already alluded to. But I confess that, on examining into the question, and looking more minutely than I had before an opportunity of doing, at the various acts of parliament by which the Church of England was constituted, and which form the foundation on which it rests, I can think of no sort of arrangement capable of being carried into execution in this country, which can add to the security of the established church.[9] . . . .

.   .   .   .

Another part of the bill has for its object the putting an end to the order of the Jesuits, and other monastic orders in this country. If your lordships will look at the act passed in the year 1791, you will probably see that at that time it was possible to make laws through which a coach-and-four might be driven (a laugh). My noble and learned friend will excuse me, I hope, for saying, that notwithstanding all the pains which he took to draw up the act of 1791, yet the fact is,—of which there cannot be the smallest doubt,—that large monastic establishments have been regularly formed, not only in Ireland, but also in this country. The measure which I now propose for your lordships' adoption will prevent the increase of such establishments, and, without oppression to any individuals, without injury to any body of men, will gradually put an end to those which have already been formed. There is no man more convinced than I am of the absolute necessity of carrying into execution that part of the present measure, which has for its object the extinction of monastic orders in this country. I entertain no doubt whatever, that if that part of the measure be not carried into execution, your lordships will very soon see this country and Ireland inundated by Jesuits and regular monastic clergy, sent out from other parts of Europe, with means to establish themselves within his majesty's kingdom.

When I recommend this measure to your lordships' attention,

[9] The Duke of Wellington then discusses possible securities such as concordats, examples of whose workings were to be found in the kingdom of Prussia, and the right of royal nomination of the Catholic bishops.

you have undoubtedly a right to ask, what are the reasons which I have for believing that it will effect the purpose for which it is intended. My lords, I believe it will answer its object, not only from the example of all Europe, but from what has occurred in a part of this kingdom on a former occasion. If I am not mistaken, at the time of the dispute between the episcopalians and the kirk of Scotland, the state of society in Scotland, was as bad as the state of society in Ireland is at the present moment. Your lordships know, that abroad, in consequence of the diffusion of civil privileges to all classes, the difference between Protestant and Catholic is never heard. I am certain that I can prove to your lordships what I state, when I say, that the state of society in Scotland, previous to the concession of civil privileges to the episcopalians, was as bad as the present state of society in Ireland. I hope your lordships will give me leave to read a petition which has been sent to me this day, and which was presented to parliament at the period when those concessions were about to be made, and your lordships will perceive, that the petition is almost a model of many of the petitions which have been read in your lordships' House, respecting the question under discussion. I am therefore in expectation, that should the present bill pass your lordships' House, there will be no longer occasion for those complaints which have been expressed to your lordships, and that the same happy and peaceful state of things which has for the last century prevailed in Scotland will also prevail in Ireland. I will with your lordships' permission, read the petition I have alluded to, and I think that after you have heard it, you will be of the same opinion as I am with respect to the similarity it bears to many of the petitions which have been presented to your lordships on the subject of the Catholic question. The petition states, that "to grant toleration to that party (the episcopalians), in the present circumstances of the church, must unavoidably shake the foundation of our present happy constitution; overthrow those laws on which it is settled; grievously disturb that peace and tranquillity which the nation has enjoyed since the late Revolution; disquiet the minds of his majesty's best subjects; increase animosity; confirm discord and tumult; weaken and enervate the discipline of the church; open a door to unheard of vices, and to popery as well as to other errors; propagate and cherish disaffection to the government, and bring the nation under the danger of falling back into those errors from which it has recovered itself." The petition in conclusion stated, "that to grant toleration to the episcopalians would be to establish iniquity by law, and they therefore prayed the members of the high court of parliament to uphold, and preserve the laws." I sincerely hope that as the prophecy contained in the petition I have just read has not been fulfilled, a similar prophecy respecting the passing of the present bill, contained in many of the petitions presented to your lordships, will not be fulfilled likewise.

But, my lords, I have other grounds besides those which I have stated for supposing that the proposed measure will answer that object in view. There is no doubt that, after this measure shall be adopted, the Roman Catholics can have no separate interest, as a separate sect; for I am sure that neither your lordships nor the other House of parliament will be disposed to look upon the Roman Catholics, nor upon any thing that respects Ireland, with any other eye than that with which you behold whatever affects the interest of Scotland and of this country. For my own part, I will state, that if I am disappointed in the hopes which I entertain, that tranquillity will result from this measure, I shall have no scruple in coming down and laying before parliament the state of the case, and calling upon parliament to enable government to meet whatever danger may arise. I shall act with the same confidence that parliament will support me then, as I have acted in the present case.

Having now explained to your lordships the grounds on which this measure is brought forward,—the state of Ireland,—the inconvenience attending the continued agitation of the question,—the difficulty, nay, the impossibility, of finding any other remedy for the state of things in Ireland,—the state of public opinion on the question,—the divisions of the government and of the parliament on this question,—the pretences, for so I must call them, which have been urged against the claims of the Catholics, founded on acts passed previous to the Revolution,—having stated likewise the provisions of the measure which I propose as a remedy for all these inconveniences, I will trouble your lordships no further, except by beseeching your lordships to consider the subject with the coolness, moderation, and temper, recommended in his majesty's most gracious Speech from the Throne.

3. Additional Problems in Church and State Relationships

A. Removal of Jewish Civil Disabilities
B. Religious Tests for Admission to Oxford and Cambridge

On August 1, 1833, the Duke of Sussex presented to the Lords a petition in favor of the Jewish Civil Disabilities Bill, signed by 7,000 inhabitants of the city of Westminster. He stated that he should give the measure his utmost support on the same principles which had led him to favor Catholic emancipation. Section A gives Wellington's reaction (HANSARD, XX [3d Ser.], 245-47). It is worthy of comment that Wellington makes a distinction between Catholics and Jews on grounds of expediency and not on grounds of principle. Section B (HANSARD, XXIX [3d Ser.], 529-33) gives Wellington's opinions on the question of whether or not the Thirty-nine Articles should be taken as a test on admission to the University of Oxford or Cambridge. The issue was debated on July 14, 1835.

A. Removal of Jewish Civil Disabilities

The Duke of Wellington observed, that the noble and learned Lord (the Lord Chancellor) [10] had said, that it was incumbent upon those who opposed this Bill, to find reasons for their opposition. This he denied. He begged to tell the noble and learned Lord, that this was a Christian country and a Christian Legislature, and that before their Lordships could fairly be called upon to agree to a measure, which at the first blush appeared to invade the principles by which the Legislature had been hitherto guided, it was requisite that some case should be brought forward to prove the necessity of the Bill. The noble and learned Lord had compared the case of the Jews to that of the Roman Catholics; but it should be remembered, that there was an essential difference in this respect. The Roman Catholic Relief Bill was adopted, because it was thought no longer necessary to continue the restrictions imposed by law on the professors of that religion, who had previously to their imposition, enjoyed all the privileges of which they had been deprived. The Catholics had a heavy ground of complaint on that head, whereas the Jews had no such complaint to make; they had never enjoyed privileges, and therefore could not claim their restoration. The conditions of

[10] Lord Brougham.

71

the Jews had, in fact, been much improved. They were formerly considered as aliens, and from the reign, he believed, of Edward the 1st, to the Commonwealth, their residence in this country was forbidden under severe penalties. The case of the Jews, therefore, stood on a very different footing from that of the Catholics and other Dissenters, to whom relief had been afforded.

The noble and learned Lord had referred to certain Acts of Parliament, by which certain indulgences were granted to Jews in the very words of the present Bill. But those indulgences were granted to Jews in the colonies—in Canada, Jamaica, and Barbadoes; and what was the reason for this? Was there no State necessity for it? Certainly there was. European inhabitants were required in the colonies, and English inhabitants especially; and it was in order to encourage their settlement in Canada, that by the 7th of George 3rd (he believed), these relaxations were made in favour of the Jews—relaxations which were also adopted in the other instances alluded to. But no such necessity existed in the present instance, nor did any reason, equally forcible, now occur. Instead, no one noble Lord who had supported the Bill, had attempted to prove any necessity for it. They had heard of other countries. Buonaparte had granted great privileges to the Jews, it was true; but it was on reasons of strong policy, and not till he had carefully inquired whether there would be any danger in so doing. Whereas, here, there was not the slightest previous examination attempted.

All that could be contended in favour of this Bill was, that the present was the age of liberal principles, and that this Bill suited the liberal principles of the age. The noble and learned Lord had contended, that by keeping up these restrictions, persons of tender conscience were excluded, whilst those who had no conscience at all, men like Shaftesbury and Bolingbroke, and Wilkes, were admitted. Certainly, there might be some persons of that kind admitted. There were men who would violate all rules, all oaths, and all safeguards; but that was no reason why society should relinquish those safeguards and securities which were, in the majority of instances, effectual. Whilst he fully admitted the respectability and propriety of conduct of a large portion of the Jewish nation, he could not, as a member of a Christian assembly, advise the Christian King of a Christian country to pass such a Bill. The noble and learned Lord had said, that the Christianity which was the law of the land, was merely the Christianity of the Church of England. He differed from the noble Lord, and thought that the law of England derived its code of morality from the Christian dispensation generally, and regarded that dispensation generally as part of that law. He felt it to be his duty to oppose this Bill.

B. Religious Tests for Admission to Oxford and Cambridge

The Duke of Wellington thought that the observations of the most reverend Prelate [11] had completely put an end to the question. The Bill which the noble Earl had brought forward was entirely different from that which was introduced last Session. The speech of the noble Earl,[12] however, and the explanation with which he introduced the measure, showed that his intention was precisely the same with the intention of the promoter of the former Bill. The noble Earl's intention—and the noble Lord [13] at the head of the Government had clearly stated this intention to be also his—was, to give the Dissenters a right to enter the Universities. That was the intention of the noble Earl, and that was the intention of the Prime Minister.

Now he had an objection to the Bill of the noble Earl for the reason stated by the most reverend Prelate. He conceived there was no cause to complain of the subscription to the Thirty-nine Articles, as practised in the University of Oxford. He would say that the explanation of the most reverend Prelate was entirely borne out by the statutes of the University, and likewise by the practice which had prevailed there. It might be desirable that there should be some other test adopted, in order to prove that the individual claiming to be matriculated was a member of the Church of England; but that which was most important at Cambridge and Oxford was, that the person to be matriculated was a member of the Church of England. That was the point; and upon that he conceived the whole question turned. The noble Earl, in his observations, alluded to something that fell from him in the course of the discussion of this question last year, viz., that he advised the most reverend Prelate not to consent to this Bill, because by such consent they would carry up to the Throne for his Majesty's assent, a measure which would tend to subvert the union between the Church and the State. That argument was neither more nor less than this—that the education of both the Universities must be education in the religion of the Church of England. That was necessary—it was the very foundation on which the Universities stood. He contended that they could not go to the King with a Bill that had for its object to establish a system of education in the Universities different in prin-

[11] The Archbishop of Canterbury.
[12] The Earl of Radnor.
[13] Viscount Melbourne.

ciple from the Church of England, without attacking the principle
of union between the Church and State.

But the noble Lord said, that the Church did not claim from
individuals any subscription to the Thirty-nine Articles. True, it
did not; nor would the University of Oxford claim the subscription
of the Thirty-nine Articles, except as evidence that the person was
a member of a family who belonged to the Established Church.
It was contended last year, and by the noble Earl this year, that
individuals might be admitted into both the Universities who were
not members of the Church of England, notwithstanding the subscription of the Thirty-nine Articles. He admitted this; but there was
a great difference between this and allowing Dissenters by right
to enter the Universities. What he contended for was, that the
system of religion taught should be that of the Established Church;
but if Dissenters were admitted of right, he was apprehensive that
not only would not the religion of the Established Church be
taught, but that no religion of any kind would be taught there.
He stated this opinion on the authority of a publication, from which
it appeared, that at a college established to teach ministers of dis-
senting persuasions it had been found impossible to adopt any creed
or any system for any considerable length of time. He confessed he
was surprised when he heard the noble Lord the first minister of the
Crown come down to this House and declare his preference for the
existence of polemical disputes in the Universities. He should have
thought the object of a Minister of the Crown would have been,
by all means to protect the Universities from all such disputes, and
to preserve any system of religion whatever from being attacked by
differences of opinion. He confessed that it appeared to him that
the Bill of the noble Earl, if it had really for its object to prevent
the signature of the Articles, did not go far enough for the attainment of the object the noble Earl had in view. As was truly stated
by the noble Viscount, the Universities were enabled to make
regulations respecting the taking of degrees, which might interfere
with a Bill like the present; the Colleges, indeed, by the will of
their founders, and by their original charters, were compelled to
make certain regulations on this subject, under which they acted.
If this measure, therefore, passed, they would have to take other
measures to insure the object they intended to attain by the signature of the Thirty-nine Articles.

The noble Earl had not only compared the two Universities with
foreign Universities, but also drew a parallel between the practice
prevailing at the present day, and that which existed in those two
learned bodies shortly after the Reformation. Now, he agreed with
the most reverend Prelate in contending that no parallel could be

drawn between the English and Foreign Universities. The sects in the two Universities were the children of the Reformation. These sects were most necessary, and were intended to preserve the standard of the religion of the Church of England. If they were to have no established religion in the country—if every man was to have his own religion in the Universities—if every man was at liberty to frame a system of religion for himself in these corporations, then let their Lordships take the Bill of the noble Earl with all its consequences, which must inevitably follow from it, namely, constant polemical disputes, and all the other consequences which the noble Viscount regarded as proper for the Universities. Supposing the object of the noble Earl to be just, and supposing it to be desirable to put an end to these subscriptions and to all tests, he (the Duke of Wellington) conceived that no mode of effecting that object could be deemed so objectionable in its nature as by the interference of Parliament with those bodies, instituted as they were by charter, and solemnly sanctioned by Acts of Parliament. He thought that those who contended in favour of the Universities had a right to complain when they found arrayed against them the Ministers of the Crown and the policy of the Government. They had a right to expect that the noble Viscount, and the other noble Lords on the bench opposite, would support inviolate the rights, the authority, and the privileges of the Universities, as granted and conferred by ancient charters. Instead of this, however, they found the Ministers of the Crown exercised their power, their influence and abilities in support of this measure, which had for its object the overthrow of the institutions and authority of the English Church.

The noble Viscount shook his head, apparently in dissent from his opinions; but did the noble Viscount think that the University of Oxford could maintain its authority if such a Bill as this became the law of the land? On what, he would ask, was the preamble of this Bill grounded, and the charges embodied in it? Had any of those charges been proved? Notwithstanding the complaints made in the preamble that individuals had been prevented from resorting to the University of Oxford, in consequence of these tests, was it not an admitted fact that at that moment there were hundreds waiting to obtain education, and to be admitted to reside in the Halls and Colleges of that University? There were many hundreds of persons now residing in the town who were unable to get residences in the various Colleges of Oxford. He contended, therefore, that there was no ground for the complaint as stated in the preamble of the Bill, and there was no ground for Parliamentary interference by means of a Bill like the present. He entirely concurred in the statement made by the most reverend Prelate as to the consequences that would flow from this measure. Would any man tell him that he believed, after this Bill passed, that the public would not understand that the meaning of it was, to proceed against the institutions of the Church of England. It was impossible that this should not be believed. The measure itself was apparent on the face of it, although it merely stated, that the Articles of the Church should be signed at a more advanced age. Noble Lords, however, must know that the Bill was not effectual for the purpose which was contended for. It extended to other views: those who attentively considered the measure would perceive that the great object of it was, to inflict a blow on the University of Oxford and against the interests of the Church. Under these circumstances he felt that it was a measure that the House should not adopt, and he earnestly recommended their Lordships to vote for the amendment [14] of the most reverend Prelate.

[14] That this bill be read a second time this day six months.

4. The State of the Country

The following speech on the distress of the country represents Wellington's defense of the Royal Address before the Lords on February 4, 1830 (HANSARD, XXII [N.S.], 34-41). An opening portion which vindicates the governmental foreign policy against the attacks of the Earl of Carnarvon (the noble earl of the first line) is omitted.

The subject of the discussion is important not only for the presentation of the continuing bad effects of the Panic of 1825 that afford some explanation of the popular demand for Parliamentary reform but also for the connotation of unpopularity which the government of Wellington received—and perhaps deserved—because of its unwillingness or inability to formulate policies for recovery from the depression.

The noble earl has thought proper to make some observations upon the Speech, as if his majesty's government had neglected to ascertain the true state of the country—as if they were ignorant of its distress, and as if I, in particular, was negligent of my duty in this instance. I can assure him that no one is more sensible than I am of the state of things, and that no one laments it more sincerely than I do: and I am certain that independently of motive or interest in this subject arising from my official situation, there is no person in the country who feels for its distress more acutely than the person who fills the situation which I have the honour to hold.

The noble earl has said that, in the Speech, the whole of the distress is attributed to the state of the seasons; but what is the statement of the Speech upon that subject? Without affecting to quote it literally, is it not, in substance, this—"that, in considering the remedies to be applied to this state of things, you are to give due weight to the unfavourable nature of the seasons, which occasioned enormous expenses in collecting the harvest, and which has, in fact, occasioned one bad harvest, if not another; so that the collection of it was excessively expensive." Surely these circumstances must not be overlooked in taking the subject of distress into consideration.

But, besides the agriculturalists, there is another class labouring under great distress—the manufacturers. I want to know whether the competition of machinery with labour in all departments of mechanics—the general application of steam—the competition abroad with our manufacturers—and the general imitation of our fabrics—have not produced very great distress amongst the manufacturers at home? These are the circumstances to which his Majesty refers as important to be considered in connection with the subject of

distress, and they are those over which parliament has no control.
Can this House prevent competition by foreign markets with our
own? Can we prevent improvements in machinery? Can we prevent steam from being applied to foreign manufacture? And yet we
all know that this injurious competition is ruinous to the manu-
facturer, by lowering his wages, or throwing the labourers out of
employ. But then, the noble earl says the distress is general—
universal. My lords, I am afraid the distress is very general; but
I must say, notwithstanding the distress which prevails, that there
are symptoms to show that the country is advancing. I say, and it
may be proved by the documents, that the exports of British manufacture have increased, have been increasing for the last few
years, and that in the last year they were larger than they ever were
before. I say, my lords, that the amount of exports of produce of
British manufacture is greater than it ever was before. (*hear*). I
say that there are, upon all sides, shown the strongest symptoms
of improvement in the condition of the country—that there is not
a rail-road, or canal, upon which the traffic has not increased of late
years, including last year. True it is, my lords, that the profits of
trade are now smaller than they were formerly; but if profit, however small, is being derived from the labour of men and animals,
surely it is impossible but that some advantage must accrue to some
one. It is true that these advantages are not so great as they were
ten or fifteen years ago (*hear*) but there is some advantage, or
would the increase of traffic exist? And where that is the case the
distress cannot be said to be universal. There is another circumstance which I would call to your lordships [*sic*] attention. There is
in this country a very large class of persons who are retail dealers;
I ask if they are distressed? (*Hear, and Yes, from the Opposition.*)
This class is very numerous in every town and village in England;
I want to know if they are distressed? Are they able to pay their
rents? Who build and rent all the new houses that one sees in all
directions? These, my lords, are circumstances, say what you please,
which every man must feel and acknowledge as indications that the
country, notwithstanding the pressure upon it, is still rising, and in
some points must continue to rise.

I will now say one word, my lords, upon the remedies proposed
by the noble earl. That noble lord has entirely misunderstood the
argument of the noble viscount (Goderich). The noble viscount
had said that the revenue in the year 1815 produced eighty millions
sterling, and that, though taxes had been reduced, first to the
amount of eighteen millions, and afterwards to the amount of nine
millions, making altogether twenty-seven millions, the revenue
produced in sound currency now the same amount as it did in a

depreciated currency before. Does not, then, this fact of the revenue keeping up, though the taxes were taken off, prove that the consumption of articles had increased one-third since the period when the taxes were taken off—a proof, also, of the better state of the country. It would be impossible for the country to increase in its consumption one-third in fifteen years if it was suffering under the universal distress which the noble Lord talks of. The noble Lord opposite and the noble Lord who spoke last (Carnarvon) have thought proper to refer the distress to a deficient circulation. Now, my Lords, I hold in my hand a paper which gives the relative amounts of the circulation at different periods. By this it appears that the largest sum ever known to be in circulation during the Bank Restriction was 64,000,000 *l.* sterling. The sum was made up of—

Bank of England notes	£30,000,000
Country-bank notes	23,000,000
Gold	4,000,000
Silver	7,000,000
Total	£64,000,000

But in the last year the circulation consisted of—

Bank of England notes	£19,900,000
Country-bank notes	9,200,000
Gold	28,000,000
Silver	8,000,000
Total	£65,100,000

Being an excess over the largest circulation ever known. (*hear*) If the question be about the actual amount of money in circulation, I beg to observe that there is more money in circulation now than there ever was at any period of the Bank restriction, and that whoever considers that there is abroad sixty-five millions, cannot say that money is scarce. Why, the truth of the matter is, that noble lords want not extended circulation, but unlimited circulation—that is—to give an unlimited power to some individuals—not the Crown, any one but the Crown—to coin as much money, in the shape of paper, as they please, that they may be enabled to lend a fictitious capital to all sorts of speculators. (*hear*) This is what the noble earl opposite wants, but what the country cannot have without exposing it to a degree of ruin from which it has so narrowly escaped in 1825 and 1826. (*hear*) If your lordships will attend to the arguments of the noble lord, you will see that this is what he wants.

For what is the language now held? "In the west of England," one says, "I inquired, and found that the farmer could not borrow any money: his corn-yards and hay-ricks were full, but he was not able to raise money upon them; and why? Because the country banker cannot coin 1 *l.* notes." (*hear*)—If these bankers, says the noble earl, cannot lend their money, they cannot get any interest upon their capital. I beg his pardon. The banker may have discount upon cashing the farmer's bill; but he is not content with the profit, he wants to be coining 1 *l.* notes, and to have profit upon those insecure notes, in addition to the discount. (*hear*)

And what is it the noble earl wants now, and will, perhaps, move for in a few days? Not to increase the circulation, for there is as much now as at any former period, but to give certain persons power to lend as much money as they please upon land or no land, upon security or no security. I submit to your lordships that the noble earl has not proved the want of money—there never was a period when money was less wanted. Is there any man, however speculative—any scheme, however visionary, provided only it is a little plausible, which now-a-days lacks support? Is there any power, however bankrupt, even Portugal and Brazil, though the creditors of these countries have been so ill-treated, but can borrow money in this city upon any security or no security? In fact, capital is more abundant now than it was ever known to be, and the evil is certainly not too limited a circulation.

I am sorry to trouble your lordships with these observations, which are rather replies to what has been said by the noble earl, and I will now pass to more important topics in his Majesty's Speech—namely, the measures which affect the permanent welfare of the country. In answer to all the declamation that we have heard to-night, as to the evils resulting from free trade, and this system of currency, I beg to state to your lordships only one fact. Since the year 1815, but principally since the bank restriction was taken off, measures have been adopted by which this country has been relieved from twenty-seven millions a year taxes, besides three millions or four millions interest of the debt, representing a capital of hundred millions of debt. I beg you to bear this in mind when you are discussing this question; and I would tell the advocates of what is called an "equitable adjustment," that, with all their measures, they could not have accomplished so much. I repeat, that since the bank restriction has been taken off, the country has been relieved to the amount of nine millions and eighteen millions besides. I wish to take no credit to myself for this; I give it to those to whom it is properly due—to my noble friend upon the cross-bench (Lord Bexley) and to the noble viscount (Goderich) opposite. Your lordships, then, perceive what may be done by economy; we give our pledge to strive to attain similar ends by the like means, and we call upon you, and count upon your giving us your aid, in putting that economy into practice which will enable us to imitate and rival our predecessors. I trust that your lordships will believe that his Majesty's ministers will do all in their power to relieve the distresses of the country.

5. Parliamentary Reform

*This speech, the omitted portions of which emphasize the problem confronting the King of the Netherlands and the existing state of affairs in Ireland, was in reply to the attacks of the Whig leader, Earl Grey, at the opening of the new Parliament in William IV's reign (1830). "You see," Earl Grey quoted, "the danger around you: the storm is in the horizon, but the hurricane approaches. Begin then at once to strengthen your houses." He continued, "The mode in which this must be done, my Lords, is by securing the affections of your fellow subjects, and . . . . I will pronounce the word— by reforming Parliament." Wellington's words (*HANSARD*, I [3d Ser.], 44-53) called forth a buzz of criticism, the cause of which he inquired about. "You have announced the fall of your government, that is all," was the reputed reply.*

He [Wellington] would now advert to a part of the discussion of that night, in allusion to a portion of his Majesty's Speech, upon a subject which gave him very great pain, he alluded to the state of the public mind in a certain part of the kingdom, and the outrages there committed. He certainly could not help agreeing with a noble Marquis (Camden) who had spoken early in the debate, that the outrages of which that country had been the scene, were not to be attributed to distress; for at a period when the population of the country had unquestionably been exposed to greater severities of condition such scenes of outrage had not taken place. He should imagine that the outrages were carried on by two different classes of people. Some of the offences had been committed by a class which was always disposed to break machines, which they thought (and certainly rightly thought) would, in the first instance, throw them out of work, although they did not see that, eventually, machinery created an additional demand for labour and bettered the condition of the labourer. But he was sorry to say that there was another class of persons who burnt and destroyed property without any visible motive whatever. Of what were the causes of these recent outrages, however, the Ministers knew no more than the gentry and magistracy of the county had told them. They were doing every thing in their power to help the gentry and magistrates of the county to discover the causes, and they were giving them every assistance they required to put the law in force, and to put down the disturbances as quickly as possible. This subject brought him to what noble Lords had said respecting the putting the country in a state to overcome the evils likely to result from the late disturbances in France.

The noble Earl had alluded to the propriety of effecting Parliamentary Reform. The noble Earl had, however, been candid enough to acknowledge that he was not prepared with any measure of reform, and he could have no scruple in saying that his Majesty's Government was as totally unprepared with any plan as the noble Lord. Nay, he, on his own part, would go further, and say, that he had never read or heard of any measure up to the present moment which could in any degree satisfy his mind that the state of the representation could be improved, or be rendered more satisfactory to the country at large than at the present moment. He would not, however, at such an unseasonable time, enter upon the subject, or excite discussion, but he should not hesitate to declare unequivocally what were his sentiments upon it. He was fully convinced that the country possessed at the present moment a Legislature which answered all the good purposes of legislation, and this to a greater degree than any Legislature ever had answered in any country whatever. He would go further and say, that the Legislature and the system of representation possessed the full and entire confidence of the country—deservedly possessed that confidence— and the discussions in the Legislature had a very great influence over the opinions of the country. He would go still further and say, that if at the present moment he had imposed upon him the duty of forming a Legislature for any country, and particularly for a country like this, in possession of great property of various descriptions, he did not mean to assert that he could form such a Legislature as they posssessed now, for the nature of man was incapable of reaching such excellence at once; but his great endeavour would be, to form some description of legislature which would produce the same results. The representation of the people at present contained a large body of the property of the country, and in which the landed interests had a preponderating influence. Under these circumstances, he was not prepared to bring forward any measure of the description alluded to by the noble Lord. He was not only not prepared to bring forward any measure of this nature, but he would at once declare that as far as he was concerned, as long as he held any station in the government of the country, he should always feel it his duty to resist such measures when proposed by others.

6. The Chartist Program

Earl Stanhope presented on June 25, 1839, several petitions that prayed practically for the application of the Chartist program to the constitution. That program called for universal manhood suffrage, equal electoral districts, vote by ballot, abolition of property qualifications for members of Parliament, payment of members of Parliament, and annually elected Parliaments.

The movement arose from the failure of the 1832 Reform Bill to produce a reformed Parliament that responded to popular needs and from continuing economic distress, which was augmented by the depression of 1837. Some of the Chartist leaders thought to effect the enactment of this program by moral suasion, others, somewhat later, by physical force. Wellington's comments are taken from HANSARD *(XLVIII [3d Ser.], 826-28).*

The Duke of Wellington agreed with the noble Viscount [15] opposite, in much that had fallen from him with respect to the inexpediency of delivering lengthened harangues in that House, on the presentation of petitions, and he could not help lamenting that the noble Earl, his noble Friend, should have taken that opportunity of delivering one of those long harangues. The petitioners stated fairly enough the grievances of which they complained, and prayed for the adoption of measures calculated to put an end to them. He could not help regretting that his noble Friend should, on that occasion, have been tempted to dilate, at so much length, upon the supposed causes of those grievances, and their present and anticipated effects, without suggesting some measure, such as the repeal of the Poor-law, or bringing forward some distinct proposition for the enactment of a new law, or the repeal of an old one. If he made some such proposition and that the House did not attend to him, then indeed might the noble Earl find some excuse for haranguing on the presentation of petitions; but it really was unworthy of the great mind of his noble Friend to endeavour to excite such a spirit as his speeches were calculated to call forth.

He was happy, however, to find that his noble Friend and he agreed in some things, that he disapproved of the arming of the people, and he hoped that if the disaffected spirit which was abroad went further, he and the noble Earl should be found on the same side, that they would stand in the same ranks. He should wish to stand near the noble Earl. Of one thing there could be no doubt, that his own place would be on the side of order and the laws, and he hoped that the noble Earl would be found near him. Let the

[15] Viscount Melbourne.

noble Earl bring forward measures upon those several subjects, and let the House decide upon them at once. That would be a more fair and manly course, and one more likely to give satisfaction to the country than the course which the noble Earl thought fit to pursue night after night.

With regard to the subject of the petition which had been presented by the noble Earl, he must confess that he had heard with great satisfaction the sentiments which the noble Viscount opposite had expressed upon these subjects. He fully concurred with the noble Viscount in the propriety of opposing the further extension of the suffrage, and upon the very same ground, namely, that such extension would be inconsistent with the best interests of the country. He likewise concurred in the sentiments which the noble Viscount had expressed upon the subject of the ballot,[16] that obnoxious, and he must say, un-English measure; at the same time he deeply regretted that the noble Viscount had thought proper to make it what was called an open question. He had had the misfortune to be in office when there were such questions, and he must say that he never could consider them as anything but a symptom of weakness on the part of those who were carrying on the service of their Sovereign—a symptom that they were not acting together, that they did not agree amongst themselves, and that there was a division, also, amongst their supporters. Instead of its being a matter of satisfaction that an important question like the ballot should be left an open question, he regarded it as a circumstance most likely to prove disastrous to the Government, and eventually so to the country. Under these circumstances, although perfectly content with the opinions delivered upon the subject by the noble Viscount, he confessed he had lamented, and did still lament most sincerely, that the question of the ballot should be considered an open question by the Government, and more particularly still did he regret that it should ever have been declared so.

[16] *I.e.,* the secret ballot.

7. The Owenite Program

The Bishop of Exeter spoke on February 4, 1840, on the motion, "viz., that an humble Address be presented to her Majesty, praying that her Majesty would be pleased to command, that inquiries should be made into the diffusion of blasphemous and unmoral publications, especially as to the tenets and proceedings of a society established under the name of Socialists; who were represented in petitions presented to this House to be a society, the object of which was by the diffusion of its doctrines to destroy the existing laws and institutions of this country." The Duke's opinions are to be found in HANSARD (LI [3d Ser.], 1210-11). The latter may, perhaps, be forgiven for his vagueness, since different emphases upon Robert Owen's ideas obtained at different times and places. Owen had come to believe, out of his life's experiences, that environment was a determinate factor in the molding of men. He himself had attempted to improve their lot by factory legislation, trade-unionism, inchoate co-operative organizations, and so-called community or socialistic experiments such as that at New Harmony, Indiana. His was a Utopian socialism.

Unfortunately for his schemes, his ideas on religion alienated many people of all classes of society and his lack of enthusiasm for Parliamentary reform estranged members of the working class.

The Duke of Wellington till lately had known nothing whatever about these Socialists. His attention was first directed to them by a petition which was sent to him to present to their Lordships' House having reference to the presentation of Mr. Owen at court by the noble Viscount [17] at the head of the Government. He declined to present the petition, because he knew nothing about the matter, and did not choose to embark himself in the support or discussion of a subject of which he had no knowledge. Having intimated this to the petitioner, he received a communication in reply, containing a full statement of what Socialism was. By this means he obtained a knowledge of the system; he saw some of the books published by the society, and became aware of the doctrines they advanced; and, having obtained this information upon the subject, he must say that the right rev. Prelate had not in any way exaggerated the viciousness of the system. It appeared to have spread itself over a great part of the country; and, upon inquiry, he found that it had taken root rather extensively in the county in which he resided. In Hampshire they had purchased 800 acres of land, and established a large institution. In reference to that institution, he had that day

[17] Viscount Melbourne.

presented a petition to their Lordships which contained statements regarding blasphemy, regarding the Holy Scriptures, regarding God Almighty, regarding all the great points of our belief, which in his estimation demanded a most serious inquiry.

When he read that petition, which he did as soon as it was placed in his hands, he felt it to be his duty as the Lord-lieutenant of the county, to call the attention of the county magistrates to the facts which it set forth. In the same way he maintained that it was the duty of the House of Lords and of the Government, now that the facts were brought before them, to take some steps in the matter. The doctrines of Socialism were rapidly gaining strength—were rapidly spreading themselves over the whole of the country—they had got beyond the point at which one could say "the thing will fall to pieces: take no notice of it." That was one way of treating an affair, but Socialism had got beyond that point. Some step must be taken. The people must be made to understand that neither the legislature nor the Government looked upon this institution in any other way than with disfavour—that they were determined to discountenance it—and that wherever, in the promulgation of its doctrines, there should be a breach of the law, that breach of the law should be punished. If the Government would undertake the matter, and institute such an inquiry as they thought fit, he should be willing to leave it in their hands; at the same time saying that, as a magistrate, a public man, and a Lord-lieutenant of a county, he would do everything in his power to assist them in carrying on their inquiries, in order to bring this system to an end.

Chapter IV

PEEL

Chapter IV

PEEL

SIR ROBERT PEEL (1788-1850) was closely connected with the Duke of Wellington in his official life, though differing from him much in disposition and characteristics. He came from a family famous in the history of calico printing. Entering Parliament in 1809, he accepted official position in 1810 and, like Pitt, was early limited by the responsibilities of office. As one of his numerous biographers has said, "Born in a Tory home, the young Peel was sent to a Tory school, graduated in a Tory university and took office in a Tory administration before he was twenty-five years of age."[1] Like a Tory he disliked the cause of revolution, believed the French Revolution, in particular, a disaster, and, perhaps, rather uncritically, connected revolution and reform. But experience gradually led him to question his inherited theories. Critics, including many contemporaries, saw in his shift of attitude merely the surrender of Tory principles one after another as opportunity permitted or demanded. More sympathetic biographers have thought him a person of great intellectual honesty who gave up early ideas as he was convinced that the needs of his country required change in policies. Perhaps his followers would have felt kindlier toward him in his opportunism had he not possessed a nature cold, reserved, and sensitive that made it difficult even for his closest colleagues to approach him.

Peel, as Chief Secretary for Ireland from 1812 to 1818, came in contact with patronage problems, the question of coercion acts, the need for establishing adequately organized police, whence the term "peelers," and in general perhaps with the advisability of schooling himself in "chilling caution."[2]

[1] J. R. Thursfield, *Peel* (London: Macmillan and Company, 1907), p. 11.
[2] George K. Clark, *Peel and the Conservative Party* (London: George Bell and Sons, Ltd., 1929), p. 11.

He was a private member after his return from Ireland until, in January 1822, he became Home Secretary with a place in the Cabinet. His attention was soon turned, therefore, to the state of the criminal law. In dealing with a problem that had called forth the energy of such reformers as Romilly and Mackintosh, he caused acts to be passed which changed more than 250 old statutes. Later, in 1827, he hoped still further to mitigate the criminal code (cf. "The Consolidation of Criminal Laws," page 95) and prevent crime through the organization of metropolitan police.[3]

In the meantime the old Liverpool Cabinet of which he was a member had broken up. Peel refused to hold office under Canning because of his own opposition to Catholic emancipation, but under Wellington he became the leader of the House of Commons. In this capacity he was obliged to introduce a measure for Catholic relief though he had habitually objected throughout his career to proposals which he now espoused. Necessity may have forced Peel, as he claimed, to surrender his earlier tenets, but in any case men of all cliques and parties never forgot his apparent inconsistency. However, in his treatment of Parliamentary reform he seems to have rewon to a degree the esteem of followers. Since Tory principles were opposed to Parliamentary reform he thought consistency demanded that he refuse to join the Duke in any endeavour to form an administration which should attempt to pass a moderate reform bill. He himself argued cleverly against Lord John Russell's measure.[4]

He accepted the Act of 1832, however, when it became a law as an essential part of the English constitution and even assisted the Whigs to a degree in the passing of the Municipal Corporations Act (cf. "Corporation Reform," page 101), thus applying to local government his idea of the deliberate and gradual improvement of every institution that needed reform. Indeed, he had already by the famous Tamworth Manifesto (1834) announced alike to his constituency and the world his intention, as the leader of his party, of undertaking, in a friendly temper, a careful review of institutions, civil and ecclesiastical, in order to correct proved abuses and redress real grievances among those

[3] His speech on the Metropolitan Police Improvement Bill (April 15, 1829) may be found in Hansard, XXI, 867-81.
[4] Cf. Hansard, II, 1330-56.

established rights which he would firmly support. In general, his concern was with the maintenance of the constitution, the safety of the church, and the economic problems of his day. He was hardly affected by popular demands as can be seen in his remarks on the national petition of the Chartists.[5]

Relying upon statistics and other data laboriously acquired he possessed sufficient abilities, however, to make a lasting place for himself in the field of economics. As early as 1819 he had passed a measure which established the principle that all bank notes should be payable on demand in gold. In times of difficulties, however, county banks had failed to cash their notes and even the Bank of England had been in danger in 1825 and 1839. Because of this situation the House of Commons had appointed committees in 1840 and 1841 that obtained important evidence upon which Peel acted in the Bank Act of 1844. "The great speech in which he introduced his measure [cf. "Bank Charter—The Currency," page 105] is the Parliamentary foundation of all sound thinking on the subject and remains to this day the most authoritative exposition of the true principles of the national currency."[6]

On the question of tariff Peel was early influenced by the advocate of a freer trade policy, William Huskisson. He did defend the Corn Laws, however, on the plea of expediency, though to a man of his family traditions there must have been some appeal in the cry that free trade meant cheap food, light taxes, better trade. After the passage of the Reform Act of 1832 Peel had not held office, except for a few months in 1834-1835, until 1841. His famous budget speech of March 1842 foretold the removal of many duties, though not those on sugar and corn. But the combination of the Anti-Corn Law League, headed by the logical Cobden and eloquent Bright, the potato blight, and the maneuvering of the Whigs, forced Peel, in spite of the strength of agricultural interests in his party, to repeal the Corn Laws (cf. page 117). Disraeli led the formidable opposition of his own party with such success that the Prime Minister, soon

---

[5] Cf. Hansard, LXIII, 76-81 (May 3, 1842).

[6] Thursfield, p. 195, but J. H. Clapham, *An Economic History of Modern Britain* (Cambridge: The University Press, 1926-1938) I, 521, declares the speech to be more noteworthy as a political effort than satisfactory from the economist's standpoint. Tresham Lever in *The Life and Times of Sir Robert Peel* (London: George Allen and Unwin, Ltd., 1942) is noncommittal.

deserted by the Whigs who had given assistance during the struggle, fell from power (cf. "Resignation of the Ministry," page 133). An accident caused his death four years later and left the way open for the development of men who possessed greater personal ambition and wider outlook on social problems—Gladstone and Disraeli.

Peel was an able speaker. His voice was clear and pleasant, and he uttered his ideas with dignity of expression and purity of diction. His eloquence, it is usually conceded, was not of the highest order, but a thorough knowledge of the subject under discussion and clearness in the development of his ideas held and moved his hearers even when he failed to set forth great philosophical truths or to display a genius versatile as that of Canning.

1. The Consolidation of Criminal Laws

The following speech is one of many which Sir Robert Peel gave before the House of Commons on the question of criminal reform. It was delivered on February 22, 1827. It can be found in HANSARD *(XVI [N.S.], 632-42).*

Sir Robert Peel came to represent the leadership of the criminal law reform movement in 1823. Previously, much effort for this reform had been expended by Sir Samuel Romilly and Sir James Mackintosh, who were anxious to alter the laws that filled the prisons and were not unmindful, therefore, of the related movement of prison reform itself. The names of John Howard, Jeremy Bentham, and Elizabeth Fry will always re-

main incised in the mind of a public concerned with the developments of this latter movement. But criminal law reform—the more important of the two movements— depended on the public's understanding that security for neither life nor property had resulted from extreme penalties, such as was implied by punishment by death for some two hundred offenses. Hence, Sir Robert's approach to the problems described in this speech is the kind of approach which engendered confidence in his leadership and which permitted him to reduce ultimately the number of offenses calling for capital punishment to a mere half dozen.

Mr. Secretary [7] Peel rose to bring forward his promised motion. He had now, he said, agreeably to that motion, to apply to the House for leave to bring in four bills, having for their object the simplification and consolidation of the statutes relating to the Criminal Laws. The first of those bills was intended to consolidate and amend the laws relating to theft, and the various offences connected therewith. The second was to amend the law relating to another class of offence against the subject, namely, a wilful and malicious injury of property. The third bill for which he should move, would be to consolidate and amend the laws relating to remedies against the hundred. And the fourth bill which he should submit to the notice of the House, would have the effect of repealing such statutes as would be superseded by the three first bills, in order not to encumber the Statute-book, by the introduction of separate acts of parliament for the attainment of that object. By this means, the three bills which he had already named would not be impeded in their operation by clauses and enactments contrary to their spirit.

He had entered last session so fully into the policy and necessity of amending the criminal statutes, that he was not sure whether it was at all necessary to enforce the reasoning which he then used,

[7] Secretary for the Home Department.

or to trouble the House with a repetition of his views, notwithstanding some of the members whom he had now the honour to
address were not in parliament on that occasion. Indeed, it required
no very powerful reasoning to show the necessity and policy of
consolidating the criminal laws of this country, and of simplifying,
as much as possible, those statutes relating to crime and misde-
meanour, which had hitherto created so much error and confusion
in our courts of justice. Such a course as that of revising and
consolidating confused and unintelligible statutes appeared so consistent with reason and common sense, that he scarcely thought it
necessary to adduce any arguments in its favour, where all whom
he had the honour to address must agree in the necessity of the
measure. He was therefore quite satisfied that the House would
sanction the part which he had taken, and confirm the support
which his predecessor had given to the subject.

The House, however, was not called upon to give a blind judgment: on the contrary, he wished and expected that honourable
gentlemen would reserve to themselves the power of expressing an
opinion on a subject of such vital importance. Although, however,
he had suggested many changes, he had not, after all, proposed any
very important alterations in the criminal statutes; because he was
desirous of proceeding gradually in the course of improvement, and
to avoid as much as possible the use of rash experiments. What he
wished was, to collect all that was valuable from existing statutes,
and to preserve from a mass of contradiction and confusion, various
clauses and provisions introduced at different periods into our
criminal laws. He was desirous of selecting all that was worthy
of being preserved, in order to present to the House a useful and
efficient statute, and thus to place as it were in juxta-position all the
law connected with the criminal jurisprudence of the country. It
was his wish to abolish every part of the criminal statutes that could
not with safety be acted on, and to accommodate the laws relating
to crime to the present circumstances of the country, and the improved state of society.

Feeling, therefore, that the House would agree, in principle at
least, to the measures which he intended to propose, he did not
think it necessary to trouble them with any further arguments, but
would proceed at once to explain the present state of the law relating to theft, which was the subject of his first bill. It was the practice, in criminal courts of justice, to distinguish between grand
and petty larceny, and to award different punishments for each
crime. It appeared, however, that the only difference between them
consisted in the amount of the property stolen; for thus the law
stood on the subject. If a man was convicted of stealing an article

under the value of one shilling, it was simple larceny, punishable at the option of the magistrate before whom the case was heard; but, if the property stolen exceeded one shilling in value, the crime was called grand larceny, to which a capital punishment was attached.

Now, after giving to the subject his best consideration, he could not see the necessity of retaining the distinction which the law laid down in these cases. There were many inferior courts spread throughout this country, which had power to take cognizance of, and to try persons charged with, the crime of petty larceny, but who had not power to try for the crime of grand larceny. The consequence of this was, that both courts and prosecutors, feeling the great expense and inconvenience of sending persons charged with these offences to be tried by the higher tribunals, agreed to evade the law, by stating in the indictment, that the value of the article stolen was less than one shilling. These instances, it was true, were not very creditable to the parties concerned, but they furnished ample reasons for abolishing all distinctions between grand and petty larceny.

He would, therefore, unite the different species of the crime of larceny under one general law; and he would fix, as the *maximum* of punishment, a sentence of transportation for seven years. It was hitherto the custom to mitigate the sentences affixed to the crime of grand larceny; but he owned he could not see the reason why, if the power existed, a criminal convicted of this crime should not be transported for stealing to the value of two shillings. There was a material difference between grand and simple larceny, when a prisoner was twice convicted. A man who repeated the crime of grand larceny, was liable to a sentence of death, without benefit of clergy. He meant to propose, that the capital punishment should be dispensed with in this instance.

He would propose also to do away with a term which had long been mixed up with the criminal law of England. He meant the "benefit of clergy." It was extremely difficult to apply the term "without benefit of clergy" to any particular crime and, to say what was a clergyable offence. It appeared to him, that the law in this particular should be simplified. Instead of saying, therefore, that the man who commits grand larceny a second time was guilty of a capital offence, without benefit of clergy, he proposed to substitute the punishment of transportation for life. This would serve to make the law more clear and intelligible; and he was sure that the House would go with him in every alteration he proposed, whereby the number of capital crimes might be lessened. Thus, the man convicted of grand larceny a second time would no longer be subject to death. In proposing this alteration he was aware, however, that it was not very material; as it rarely occurred that the penalty of death was put in force when a man was convicted of grand larceny a second time; but it was right at the same time, that the law in this particular should be clear and determinate; for it was one of the just objections brought by foreigners against the criminal laws of England, that we condemned men to death for crimes, who were never executed, and whose sentence was, in fact, never intended to be carried into effect. It would therefore be a material improvement, if, in every available instance, we could erase capital punishments from the Statute-book, and provide milder punishments, and thereby avoid the mockery of condemning men to death, merely because that penalty was attached to the crime which they had committed.

He proposed also to mitigate the penalty for stealing in a dwelling-house to the value of forty shillings. According to the law, as it now stood, the penalty of death was attached to that crime. A distinction, however, he conceived should be made; and there were cases in which the punishment of death might be considered harsh and unnecessary. He therefore meant to propose, that the sum of forty shillings should be raised to a higher amount; by which means the number of capital convictions for this species of crime would be considerably diminished.

He was not prepared to say whether or no it might not be necessary to go further in the plan of reducing the number of capital convictions. Much had lately been done, and much remained to do; but he thought he might claim some credit to himself for having done more towards the great and important object of improving and consolidating the criminal statutes of this country, than any other individual who had gone before him. He never was an advocate for the infliction of capital punishments, and he thought it would be found, on comparing the executions for the last five years, in which he had presided at the home department, that they had not increased in number, as compared with those that had taken place in former years. Willing as he felt, however, to reduce the amount of capital convictions, he advised the House not to be led away too far by mistaken feelings. If parliament were to proceed too rapidly to overthrow the existing enactments, a strong prejudice might arise in the country against measures that were intended for the public good; and thus the great object of justice and humanity might be defeated.

With respect to the law relative to malicious injuries to property, which his second bill was intended to embrace, he conceived that it might be beneficially altered, and confined within proper limits. He conceived the punishment attached to the crime of cutting down hop-fences, stakes, hedges, etc., was neither clearly nor properly defined; and therefore he proposed to abrogate the law altogether, and try the effects of a milder punishment. Without entering more fully into the particular clauses of each bill, of which the committee, whose appointment he anticipated, could best judge; he would now only refer to the general principles upon which he came forward to claim the countenance and support of the House. Notwithstanding the very able assistance he had had, he felt considerable difficulty in drawing up the bills which he hoped to be allowed to introduce; owing to the number of abstruse and unintelligible phrases which he found it necessary to use, in compliance with the usage of the law in this particular. The endless repetition of words; the confusion of the singular and plural number; the frequent use of the words "party or parties," "defendant or defendants," "corporations," or "persons," had always, he confessed, puzzled him beyond measure, whenever he had occasion to refer to an act of parliament. He had, therefore, in the bills which he had framed, avoided as much as possible the confusion arising from the frequent introduction of words and phrases; and at the commencement of each bill, he had defined the precise punishment for each particular crime, adding to the end of the bill, in order to remove any doubt occasioned by the ambiguity of the language, that the word "person," when mentioned in the body of the bill, should be taken to mean the party accused, whether man, woman, or child, and that the same should hold good, with regard to owner, defendant, or defendants, or by whatever term the accused party might be designate.[8] . . . .

. . . .

He must also say, that he had another motive for proceeding gradually and slowly in this matter. It was necessary to carry along with him all the instruments engaged in the administration of justice; for if too many changes were suddenly made in the laws of daily and ordinary occurrence, and if what was declared law was not executed well, no advantage would result to the country. He was aware, that a more splendid fame might be acquired by attaching his name to the introduction of a new code of law, as had been done elsewhere; but greater advantage to the country would be gained by convincing the people, who were justly attached to their ancient institutions, that the circumstances which had given rise to them, were either altered or gone by; that they

---

[8] There is omitted a discussion of fees and improvement in the office of coroner and other offices.

could be amended and improved; and that the rust and impurity which they had acquired, by the lapse of time and carelessness of legislation, could be removed without injuring their substance or impairing their strength. The House would confer greater benefits on the people by reconciling them to the improvements which it sanctioned, and by showing them that those improvements could be made without any practical inconvenience, than by attempting too much at once in the shape of innovation, and by leading them away by splendid illusions of general improvement. He would be content, if by his humble efforts, a gradual reform could be effected in our criminal law, without leading to any great practical inconvenience: and he trusted that, so far from dissatisfaction being excited by the attempts of the House to accommodate ancient usages to the necessities of modern times, the attachment of the people to those usages would be increased, by their being convinced that the foundations of those usages were only widened to receive additional strength, and that it was wiser to amend them where they were defective, than to maintain them steadily because they were antiquated imperfections. He would now move, "That leave be given to bring in a bill for consolidating and amending the laws in England, relative to Larceny, Burglary, and Robbery."

2. Corporation Reform

Lord John Russell rose on June 5, 1835, to ask leave of the House of Commons "to bring in a Bill, to provide for the regulation of Municipal Corporations in England and Wales." Sir Robert Peel followed with the address, a portion of which is given (HANSARD, XXVIII [3d Ser.], 558-71).

*The Municipal Corporations Act of 1835 was, perhaps, a corollary of the Great Reform Bill of 1832: as there had been public demand for the removal of numbers of anomalies in the Parliamentary representative system, so was there outcry for the abolition of abuses and corruption in the municipal corporations. A municipal commission, which was appointed in 1833 to study the situation, concluded its work in 1835. A bill based on its recommendations was the bill which Lord John Russell was per-*mitted to bring before the House of Commons. The terms did give uniformity of government to most boroughs and cities, except London and a few nonpopulous places, increased representative authority to the local populace in a large number of cases, but also excluded individuals as electors of town councils if they had not regularly paid their poor rates during a preceding three years. The terms, therefore, were regarded with hostility by both the Radicals and the Tories. Sir Robert Peel, however, had already concluded that the nation would benefit from some kinds of changes, and, even though he pointed out that corruption was not concentrated in places where the few rather than the many, or where Tories rather than Whigs, controlled, he made "no opposition whatever" to the motion.*

Although, Sir, I have resolved to avail myself of every advantage in the discussion of this most important question, which additional time and opportunities of reference, not only to documents already in the possession of the House, but to others which are not yet laid before it will afford me, and to decline entering, therefore, into any detailed discussion of the measure which the noble Lord has this night proposed: yet, Sir, on account of its vast importance, I should be unwilling to allow the Motion to be put from the Chair without a single observation having been offered on the subject except those contained in the speech of the noble Lord. I shall make no opposition whatever to that Motion; I shall throw not the slightest impediment in the way of the introduction of this Bill—and, moreover, I am about to state opinions upon the subject of Municipal Reform generally—though not in immediate reference to this measure, the details of which are so important that each is entitled to separate discussion—which will prove that an opposition on my part, to the introduction of this measure would be quite inconsistent with the opinions which I entertain.

Sir, when I look to the state of the population of the larger towns of this kingdom—when I contemplate the rapidity with which places, which at no remote period were inconsiderable villages, have through manufacturing industry, started into life and into great wealth and importance—when I look, too, to the imperfect provision which is now made for the preservation of order and the administration of justice in most of those towns—I cannot deny that the time has arrived when it is of the utmost importance to the well-being of society, to establish within societies so circumstanced a good system of Municipal government. In some of these towns no permanent and regular provision is, at present, made for the maintenance of public order, and the general purposes of good government; in others the provision which was originally intended to be made through the instrumentality of the Corporate system, has become utterly inefficient for the purpose; and I am bound to admit therefore, that on account of the change of circumstances, and on that account singly, there is ample ground for now considering whether such provision ought not to be made in towns not corporate; and whether in those towns which have Corporations, the provision at present in force be not inadequate!

Sir, I am bound also to state that, on referring as fully as I have been able to do since they were presented, and amid the great pressure of other business, to the reports on the state of Corporations, the general impression left on my mind is, that, independently of the considerations above mentioned, the general purport of the evidence adduced before the commission,[9] shows that the time is also arrived, when it is necessary for Parliament to interfere, for the purpose of providing some effectual checks against the abuses, which have been proved to prevail in some of the corporate bodies of this country. I therefore, Sir, without hesitation admit, that it is of the utmost importance to the well-being of society, that a good system of municipal government should be provided for the larger towns of this country, whether they be corporate or not, by the means of which the regular and pure administration of justice may be extended and secured, and the maintenance of public order promoted through the means of a well-regulated police.

And, Sir, after having made that admission, I think it follows, almost as a matter of course, that corporations where they exist, ought to be made mainly instrumental in effecting those objects. To leave the corporations precisely on their present ground, and to establish new rates (where they may be necessary) for municipal

---

[9] The commission had spent a year and a half in investigating two hundred corporations.

purposes by new laws to be now passed, making no new provision for the application of these revenues, placing them under the sole control of corporate bodies existing on the old principle, would have a great tendency to defeat the object in view. If we admit the fact that the well-being of society requires the consideration of a good system of Municipal government, it is impossible to exclude from simultaneous consideration the existing state of the corporate bodies themselves. I think Parliament has a right to require, by laws to be now passed, that the revenues of these Corporations, excepting where they are applied under particular bequests to special purposes, shall be henceforth devoted to public purposes, connected with public municipal interests. I must say, that if I were a member of any corporation, so far from looking at this question in a mere narrow, party light, I should feel a much greater interest, a much stronger, direct, personal, pecuniary interest, in seeing the corporate funds applied to public purposes, than in seeing them applied to any system of public feasting, or to any objects of mere electioneering and party interest.

At the same time it is due to the existing corporations to admit at once, that while I have not the slightest objection to any new provision to be made by law which should impose some check on the appropriation of corporate revenues, such check will involve a new principle of law. The principle of the law heretofore has been, that these corporate bodies have had a legal right to apply their funds to other than public municipal purposes: they clearly had a right to apply their funds to corporate purposes as distinguished from municipal; and I apprehend that it has been ruled by the highest authorities, that excepting so far as the restraining statutes interfered with the powers of ecclesiastical corporations, the corporations of this country had a right to regulate at their discretion, the application of their property, and even to alienate it, if they thought proper. The report made by the Commissioners has not sufficiently referred to the principles of law in conformity with which the corporations have hitherto acted. I think, also, there is ground for complaint that this report involves all the corporations in too indiscriminate a censure, that it does not sufficiently point out the many cases in which corporations have acted honestly in the performance of their trust, but that it has thrown a general reflection upon all corporations, in consequence of the abuse of their functions by a limited number.

The noble Lord did wisely in laying down the principle that we had much better defer to a future opportunity any attempt to cite particular instances in which corporations may not have been justly dealt with. It is much more convenient on this occasion to refer to the general principle of the measure than to enter into the consideration of any special and individual cases. The noble Lord's precepts, however, were, as it often happens, much sounder than his practice.[10]

[10] Sir Robert then shows that corruption on the part of members of corporations was not confined to Tories. Finally, discussing terms of Lord John Russell's bill, he pronounced his fundamental assumption: "Of this I am satisfied, that no system of Municipal Government, however specious in its theory, will promote the object for which alone it ought to be designed, will ensure the maintenance of public order, the pure administration of justice, or the harmony and happiness of the societies to which it is to be applied, unless its direct tendency be to commit the management of Municipal affairs to the hands of those who from the possession of property have the strongest interest in good government, and, from the qualifications of high character and intelligence, are most likely to conciliate the respect and confidence of their fellow citizens."

3. Bank Charter—The Currency

The House of Commons, on the motion of Sir Robert Peel, resolved itself (May 6, 1844) into a committee on the Bank of England Charter Act. Peel's speech is to be found in HANSARD *(LXXIV [3d Ser.], 720-54). As a basis for this exposition of orthodox monetary theory Peel and his listeners could go back to the arrangement which existed between the nation and the Bank of England from the establishment of the bank in 1694. In the early part of the eighteenth century a law had forbidden any association having more than six partners to carry on banking but laws of the early nineteenth century had permitted creation of joint-stock banks, such banks possessing the right to issue bank notes subject to legislative restrictions. Joint-stock banks increased tremendously in their own numbers and in the amount of paper money which they caused to circulate. Speculations in the form of new companies became rampant, fears were expressed on the part of economists concerning the stability of business, while export of gold for ventures in the United States assisted to effect a decline of bullion in the Bank of England; a resulting recession in England and a depression in America gave the opportunity to Peel to show patently his distrust of a system that allowed quantities of paper money to be issued on no adequate basis of bullion. His own plans are clearly expressed in the latter part of his speech. Perhaps his ideas should be considered in conjunction with those of William E. Gladstone (cf. chapter 7, "International Monetary Conference," page 299).*

Sir R. Peel rose, and addressing Mr. Greene, who was in the Chair, said—Sir, there are occasionally questions of such vast and manifest importance, and which prefer such a claim, I should rather say such a demand, on the attention of the House, that all rhetorical prefaces, dilating on their magnitude or enjoining the duty of patient consideration, are superfluous and impertinent. I shall, therefore, proceed at once to call the attention of this Committee to a matter which enters into every transaction of which money forms a part. There is no contract, public or private,—no engagement, national or individual, which is unaffected by it. The enterprises of commerce, the profits of trade, the arrangements made in all the domestic relations of society, the wages of labour, pecuniary transactions of the highest amount and of the lowest, the payment of the national debt, the provision for the national expenditure, the command which the coin of the smallest denomination has over the necessaries of life, are all affected by the decision to which we may come on that great question which I am about to submit to the consideration of the Committee.[11]

. . . .

My immediate proposition relates to Banking Concerns, and to the issue of Promissory Notes; but, considering that ten years have now elapsed since this subject was brought under consideration, I hope I shall be excused, if I take a wider range than the immediate questions for decision might seem to justify, and if I advert at the outset to the great principles which govern, or ought to govern, the Measure of Value, and the Medium of Exchange. They lie, in truth, at the very foundation of our discussion. We cannot hope to agree on the Measure to be adopted with regard to Paper Currency, unless we are agreed on the principles which determine the value of that of which Paper is the representative, and on the nature of the obligation which is imposed upon the issuer of Promissory Notes. Now I fear there is not a general agreement on those fundamental principles—that there is still a very material difference of opinion as to the real nature and character of the Measure of Value in this country.

My first question, therefore, is, what constitutes this Measure of Value? What is the signification of that word "a Pound," with which we are all familiar? What is the engagement to pay a "Pound"? Unless we are agreed on the answer to these questions, it is in vain we attempt to legislate on the subject. If a "Pound" is a mere visionary abstraction, a something which does not exist either in law or in practice, in that case one class of measures relating to Paper Currency may be adopted; but if the word "Pound," the common denomination of value, signifies something more than a mere fiction—if a "Pound" means a quantity of the precious metals of certain weight and certain fineness—if that be the definition of a "Pound," in that case another class of measures relating to Paper Currency will be requisite. Now, the whole foundation of the proposal I am about to make rests upon the assumption that according to practice, according to law, according to the ancient monetary policy of this country, that which is implied by the word "Pound" is a certain definite quantity of gold

[11] Peel explained that Parliament had the power, in terms of the Act of 1833, to reconsider the charter of the Bank of England, provided it did so within a few months. The state of the nation demanded, in his opinion, that Her Majesty's Government should accept this opportunity. He therefore asked members of the House to give consideration to the subject no matter what pressure should be applied to them by country bankers who feared curtailment of their existing privileges.

with a mark upon it to determine its weight and fineness, and that the engagement to pay a Pound means nothing, and can mean nothing else, than the promise to pay to the holder, when he demands it that definite quantity of gold.

What is the meaning of the "Pound" according to the ancient monetary policy of this country? The origin of the term was this:— In the reign of William the Conqueror a pound weight of silver was also the pound of account. The "Pound" represented both the weight of metal and the denomination of money. By subsequent debasements of the currency a great alteration was made, not in the name, but in the intrinsic value of the Pound sterling, and it was not until a late period of the reign of Queen Elizabeth that silver, being then the standard of value, received that determinate weight which it retained without variation, with constant refusals to debase the standard of silver, until the year 1816, when gold became the exclusive standard of value. The standard of silver was fixed about 1567; but in 1717, the value of the guinea was determined to be 21s., and for a certain period, both gold and silver constituted the mixed standard of value. In the year 1774, it being then enacted that no legal contract should be discharged in silver for any sum of more than 25 l., gold became substantially the measure of value, and so it continued to be legally and practically until 1797, when that fatal measure for restricting cash payments by the Bank was passed, and parties were enabled to issue at their discretion Paper Money not convertible into coin at the will of the bearer. From 1797 to 1810 public attention was not much directed to this important subject; but in 1810 men of sagacity observed that the exchanges had been for a considerable period unfavourable to this country—more unfavourable than could be accounted for by the balance of trade or the monetary transactions of the country.

A Committee was appointed to inquire into the subject, and opinions, not really novel, but at that time very startling, were enounced, to the effect that the "Pound" meant, in fact, nothing else than a definite quantity of the precious metals, and that those who promised to pay a Pound ought to pay that quantity. That theory was very much contested at the time. The House of Commons was not convinced by the arguments used in favour of it. The public mind, confused by the practice that had prevailed since the issue of inconvertible paper, would not admit the doctrine of a metallic standard. Those who contested it were, however, called upon to give their definition of the Pound Sterling, and it must be admitted that they responded to the call. They did not evade the question, as is now the practice, by writing long and unintelligible pamphlets, but, confident in their own theories, gave, in brief and compendious forms, their definitions of the standard of value. One writer said, "that a Pound might be defined to be a sense of value in reference to currency as compared with commodities." Another writer was dissatisfied with that definition, thinking the public had a right to something more definite and tangible, and that the meaning of "a reference to currency as compared with commodities", was not very obvious to enlightened minds. This writer said, "There is a standard and there is an unit which is the measure of value, and that unit is the interest of 33 *l.* 6*s.* 8*d.* at 3 per cent, that being 1 *l.*, and being paid in a Bank-note as money of account." The last definition of the standard of value which I shall quote is this:—"The standard is neither gold nor silver, but it is something set up in the imagination, to be regulated by public opinion."

Such were the absurdities into which ingenious men were betrayed, in the attempt to set up some other standard of value, more consistent with inconvertible paper than a metallic standard. It was supposed at that time that the doctrines propounded by the Bullion Committee were the visionary speculations of theorists, and were unknown in the former monetary history of this country. But that is not the case. Refer to every writer of eminence—to Mr. Locke, to Sir W. Petty, to any one who wrote before 1797, and who had not been familiar with inconvertible paper currency, and you will find they arrive at precisely the same conclusions with the Bullion Committee. Take the opinion of Mr. Harris, an officer of the Mint, and an eminent writer on the subject a century before the Bank Restriction Act:—

"In all countries (says Mr. Harris) there is established a certain standard both as to weight and fineness of the several species of those coins.

"In England, the silver monies are to contain 111 parts of fine silver, and 6 parts of alloy. That is, the pound troy with us contains 11 oz. 2 pennyweights of fine silver, and 18 pennyweights of alloy; and of a pound troy of this standard silver, our money pound contains $^{20}\!/_{62}$ parts, that is to say a pound of this silver is coined into 62s. This standard has continued invariable ever since the 43rd Elizabeth.

"By the standard of money is always meant the quantity of pure or fine metal contained in a given sum. In England accounts are kept by the pound sterling, which is a certain quantity of fine silver appointed by law for a standard." (He was writing at a time when silver was the standard in England.) "All payments abroad are regulated by the course of exchange, and that is founded upon the intrinsic value, and not on the mere names of coins.

"We may break the public faith here, and curtail the long-established measure of property, but foreigners will make ample allowance for what we may do, and however we may rob and cheat one another, will secure themselves, and make an advantage of our discredit, by bringing the exchange against us beyond the part."

These are the true doctrines as to the measures of value, doctrines delivered one hundred years before the Report of the Bullion Committee was made, but in precise conformity with that Report. The truth of them is not, I fear, even now admitted. Publications daily issue from the press contesting it. Here is a volume published at Birmingham since the commencement of the present year, not the production, I presume, of a single author, for it professes to be written by Gemini. I have no wish to withhold justice from writers who gave that proof of their sincerity, which is implied by the publication of an octavo volume. And I admit at once, that I do not believe this work could have proceeded from any other town in the Queen's dominions than Birmingham, and that the efforts of no single writer are equal to the production of so much nonsense. This volume collects and repeats all the old exploded fallacies on the subject of the standard of value and the currency. Its authors bewail the darkness of the age which adheres to a standard which was adopted in the reign of Queen Elizabeth, and which they consider wholly unsuitable as a measure of value now, considering the extent of our commerce, and the increase of all pecuniary transactions in number and amount. They might with equal justice complain, that since travelling has been increased by the completion of railways, the foot measure is still adhered to. There is no better reason for making the sovereign pass for twenty-five shillings instead of twenty, than for making the foot consist of sixteen inches instead of twelve. They consider it absurd, that with the progress we have made in wealth and knowledge, we should still coin the ounce of gold into a sum represented by 3*l.* 17*s.* 10½*d.* "Coin the ounce of gold," say they, "into 5*l.* and we shall then have relief from our burthens, and encouragement to industry and trade."

Now, let us consider what is meant by affixing to the ounce of gold a value, represented in coin by the sum of 3*l.* 17*s.* 10½*d.*? According to the regulations of the Mint, before the alteration of the silver coin in 1816, a pound weight of standard gold was coined into 44½ guineas; a pound weight of standard silver was coined into 62*s.*; and a guinea was made current for 21*s.* We are thus enabled to calculate the relative value of gold and silver according to the Mint regulations. The sum of 44½ guineas in gold, that is a pound of gold, was equivalent to 1,869 sixpences in silver, and the pound of silver being equal to 124 sixpences in coin, the value of gold was to that of silver, as 1,869 to 124, or as $15\frac{9}{124}$ to 1. The ounce of gold in coin was equivalent to the corresponding amount in silver, namely, the twelfth part of 1,869 sixpences, that is to say, to 155 sixpences and $\frac{9}{12}$ of a shilling, or 3*l*. 17*s*. 10½*d*. There was, indeed, a small difference in the amount of alloy in a pound of coined gold and a pound of coined silver, for which it is necessary to make allowance, and that allowance being made, the relative value of pure gold to pure silver in the coins of the two metals was as $15^{2855}\!/_{13460}$ to 1. Silver has ceased to be a standard of value, and the silver coin being now a mere token, the former relative value of gold coin to silver coin is not now preserved.

The above calculations explain our meaning when we say that the ounce of gold is coined into the sum of 3*l*. 17*s*. 10½*d*. These terms express the relation of gold and silver coin, according to the Mint regulations at the time that silver coin was made of standard silver. You may now enact, no doubt, that the ounce of gold shall be coined into 5*l*. in money of account, that is to say, you may debase the standard to that extent. And what will be the effect of this? All debtors will no doubt gain by it. In the case of all unfulfilled contracts, he who has to receive payment will receive much less in point of real value than he stipulated for. The creditor will be defrauded—the debtor will have a corresponding advantage. But this will be the whole effect. No new transactions will be affected by your choosing to call an ounce of gold 5*l*. As Mr. Harris says, you may cheat each other at home, but foreign countries will adjust their dealings with you, not on account of the name to be given to your coin, but according to its real value. All new contracts at home will be regulated by the same principle. The real and not the nominal value of that which is made by law the medium of exchange, will regulate prices and all future contracts. Even the relative value of gold and silver will not be adjusted by your laws. You may insist on coining the ounce of gold into 5*l*. instead of 3*l*. 17*s*. 10½*d*., that is to say, into 200 sixpences instead of, as at present, into 155 sixpences and fourpence halfpenny, but silver will disobey your law, and will insist on finding its own value in the market on principles which you cannot control. The Mint regulations do not, it is true, correctly express the present relative value of gold and silver in the bullion market. Silver is not worth 5*s*. 2*d*. an ounce, not more. I believe, than 5*s*. an ounce, and there would be an apparent present advantage to the debtor in taking silver rather than gold as the standard, since the relative value of gold to silver when standard-silver is 5*s*. per ounce, is 15.575 to 1, instead of $15^{285}\!/_{1346}$ to 1.

But there is reason to doubt whether those who wish for a relaxation of the standard, and who, for the purpose of benefiting the debtor, recommend either a joint standard of silver and gold, or the substitution of silver for gold as the standard, would attain their object were either of those Measures adopted. There is reason to believe, adverting particularly to the rapid increase of the annual supply of gold from mines within the dominions of the Emperor of Russia, that the value of gold in the general markets of the world is on the decrease, and that the interest of the debtor would not be permanently advanced by the abandonment of gold for silver as the standard of value in the country.

But to revert to the errors of those who are the advocates of some measure of value other than the precious metals. They object to the selection of gold as the standard of value, because gold is an article of commerce,—because there is demand for it as bullion, affecting, therefore, its value as coin, and disqualifying it to be the measure of value. Now, no one contends that there is or can be an absolutely fixed and invariable standard of value. No one denies that the value of gold, with reference to all commodities, excepting gold itself, may be subject to slight variations. But what other substance is not more subject to variations in value than the precious metals? What other substance possessing intrinsic value will not also be in demand as an article of commerce? It is because gold is an article of commerce, because there are no restrictions upon its export or its import, that you can at all times depend upon such a supply of gold for the purposes of coin as may be sufficient for the wants of this country. The precious metals are distributed among the various countries of the world in proportion to their respective necessities, by laws of certain though not very obvious operation, which, without our interference, will allot to our share all that we require. Some entertain the apprehension that we may be drained of all our gold in consequence of a demand for gold from foreign countries, either for the payment of their armies in time of war, or in consequence of sudden and unforeseen demand for foreign corn for our own internal consumption. It is supposed that gold, being an article in universal demand, and having at all times and in all places an ascertained value, is more subject to exportation than anything else. But the export of gold, whether coin or bullion, is governed by precisely the same laws by which the export of any other article is governed. Gold will not leave this country unless gold be dearer in some other country than it is in this. It will not leave this country, merely because it is gold, nor while there is any article of our produce or manufacture which can be exported in exchange for foreign produce with a more profitable return. If gold coin be in any country the common medium of exchange; or if the promissory notes, which perform in part the functions of gold coin, are at all times and under all circumstances of equal value with gold, and are instantly convertible into gold; there are causes in operation which, without any interference on our part, will confine within known and just limits the extent to which gold can be exported. There may no doubt be temporary pressure from the export of gold, even when it is confined within those limits; but none for which you may not provide, none to which you would not be subject, in a higher degree probably, were any other standard of value adopted in preference to gold.

I have thus stated the grounds which justify the conclusion, that, according to the ancient monetary policy of the country, according to the law, according to the practice that prevailed at all times, excepting during the period of inconvertible paper currency, a certain quantity of the precious metals, definite in point of weight and fineness, has constituted, and ought to constitute, the measure of value. The minds of men, habituated during the Bank Restriction to a departure from that measure of value, were loath to admit those great elementary truths which are at the foundation of the whole system of currency, paper credit, and foreign exchange. Ingenious writers have from time to time laboured to prove the unsoundness of these doctrines, to show that a metallic standard was neither practically nor theoretically the measure of value in this country, and have cited various facts apparently irreconcilable with the theory. But when all the circumstances attending each fact have been fully stated, they have been sufficient to account for the seeming contradiction. When Sir Isaac Newton had established the planetary system on the principle of gravitation and attraction, there were phenomena apparently at variance with the theory. But succeeding philosophers, starting from the point which in the progress of science had been reached by Sir Isaac Newton, applying his principles with improved means of investigating truth, solved the doubts which he had not been able to solve, and showed that the apparent contradictions, when all the disturbing influences were taken into account, became in fact new demonstrations of the soundness of the original theory. And the same result has followed, and will follow, in the case of objections which have been, and will continue to be, urged against the principle of the metallic standard.

It must at the same time be admitted that it would be quite consistent with that principle to adopt some other measure of value than that which we have adopted. It would be consistent with that principle to select silver instead of gold as the standard,—to have a mixed standard of gold and silver, the relative values of the two metals being determined,—to dispense with gold coin altogether, and regulate the amount and value of paper currency by making it convertible only, according to the proposal of Mr. Ricardo, into gold bullion of a given minimum amount.

I trust, however, this House will adhere to the present standard,— will resolve on the maintenance of a single standard, and of gold as that standard. All the great writers on this subject, Sir William Petty, Mr. Locke, Mr. Harris, and Lord Liverpool, have been decidedly in favour of a single, in preference to a double standard. Mr. Locke, indeed, was of opinion that silver ought to be the standard; but there appears good ground to doubt the soundness of that opinion; and there are, at any rate, the most cogent reasons, since gold has been for a long course of years the standard in this country, for the continued maintenance of it. They are well stated in the admirable Treatise on Coins,[12] written by the first Lord Liverpool. In that treatise a system of coinage is recommended, which is in exact conformity, both in point of principle and detail, with the system which we have adopted. Lord Liverpool observes:—

"After full consideration of this extensive, abstruse, and intricate subject, I humbly offer to your Majesty, as the result of my opinion,

"First, That the coins of this Realm, which are to be the principal measure of property and instrument of commerce, should be made of one metal only.

"Secondly, That in this Kingdom the gold coins only have been for many years past, and are now, in the practice and opinion of the people, the principal measure of property and instrument of commerce.

. . . .

"It has been shown that, in a country like Great Britain, so distinguished for its affluence and for the extent of its commercial connections, the gold coins are best adapted to be the principal measure of property; in this Kingdom, therefore, the gold coin is now the principal measure of property and standard coin, or, as it were, the sovereign archetype by which the weight and value of all other coins should be regulated.

"It is the measure of almost all contracts and bargains; and by it, as a measure, the price of all commodities bought and sold is adjusted and ascertained. For these reasons the gold coin should be made as perfect and kept as perfect as possible.

. . . .

"Thirdly. It is evident, that where the function of the gold coins as a measure of property ceases, there that of the silver coins should begin; and that where the function of the silver coins, in this respect, ceases, there that of copper should begin: it is clear, therefore, that so far only

[12] *The Coins of the Realm* was published in 1805.

these silver and copper coins should be made legal tender and no further, at least not in any great degree; and it follows that the coins, both of silver and copper, are subordinate, subservient, and merely representative coins; and must take their value with reference to the gold coins according to the rate which the sovereign sets upon each of them."

These are, in fact, the principles which regulate our present coinage. We have a single standard, and that standard gold,—the metal which was practically the standard for many years previously to the suspension of cash payment. The silver coin is a mere token, auxiliary and subordinate to the gold coin; the ounce of silver being now coined into 66s. instead of 62s., and silver coin not being a legal tender for any greater sum than 40s. By the abolition, in this part of the United Kingdom, of the promissory notes below 5l., you introduce the gold coin into general use for the purpose of effecting small payments; you enable the holder of the smallest note to demand payment in gold, and thus insure the maintenance of a very considerable quantity of gold as a part of the circulating medium. There is, no doubt, some expense in the maintenance of a metallic circulation, but none, in my opinion, sufficient to countervail the advantage of having gold coin generally distributed throughout the country, accessible to all, and the foundation of paper credit and currency. It is contended by some, that if you were to dispense with coin altogether, to adopt the principle of Mr. Ricardo's plan,[13] and make bank notes not convertible into gold at the will of the holder, excepting when presented to the amount of a very considerable sum (300l. or 400l. for instance), and then convertible into bullion and not coin, you would provide a security against the effects of a panic connected with political causes, causing a sudden demand for gold. I very much doubt the policy of taking such precautions against such a contingency, and consider that the most effectual measure for promoting permanent confidence in the paper circulation of the country, is to require that the gold coin shall be in general use for small payments, and that the promissory note shall be of equal value with the coin which it professes to represent. I shall here close my observations on the measure of value and the coinage, and proceed to the more immediate subject for consideration, namely, the state of the paper circulation of the country, and the principles which ought to regulate it.[14] . . . . .

. . . . . Permit me, before I conclude, briefly to recapitulate the outlines of the plan recommended by Her Majesty's servants. It is proposed that the Bank of England shall continue in possession of its

[13] The noteworthy economist presented his plan in a pamphlet of 1816.
[14] The section of the speech dealing with this subject is omitted.

present privileges—that it shall retain the exclusive right of issue,
within a district of which sixty-five miles from London as a centre
is the radius. The private banks within that district, which now
actually issue notes, will of course be permitted to continue their
issues to the amount of the average of the last two years. Two
Departments of the Bank will be constituted: one for the issue of
notes, the other for the transaction of the ordinary business of banking. The bullion now in the possession of the Bank will be transferred to the Issue Department. The issue of notes will be restricted
to an issue of 14,000,000*l.* upon securities—the remainder being
issued upon bullion—and governed in amount by the fluctuations
in the stock of bullion. If there be, under certain defined circumstances, an increase of the issues of securities, it can only take place
with the knowledge and consent of the Government; and the profit
derivable from such issue will belong to the public. Bankers now
actually enjoying the privilege of issue, will be allowed to continue
their issues, provided the maximum in the case of each bank does
not exceed the average of a certain prescribed period. A weekly
publication of issues will be required from every Bank of Issue.
The names of shareholders and partners in all banks will be regis-
tered and published. No new Bank of Issue can be hereafter
formed, and no Joint-stock Company for banking purposes can be
established, except after application to the Government and compliance with various regulations which will be hereafter submitted
to the consideration of Parliament.

I have now concluded the duty which I have to perform, and
trust I have clearly explained to the House the principle and details
of the plan which the Government proposes for the future regulation of the currency, and the grounds upon which it is founded. I
ask for no vote tonight on the resolutions which I shall propose,
pro forma, and, if I might give advice on such a subject, would
recommend the postponement of discussion to a future day. To-
morrow the correspondence which has taken place with the Bank,
explaining more in detail our communications with the Bank, and
the nature of the pecuniary arrangements between the Bank and
the Government, will be laid upon the Table. The knowledge of
that correspondence is important as a preliminary to full and satisfactory discussion on the merits of our proposal. Considering the
part which I took in the year 1819 in terminating the system of
inconvertible paper currency, and in re-establishing the ancient
standard of value, it will no doubt be a source of great personal
satisfaction to me, if I shall now succeed, after the lapse of a quarter
of a century since those measures were adopted, in obtaining the
assent of the House to proposals which are, in fact, the complement

of them, and which are calculated to guarantee their permanence, and to facilitate their practical operation.

But my gratification will be of a higher and purer nature than any connected with the satisfaction of personal feelings, if I may look forward to the mitigation or termination of evils, such as those which have at various times afflicted the country in consequence of rapid fluctuation in the amount and value of the medium of exchange. When I call to mind the danger to which the Bank of England has been exposed, the various effects of a sudden change from an overabundant to a contracted circulation, the reckless speculation of some of the Joint Stock Banks, the losses entailed on their shareholders, the insolvency of so many private banks, the miserable amount of the dividends which have in many cases been paid, the ruin inflicted on innocent creditors, the shock to public and private credit, then indeed I rejoice on public grounds in the hope, that the wisdom of Parliament will at length devise measures which shall inspire just confidence in the medium of exchange, shall put a check on improvident speculations, and shall ensure, so far as legislation can ensure, the just reward of industry, and the legitimate profit of commercial enterprise conducted with integrity and controlled by provident calculations. The right hon. Baronet concluded by moving—

"That it is expedient to continue to the Bank of England, for a time to be limited, certain of the privileges now by law rested in that Corporation, subject to such conditions as may be provided by any Act to be passed for that purpose."

4. The Corn Laws

Sir Robert Peel gave, in the midst of the discussion on the address in answer to the royal speech (January 22, 1846), the following account of the causes which impelled him no longer to maintain the Corn Law. This selection can be found in HANSARD (LXXXIII [3d Ser.], 67-95).

Peel modified in 1842 the sliding scale of 1828 (cf. Canning's speech, "The Corn Trade," page 46) in order to stimulate importation of grain, and he also reduced the tariff on a large number of articles. The results of this program impressed the Conservative leader, as he stated in his speech, so that he was prepared to go much farther in the direction of free trade should an emergency, such as came with the potato blight, occur. With the arrival of

the dread emergency Peel could neither get united support on policy from members of his own cabinet nor obtain, upon his resignation, a Whig successor; Lord John Russell, who might have assumed responsibility and who was, in reality, for the repeal of the Corn Laws, found himself unable to form a ministry. Peel therefore reassumed the burdens of office.

The political maneuvers of the day gave Peel an opportunity to discuss in the latter part of the speech the relationship between the Prime Minister and other agencies of government. The subheading which is inserted (cf. page 129) is not to be found in the original presentation of the speech. In explanation of the situation this part should be read with "Resignation of the Ministry" (page 133).

Sir, I would fain hope, that although the course which I take is an unusual one, yet that I am acting in conformity with the general wish of the House, in availing myself of the very earliest opportunity of giving that explanation which at no remote period the House will require from me. I would fain hope that I am not obstructing the course of this discussion upon the Address by giving that explanation at this period. But, if no consideration of public advantage could justify me in taking this course, I am sure the generous feelings of the House will deem it only natural that I should desire that not a moment should elapse before I explain to the House the motives by which I have been actuated, and the principles which have governed my conduct. I may feel hurt at having been the object of much accusation upon vague surmise; I may think it unjust to have been condemned without a hearing— I say nothing upon that head; if any momentary feelings of indignation were aroused, the recollection of great indulgence and of great confidence was quite sufficient to efface those temporary feelings. I shall make no allusion, therefore, to particular expressions, or particular accusations; but this I do ask, even while I do not require the reversal of the sentence; I ask for the opportunity, after condemnation, of explaining the motives of my conduct. I ask you to listen at least with patience and indulgence to those facts and that evidence which I shall this night adduce, and which will form the materials on which other tribunals, judging under less excitement, will ultimately pronounce upon the motives and the conduct of men charged with deep responsibility in critical times. I wish to explain what were the grounds which led me and those with whom I acted humbly to tender to a gracious Sovereign the resignation of the trust which was committed to us. I wish also to explain what were the circumstances under which the trust was reassumed, and under which I now appear in the House as the Minister of the Crown.

Sir, the immediate cause which led to the dissolution of the Government in the early part of last December, was that great and mysterious calamity which caused a lamentable failure in an article of food on which great numbers of the people in this part of the United Kingdom, and still larger numbers in the sister kingdom, depend mainly for their subsistence. That was the immediate and proximate cause, which led to the dissolution of the Government. But it would be unfair and uncandid on my part, if I attached undue importance to that particular cause. It certainly appeared to me to preclude further delay, and to require immediate decision—decision not only upon the measures which it was necessary at the time to adopt, but also as to the course to be ultimately taken with regard to the laws which govern the importation of grain. I will not assign to that cause too much weight. I will not withhold the homage which is due to the progress of reason and to truth, by denying that my opinions on the subject of protection have undergone a change. Whether holding a private station, or placed in a public one, I will assert the privilege of yielding to the force of argument and conviction, and acting upon the results of enlarged experience. It may be supposed that there is something humiliating in making such admissions; Sir, I feel no such humiliation. I have not so much confidence in the capacity of man, to determine what is right or wrong intuitively, as to make me feel abashed at admitting that I have been in error. I should feel humiliation, if, having modified or changed my opinions, I declined to acknowledge the change for fear of incurring the imputation of inconsistency. The question is whether the facts are sufficient to account for the change, and the motives for it are pure and disinterested. Nothing could be more base on the part of a public man than to protect himself from danger by pretending a change of opinion; or more inconsistent with the duty he owes to his Sovereign and country than if, seeing reason to alter his course, he forebore to make the alteration by the fear of being taunted with a charge of inconsistency. The

real question, as I have said, is, whether the motives for the modification of opinion are sufficient and sincere.

Sir, those who contend for the removal of impediments upon the
import of a great article of subsistence, such as corn, start with an
immense advantage in the argument. The natural presumption is
in favour of free and unrestricted importation. It may, indeed, be
possible to combat that presumption; it may be possible to meet its
advocates in the field of argument, by showing that there are other
and greater advantages arising out of the system of prohibition than
out of the system of unrestricted intercourse; but even those who
so contend will, I think, admit that the natural feelings of mankind
are strongly in favour of the absence of all restriction, and that the
presumption is so strong, that we must combat it by an avowal of
some great public danger to be avoided, or some great public benefit
to be obtained by restriction on the importation of food.

We all admit that the argument in favour of high protection or
prohibition on the ground that it is for the benefit of a particular
class, is untenable. The most strenuous advocates for protection
have abandoned that argument; they rest, and wisely rest, the defence of protective duties upon higher principles. They have alleged, as I have myself alleged, that there were public reasons for
retaining this protection. Sir, circumstances made it absolutely
necessary for me, occupying the public station I do, and seeing the
duty that must unavoidably devolve on me—it became absolutely
necessary for me maturely to consider whether the grounds on
which an alteration of the Corn Laws can be resisted are tenable.
The arguments in favour of protection must be based either on the
principle that protection to domestic industry is in itself sound
policy, and that, therefore, agriculture being a branch of domestic
industry, is entitled to share in that protection; or, that in a country
like ours, encumbered with an enormous load of debt, and subject
to great taxation, it is necessary that domestic industry should be
protected from competition with foreigners; or, again—the interests
of the great body of the community, the laborious classes, being
committed in this question—that the rate of wages varies with the
price of provisions, that high prices implies high wages, and that
low wages are the concomitants of low prices. Further, it may be
said, that the land is entitled to protection on account of some
peculiar burdens which it bears. But that is a question of justice
rather than of policy; I have always felt and maintained that the
land is subject to peculiar burdens; but you have the power of
weakening the force of that argument by the removal of the burden,
or making compensation. The first three objections to the removal
of protection are objections founded on considerations of public

policy. The last is a question of justice, which may be determined by giving some counterbalancing advantage.

Now, I want not to deprive those who, arguing *a priori*, without the benefit of experience, have come to the conclusion that protection is objectionable in principle—I want not to deprive them of any of the credit which is fairly their due. Reason, unaided by experience, brought conviction to their minds. My opinions have been modified by the experience of the last three years. I have had the means and opportunity of comparing the results of periods of abundance and low prices with periods of scarcity and high prices. I have carefully watched the effects of the one system and of the other—first, of the policy we have been steadily pursuing for some years, viz., the removal of protection from domestic industry; and next, of the policy which the friends of protection recommend. I have also had an opportunity of marking from day to day the effect upon great social interests of freedom of trade and comparative abundance. I have not failed to note the results of preceding years, and to contrast them with the results of the last three years; and I am led to the conclusion that the main grounds of public policy on which protection has been defended are not tenable; at least I cannot maintain them. I do not believe, after the experience of the last three years, that the rate of wages varies with the price of food. I do not believe, that with high prices, wages will necessarily rise in the same ratio. I do not believe that a low price of food necessarily implies a low rate of wages. Neither can I maintain that protection to domestic industry is necessarily good. I said last year on the Motion of the noble Lord (Lord J. Russell) that I thought protective duties were evils in themselves. But I also said, that as they had grown with our system, and not being incompatible with a high degree of prosperity, I thought they ought not to be lightly abolished, and must be tenderly and cautiously dealt with. It is now, however, impossible for us, after we see the results of the change in the Tariff during the last four years, to contend that protection to industry is in itself, and abstractedly, a public good.

Then, as to the other argument, which I confess made a great impression on me in the first instance, and which is sanctioned by great authority—that because we have a heavy debt and a high rate of taxation, we must be protected from competition with foreign industry—that argument has also been submitted to the test of the last three years, and, so far as the experience of that period can supply an argument, it is this—that a large debt and heavy taxation are best encountered by abundance and cheapness of provisions; which rather alleviate than add to the weight of the burden.

Let us take the result of that experience of constantly diminished protection—on wages—on trade, and on revenue. First, as to wages. Who can deny the fact that during the three years that preceded the month of October last, prices were comparatively low? There was comparative cheapness and plenty, and yet at no period were the wages of labour higher. If you take the three preceding years, you will find high prices, and coexistent with high prices you will find low wages. Well, then, I have six years experience; I have during the first three years high prices and low wages; I have during the last three years low prices and high wages; and I cannot resist the conclusion that wages do not vary with the price of provisions. They do vary with the increase of capital, with the prosperity of the country, with the increased power to employ labour; but there is no immediate relation between wages and provisions—or if there be a relation, it is an inverse ratio.

Now as to the Tariff; as I said before during the last four or five years we have been acting on the admitted principle of removing prohibitions—reducing duties, or abating, and in some cases destroying protection to native industry. That has been the principle, whether right or wrong, on which we have acted—the removal of protection to native industry. Now, what has been the result? I will give you the total amount of exports since the year 1839. The total value of British produce and manufactures exported from the United Kingdom was, in 1839, 53,000,000*l*.; in 1840, 51,000,000*l*.; in 1842, 47,000,000*l*.; in 1843, 52,000,000*l*.; in 1844, 58,000,000*l*.; that is, the rise from the year when the great invasion upon the protection of domestic industry was made by Parliament was from 47,381,000*l*. in 1842, to 58,500,000*l*. in 1844. But it may be said the China trade made all the difference. Now let us deduct the whole of that trade. In 1842, our exports to all the countries, except China, amounted to 46,411,000*l*.; and in 1844, they increased by 10,000,000*l*., amounting to 56,000,000*l*. For the last year we can only have the account for eleven months preceding December. In 1843, the exports of our principal articles of manufacture to all parts of the world, including China, amounted to 41,011,000*l*.; in 1844, to 47,312,000*l*., and during the first eleven months of 1845, to 47,-764,000*l*. Such is the state of our foreign exports under this system of continued removal of protection.

Now let me take the returns of the revenue as bearing on this question—ought there to be high protection in a country encumbered with an immense public debt and heavy taxation? In 1842, I proposed a reduction in the Customs to an estimated amount of 1,438,000*l*.; in 1844, I proposed a further reduction in the Customs' duties to the amount of 273,000*l*.; in 1845, to the large amount of 2,418,000*l*. I estimated the total loss from these several reductions at 4,129,000*l*., and let it be remembered that I discarded altogether the revenue from corn. How have these calculations been verified? Have 4,000,000*l*. been lost? No. The total amount of the loss has been 1,500,000*l*. I dealt with the Excise last year, and made a reduction of a million of Excise duties; the whole of the glass duties, the whole of the auction duty was taken off; the loss on that occasion was estimated at 1,000,000*l*. Observe, that was not a mere reduction of duties; there was no expection, therefore, that increased consumption would make up for a diminished rate of taxation, for these duties were totally abolished. I felt confident, that although the glass and auction duties were abolished, still by vivifying other branches of industry, the revenue would derive some compensation. What will be the fact on the 5th of April? I believe, that notwithstanding the total reduction, the absolute loss of a million, my firm belief is, that the revenue from the Excise will this year be greater than ever. Notwithstanding these reductions there has been a salient spring of prosperity which has supplied the void you caused by the remission of taxation. Well, then, with that evidence before me, could I contend that on account of high taxation or great debt you must necessarily continue high protective duties? I have shown you that my estimates as to a loss in the Customs have been already falsified; that the Customs this year amount to nearly 20,000,000*l*.; that, comparing the Customs' revenue of 1845 with the Customs' revenue of 1842, after that diminution of taxation to the extent of 4,000,000*l*., the Customs of this year, excluding from both years the revenue from foreign corn, are better by 100,000*l*. than in the former year. But I will now refer to more important considerations than those either of trade or revenue; I will take the state of crime in the country.[15]

. . . . . I think, as far as we have had experience within the last four years, I have shown that, by the removal of protection, domestic industry and the great social interests of the country have been promoted; crime has diminished, and morality has improved. I can bring the most conclusive proof that the public health has been improved, yet the national trade has been extending, our exports have increased; and this—and I rejoice in it—has been effected, not only without serious injury to those interests from which protection was withdrawn, but I think I have shown that it has been concurrent with an increase in the prices of those articles.

Now, it is right I should state, that notwithstanding the conviction which this experience has brought home to my mind, yet my

[15] Data on this subject as well as on the diminution of protection are omitted.

decided impression was, that on other grounds the charge of considering the change in the present Corn Law ought not to have devolved upon me. This I was firmly resolved upon, that I could not this Session, on the Motion of the honourable Gentleman (Mr. Villiers), for the consideration of the Corn Laws—I could not, with these convictions, which, say as you will, I cannot withstand, have met that Motion with a direct negative. Now, Sir, let me again repeat that I claim no credit whatever for having drawn my conclusions from abstract reasoning. My conviction has been brought about by observation and experience; and I could not, with this conviction, have undertaken the defence of the Corn Laws, either upon the public ground that this country being highly taxed the continuance of protection was necessary, or upon the ground that it was for the interest of the labouring classes that high prices should continue as a guarantee of high wages; and I could not have undertaken it upon the ground that the removing protection from domestic industry must necessarily paralyse commerce, lower prices, and undermine our national prosperity.

But this I wish more ardently—I wish to have the opportunity of frankly stating to those Gentlemen who have honoured me upon so many occasions with their confidence, that I can continue this contest no longer—that they must devolve the duty of maintaining protection upon other persons, who can adduce better arguments in its favour than I can. I doubted whether it would not have been advantageous if, in another Parliament, this question should have been considered; but it would have been my bounden duty to have committed the defence, if a defence were undertaken, of protection to other hands more able to maintain the conflict.

I should have wished, I say, that another Parliament should have had an opportunity of considering this question; but there did occur, during the course of the last autumn, that which precluded me from taking the course which would have been most agreeable to my personal feelings. A great calamity befell us, the limits of which it was difficult to divine, the consequences of which, though felt, it may still be difficult to describe. There occurred a great visitation of Providence, extending not to Ireland [16] only, but Great Britain, America, and many parts of the world; and we, Her Majesty's servants, constituting the Government of the country, were called upon to consider what should be done to lessen the calamity. There appeared to be a great and a pressing danger, and it was our duty towards our Sovereign and towards the country to meet the danger. If it was advisable, from the pressure of the deficiency to

[16] The potato blight.

take immediate measures, it would have been impossible, with our conviction of the necessity, to abstain; with our convictions, we could not, consistently with the duty we owed to the Sovereign and the country. If we had, indeed, pretended apprehensions of a scarcity for the purpose of effecting an alteration in the Corn Laws, nothing could have been more base or dishonest than to have taken such a step; but you shall have the opportunity of judging of the motives upon which I and others have acted, and you shall determine whether or no, with the information we were in possession of, we were not justified in drawing the conclusion that it was impossible to maintain the existing commercial system.

My own opinion was founded upon the evidence which I shall now adduce; and it was impossible, upon that evidence to come to any other opinion. The advice which I individually offered at an early period—so early as in the month of November, was to meet this emergency by a suspension of the import duties on foreign corn. I came to that conclusion; and I was adduced to advise that unusual—not unprecedented, but I admit unusual—course, upon the following considerations.

I will proceed first to an explanation of the circumstances under which, early in December, the Government was temporarily dissolved, and under which the Government, as now constituted, resumed office. There are two important periods in giving that explanation, to which I must draw attention—first, the period which elapsed between the 1st of November, 1845, and the 6th of November; and, second, the period which elapsed between the 25th of November and the 6th of December. I propose to read consecutively the information that was received from different parts of this country and the Continent which appeared to me to justify the conclusion to which I came, both in the early part of November, and towards the close of that month and the beginning of the following month. I will give the date of each letter that I shall quote; but, of course, the letters which were received subsequently to November 6th, can form no justification of the advice; but though I shall give the date of each letter, I will not divide the evidence into two periods, but I will give the whole of it consecutively. The disease which affected the potato crop in this country was also felt in other parts of the world; and there were in other parts of Europe apprehensions of scarcity. For instance, the Resident Agent of the Government, writing from Poland, on the 22nd of October, said—

"The cost of articles of food is stated to be higher than it has been since 1813 and 1814. The unfavourable results of the harvests in Podolia, Lithuania, Gallicia, the German Baltic provinces, preclude the hope of foreign aid. No alleviation of the general distress is expected before next autumn."

In a letter, dated the 14th of December, Colonel Wynford, writing from Riga, says—

"The supply of rye and rye-flour sent from St. Petersburg is insufficient for the relief of the Livonians, and discontent prevails."

. . . . . Here is a letter from Mr. Wood, Chairman of the Excise, who, writing on the 2nd December from Yorkshire, thus addressed the Chancellor of the Exchequer:—

"You will regret to hear that the potato disease has now manifested itself in the most extensive manner in this district. Potatoes were selling ten days since at 2s. to 2s. 6d. a bushel of 70 lbs., in York. Yesterday, the same weight sold at 1s. 2d., owing to the farmers bringing an extra quantity to market. I have, consequently, had several pits opened on this estate, and I fear that before Christmas we shall not have a sound one; what the poor are to live on, I cannot guess. I know you will be anxious to have accurate information, and therefore have ventured to give you this account."

From Scotland, I received a letter from my honourable Friend the Member for the County of Dumfries, which gave us as unfavourable an account as any I had seen from that part. Mr. Hope Johnstone, writing on the 22nd November, says—

"I am sorry to say, that in so far as my own observation has gone, the disease appears to be progressing. I have today examined a large quantity of potatoes grown on some of the best and dryest soils in this neighborhood, and have not found one potato in twenty untainted, while three-fourths are quite unfit for human food. These have been carefully housed, and have never been exposed to damp since they were taken out of the ground. In Dumfries-shire also the decay is going on rapidly."

These were the accounts which reached me in the months of October and November, with respect to the extent of this disease in parts of Great Britain.

Now as to the accounts from Ireland, because the pressure appeared to be the greatest in that country, the people there chiefly subsisting upon potatoes. It is difficult to estimate the numbers who subsist upon potatoes. But here is the Report made to the Government, presented by Mr. Lucas, who was Member for Monaghan, Sir. R. Routh, and Professor Kane. They say that the numerical proportion of the Irish population that live exclusively upon potatoes, included, certainly, four millions. It was, therefore, a calamity which threatened the subsistence of not less than four millions in

Ireland that the Government had to provide against. Now, first I will read to the House the information which came to us from the chief authority in Ireland—the Lord Lieutenant, who remitted to us every day the principal information which he received. It was the duty of my right honourable Friend and myself to read the reports thus received, and to that duty we did devote many anxious days and nights. I will not refer to the detailed reports received in great numbers from Ireland. They were nearly all concurrent; but I will state at once the impressions of the chief authority, and the communications which he made to the Government.[17]

.   .   .   .

. . . . . I thought that there was a perfect justification at the time for extraordinary measures, and that the adoption of extraordinary measures would compel the reconsideration of the Corn Law. My noble Friend [18] was not the only Member of the Administration who would have refused me the inestimable aid of his counsel and support; and that being the case—believing as I did that his resignation would be followed by that of others—thinking that under such circumstances the attempt to settle the question, which I thought to settle, would fail, and that I should fail after having made new combinations, and that I should be compelled to offer worse terms than the interests in question were entitled to claim at my hands.

I felt it to be my duty, not being supported by the unanimous voice of my Colleagues, humbly to tender to Her Majesty my resignation. That resignation Her Majesty was pleased to accept; and as my late Colleagues were not themselves prepared to carry on the Government, Her Majesty, of Her own choice, sent for the noble Lord. The noble Lord undertook the task of forming an Administration—I believed then that I was in the situation of a private Member—that I was reduced to the ranks, and that I was at entire liberty to act on the suggestions of my own conscience; and I do not hesitate to say that in that capacity I would have done all in my power to promote the settlement of this question. The duty of adjusting would then have been left to the noble Lord, and in my capacity as a private Member I repeat that I would have done all I could to facilitate a fair and final settlement of the question. I remained under the impression that my functions had ceased until Saturday, the 20th of December. On Thursday, the 18th, it was intimated to me by Her Majesty that the noble Lord had under-

[17] Additional statements on this topic and the effects of the reports upon the Cabinet are omitted.
[18] Lord Stanley.

taken the duty of forming an Administration, and on the 19th I received a gracious communication from Her Majesty stating that, as my relation to Her Majesty was about to terminate, she wished again to see me, for the purpose of taking a final farewell; and Saturday, the 20th of December, was the day appointed for that purpose. Upon waiting on Her Majesty—having heard through the courtesy of the noble Lord that he had found all his efforts to form an Administration were in vain—upon waiting on Her Majesty she was pleased to inform me, that so far from taking my final leave, She was obliged to demand of me that I should withdraw my offer of resignation. Her Majesty had understood from those of my Colleagues who had differed from me that they were unprepared to form, and did not advise the formation, of a Government on the principle of the existing protective system. That the noble Lord, having undertaken the formation of a Government, had failed, from causes which it is unnecessary for me to notice; and the noble Lord having signified to Her Majesty that he had failed in his attempt to form a Government, Her Majesty requested that I should not persist in the tender of my resignation. I do not hesitate to say that I informed Her Majesty on the instant, and without a moment's hesitation, that the noble Lord having failed, and the Colleagues with whom I had heretofore acted not thinking it advisable to form an Administration, I did inform Her Majesty on the instant that I would return to town as Her Majesty's Minister—that I would withdraw my resignation, and inform my Colleagues of my determination, and urge them to assist me in carrying on the business of the country.

I resolved, therefore, to meet them in the capacity of the Minister of the Crown, and to submit to them the measures I proposed to bring before Parliament. My noble Friend at once expressed the regret he felt that he could not co-operate with me in the difficult circumstances in which I was placed; but my Colleagues generally thought it was their duty to assist me in the arduous task I had undertaken. I have now, Sir, stated to the House the circumstances under which I felt it my duty to tender my resignation, and also the circumstances under which I again returned to office.

Sir, I have given, on the earliest day on which it is possible, notice, that it is my intention, on the part of the Government, to submit to the consideration of the House measures connected with the commercial and financial affairs of the country. My firm determination is not to anticipate discussion. I know that the information I have given must be imperfect—I know that it may give rise to some misconception, and that I must ask for a suspension of the judgment of the House; but my desire is to disconnect a great political question from the mere personal and party one; to keep my explanation, so far as it refers to personal matters, distinct from the great question itself, and my explanation therefore is necessarily imperfect.

Therefore I do hope, that after having referred to the evidence in the possession of the Government, although many may think that the conclusions to which I and others have come as to the danger have been erroneous, I advise them not to be too confident, as we have yet seven months to pass before a new supply of food can be obtained for the people. I remember the accounts that have been lately coming in; but I ask the House not to form too precipitate a conclusion that the danger has passed. It is not so. Sir, I trust I may have satisfied some of those who think the con- clusions were erroneous, that, at least, the advice was honest, for advising a resort to extraordinary measures.

Sir, you can hardly estimate what a painful position it is for those whose public duty requires them to take precautions against so fearful a calamity as famine. I am charged with treason towards the agricultural interest—treason, indeed, it would be, if, with my deep conviction and solemn impressions of the position in which the country was placed, I subjected the agricultural interest to the odium of claiming protection against the hazard of scarcity—of calling for votes of public money for purchasing oats and other grain, while at the same time I resisted on their part any relaxation of the protective duties. Why, there are some points in which you could not possibly resist it. I take the law as it applies to the introduction of Indian corn. It is in a most anomalous state, be- cause the present amount of duty on Indian corn depends on the price of barley. There is no connexion between them. There is no reason why it should rise and fall with the price of barley. Sup- pose a proposition had been made at the meeting of Parliament for the admission of Indian corn, what would be the consequence? Suppose the worst of things arises in Ireland, which I anticipate as possible, which I am afraid is probable, what would be the feel- ing with regard to the great agricultural interests of this country, if I, a member of it, had positively refused to make the slightest relaxation in the law?

But this I tell you, to touch the Corn Law in some slight point, like that of Indian corn, would be dangerous to it. I thought it would be unjust to relax it upon one article, and to confine it to the nobler species of grain, oats, and wheat. Sir, I would rather keep the law intact and refuse to admit Indian corn, than come down to the House with such a proposition, and refuse to relax the duties on other descriptions of grain. I recollect the notice given by the Honourable Member for Winchester,[19] which was brought forward for the special benefit of the agricultural interest. Would it be possible to relax the law in that instance and refuse it in the others? Sir, I venture to think that it would be impossible, consistently with the true interests of agriculture, to take such a step. Sir, I have felt, as I said before, that when after the severe labour of the last Session of Parliament, almost every hour of the recess was devoted to calculating the chances that might result from the disease, and to collecting evidence on the subject, night and day, and adopting precautions against the possibility of the calamity which might result from such a state of the crop—I felt it rather hard to find myself the object of accusations that I was unfaithful to the interests of the country, or to any special and peculiar interest. I cannot, of course, but recollect the repeated manifestations of great confidence which I have at various times experienced— those manifestations cannot be without their effect on my mind— but notwithstanding those manifestations of confidence, the constant repetition of those observations to which I have adverted, of those accusations that I have been unfaithful renders it absolutely necessary that I should allude to them.

The Prime Minister and Other Agencies of Government

I have over and over again attempted to define the relation in which I conceived myself to stand with respect to party, to my country, and to my Sovereign, and it is necessary that I should again describe that relation. I see it over and over again repeated, that I am under a personal obligation for holding the great office which I have the honour to occupy. I see it over and over again repeated, that I was placed in that position by a party, and that the party which elevated me to my present position is powerful enough to displace me. I see constantly put forth allusions to the power of those men to remove me from office. I am afraid that, with respect to holding the office that I hold, there is a very material difference between the extent of the obligation and the amount of the penalty. I am not under an obligation to any man, or to any body of men, for being compelled to submit to the sacrifices which I have submitted to, and to undergo the official duties and labour which I have undertaken. I do not underrate the distinction and importance of the position; but let us understand—and I am speaking not for myself, but for the many honourable men who have

[19] Bickham Escott.

preceded me of different parties—let us understand what is the nature of the obligation we owe for being placed in office. As I said before, I do not undervalue the distinction and the power which are attached to the occupation of that office; but what, I ask, is its real value? It does not consist in the power of distributing honours, or conferring appointments. That power, it is true, is inseparable from the office of Prime Minister, and cannot be separated from it without injuring its authority; but the power of giving the highest rewards and the highest offices, is constantly accompanied by the invidious duty of selection, and the disappointment of those who may not have been selected. For my part, I value power not one farthing for any such privilege. I have served four Sovereigns; George III, and his three successors. In the reign of George III, the office which I held was so subordinate, that it was impossible my services could have attracted his notice; but, as I have said, I also served his three successors—George IV as Regent and King, King William IV, and Queen Victoria; and during the reigns of those Sovereigns, it has been my fate to hold some of the highest offices in the State. I served each of those Sovereigns at critical times and in critical circumstances—I did so with constant truth to each, and I constantly said to each of those Sovereigns that there was but one favour, but one distinction, one reward which I desired, that it was in their power to offer me—namely, the simple acknowledgment, on their part, that I had been to them a loyal and faithful Minister.

I have now stated my view of the obligations which are conferred on those in power; but let me remark that there is that valuable privilege in power, that it gives constant and favourable opportunities for exertion; and affords great facilities to the holder of it to render his country service, according to his sense of the public good. That, in my mind, constitutes the real value of official power; and I can say with truth, that I have never abused that power for any unworthy object. I have tried to use it for the promotion of the public interests and the advancement of the public good. I used it for the public advantage, and in doing so I cannot charge myself with any conduct at variance with the true and comprehensive policy of a Conservative Minister. Sir, I do not think it at variance with Conservative policy, that I and my Colleagues have attempted to repair the disasters of Cabul [20]—that

[20] Cabul or Kabul, seat of the Afghan ruler, had been the place of British tragedy. A British official, suspecting the emir of duplicity, placed a rival in power (1838) only to beget a native revolt (1841) which caused a disastrous retreat. In Peel's administration a successful return to Cabul was made.

we have attempted to infuse into the Indian army that spirit which had been checked by the defeats and misfortunes of Affghanistan. Nor do I think it inconsistent with true Conservative policy, that I have laboured to assuage that feeling of animosity which for a long time prevailed between this country and another powerful and great nation; and I cannot think that this paragraph in the Speech of the Sovereign—

"The Convention concluded with France in the course of last year, for the more effectual suppression of the Slave Trade,[21] is about to be carried into immediate execution by the active co-operation of the two Powers on the coast of Africa. It is my desire that our present union, and the good understanding which so happily exists between us, may always be employed to promote the interest of humanity, and to secure the peace of the world;"—

I cannot, I repeat, think it inconsistent with true Conservative policy, that we should be enabled to insert that paragraph, and that we should be engaged in trying to efface the recollections of the exploits of both countries in war, or extracting from those recollections everything which savours of bitterness; that we should be trying to engage in a rivalry, not in exploits on the field of blood, but in an honourable competition for the advancement of commerce and civilization, and the improvement of the social condition of the people. It is not inconsistent with true Conservative policy, that we should increase the trade of the country by removing restrictions; nor is it inconsistent with sound Conservative policy, that we should reduce the taxation of the country whilst we increased its revenue. It is not, in my mind, inconsistent with true Conservative policy, that we have extinguished agitation and discouraged sedition, not by stringent coercive laws, but by encouraging the idea amongst the great body of the people, that we, the rich and powerful, are willing to take a more than ordinary share of the public burdens, and to remove those burdens from the people so far as it is possible.

Sir, believe me, to conduct the Government of this country is a most arduous duty; I may say it without irreverence, that these ancient institutions, like our physical frames, are "fearfully and wonderfully made." It is no easy task to ensure the united action of an ancient monarchy, a proud aristocracy, and a reformed constituency. I have done everything I could do, and have thought it consistent with true Conservative policy to reconcile these three branches of the State. I have thought it consistent with true Con-

[21] For background, see "The Slave Trade," p. 166.

servative policy to promote so much of happiness and contentment among the people that the voice of disaffection should be no longer heard, and that thoughts of the dissolution of our institutions should be forgotten in the midst of physical enjoyment. These were my attempts, and I thought them not inconsistent with true and enlarged Conservative policy. These were my objects in accepting office—it is a burden too great for my physical, and far beyond my intellectual structure; and to be relieved from it with perfect honour would be the greatest favour that could be conferred on me. But as a feeling of honour and strong sense of duty require me to undertake those responsible functions, I declare, Sir, that I am ready to incur these risks, to bear these burdens, and to front all these honourable dangers. But, Sir, I will not take the step with mutilated power and shackled authority. I will not stand at the helm during such tempestuous nights as I have seen, if the vessel be not allowed fairly to pursue the course which I think she ought to take. I will not, Sir, undertake to direct the course of the vessel by the observations which have been taken in 1842. I will reserve to myself the marking out of that course; and I must, for the public interest, claim for myself the unfettered power of judging of those measures which I conceive will be better for the country to propose.

Sir, I do not wish to be the Minister of England; but while I have the high honour of holding that office, I am determined to hold it by no servile tenure. I will only hold that office upon the condition of being unshackled by any other obligations than those of consulting the public interests, and of providing for the public safety.

5. Resignation of the Ministry

This extract contains the peroration of Sir Robert Peel's speech which announced to the House of Commons the resignation of his ministry. It can be found in HANSARD *(LXXXVII [3d Ser.] 1053-55 [June 29, 1846]).*

During the five months which elapsed between the speech, "The Corn Laws," and this speech, Peel had endeavored to win back followers who considered him an apostate by arguing for free trade in food as a concomitant of a reduction of duties on manufactured and half-manufactured goods and the removal of the whole import from raw materials. He met with little but obstruction. At the end, after his legislation was passed with the help of members of other political leanings, he was left without adequate political support.

Sir, I have now executed the task which my public duty imposed upon me. I trust I have said nothing which can lead to the revival on the present occasion of those controversies which I have deprecated. Whatever opinions may be held with regard to the extent of the danger with which we were threatened from the failure in one great article of subsistence, I can say with truth that Her Majesty's Government, in proposing those measures of commercial policy which have disentitled them to the confidence of many who heretofore gave them their support, were influenced by no other motive than the desire to consult the interests of this country. Our object was to avert dangers which we thought were imminent, and to terminate a conflict which, according to our belief, would soon place in hostile collision great and powerful classes in this country.

The maintenance of power was not a motive for the proposal of these measures; for, as I said before, I had not a doubt, that whether these measures were accompanied by failure or success, the certain issue must be the termination of the existence of this Government. It is, perhaps, advantageous for the public interests that such should be the issue. I admit that the withdrawal of confidence from us by many of our friends was a natural result. When proposals are made, apparently at variance with the course which Ministers heretofore have pursued, and subjecting them to the charge of inconsistence—it is perhaps advantageous for this country, and for the general character of public men, that the proposal of measures of that kind, under such circumstances, should entail that which is supposed to be the fitting punishment, namely, expulsion from office. I, therefore, do not complain of that expulsion. I am sure it is far preferable to the continuance in office without a full assurance of the confidence of this House. I said before, and I said truly, that in proposing our measures of commercial policy, I had no wish to rob others of the credit justly due to them. I must say, with reference to honourable Gentlemen opposite, as I say with reference to ourselves, that neither of us is the party which is justly entitled to the credit of them. There has been a combination of parties generally opposed to each other, and that combination, and the influence of Government, have led to their ultimate success; but the name which ought to be associated with the success of those measures is not the name of the noble Lord,[22] the organ of the party of which he is the leader, nor is it mine. The name which ought to be, and will be, associated with the success of those measures, is the name of one who, acting, I believe, from pure and disinterested motives, has, with untiring energy, made appeals to our reason, and has enforced those appeals with an eloquence the more to be admired because it was unaffected and unadorned; the name which ought to be chiefly associated with the success of those measures, is the name of RICHARD COBDEN.

Sir, I now close the observations which it has been my duty to address to the House, thanking them sincerely for the favour with which they have listened to me in performing this last act of my official career. Within a few hours, probably, that power which I have held for the period of five years will be surrendered into the hands of another—without repining—without complaint on my part—with a more lively recollection of the support and confidence I have received during several years, than of the opposition which during a recent period I have encountered. In relinquishing power, I shall leave a name, severely censured I fear by many who, on public grounds, deeply regret the severance of party ties—deeply regret that severance, not from interested or personal motives, but from the firm conviction that fidelity to party engagements—the existence and maintenance of a great party—constitutes a powerful instrument of government: I shall surrender power severely censured also, by others who, from no interested motive, adhere to the principle of protection, considering the maintenance of it to be essential to the welfare and interests of the country: I shall leave a name execrated by every monopolist who, from less honourable motives, clamours for protection because it conduces to his own individual benefit; but it may be that I shall leave a name sometimes remembered with expressions of good will in the abodes of those whose lot it is to labour, and to earn their daily bread by the sweat of their brow, when they shall recruit their exhausted strength with abundant and untaxed food, the sweeter because it is no longer leavened by a sense of injustice.

[22] Lord John Russell.

Chapter V

PALMERSTON

Chapter V

PALMERSTON

Henry John Temple, third Viscount Palmerston (1784-1865), had his family title from an Irish peerage and was not disqualified for election to the House of Commons throughout his political career. Educated at Harrow, Edinburgh, and Cambridge he came to Parliament at twenty-three years of age and at twenty-five was a minister of state. His appointment as Secretary at War did not give him a seat in the Cabinet, however, although it meant that he was burdened with the task of keeping accounts and attempting to control military expenditures without directing military policies. For almost twenty years he was connected with the War Office and finally under Canning entered the Cabinet.

Palmerston's political tenets during his early years were comprised in "those constitutional principles upon which the administration of this country has been fortunately conducted by Mr. Pitt and those who have succeeded him." [1] He deviated from the more conservative Tories in standing for Catholic emancipation and a degree of free trade and even from Canning in admitting the necessity for moderate Parliamentary reform. When Huskisson left Wellington's government, Palmerston was one of those who went with him. Although the Duke tried to regain his services, Palmerston did not accept office until he was appointed by Earl Grey, the Whig leader, to the Foreign Office in 1830. At this post which he retained for eleven years (except for the four months when Peel was in power) he won fame. He believed, like a true disciple of Canning, that the dignity, prestige, and power of England should be maintained and that a strong foreign policy was in reality a policy of peace. Interfering frequently abroad, he sometimes gave friendly counsel and good

[1] Cf. Philip Guedalla, *Palmerston* (London: Ernest Benn, Ltd., 1927), p. 99.

advice and sometimes excited toward warfare those whom he had no means of supporting. In any case he probably was not unmindful of British interests or what he conceived to be British interests. As a matter of actual accomplishment from 1830 to 1841 he had, in the words of one biographer,[2] "created Belgium, saved Portugal and Spain from absolutism, rescued Turkey from Russia and the highway to India from France."

During Peel's administration from 1841 to 1846 opposition claimed Palmerston but the Foreign Office saw him again in July of the latter year. He continued, on the one hand, to sympathize with oppressed nationalities and to stand for constitutional principles and, on the other, to defend secret diplomacy (cf. "International Arbitration," page 141). His whole foreign policy was tested in the famous Don Pacifico case. Who Don Pacifico was may perhaps be gleaned from "Foreign Policy—Affairs of Greece" (page 153), but his identity is a matter of little importance for as Palmerston's secretary explains:

Just as some unsightly knoll or insignificant stream has won imperishable fame by the accident of its crest or banks being the scene of a great battle, so did the name of a paltry adventurer become famous, in 1850, by its connection with a memorable debate. The fate of the Ministry, as well as that of a minister, was involved, for the wrongs of Don Pacifico and the manner of their redress were only the battle-field on which a policy was attacked and bitter antagonisms fought out.[3]

The debate lasted for four nights on the second of which Palmerston, attempting to vindicate himself, spoke for four hours and thirty-five minutes without notes and ended with the finest peroration he ever delivered ("Foreign Policy—Affairs of Greece," page 153). Sustained by the House of Commons, he enjoyed an enhanced reputation throughout the country. His supremacy was cut short, however, when he expressed himself too joyously and independently, without consultation with Cabinet colleagues and the Queen, on Louis Napoleon's *coup d'état* in 1851. Palmerston in reality had caused the Queen's resentment on former occasions by withholding data to which Victoria

---

[2] Lloyd C. Sanders, *Life of Viscount Palmerston* (London, 1888), p. 79.
[3] Evelyn Ashley, *The Life of Henry John Temple, Viscount Palmerston: 1846-1865* (London, 1876), I, 176.

and the Prince Consort felt themselves entitled. Taking advantage of a confused situation, Russell as head of the ministry dismissed Palmerston.

A few weeks later Palmerston opposed Russell on a militia bill and turned him out. He had played tit-for-tat with Lord John.

He was in opposition to Derby (1852) but under Aberdeen's coalition government took the Home Office. Since 1840 he had shown an interest in questions other than those strictly related to foreign affairs. Influenced by Lord Shaftesbury he spoke for factory and mines and colliery legislation; his activity for the suppression of the slave trade (cf. page 166) was a matter of pride to himself to his dying day. He now—in the decade of the fifties —gave himself over to public health and related questions. The Crimean War, however, broke across a country to which Tennyson had preached the brotherhood of man and to which victories soon became so essential that it called for a bold, active man to replace the impotent Aberdeen in the Eastern crisis. Palmerston with his reputation for hostility to Russia and for energy in foreign affairs and with an ability to radiate cheerfulness during the most trying of times (cf. "Sir Charles Napier," page 176) found himself on February 6, 1855, at seventy years of age the Prime Minister. The Crimean War was hardly over before the Indian Mutiny occurred. Again Palmerston showed ability at arousing the national spirit.[4]

In 1857 a general election that provided Palmerston with a large majority had been held. But at the very height of popularity he found his power waning when the public thought him yielding to foreign dictation in offering a bill which was designed to prevent foreign refugees from abusing the hospitality of the country as had been done by those who plotted against Louis Napoleon. Turned out himself, Palmerston had the satisfaction of seeing Derby and Disraeli wrecked in the question of Parliamentary reform. For his own attitude on the subject,[5] stated in his own peculiar way, see "Constitutional Reforms" (page 179).

By 1859 Palmerston was in leadership again—a leadership which he retained until his death in 1865. The country remained tranquil during this era and Palmerston found himself

[4] Cf. speech at Lord Mayor's banquet, November 9, 1857.
[5] Herbert C. Bell, in the *Journal of Modern History*, IV, No. 2 (June 1932), gives able consideration to this topic.

guiding one great political party and unopposed by the other. It was an era of "rest and be thankful" with the head of the nation unwilling to accept the Radicalism of Bright and Cobden. Rather he talked on defense [6] or guided his colleagues through the maze of the Schleswig-Holstein affair ("Denmark and Germany," page 180) in a speech which probably was second in power only to the *Civis Romanus sum* speech. Holding position for such a length of time, he might well quote an eminent physician that continuance in office, with the resulting employment, was food for the health. And, questioned as to whether active opposition might not do as well, he gave a characteristic reply: "No, no; that stirs up the bile and creates acidity. Ask Disraeli if it does not." [7]

There seems to be little doubt of Palmerston's popularity with his countrymen. They liked him for his lack of affectation and for his genial dignity, for his love of sport and horses, for his rough English satire and spontaneous jokes, for his merry "Ha! Ha!" and his pluck, for his reliance upon experience rather than books, and for his loyalty to things English. And in addressing his countrymen Palmerston knew how to gauge the temper of his audience (cf. "Constitutional Reforms," page 179). But he was no orator, no great master of phrasing like W. E. Gladstone, no symbolic representative of eloquence like John Bright. Seldom formally prepared for a speech, he hesitated for word or phrase—using ahems—so that Disraeli was almost justified in poking fun at him. [8] If the art of speaking well was indeed not the forte of Palmerston, his power and effectiveness in oratory were produced, it is said, [9] "more because it proceeded from the man than because it was beautiful either in sound of voice or eloquence of expression."

---

[6] Cf. Hansard, CXL, 17-32 (July 23, 1860).
[7] The Marquis of Lorne, *Viscount Palmerston* (New York, 1892), p. 22.
[8] Guedalla, *Palmerston*, p. 403.
[9] Lorne, *Viscount Palmerston*, p. 13.

1. International Arbitration

Richard Cobden, member for the West Riding of Yorkshire, made a motion, in which he was fortified by petitions, for international arbitration on June 12, 1849. Palmerston's reactions appear in Hansard *(CVI [3d Ser.], 78-90).*

The House of Commons just previously had been informed of American and Russian efforts to assist in the search for a Polar expedition of one hundred thirty-eight men that had left British shores four years before. Cobden made use of the occasion to remark that this type of co-operation was proof that existing days differed from those of the past. Following a patent line of argument, he continued: "I think there is nothing unreasonable in our seeking to take another step towards consolidating the peace of nations, and securing us against the recurrence of the greatest calamity that can afflict mankind." As a representative of Christianity as well as of a great portion of the middle class

and the great bulk of the working classes, he expressed his abhorrence of war and pressed forward with the idea of resorting "to that mode of settling disputes in communities which individuals resort to in private life."

Specifically he wished agreements between nations to bind themselves in the case of any misunderstanding that could not be settled by mutual representation or diplomacy to refer the dispute to the decision of arbitrators—not necessarily crowned heads or neutral states but preferably individuals (regardless of title or designation) who should be appointed from one country to meet men appointed from another country with right to inquire into the matter and deal with it and with authority, if their efforts availed nothing, to call in an umpire. Cobden proposed, therefore, an address to the Crown praying that Her Majesty would instruct her Foreign Secretary to propose to foreign powers to enter into treaties, etc.

Sir, I beg to assure my honourable Friend the Member for the West Riding, that in rising to state my intention of opposing his Motion, I am far from wishing to speak either of the sentiments he has himself expressed, or of the opinions of those whose organ he is, with anything but the greatest possible respect. I entirely agree with my honourable Friend, and with those of whose opinion he has been on this occasion the organ, in attributing the utmost possible value to this Motion, and in feeling the greatest dislike, and I may say horror, of war in any shape. I will not go into those commonplace remarks which must be familiar to the mind of every man who has contrasted the calamities of war with the various blessings and advantages which attend upon peace. I cannot conceive that there exists in this country the man who does not attach the utmost value to the blessings of peace, and who would not make the greatest sacrifices to save his country from the calamities attendant upon war. And although I differ from my honourable Friend, and although I am not ready to accede to his Motion, yet I cannot but say that I am glad he has made the proposition, because it will be useful for this country and for Europe at large that every man should know that in this assembly, and among the vast masses of men of whom we are the representatives, there is a sincere and honest disposition to maintain peace.

But that which I wish to guard against—the impression that I wish should not be entertained anywhere, either in this country or out of it—is, that while there is in England a fervent love of peace, an anxious and steady desire to maintain it, there should not exist the impression that the manly spirit of Englishmen is dead—that England is not ready, as she is ever, to repel aggression and resent injury, and that she is ready to defend her rights, although she never will be found acting aggressively against any other Power. Sir, it would be most dangerous indeed to the interests of peace, that a contrary opinion should prevail. I can conceive nothing that would bring more into jeopardy the peaceful relations of this country, than that an idea should prevail among foreign nations that we are so attached to peace that we dare not make war, and that, therefore, any aggression or any injury may be safely ventured against English subjects, because England has such a rooted aversion to war that she will not repel it. That is the principle on which I differ from the observations made by my honourable Friend, when he condemned those provident supplies—so I may call them—for military defence, which, he said, he had found by his examination in a Committee above stairs had been laid up in store by this and the last Government.

I quite agree with those who think that it is a useless expenditure of the public money to keep in pay an excessive number of men, either by sea or by land, beyond what the existing service of the country may demand, on an imaginary expectation of future and contingent hostilities. I think that is a wasteful application of the public money; but I cannot go along with the honourable Member in condemning that provident provision of things which cannot be created at a moment's notice—which would be necessary if we were called on to defend ourselves from foreign aggression—and the absence of which, if known to foreign countries, would form an incitement and temptation to commit wrong against this country. Therefore I think that a Government acts wisely and prudently when they gradually, and without overstraining the burden on the country, lay up a store of those things which may be wanted on the first outbreak of war, if it should unfortunately occur, and which must be provided beforehand, while they abstain from useless augmentations of men, which can be raised when the emergency arises, and in a short period would be just as effective as if they had been longer in military training.

Sir, I cannot agree with the proposal of my honourable Friend, because I think it is founded on an erroneous principle, and that it would be impracticable if attempted to be carried out. My honourable Friend comes to his conclusion by an analogy which he draws between private life and the intercourse of nations. He says, in the ordinary transactions between man and man, what is so common as an agreement between individuals, that in the event of disputes occurring they shall be referred to arbitration? It is very true that is a common and very advantageous practice; but how stand these individuals? Why, if the sentence of arbitration is not conformable to the opinion of both parties, there is a higher and superior authority—the authority of some legal tribunal, which enforces concurrence; to that tribunal the parties previously agree to submit, and it is this superior force that gives value and efficacy to the agreement for arbitration. But my honourable Friend at once perceives, and fairly acknowledges, that that element is wanting in the machine by which he proposes to settle international differences; and, unless we have recourse to the plan of my honourable Friend who spoke last for a general tribunal of nations, with a military force to compel compliance with its decrees, it is plain that the arbitration of my honourable Friend the Member for the West Riding would, in truth, simply, and in most cases, resolve itself into mediation, that is, the proposal by a third party of an arrangement of differences between two other parties. Honourable Members ought not to lose sight of the distinction, which is frequently forgotten, between arbitration and mediation—arbitration consisting in the pronouncing of a final decision by a third party, which is to be binding on the other two; mediation consisting in the good offices of a third party to bring about, by the consent and acquiescence of the other two, an amicable termination of differences that may have arisen between them.

Now, Sir, my honourable Friend is so internally aware of the difficulty attending the practical execution of his own idea, that he has been obliged to abandon that which most persons imagined to be his plan.

Mr. Cobden: I beg pardon. I never altered or abandoned my Motion in the slightest degree.

Viscount Palmerston: I will not say my honourable Friend has abandoned, but he has been obliged not to propose, what many persons, myself included, imagined to be his plan—namely, that the court of arbitration should consist of some foreign Government or Governments: in turning over the matter, and bringing it to a practical bearing, he has found it necessary to substitute commissioners taken from private life. Now, Sir, it is obvious that that which would be to any person thinking of this matter for the first time the natural arrangement—and whenever the principle of my honourable Friend has been acted upon the plan that has been fully practised—is that of making the arbitrator the Government of some foreign State. The plan of my honourable Friend, so far as I am aware, has never been attempted. It is perfectly true that there are cases in which arbitration has been resorted to, but in those cases the arbitrator chosen has been a Sovereign or a Government; in no case has final arbitration been consented to resting on private individuals. What are the reasons why my honourable Friend abstained from that proposal which was generally expected to come from him on the present occasion? My honourable Friend who has just sat down said, that it would be a very desirable thing if a European tribunal could be composed that would act invariably on the principles of justice and of right, which would always give equitable decisions, and which, of course, should have force to compel acquiescence in its judgments; but unfortunately the world is not yet come to that happy state of things. If you could find the Governments of Europe all perfectly just, perfectly impartial, perfectly disinterested, and, by the possession of these qualities, competent to form the tribunal my honourable Friend imagines, why, such a tribunal would supersede itself; because if all Governments were perfectly just, impartial, and disinterested, they would settle any little disputes that might arise between their respective subjects without having recourse to the extreme of war, which this tribunal was intended to prevent. But, unfortunately, it so happens that in the present imperfect condition of human nature, Governments, like individuals, are actuated by unfounded and suspicious jealousies of each other—by that which, in men, is called covetousness, which in nations is called ambition—by interested motives of various kinds, interests conflicting with each other; and it is a matter so difficult that it may almost be deemed impossible to find, in a quarrel between two nations, a third party whose judgment each of the two contending parties would place confidence in. If you were to propose to the Governments of Europe to enter now, today or tomorrow, into a prospective agreement that in cases of difference they would submit their disputes to any third party to be named now or to be named afterwards—if the engagement were that the third party should be named now, you never would get them to consent; and if the engagement were to name the third party when the dispute arose, you would have made very little progress towards the establishment of your arbitration.

There is one case where a dispute arose between this country and the Government of the United States, with respect to the Maine boundary, which was by the Treaty of Ghent submitted to arbitration. My honourable Friend would have said, "You only want geographers for such a purpose; two members of the Geographical Society have only to draw the line, and there it is." But my honourable Friend can hardly imagine how much time elapsed before we could come to any agreement as to the choice of the Sovereign who was to be the arbitrator in that case, which certainly is not a happy illustration of the results of arbitration; because the King of the Netherlands, having been chosen by the two Powers as arbitrator in that difference, did, after a very long period of time, pronounce an award, which the United States, not finding suitable to their notions of the terms of reference, refused to submit to; the matter was left in a worse condition than before the arbitration began; and if that arbitration did not lead to war, I can assure my honourable Friend it was no merit of the principle of arbitration, but only because the two Governments were mutually inspired by a most intense desire to settle the question without having recourse to arms.

Well, then, I say, if my honourable Friend had proposed, as men generally thought he intended to propose, a court arbitration, to consist of some third or foreign Governments, the answer would have been that the mutual jealousies of Governments, the rivalry of conflicting interests, the—I was going to say—intrigues, but the hostile policy of nations towards each other, would make it, I am satisfied, perfectly impossible to bring countries to acquiesce in the prospective arrangement; and I, for one, must say, it would be dangerous to the interests of this country to submit the vital rights and interests of England to the chances of a decision by the judgment of any foreign Power.

Well, but my honourable Friend very wisely steers clear of that difficulty, and proposes the appointment of commissioners. I am not sure that I quite comprehend the proposal of my honourable Friend, but he will correct me if I am quite wrong. I understand him to propose that a treaty should be made containing a stipulation that, in the event of differences, each Government should name commissioners of its own to discuss the point at issue, and that they, either before they met, or after they met, should name some third person not in the employment of either Government; but a man of science, or a man in private life, to be the arbitrator between the commissioners in case they should not be able to agree.

That, so far as I understood, was the manner in which the proposal of my honourable Friend was to be carried out.

Now, Sir, if it is objectionable, as I think it is, to commit the interests of a great country to the decision of what may be a rival Power, upon matters of vital interest, or upon matters concerning most important and essential rights, I must say my objection to submit such matters to the arbitration and final decision of a third party would not be removed by substituting for a Government, which at least is a public and responsible body, persons irresponsible, and taken from private life. At all events, a Government acts in the face of the world; it is accustomed to deal with matters of the kind submitted to it for decision; but if you take a man from private life he is perfectly irresponsible in any public way; his habits and pursuits may have been very different from those that would qualify for the decision of questions submitted to him; in my humble opinion almost all the same objections would apply, and other objections apply, which would not apply to a Government. There was one instance, to be sure, to show that these learned men are not always persons who are the readiest to come to a decision on a simple matter. There is one well-known problem the difficulty of solving which is universally acknowledged. No one denies the difficulty of finding the longitude. But if a man be required to ascertain the latitude of any given place, or the position of any parallel of latitude, it is deemed to be a very simple process. Now, by the Treaty of Ghent, the commissioners appointed to settle the boundary dispute, were to trace a line which should coincide with or come within a specified distance of a certain given parallel of latitude. Of course it will be said that nothing could be more easy than that; nothing was easier, it might be said, than to appoint two geographers as two commissioners, who would at once determine the matter, it being the simplest thing possible: they had only their boundary to mark along the line indicated by the treaty: that was precisely the sort of thing that suited the views of my honourable Friend the Member for the West Riding—nothing seemed easier than to find two learned men such as he would elect, and put them at once to find the parallel of latitude. But it so happened that there was not a chance of agreeing upon any such point, for one maintained that the parallel was to depend upon calculations commencing at the centre of the earth, and the other that the computations were to be made from the centre of the sun; they were, therefore, as far apart as the earth from the sun—they were further than the poles asunder—they were unable to agree about that which might be settled at once by any one who was able to set a village sundial. Neither Baron von Humboldt [10] nor Professor Tiarcks, who was associated with him in the undertaking, could arrive at any satisfactory result. (Mr. Cobden: The question is settled.) True, but not by geographers. However, I feel assured the House will agree with me when I say that it would not be safe to trust such interests as those, or at all events such interests as usually give rise to differences between nations—it would not be safe to leave them to arbitration; and, though the matter was eventually settled in the usual way, I do think that the case is less of an example to be followed, than of a beacon to be avoided.

Then my honourable Friend says there is nothing new at bottom in the proposition which he has made to the House, for he says that the powers which we were accustomed to give to negotiators we might in future give to two commissioners, one to be appointed by either nation concerned, giving them power to call in a third as final arbitrator; and my honourable Friend instanced the case of Lord Castlereagh, who, on behalf of this country, attended the Congress of Vienna, and took a part in the transactions which occurred on that memorable occasion. Lord Castlereagh was there enabled to say *adsum qui feci;* he might say he had done it; he was there upon his own responsibility, at least to a considerable extent upon his own responsibility, for Lord Castlereagh at that time held the office of Secretary of State for Foreign Affairs. But here it may be necessary for me to mention a matter well deserving to be borne in mind during the discussion which now occupies the attention of the House. It is this—that no person goes out from this country, or usually from any other, with full powers in the strict sense of those words. Some discretion may be left to him, but he does not go out with full and entire discretion—quite the contrary. Every Minister Plenipotentiary receives instructions. He is always told what he may agree to and what he may not, and he has opportunities, of which Ministers often avail themselves, to send home for further instructions. As long as he confines himself to his instructions he may proceed with some degree of confidence; but the Government by which he is accredited is still not finally bound by his acts, and everything that an Ambassador does he does subject to the approbation of the Government which he represents. It is perfectly competent to that Government to disavow the acts of the Minister whom they have sent out as an Ambassador, and to disavow and reject all that he has done, if they think it expedient to do so . . . . . It is, therefore, quite a mistake to suppose that,

[10] His name had been used by Cobden in connection with umpireship in a geographical question.

according to the present and prevailing practice, Governments are at the mercy of their envoys; nothing is binding upon a Government unless it be in strict accordance with communications made to other Governments in the precise words of the instructions. A treaty may be signed and concluded, but it is of no value without ratification, and this sort of provision is necessary in order that no Government may be bound by the indiscreet or unauthorized act of any of its agents; and therefore if an envoy should go against his instructions, the arrangements he may make are of no value beyond the paper on which they are written. Therefore do I state that my honourable Friend the Member for the West Riding makes an admission that his plan is new in principle. The House will not have forgotten that my honourable Friend quoted several cases of international transactions; but he did not succeed in making out the case which he appeared to think was necessary for his purpose. The cases which he mentioned were not cases of arbitration but of mediation, or else they were cases of no mediation at all, settled neither by arbitration nor by intervention—such as those which he mentioned between Russia and England, and the case also of the *Vixen.*[11] In the boundary case it seemed as if there had been some show of arbitration; but it was notorious that in that case arbitration failed; and when arbitration had totally failed, the parties concerned settled the matter for themselves in the usual manner: and let the fact not be overlooked, that the Oregon question was settled in pretty nearly the same way; at all events it was not settled by geographers, in the manner that my honourable Friend would propose. If it were to have been settled by geographers, I confess I should not very much envy the gentlemen who might be employed upon such an undertaking; for I believe there can be no doubt that the district through which they would have had to penetrate is one of extraordinary wildness and difficulty, where the means of subsistence are hardly to be obtained.

Now, the case of the *Caroline* [12] was a remarkable one in reference to the question of arbitration, and it was one of those few cases in which it was manifest that it would be unavailing to arbitrate. It was not a case of dispute between this country and the United States, for the federal authority of that Government was not suffi-

[11] A case of 1837 when a dispute arose with Russia about the confiscation of a ship in the Black Sea called the "Vixen." Cf. Cobden's speech, Hansard (CVI, 62).

[12] Cobden had explained (Hansard [CVI, 63-64]) "the case of Mr. M'Leod, who had been taken and imprisoned by the State of New York, and tried for his life, for having . . . . taken part in the burning of the *Caroline,* in which an American citizen lost his life."

cient to meet the exigency of the case. The Government of the United States said they were sorry for what occurred, but they had no power to interfere—the supreme Government of the United States possessed no power over the local authority or government with which the dispute arose. Now, if we in that case possessed a treaty of arbitration, of what use would it be to us? For the Government of the United States would repeat its declaration that it could not interfere with the local government. They would say, "We are very sorry, but we can obtain you no redress from the State of New York." Your principle then of arbitration would be of not the slightest avail in such a case; it leaves you precisely where you were before the introduction of such a plan.

The cases then which my honourable Friend has quoted, are cases in which the principle of arbitration proved useless, or they are cases which have been settled by the ordinary authorities, or they are cases of mediation in which a friendly Power has exercised its good offices, as in the sulphur question with France, or they are cases settled in the usual way after arbitration has wholly failed. I do think, however, and I have always thought, that when two nations have had any difference capable of being settled by arbitration, it is most desirable that they should allow a third party to come in to assist them in the good work of making a satisfactory arrangement—it is at all times most desirable that a third party not actuated by the same passions which heat those immediately concerned, should step in, and bring the disputants to something like a compromise; for in all such cases there must be an arrangement in the nature of a compromise—there must be a giving and taking on both sides, for neither party in such cases can expect to get all that he may reasonably or fairly demand, and all such negotiations should therefore be entered upon in a spirit of accommodation and mutual concession, with a view to prevent an appeal to arms, and with a view to open the door to that kind of negotiation which may lead to peace, in the course of which the Ministers engaged on both sides may receive from their respective Governments fresh instructions, in which answers may be received, in which remonstrances may be made, further replies given, and thus a long time elapses before any actual rupture occurs, and before recourse is had to that appeal which arms alone afford. In the course of those proceedings opportunities occur for one or other of the parties to obtain the opinion of a third nation friendly to both, and having no private or separate interest to promote. A nation so circumstanced may, I think, well offer its mediation, and I have incurred no small amount of obloquy, and perhaps ridicule also, on the ground that I have been too forward to offer mediation in such cases as those which I have just been describing. But I confess that I feel perfectly easy under the influence of such attacks, for I feel quite persuaded that the goodwill, at least, manifested in such attempts cannot fail eventually to be appreciated, and that in cases where England has nothing either to gain or to lose, a sincere desire to prevent war must, sooner or later, be attended with beneficial results; and I cannot help thinking that it must be most satisfactory to my honourable Friend the Member for the West Riding, and to those who support his Motion, to know that mediation has been of much more frequent occurrence of late years than in times past; but those honourable Gentlemen must, at the same time, bear in mind that the principle of arbitration is not applicable to the present state of Europe. Wars are now proceeding in various parts of the Continent, blood is being shed, lives being sacrificed; but these occurrences do not arise from international wars. It is to civil wars that they must be imputed, and, except in very rare instances indeed, the intervention of foreigners, or third parties, or arbitrators, would be either impracticable, or, if possible, might be mischievous; and it must be obvious to every one that the kind of war now prevailing on the continent of Europe is not the species of hostility to which the principle of arbitration can be applied.

In those wars, however, I am happy to be able to perceive striking evidence of the improved civilisation of the people of Europe—evidence not only of improvement in the Governments of Europe, but of advancing civilisation amongst the masses of the people. If such events as have recently taken place in Europe, had occurred half a century ago, we should have had not only civil wars, but conflicts between nations of the most fatal character—fatal alike to prosperity and civilisation. It is consoling, then, to see that great masses of men, instead of standing forth as the aggressors of their neighbours, confine their disputes to their own territories, to the communities to which they properly belong, and to their own internal affairs. It is gratifying to think that they have not been led into warfare with other nations, either by feelings of ambition or by any different description of impulse.

I hope, then, that now sufficient proof has been given that we should not advance the interest of nations by recognising the principle for which my honourable Friend contends, at the same time that I cannot find fault with him for introducing this question, or for affording an opportunity for the expression of that general feeling which animates Members of this House upon the present occasion. The cultivation of that feeling forms a great example to the rest of Europe—it tends to inspire not only Governments but nations with the sentiments which my honourable Friend feels and has made known to the House this evening; and I conceive that it will take away nothing from the force of those sentiments, but rather add to their influence, when I say that ever since the year 1825 down to the present period, the practice of mediation has been preferred by many Governments, and several cases have arisen in which it has been advantageously adopted. I believe that the present Government, and any other which may succeed to the task of conducting the affairs of this country, would feel it not only their duty, but their pride, to avail themselves of every occasion when they think they can do good by softening the asperities between conflicting Powers, and by effecting between Governments and countries that may differ, an amicable settlement of their disputes, either without war, or by shortening war if war should unfortunately arise.

The proposition of my honourable Friend, however, is not one to which I can advise the House to accede. I do not quarrel with the principle upon which it is founded; but I think its practical effect would be dangerous to this country, and that its practical adoption by other countries would be impossible. Indeed, I believe that no country would agree to such a proposal. No country would consent blindfold to submit its interests and its rights on all future occasions to the decision of any third party, whether public or private, whether Governments or men of science; and I think, therefore, the proposition is one which would be attended with no possible result as regards foreign countries. I confess also that I consider it would be a very dangerous course for this country itself to take, because there is no country which, from its political and commercial circumstances, from its maritime interests, and from its colonial possessions, excites more envious and jealous feelings in different quarters than England does; and there is no country that would find it more difficult to discover really disinterested and impartial arbiters. There is also no country that would be more likely than England to suffer in its important commercial interests from submitting its case to arbiters not disinterested, not impartial, and not acting with a due sense of their responsibility. For these reasons it is not in my power to assent to the Motion. I should, however, be sorry to meet it in a way that might, even by misconstruction, be considered as negativing the principle upon which it is founded. I shall not, therefore, propose a direct negative, although that is the mode which, according to the usual practice of the House, ought to be adopted by those who differ from my honourable Friend. The "previous question" is not technically applicable to this case; but the previous question being the most courteous mode of disposing of such a Motion as that before the House, and one less liable than any other to the imputation—however unfounded it may be—of negativing the principle of peace, which is the foundation of my honourable Friend's proposal, I beg leave to move the previous question.

2. Foreign Policy—Affairs of Greece

The following speech was delivered on June 25, 1850 (HANSARD, CXII [3d Ser.], 380-444). In reply to a censure of the ministerial foreign policy on the part of the House of Lords, Mr. Roebuck, member for Sheffield, moved a resolution which should test the confidence of the House of Commons and therefore of the people of England in the government: "That the principles which hitherto have regulated the foreign policy of Her Majesty's Government are such as were required to preserve untarnished the honor and dignity of this country, and in times of unexampled difficulty the best qualified to maintain peace between England and the various nations of the world."

For background it may be well to point out that Palmerston had behaved in a fashion that many persons believed might have led to war with France. Feeling that the Russian and French Ambassadors to Greece were playing their own game against British interests and realizing that outrages such as the Fantome case which he describes in the speech were serious matters, he peremptorily ordered the British fleet to the Piraeus with the idea of getting settlement of the claims of Don Pacifico, a Jew from Gibraltar and a British subject, whose house had been invaded and damaged by a Greek mob in 1847. The Greek Government was slow in meeting British demands, and France tendered her good offices. Unfortunately, terms applied by the British local representative upon the Greeks rather than terms which the French and British representatives agreed upon in London implied discourtesy to France. A risk of war had been run for a purpose, the inferences concerning which did not please many Englishmen.

The Lords offered their censure and Mr. Roebuck moved his resolution. Palmerston defended himself with skill and verve, cleverly playing upon the susceptibilities of his countrymen. Indeed, Lord Robert Cecil (Lord Salisbury of later date) remarked subsequently, "I am aware that, whatever folly or madness an English Government may commit, the appeal to the Civis Romanus doctrine is rarely without its effect upon an English audience."

Sir, anxious as many Members are to deliver their sentiments upon this most important question, yet I am sure they will feel that it is due to myself, that it is due to this House, that it is due to the country, that I should not permit the second night of this debate to close, without having stated to the House my views upon the matters in question, and my explanation of that part of my conduct for which I have been called to account.

When I say that this is an important question, I say it in the fullest expression of the term. It is a matter which concerns not merely the tenure of office by one individual, or even by a Government; it is a question that involves principles of national policy, and the deepest interests as well as the honour and dignity of England. I cannot think that the course which has been pursued, and by which this question has assumed its present shape, is becoming those, by whose act it has been brought under the discussion of Parliament, or such as fitting the gravity and the importance of the matters which they have thus led this House and the other House of Parliament to discuss. For if that party in this country imagine that they are strong enough to carry the Government by storm, and to take possession of the citadel of office; or, if without intending to measure their strength with that of their opponents, they conceive that there are matters of such gravity connected with the conduct of the Government, that it becomes their duty to call upon Parliament solemnly to record its disapprobation of what has passed, I think that either in the one case or in the other, that party ought not to have been contented with obtaining the expression of the opinion of the House of Lords, but they ought to have sent down their resolution for the consent and concurrence of this House; or, at least, those who act with them in political co-operation here, should themselves have proposed to this House to come to a similar resolution. But, be the road what it may, we have come to the same end; and the House is substantially considering whether they will adopt the resolution of the House of Lords, or the resolution which has been submitted to them by my honourable and learned Friend the Member for Sheffield.

Now, the resolution of the House of Lords involves the future as well as the past. It lays down for the future a principle of national policy, which I consider totally incompatible with the interests, with the rights, with the honour, and with the dignity of the country; and at variance with the practice, not only of this, but of all other civilised countries in the world. Even the person who moved it was obliged essentially to modify it in his speech. But none of the modifications contained in the speech were introduced into the resolution adopted by the other House. The country is told that British subjects in foreign lands are entitled—for that is the meaning of the resolution—to nothing but the protection of the laws and the tribunals of the land in which they happen to reside. The country is told that British subjects abroad must not look to their own country for protection, but must trust to that indifferent justice which they may happen to receive at the hands of the Government and tribunals of the country in which they may be.

The House of Lords has not said that this proposition is limited to constitutional countries. The House of Lords has not said that the proposition is inapplicable, not only to arbitrary and despotic countries, but even to constitutional countries where the courts of justice are not free; although these limitations were stated in the speech. The country is simply informed by the resolution, as it was adopted, that, so far as foreign nations are concerned, the future rule of the Government of England is to be, that, in all cases, and under all circumstances, British subjects are to have that protection only, which the law and the tribunals of the land in which they happen to be, may give them.

Now, I deny that proposition; and I say it is a doctrine on which no British subjects are bound to have recourse for redress to the means which the law of the land affords them, when that law is available for such purpose. That is the opinion which the legal advisers of the Crown have given in numerous cases; and it is the opinion on which we have founded our replies to many applications for our interposition in favour of British subjects abroad.[13]. . . . . But there may be cases in which no confidence can be placed in the tribunals, those tribunals being, from their composition and nature, not of a character to inspire any hope of obtaining justice from them. It has been said, "We do not apply this rule to countries whose Governments are arbitrary or despotic, because there the tribunals are under the control of the Government, and justice cannot be had; and, moreover, it is not meant to be applied to nominally constitutional Governments, where the tribunals are corrupt." But who is to be the judge in such a case, whether the tribunals are corrupt or not? The British Government, or the Government of the State from which you demand justice?

I will take a transaction that occurred not long ago, as an instance of a case in which, I say, the people of England would not permit a British subject to be simply amenable to the laws of the foreign country in which he happened to be. I am not going to talk of the power of sending a man arbitrarily to Siberia; nor of a country, the constitution of which vests despotic power in the hands of the Sovereign. I will take a case which happened in Sicily, where not long ago a decree was passed, that any man who was found with concealed arms in his possession should be brought before a court-martial, and, if found guilty, should be shot. Now, this happened. An innkeeper of Catania was brought before a court-martial, accused under this law by some police officers, who stated that they had discovered in an open bin, in an open stable in his inn-yard, a knife, which they denounced as a concealed weapon. Witnesses having been examined, the counsel for the

---

[13] A personal reference is omitted.

prosecution stated that he gave up the case, as it was evident there was no proof that the knife belonged to the man, or that he was aware it was in the place where it was found. The counsel for the defendant said, that such being the opinion of the counsel for the prosecution, it was unnecessary for him to go into the defence, and he left his client in the hands of the court. The court, however, nevertheless pronounced the man guilty of the charge brought against him, and the next morning the man was shot.

Now, what would the English people have said if this had been done to a British subject? and yet everything done was the result of a law, and the man was found guilty of an offence by a tribunal of the country. I say, then, that our doctrine is, that, in the first instance, redress should be sought from the law courts of the country; but that in cases where redress cannot be so had—and those cases are many—to confine a British subject to that remedy only, would be to deprive him of the protection which he is entitled to receive.

Then the question arises, how does this rule apply to the demands we have made upon Greece? And here I must shortly remind the House of the origin of our relations with Greece, and of the condition of Greece; because those circumstances are elements that must enter into the consideration of the course we have pursued.

It is well known that Greece revolted from Turkey in 1820. In 1827, England, France, and Russia determined upon interposing, and ultimately, in 1828, they resolved to employ forcible means in order to bring Turkey to acknowledge the independence of Greece. Greece, by protocol in 1830, and by treaty in 1832, was erected into a separate and independent State. And whereas nearly from the year 1820 up to the time of the treaty of 1832, when its independence was finally acknowledged, Greece had been under a republican form of government, with an Assembly and a President, the three Powers determined that Greece should thenceforth be a monarchy. But while England assented to that arrangement, and considered that it was better that Greece should assume a monarchial form of government, yet we attached to that assent an indispensable condition, that Greece should be a constitutional monarchy. The British Government could not consent to place the people of Greece, in their independent political existence, under as arbitrary a government as that from which they had revolted. Consequently, when the three Powers, in the exercise of that function which had been devolved upon them by the authority of the General Assembly of Greece, chose a Sovereign for Greece (for that choice was made in consequence of, and by virtue of the authority given to them by the General Assembly of Greece), and when Prince Otho of Bavaria, then a minor, was chosen; the three Powers, on announcing the choice they had made, at the same time declared that King Otho would, in concert with his people, give to Greece constitutional institutions.

The choice and that announcement were ratified by the King of Bavaria in the name, and on the behalf, of his son. It was however understood, that during the minority of King Otho, the establishment of the constitution should be suspended; but that when he came of age, he should enter into communication with his people, and, together with them, arrange the form of constitution to be adopted. King Otho came of age, but no constitution was given. There was a disinclination on the part of his advisers to counsel him to fulfill that engagement. The Government of England expressed an opinion, through various channels, that that engagement ought to be fulfilled. But opinions of a different kind reached the Royal ear from other quarters. Other Governments, naturally—I say it without implying any imputation—are attached to their own forms. Each Government thinks its own form and nature the best, and wishes to see that form, if possible, extended elsewhere. Therefore, I do not mention this with any intention of casting the least reproach upon Russia, or Prussia, or Austria. Those three Governments at that time were despotic. Their advice was given, and their influence was exerted to prevent the King of Greece from granting a constitution to his people. We thought, however, that in France we might find support in the advice which we wished to give. But we were unfortunate. The then Government of France, not at all undervaluing constitutional institutions, thought that the time was not yet come when Greece could be ripe for representative government. The King of Bavaria leaned also to the same side. Therefore, from the time when the King came of age, and for several years afterwards, the English Government stood in this position in Greece with regard to its Government—that we alone were anxious for the fulfillment of the engagement of the King, while all the other Powers who were represented at Athens, were averse to its being made good, or at least were not equally desirous of urging it upon the King of Greece. This necessarily placed us in a situation, to say the least of it, of disfavour on the part of the agents of those Powers, and on the part of the Government of Greece. I was sorry for it; at the same time, I don't think the people of this country will be of opinion that we ought, for the sake of obtaining the mere good-will of the Greek Government, to have departed from the principle which we had laid down from the beginning. But it was so; and when people talk of the antagonistic influences which were in conflict at the Greek Court; and when people say, as I have heard it said, that our Ministers, and the Ministers of foreign Governments, were disputing about the appointments of mirarchs and nomarchs, and God knows what petty officers of the State, I say that, as far as our Minister was concerned, that is a statement entirely at variance with the fact. Our Minister, Sir Edmund Lyons, never, during the whole time he was in Greece, asked any favour of any sort or kind, for himself, or for any friend. No conduct of that mean, and low, and petty description was carried on by any person connected with the English Government. It was known that we wished the Greek nation should have representative institutions, while, on the other hand, other influences were exerted the other way; and that, and that only, was the ground of the differences which existed.

One of the evils of the absence of constitutional institutions was, that the whole system of government grew to be full of every kind of abuse. Justice could not be expected where the judges of the tribunals were at the mercy of the advisers of the Crown. The finances could not be in any order where there was no public responsibility on the part of those who were to collect or to spend the revenue. Every sort of abuse was practised.

In all times, in Greece, as is well known, there has prevailed, from the daring habits of the people, a system of compulsory appropriation—forcible appropriation by one man of that which belonged to another; which, of course, is very disagreeable to those who are the victims of the system, and exceedingly injurious to the social condition, improvement, and prosperity of the country. In short, what foreigners call brigandage, which prevailed under the Turkish rule, has not, I am sorry to say, diminished under the Greek Sovereignty. Moreover, the police of the Greek Government have practised abuses of the grossest description; and if I wanted evidence on that subject, I could appeal to the honourable Gentleman,[14] who has just sat down, who, in a pamphlet, which all must have read, or ought to read, has detailed instances of barbarity of the most revolting kind practised by the police. I have here depositions of persons who have been subjected to the most abominable tortures which human ingenuity could devise—tortures inflicted upon both sexes most revolting and disgusting. One of the officers, a man of the name of Tzino, at the head of the police, was himself in the habit of inflicting the most diabolical tortures upon Greeks and upon foreigners, Turks, and others. This man Tzino, instead of being punished as he ought to have been, and as he deserved to be, not only by the laws of nature, but by the laws of Greece—this

[14] B. Cochrane.

person, I am sorry to say, is held in great favour in quarters where he ought to have received nothing but marks of indignation.

Well, this being the state of things in Greece, there have always been in every town in Greece a great number of persons whom we are bound to protect—Maltese, Ionians, and a certain number of British subjects. It became the practice of this Greek police to make no distinction between the Maltese and Ionians and their own fellow-subjects. We shall be told, perhaps, as we have already been told, that if the people of the country are liable to have heavy stones placed upon their breasts, and police officers to dance upon them; if they are liable to have their heads tied to their knees, and to be left for hours in that state; or to be swung like a pendulum, and to be bastinadoed as they swing, foreigners have no right to be better treated than the natives, and have no business to complain if the same things are practised upon them. We may be told this, but that is not my opinion, nor do I believe it is the opinion of any reasonable man. Then, I say, that in considering the cases of the Ionians, for whom we demanded reparation, the House must look at and consider what was the state of things in this respect in Greece; they must consider the practices that were going on, and the necessity of putting a stop to the extension of these abuses to British and Ionian subjects by demanding compensation, scarcely indeed more than nominal in some cases, but the granting of which would be an acknowledgment that such things should not be done towards us in future.

In discussing these cases, I am concerned to have to say that they appear to me to have been dealt with elsewhere in spirit, and in a tone, which I think was neither befitting the persons concerning whom, nor the persons by whom, nor the persons before whom, the discussion took place. It is often more convenient to treat matters with ridicule, than with grave argument; and we have had serious things treated jocosely; and grave men kept in a roar of laughter, for an hour together, at the poverty of one sufferer, or at the miserable habitation of another; at the nationality of one injured man, or the religion of another; as if because a man was poor he might be bastinadoed and tortured with impunity; as if a man who was born in Scotland might be robbed without redress; or, because a man is of the Jewish persuasion, he is fair game for any outrage. It is a true saying, and has often been repeated, that a very moderate share of human wisdom is sufficient for the guidance of human affairs. But there is another truth, equally indisputable, which is, that a man who aspires to govern mankind ought to bring to the task, generous sentiments, compassionate sympathies, and noble and elevated thoughts.

Now, Sir, with regard to these cases, I would take first, that which I think would first present itself to the mind of an Englishman—I mean the insult offered by the arrest of the boat's crew of Her Majesty's ship *Fantome*. The time has been, when a man aspiring to a public situation, would have thought it his duty to vindicate the honour of the British Navy. Times are changed. It is said that in this case there were only a few sailors taken out of a boat by some armed men—that they were carried to the guard-house, but were soon set at liberty again—and why should we trouble our heads about so small a matter? But did we ask anything extraordinary or unreasonable on account of this insult? What we asked was an apology. I really did not expect to live to see the day, when public men in England could think that in requiring an apology for the arbitrary and unjustifiable arrest of a British officer and British seamen in the performance of their duty, we were making a demand "doubtful in its nature, and exaggerated in its amount." Now, what is the history of this case? for circumstances have been referred to, in connexion with it, which do not appear from the statement of the case itself. The son of the Vice-consul, who had dined on board the *Fantome,* was taken ashore in the evening by the coxswain and a boat's crew, and landed on the beach. The coxswain accompanied the young gentleman to his father's house, and on returning to the boat, was taken prisoner by the Greek guard. The guard went down to the boat, and, finding the seamen in it were without arms, began thumping them with the butt-ends of their muskets, and wounded one man in the hand by a thrust with a bayonet. The guard then took the seamen prisoners, and carried them to the guard-house where after a certain time they were released, through the interposition of the Vice-consul, and they returned to their ship. Excuses were given for this proceeding, and the gist of them was this—that the guard thought the boat belonged to the *Spitfire,* and that it had been seen landing rebels, one of whom had escaped; this supposed rebel being a boy of fourteen years old, who had returned quietly to his father's house.

The matter to which these excuses related, occurred a little while before, in consequence of the disorganised state of Greece—a disorganisation, by the by, which arises entirely from the acts of the Government; because it has been, and still is, the practice of the Government, instead of punishing brigands, to amnesty and pardon them; and indeed it is even supposed that the officers of police sometimes go shares in the plunder. That, however, is a matter of opinion; but it is a fact that the robbers are almost always pardoned; and such is the encouragement thereby given to the system of plunder, that the robbers go about armed in bands, and sometimes actually attack and occupy towns.[15]

. . . .

Then we come to the claim of M. Pacifico—a claim which has been the subject of much unworthy comment. Stories have been told, involving imputations on the character of M. Pacifico; I know nothing of the truth or falsehood of these stories. All I know is, that M. Pacifico, after the time to which those stories relate, was appointed Portuguese consul, first to Morocco and afterwards at Athens. It is not likely that the Portuguese Government would select for appointments of that kind, a person whose character they did not believe to be above reproach. But I say, with those who have before had occasion to advert to the subject, that I don't care what M. Pacifico's character is. I do not, and cannot, admit that because a man may have acted amiss on some other occasion, and in some other matter, he is to be wronged with impunity by others.

The rights of a man depend on the merits of the particular case; and it is an abuse of argument to say, that you are not to give redress to a man, because in some former transaction he may have done something which is questionable. Punish him if you will— punish him if he is guilty, but don't pursue him as a Pariah through life.

What happened in this case? In the middle of the town of Athens, in a house which I must be allowed to say is not a wretched hovel, as some people have described it; but it does not matter what it is, for whether a man's home be a palace or a cabin, the owner has a right to be there safe from injury—well, in a house which is not a wretched hovel, but which in the early days of King Otho was, I am told, the residence of the Count Armansperg, the Chief of the Regency—a house as good as the generality of those which existed in Athens before the Sovereign ascended the throne—M. Pacifico, living in this house, within forty yards of the great street, within a few minutes' walk of a guard-house, where soldiers were stationed, was attacked by a mob. Fearing injury, when the mob began to assemble, he sent an intimation to the British Minister, who immediately informed the authorities. Application was made to the Greek Government for protection. No protection was af- forded. The mob, in which were soldiers and gens-d'armes, who, even if officers were not with them, ought, from a sense of duty, to have interfered and to have prevented plunder—that mob, headed

[15] About five additional pages dealing with abuses are omitted.

by the sons of the Minister of War, not children of eight or ten
years old, but older—that mob, for nearly two hours, employed
themselves in gutting the house of an unoffending man, carrying
away or destroying every single thing the house contained, and left
it a perfect wreck.

Is not that a case in which a man is entitled to redress from somebody? I venture to think it is. I think that there is no civilised
country where a man subjected to such grievous wrong, not to
speak of insults and injuries to the members of his family, would
not justly expect redress from some quarter or other. Where was
he to apply for redress at Athens? The Greek Government neglected its duty, and did not pursue judicial inquiries, or institute
legal prosecutions as it might have done for the purpose of finding
out and punishing some of the culprits. The sons of the Minister
of War were pointed out to the Government as actors in the outrage. The Greek Government were told to "search a particular
house; and that some part of M. Pacifico's jewels would be found
there." They declined to prosecute the Minister's sons, or to search
the house. But, it is said, M. Pacifico should have applied to a
court of law for redress. What was he to do? Was he to prosecute
a mob of five hundred persons? Was he to prosecute them crim-
inally, or in order to make them pay the value of his loss? Where
was he to find his witnesses? Why, he and his family were hiding
or flying, during the pillage, to avoid the personal outrages with
which they were threatened. He states, that his own life was saved
by the help of an English friend. It was impossible, if he could
have identified the leaders, to have prosecuted them with success.

But what satisfaction would it have been to M. Pacifico to have
succeeded in a criminal prosecution against the ringleaders of that
assault? Would that have restored to him his property? He wanted
redress, not revenge. A criminal prosecution was out of the question, to say nothing of the chances, if not the certainty, of failure
in a country where the tribunals are at the mercy of the advisers of
the crown, the judges being liable to be removed, and being often
actually removed upon grounds of private interest and personal
feeling. Was he to prosecute for damages? His action would have
lain against individuals, and not, as in this country, against the
hundred. Suppose he had been able to prove that one particular
man had carried off one particular thing, or destroyed one particular
article of furniture; what redress could he anticipate by a lawsuit,
which, as his legal advisers told him, it would be vain for him to
undertake? M. Pacifico truly said, "If the man I prosecute is rich,
he is sure to be acquitted; if he is poor, he has nothing out of which
to afford me compensation if he is condemned."

The Greek Government having neglected to give the protection they were bound to extend, and having abstained from taking means to afford redress, this was a case in which we were justified in calling on the Greek Government for compensation for the losses, whatever they might be, which M. Pacifico had suffered. I think that claim was founded in justice. The amount we did not pretend to fix. If the Greek Government had admitted the principle of the claim, and had objected to the account sent in by M. Pacifico—if they had said, "This is too much, and we think a less sum sufficient," that would have been a question open to discussion, and which our Ministers, Sir E. Lyons at first, or Mr. Wyse afterwards, would have been ready to have gone into, and no doubt some satisfactory arrangement might thus have been effected with the Greek Government. But the Greek Government denied altogether the principle of the claim. Therefore, when Mr. Wyse came to make the claim, he could not but demand that the claim should be settled, or be placed in train of settlement, and that within a definite period, as he fixed it, of twenty-four hours.

Whether M. Pacifico's statement of his claim was exaggerated or not, the demand was not for any particular amount of money. The demand was, that the claim should be settled. An investigation might have been instituted, which those who acted for us were prepared to enter into, fairly, dispassionately, and justly.

M. Pacifico having, from year to year, been treated either with answers wholly unsatisfactory, or with a positive refusal, or with pertinacious silence, it came at last to this, either that his demand was to be abandoned altogether, or that, in pursuance of the notice we had given the Greek Government a year or two before, we were to proceed to use our own means of enforcing the claim. "Oh! but," it is said, "what an ungenerous proceeding to employ so large a force against so small a Power!" Does the smallness of a country justify the magnitude of its evil acts? Is it to be held that if your subjects suffer violence, outrage, plunder in a country which is small and weak, you are to tell them when they apply for redress, that the country is so weak and so small that we cannot ask it for compensation? Their answer would be, that the weakness and smallness of the country make it so much the more easy to obtain redress. "No," it is said, "generosity is to be the rule." We are to be generous to those who have been ungenerous to you; and we cannot give you redress because we have such ample and easy means of procuring it.

Well, then, was there anything so uncourteous in sending, to back our demands, a force which should make it manifest to all the world that resistance was out of the question? Why, it seems

to me, on the contrary, that it was more consistent with the honour
and dignity of the Government on whom we made those demands,
that there should be placed before their eyes a force, which it
would be vain to resist, and before which it would be no indignity
to yield. . . . . .[16]

.   .   .   .

I believe I have now gone through all the heads of the charges
which have been brought against me in this debate. I think I have
shown that the foreign policy of the Government, in all the transactions with respect to which its conduct has been impugned, has
throughout been guided by those principles which, according to
the resolution of the honourable and learned Gentleman the Member for Sheffield, ought to regulate the conduct of the Government
of England in the management of our foreign affairs. I believe that
the principles on which we have acted are those which are held by
the great mass of the people of this country. I am convinced these
principles are calculated, so far as the influence of England may
properly be exercised with respect to the destinies of other countries,
to conduce to the maintenance of peace, to the advancement of civilization, to the welfare and happiness of mankind.

I do not complain of the conduct of those who have made these
matters the means of attack upon Her Majesty's Ministers. The
government of a great country like this, is undoubtedly an object
of fair and legitimate ambition to men of all shades of opinion. It
is a noble thing to be allowed to guide the policy and to influence
the destinies of such a country; and, if ever it was an object of
honourable ambition, more than ever must it be so at the moment
at which I am speaking. For while we have seen, as stated by the
right Baronet the Member for Ripon,[17] the political earthquake
rocking Europe from side to side—while we have seen thrones
shaken, shattered, levelled; institutions overthrown and destroyed—
while in almost every country of Europe the conflict of civil war
has deluged the land with blood, from the Atlantic to the Black Sea,
from the Baltic to the Mediterranean; this country has presented a
spectacle honourable to the people of England, and worthy of the
admiration of mankind.

We have shown that liberty is compatible with order; that individual freedom is reconcilable with obedience to the law. We have
shown the example of a nation, in which every class of society

[16] There is omitted some forty of the Hansard columns that attempt to
justify the British Government in its actions.
[17] Sir J. R. G. Graham.

accepts with cheerfulness the lot which Providence has assigned to it; while at the same time every individual of each class is constantly striving to raise himself in the social scale—not by injustice and wrong, not by violence and illegality—but by persevering good conduct, and by the steady and energetic exertion of the moral and intellectual faculties with which his Creator has endowed him. To govern such a people as this, is indeed an object worthy of the ambition of the noblest man who lives in the land; and therefore I find no fault with those who may think any opportunity a fair one, for endeavouring to place themselves in so distinguished and honourable a position. But I contend that we have not in our foreign policy done anything to forfeit the confidence of the country. We may not, perhaps, in this matter or in that, have acted precisely up to the opinions of one person or of another—and hard indeed it is, as we all know by our individual and private experience, to find any number of men agreeing entirely in any matter, on which they may not be equally possessed of the details of the facts, and circumstances, and reasons, and conditions which led to action. But, making allowance for those differences of opinion which may fairly and honourably arise among those who concur in general views, I maintain that the principles which can be traced through all our foreign transactions, as the guiding rule and directing spirit of our proceedings, are such as deserve approbation. I therefore fearlessly challenge the verdict which this House, as representing a political, a commercial, a constitutional country, is to give on the question now brought before it; whether the principles on which the foreign policy of Her Majesty's Government has been conducted, and the sense of duty which has led us to think ourselves bound to afford protection to our fellow subjects abroad, are proper and fitting guides for those who are charged with the Government of England; and whether, as the Roman, in days of old, held himself free from indignity, when he could say *Civis Romanus sum;* so also a British subject, in whatever land he may be, shall feel confident that the watchful eye and the strong arm of England, will protect him against injustice and wrong.

3. The Slave Trade

This address appears in HANSARD (LXXVI [3d Ser.], 922-48) under the date July 16, 1844. Sir Robert Peel who spoke immediately after Palmerston agreed with the part of the speech which is given. He did not concur with certain reflections which Palmerston cast on the policy of the government in dealing with slave traders and which are omitted in the extract.

The names of many famous Englishmen are connected with the endeavor to abolish the slave trade, the traffic in which augmented English commercial developments after the Treaty of Utrecht: Thomas Clarkson, William Wilberforce, Pitt the Younger, Charles James Fox, and others worked toward the suppression act which was passed in 1807. By an act of 1833 arrangements were made for abolition of slavery in the colonies. But so far as the slave trade was concerned, an illegal traffic persisted. Arab slave traders of Africa could not be forced to obey English laws, and, though the European powers made the slave trade the subject of treaties in the early nineteenth century, France as late as 1841 refused to co-operate with other European countries in the plans which, it was hoped, might be effective in limiting the traffic. Palmerston is treating of a theme, familiar and dear to the English, in this speech.

Sir, in rising to move for the Returns connected with the Slave Trade, of which I have given notice, and to the production of which I presume that no objection will be offered, I wish to make some observations upon the Slave Trade itself; a subject of great interest and importance, not indeed new to this House, but which has now, for nearly half a century engaged the attention of the Parliament and people of this country. Almost all the men who, during that period of time, have been most eminent and distinguished in this country, whether on one side or on the other of this House, whether within or without these walls, have exerted the best energies of their minds to put an end to this abominable crime. And their labours have not been vain. They succeeded in rescuing the country from the foul stain of Slave Trade, and as a natural and necessary consequence soon followed the abolition of the condition of Slavery itself, throughout the dominions of the British Crown. These great results, however, were not accomplished without much labour, and a long lapse of time; the descent to evil is rapid and easy; the return to good is hard and slow; and if there are nations who are still imitating our downward course, and who have not yet resolved to follow our upward footsteps, we should look upon their errors with more indulgence than we might otherwise feel, when we remember what long and painful efforts it cost us, to wean ourselves from these detestable practices. But, on the other hand, if there be nations, and many there are, who have entered with us, by the stipulations of treaties, into engagements, having for their object the putting down of this crime, we should be making ourselves again partakers in this guilt, if we were to release any of those nations from the smallest particle of their engagements.

Many years have now passed away since those investigations took place, which, by laying bare in all their hideous deformity the disgusting atrocities connected with the prosecution of the Slave Trade, brought round the minds of men in this country to resolve that England at least should cease to be polluted with this crime. Those details are now well nigh forgotten; and though most men have a general knowledge that Slave Trade is a cruel thing, and that it is barbarous to tear men by violence from their homes, their families, and their country; to transport them by force across the Atlantic; and to doom them to pass the remainder of their shortened lives in painful toil, under the lash of a foreign tyrant;—though these things are known and felt by all, yet few can form to themselves any adequate conception how intense is the degree, and how extensive the range, of the cruelties of which the Slave Trade is the cause.

It is difficult to ascertain, with any approach to certainty, the number of negroes who are annually landed on the islands and continent of America, to be there consigned to slavery. The Returns for which I am about to move will furnish the best information that can be obtained on this subject; but that information can only be acquired through our consular agents, our Slave Trade Commissioners, and our naval officers. The governments of the countries in which those negroes are landed, publish no returns; but, on the contrary, endeavour to throw the veil of secrecy over such transactions. These Governments are those of Spain and Brazil, for it is to Cuba and to Brazil that these importations take place. But both Spain and Brazil are bound by treaties concluded with us, to prohibit all their subjects from engaging in, or being concerned with the Slave Trade in any manner whatsoever, and they have, in pursuance of those treaties, promulgated laws denouncing severe punishments upon such of their subjects as may have anything to do with the Trade.

But these Governments notoriously set at nought their engagements, and systematically disregard them, while they permit their own laws to be daily and openly violated with impunity. They endeavour, therefore, to conceal the importations which they connive at, and the information which we obtain about them must be necessarily imperfect. One thing, therefore, is certain, that the

Returns which we receive must fall short of the truth; they cannot exceed it. Now, what is the number of negroes supposed to be annually landed in America? Mr. Bandinell, of the Foreign Office, in his able and valuable work on the Slave Trade, compiled from official documents, and comprising, in a small compass, more useful and authentic information than almost any work that has yet been published, calculates the number at something between 120,000 and 130,000. Sir Fowell Buxton, in his most interesting work on the Slave Trade, states the number at 150,000; but whether the one or the other number be assumed to be correct, what an enormous amount of human misery and of human crime does this single statement involve.

When we look at an abstract statement on paper, conveyed in arithmetical figures, the mind is scarcely able to embrace within its grasp all the details and the full extent of the facts of which the knowledge may be so communicated. But let any man consider for a moment what an enormous mass of people 150,000 men amount to, and what an extent of ground they would cover. Many may have seen large armies; but few have seen an army of 150,000 men assembled in one spot, and at once within the reach of the eye. But let any one imagine that he saw 150,000 human beings drawn up on a great plain, and that he was told as they marched past him that they were all travelling to the same doom; that this vast living mass of fellow creatures was driven on to suffer painful and premature death, under every variety of bodily and mental torture. Let him further fancy himself told that this was not a single or an accidental calamity, but that every succeeding year the same ground would again be trodden by the same number of victims hurried forward to the same melancholy fate. What would be the just indignation that would burn within his bosom, and what would be the fervour with which he would call down the vengeance of Heaven, not only upon the authors of such enormities, but upon those who having the power to prevent such crimes, had culpably neglected to do so!

But any man would be much deceived who should suppose that the number of negroes annually landed on the coast of America, could be taken as a full measure of the number of human victims annually sacrificed to the avarice and cruelty, I will not say of Christian men, for Christians they deserve not to be called, but of men belonging to Christian nations. It is calculated, and I believe not without good reason, that for every negro thus landed in America, two others have perished in the preceding stages of the slave-making process; so that we must multiply by three the number actually landed, to arrive at the total number annually swept away by the Slave Trade from the population of Africa. It is well known that the negroes are not in general collected from the immediate neighborhood of the place where they are embarked. They come from the interior, and are marched down great distances to the coast. Some are captives taken in wars; in wars often waged for the express purpose of acquiring the gain to be made by the sale of prisoners. But the greatest number are obtained by the system of slave-hunting and man-stealing, which for the supply of the Slave Trade prevails all over the interior of Africa.

The way in which that system is carried on, is this: when the time of year comes round for sending down the slave caravan to the coast; at the dead of night, some peaceful African village, whose unsuspecting inhabitants are buried in that repose, which nature has kindly bestowed upon man to fit him again for the useful occupations and for the innocent enjoyments of the succeeding day; at the dead of the night, some such African village is suddenly surrounded by the armed ruffians of some neighbouring chief. The huts of which the village consists are set on fire; the inhabitants, roused from their sleep by the flames by which they are enveloped, rush forth; see their assailants and endeavour to escape capture, some by flight, others by resistance; but all equally in vain. The fugitives are intercepted and caught. Those who resist are overpowered, and either slain or made prisoners. Sometimes a hill village is attacked; there the intricacies of the ground afford greater facilities for escape, and some make good their flight to neighbouring caverns, or to hiding-places on the summit. The caverns are besieged, fires are lighted at their mouths, and those who have sought shelter there, are forced to choose between suffocation within and captivity without. The wells and springs upon which the people depend for their supply of water, are occupied; and those who have found a temporary safety in the higher grounds are compelled by the unendurable torments of thirst to come down, and barter their liberty for a few drops of water. Then comes the selection. The hale and healthy of either sex, and children above six or seven years old, are set apart for the slave caravan. The aged and the infirm, the infant torn from its mother's breast, the child wrenched from its parent's grasp, are murdered. To march these down to the coast would be impossible, and if possible, profitless; to maintain them would be costly; and to leave them to die of hunger when deprived of those by whose labour they had been supported, would be too cruel even for slave-hunters. They are, therefore, at once despatched, and they are the least to be pitied. Their sufferings are over, those of their surviving friends and relations are only about to begin.

When a sufficient number have thus been selected, the caravan sets out. Men, women, children, half naked, barefooted; the weak urged on by the goad and lash, the strong restrained from escape by yokes and chains, are driven hundreds and hundreds of miles across the burning sands of the plain, and over the stony passes of the mountain to the place of embarkation. Hunger, thirst, fatigue, despair, disease of body, and agony of mind, make dreadful havoc in the caravan. Some drop down dead as they go; others, unable to keep up, are left behind to die the lingering death of hunger and of thirst, or to become the prey of the wild beasts of the desert; others, more mercifully treated, when sinking under their fatigue, are knocked on the head and put out of their pain at once. Multitudes thus perish, and travellers who have visited the interior of the country tell you, that you may trace the march of these slave caravans across the pathless desert, and find your way to the wells that make their halting places, by the hundreds and thousands of human skeletons that lie bleaching and mouldering on the ground.

At last the caravan reaches the place of embarkation, but it often happens that the slave ship is not arrived, and the negroes have to wait many days, and perhaps weeks, for its arrival. In the interval they are cooped up in crowded huts called barracoons, imperfectly clothed, fed, and medically cared for. The fatigue of the march begins to tell even upon those whose strength had held on to the end of it; diseases break out, and many deaths ensue.

At length the slave ship arrives; the captain lands, and inspects the negroes. He picks out those whose apparent health and strength give promise that they will outlive the voyage, and be saleable at the market; the weak and sickly he rejects. Those whom he selects are embarked; those whom he rejects are either put out of the way at once, or left to perish on the coast by disease and want. It is reckoned that whatever may be the number of negroes thus embarked, at least an equal number have previously perished, in the seizure, the march, and the detention; and thus, if 500 are put on board the slave ship, 500 others have already been sacrificed in the preceding stages of the process.

Then comes the voyage; and then begins a scene of suffering and of horrors, greater than anything that has gone before, and greater than any man who has not been an eye-witness, can either imagine, or attempt to describe. Whatever the size of the slave ship may be, whether great or small, whether fifty tons or five hundred, the slave captain takes on board a fourth or a third more negroes than the vessel can properly contain. Such is, and such always has been the practice. It is founded upon a dry arithmetical calculation. It is done on the same principle according to which a man who sends a pipe of wine from Madeira to England to go round by the

East Indies, sends a quarter cask with it, in order that the waste by leakage and evaporation may be filled up, and that the pipe may still be full when it reaches its destination. The slave captain knows, that however careful he may be in choosing his negroes, some, who are apparently healthy, will yet have imbibed the seeds of diseases which will break out and prove fatal during the voyage; and that others who are quite sound when they embark, will yet, from change of food, of habits, and of temperature, sicken during the passage, and die before they reach the port. He, therefore, takes on board a number of supernumeraries, to fall into the vacancies to be created by those casualties, so that he may still have a full cargo on arriving at his market. But this very arrangement aggravates the evils, against the effects of which it is intended to provide. The crowded state of the vessel makes all the causes of disease act with infinitely greater force; sea-sickness, ophthalmia, fever, dysentery, small-pox, make ravages among the negroes, and hardly a day passes but the bodies are thrown overboard. But is it dead bodies only that are thrown overboard? I am sorry to say not. The living as well as the dead are often consigned to the bosom of the deep. Sometimes the progress of disease is rapid. The negro who is well today, sickens at night, and is a corpse tomorrow, and in such cases the course is plain. But it often happens that the disease is of a more lingering kind; and then the keen and experienced eye of the slave captain foresees in the early stage of the malady that the poor negro, though he may struggle on for a week or a fortnight, must inevitably die before the ship reaches the port, or if he should live till then, would be unsaleable in the market. But he also knows that during the remaining days of his suffering the negro will go on consuming provisions which are valuable, and money's worth; he will at all events lose the price he has paid for the negro and the cost of his subsistence up to that time; why should he needlessly increase that loss? He resolves not to do so; he determines to save his provisions; and overboard goes the living negro. This is by no means an un-common occurrence; it was not uncommon, I am ashamed to say, even in ships of this country, before our slave-trade was abolished.

There is on record the case of the ship Zong, commanded by a man of the name of Collingwood, which sailed for Jamaica in 1781, on board of which it was proved by a Court of Justice, that a trans-action of this kind took place. The ship had a large cargo of negroes; she missed her course; her water ran short, and her negroes grew sickly. The captain reflected that the negroes who died would be a loss to the owners; but he thought that if he could make it appear that a certain number were necessarily thrown overboard for the safety of the ship, their value might be recovered from the insurers; accordingly, he resolved to throw overboard those who were the most sickly, and the least likely to live to reach the port; and in three nights 132 of the negroes were thrown overboard alive.

Many negroes are lost by shipwreck, and a remarkable instance of this kind happened in 1819. I have stated that the ophthalmia often breaks out in the slave ships. In 1819, this disorder raged on board the French slave ship, the Rodeur, bound with a cargo of negroes to Guadaloupe; the disease was so virulent, that only one man in the ship's company retained his eyesight sufficiently to be able to steer the ship. In this condition the Rodeur fell in with another large vessel, full of people, but apparently drifting at the mercy of the winds and waves. The vessels came within hail; the strange ship was St. Leon, a Spanish slaver, full of negroes; the people on board said that the ophthalmia had broken out also among them, and that there was not a single man on board who could see well enough to steer or work the ship. They begged for assistance, but none could be given them. The ships parted; the Rodeur reached Guadaloupe; the St. Leon was never heard of more.

Sometimes calamities of a different kind occur. I have already stated how small and inconvenient the places are, in which the negroes on board these slave ships are confined. The bottom of the hold is filled with the casks, which contain the water and provisions for the people on board; over these casks is spread a platform, composed of rough unplaned boards, laid loosely together, and upon this rough and splintery surface the naked negroes are obliged to lie. Sometimes even this poor accommodation is denied them, and nothing but a few mats are spread over the uneven surface of the casks, and the negroes are to fit themselves to the inequalities of the surface as they can. The distance between this platform and the upper deck of the vessel varies according to the size of the ship; it is scarcely ever more than three feet and a half, and sometimes it is barely two feet and a half. Into this black hole the negroes are thrust like so many bales of goods; linked two by two, with fetters, to prevent them from crushing each other by moving about; and so crowded together, that, as stated by a witness examined before a Committee of this House, in 1791, the negro in the hold of a slave ship has not as much room as a man has in his coffin. It may well be imagined how vitiated must be the air breathed by so many lungs; how intense must be the heat created by such an aggregation of living bodies in so small a space, under the vertical rays of a tropical sun; and how pestilential the effluvia occasioned by the circumstances of their confinement and condition. In order to mitigate these inconveniences, by admitting as much air as possible below, the hatch-ways of slave-ships are made larger than those of merchantmen, and are covered by open gratings, instead of with closed hatches, and some have air-ports beside. In fine and even in moderate weather, these arrangements, to a certain degree, answer their purpose; but the slave-ships sometimes encounter a violent storm, the sea runs high and breaks over the vessel, and then the hatchways must be nearly closed, or the ship would fill and go down. Then ensues a scene of horror, of struggle, of agony, of death, which I will not attempt to describe. The results of such a calamity are related by the rev. Mr. Hill, in his pamphlet, called "Fifty Days in a Slaver." The captured slave-ship he was on board of, was overtaken by a storm; the hatchways were closed, and fifty-two negroes out of about four hundred died in one night, suffocated by want of air, or strangled in their struggle to get near to the small opening still left for the admission of air. Mr. Hill imagines that this was a singular instance, and that the misfortune arose from the inexperience of the prize crew, who were not accustomed to deal with such emergencies. But I fear he is mistaken. The loss of life was, indeed, greater, in consequence of the negroes not having been released from their fetters, which would have prevented them from struggling so much with each other; but when slave-ships meet with storms, which not unfrequently happens, the hatchways must be partially closed up, and many negroes die by suffocation.

It is calculated, that from all these causes, about a third of the negroes that are embarked die during the passage; and if this third of the 500 embarked be added to the 500 assumed to have died in the seizure, the march, and the detention, it will be seen that for every negro landed, two others will have perished in the previous stages of the slave-making process; and thus, if 130,000 or 150,000 negroes have been landed annually in America, the yearly ravage committed on the African nations must amount to something like 400,-000; and if this has been going on for the last century, how many millions must during that period have been swept away from the population of Africa. Why I will venture to say, that if all the other crimes which the human race has committed, from the creation down to the present day, were added together in one vast aggregation, they would scarcely equal, I am sure they could not exceed, the amount of guilt which has been incurred by mankind, in connexion with this diabolical Slave Trade.

And is it not, then, the duty of every government, and of every nation on whom Providence has bestowed the means of putting an end to this crime, to employ those means and to the greatest possible extent? And if there is any government and any nation upon whom that duty is more especially incumbent, is not that government the government of England, and are we not that nation?

Political influence and naval power are the two great instruments by which the Slave Trade may be abolished; our political influence, if properly exerted, is great, our naval power is pre-eminent.[18]

.   .   .   .

. . . . . The right honourable Baronet at the head of the Government [19] stated on a former occasion that one of the great motives which led him and his Colleagues to undergo the toils, and vexations, and harassments of office, (and they who have been themselves in office know that burthen is not light), was the desire and hope of obtaining thereby posthumous fame. I am sure the right honourable Baronet did not by that expression exclude from his view the desire and the hope also of that approval of a satisfied conscience, which is the certain reward for duties well performed; I am sure he did not mean to exclude that higher sanction, in comparison with which all human approbation sinks into utter insignificance; but the right honourable Baronet stated, that one of his objects, and a fair and honourable one it is, was the hope of acquiring fame in after ages. They, however, who are charged with the Government of a great nation, can obtain fame only by conferring some great benefits on their own country, or on the rest of mankind. Now the peculiar position in which the present Government stands renders it difficult for them to do the first. They cannot emancipate the commercial industry of the country, nor open to us that full career of prosperity on which we might be able to enter; they are prevented from doing that, by the prejudices of the great body of their supporters. They cannot lay the foundations of any large and liberal system of education for the great numbers who are every year rising up in the manufacturing districts in the darkest ignorance, intellectual, moral, and religious; they are prevented from doing that by prejudices which they themselves partake. They cannot give contentment to the six millions of Catholics who inhabit Ireland: they are prevented from doing that by obstacles which they themselves in former times have contributed to create. They cannot take a leading part in the settlement of any great European question, if any such should arise in their time, because, dissatisfied apparently with the front rank position in which they found the country when they took the helm, they thought it more consistent with the modesty of our national character that Great Britain, under their command, should drop quietly astern, and take up her berth in the wake of all the great

[18] A lengthy discussion on the history of the attitude of foreign states toward the slave trade is omitted.

[19] Sir Robert Peel.

Foreign Powers. But there is one field still open in which they may gather unfading laurels; they may abolish the Slave Trade. In their efforts to accomplish that great end they will be thwarted by no resentful supporters, by no disapproving opponents. They will have the country unanimously with them, and the will of this great nation, when unanimously expressed for a noble cause, is able to accomplish great results. If the present Government shall have to say that they succeeded, in their time, in extinguishing a foul traffic, for the suppression of which those who had gone before them had laboured for many years, and with only partial success, they will bequeath to posterity a name that will live in the grateful remembrance of the most distant ages. But if it shall justly be laid to their charge, that whereas the Slave Trade had been much checked, and nearly extinguished by the efforts of those who preceded them, it had in their time acquired fresh life, and had again reared aloft its hideous and gigantic head, they will indeed attain an everlasting fame, but it will be a fame in comparison with which the most perfect and entire oblivion would be deemed an enviable lot.[20]

[20] The noble Viscount concluded by moving an Address for—"Return, showing the total number of African Negroes landed for the purposes of Slavery on the Islands and on the Continent of America, from the year 1815 to the year 1843, both inclusive; distinguishing the number so landed in each of those years, and distinguishing also the number landed in each year on the territory of each separate State or Power, so far as the same can be made up from Documents in the possession of Her Majesty's Government, also, Cases adjudged under Slave Trade Treaties, and number of Slaves emancipated in consequence at Sierra Leone, Rio de Janeiro, Havannah, Surinam, and other places respectively, from the year 1829 to the year 1844."

4. Sir Charles Napier

A banquet was given to Sir Charles Napier at the Reform Club on March 7, 1854, just before his departure with the fleet to the Baltic. Palmerston had the chair. After toasts to various sovereigns and countries had been drunk, Palmerston gave the following speech which may be found in The Times (London) of March 8, 1854, and in Ashley's Life of Henry John Temple, Viscount Palmerston (London, 1876), Vol. II.

It is inserted to show the effectiveness of Palmerston's levity—a levity that may now appear as a strange thing inasmuch as England was destined to enter formally the Crimean War three weeks later.

There was a very remarkable entertainer of dinner company, called Sir R. Preston, who lived in the city, and who, when he gave dinners at Greenwich, after gorging his guests with turtle, used to turn round to the waiters and say, "Now bring dinner." Gentlemen, we have had the toasts which correspond with the turtle, and now let's go to dinner. (Laughter.) Now let us drink the toast which belongs to the real occasion of our assembling here. I give you "The health of my gallant friend Sir Charles Napier," who sits beside me. If, gentlemen, I were addressing a Hampshire audience, consisting of country gentlemen residing in that county, to which my gallant friend and myself belong, I should introduce him to your notice as an eminent agriculturist. (Laughter.) It has been my good fortune, when enjoying his hospitality at Merchistoun Hall, to receive most valuable instructions from him while walking over his farm about stall-feeding, growing turnips, wire fencing, under-draining, and the like. (Laughter.) My gallant friend is a match for everything, and whatever he turns his hand to he generally succeeds in it. (Cheers and laughter.)

However gentlemen, he now, like Cincinnatus, leaves his plough, puts on his armour, and is prepared to do that good service to his country which he will always perform whenever an opportunity is afforded to him. I pass over those earlier exploits of his younger days, which are well known to the members of his profession; but, perhaps, one of the most remarkable exploits of his life is that which he performed in the same cause of liberty and justice in which he is now about to be engaged. In the year 1833, when gallantly volunteering to serve the cause of the Queen of Portugal against the encroachments and the usurpations of Don Miguel—to defend constitutional rights and liberties against arbitrary power—he took the command of a modest fleet of frigates and corvettes, and, at the head of that little squadron, he captured a squadron far superior

176

in force, including two line-of-battle ships, one of which my gallant friend was the first to board. But on that occasion my gallant friend exhibited a characteristic trait. When he had scrambled upon the deck of this great line-of-battle ship, and was clearing the deck of those who had possession of it, a Portuguese officer ran at him full dart with his drawn sword to run him through. My gallant friend quietly parried the thrust, and, not giving himself the trouble to deal in any other way with his Portuguese assailant, merely gave him a hearty kick, and sent him down the hatchway. (Roars of laughter.) Well, gentlemen, that victory was a great event—(much laughter)—I don't mean the victory over the officer who went down (renewed laughter), but the victory over the fleet, which my gallant friend took into port; for that victory decided a great cause then pending. It decided the liberties of Portugal; it decided the question between constitutional and arbitrary power—a contest which began in Portugal, and which went on afterwards in Spain, when my gallant friend Sir De Lacy Evans lent his powerful aid in the same cause, and with the same success. My gallant friend Sir Charles Napier, however, got the first turn of fortune, and it was mainly owing to that victory of his that the Queen of Portugal afterwards occupied the throne to which she was rightfully entitled, and the Portuguese nation obtained that Constitution which they have ever since enjoyed. (Cheers.) A noble friend of mine, now no more, whose loss I greatly lament, for he was equally distinguished as a man, as a soldier, and as a diplomatist, the late Lord William Russell—an honour to his country, as to his family—told me that one day he heard that my gallant friend Sir Charles Napier was in the neighbourhood of the fortress of Valenza, a Portuguese fortress some considerable distance from the squadron which he commanded. Lord W. Russell and Colonel Hare went to see my gallant friend, and Lord W. Russell told me that they met a man dressed in a very easy way (great laughter), followed by a fellow with two muskets on his shoulders. (Renewed laughter.) They took him at first for Robinson Crusoe (roars of laughter); but who should these men prove to be but the gallant admiral on my right and a marine behind him. (Laughter.) "Well, Napier," said Lord W. Russell, "what are you doing here?" "Why," said my gallant friend, "I am waiting to take Valenza." "But," said Lord William, "Valenza is a fortified town, and you must know that we soldiers understand how fortified towns are taken. You must open trenches; you must make approaches; you must establish a battery in breach; and all this takes a good deal of time, and must be done according to rule." "Oh," said my gallant friend, "I have no time for all that. (Cheers and laughter.) I have got some of my bluejackets up here and a few of my ship's guns, and I mean to take the town with a letter." (Laughter.) And so he did. He sent the governor a letter to tell him he had much better surrender at discretion. The governor was a very sensible man (cheers and laughter); and so surrender he did. So the trenches and the approaches, the battery, breach, and all that were saved, and the town of Valenza was handed over to the Queen of Portugal. Well, the next great occasion in which my gallant friend took a prominent and distinguished part—a part for which I can assure you that I personally, in my official capacity, and the Government to which I had the honour to belong, felt deeply indebted and obliged to him—was the occasion of the war in Syria. There my gallant friend distinguished himself, as usual, at sea and on shore. All was one to him, wherever an enemy was to be found; and I feel sure that when the enemy was found, the enemy wished to Heaven he had not been found. (Great laughter and cheering.) Well, my gallant friend landed with his marines, headed a Turkish detachment, defeated the Egyptian troops, gained a very important victory, stormed the town of Sidon, captured three or four thousand Egyptian prisoners, and afterwards took a prominent part in the attack and capture of the important fortress of Acre. I am bound to say that the Government to which I belonged, in sending those instructions which led to the attack upon Acre, were very much guided by the opinions which we had received of the practicability of that achievement in letters from my gallant friend.

5. Constitutional Reforms

In 1852 and periodically thereafter the question of Parliamentary reform had been presented before Parliament and the nation. During the electioneering of 1859, Mr. Rowcliffe, a Radical, attacked Palmerston in remarking that his lordship had talked a great deal about Lord Derby's proposed reform act of 1859 but had not favored the electors and nonelectors with his own views on reform. Would his lordship vote for the ballot, did he prefer manhood suffrage or a £6 franchise or a rating franchise? For himself, he had refused to remain a member of the noble Lord's committee because he considered the noble Lord to be not a Liberal but a downright Tory and the best representative the Conservatives could possibly have. He hoped to hear his questions answered in a straightforward and honest manner.

Palmerston gave his reply (cf. Ashley's Life, Vol. II) in a manner exasperating to his opponent, embarrassing to some of his Liberal colleagues, stimulating to his public, and puzzling to historians. Short as the reply is, it is very suggestive of Palmerston's politics.

Lord Palmerston said he was delighted to find that his old friend however far advanced in years, retained that youthful vigour which he possessed when first he knew him, and with his vigour he had retained also his prejudices and opinions. (Laughter, and a cry of "No chaff.") His friend asked for a straightforward answer, and he would give one. He totally disagreed with him in almost all his opinions. (Laughter.) He (the noble lord) thought the day would never come when he and his friend would agree in political faith. (Much laughter.) His friend asked him what he thought on many points. In the first place he would say he was opposed to the ballot. He was against manhood suffrage. (Rowcliffe: "How far will you go with the franchise?") He would give a straightforward answer to that. He would not tell him. (Laughter.) He held it was his duty, after the confidence they had reposed in him, to act according to his judgment in any measure relating to Reform. (Cheers.) He hoped that the political difference of Mr. Rowcliffe and himself would not alter their private friendship. (Loud laughter.) He was sorry to disagree with his friend, but no man could agree with everybody. The man who did agree with everybody was not worth having anybody to agree with him. (Cheers and laughter.)

6. Denmark and Germany

Disraeli, mindful of the success of a Conservative attack in the House of Lords upon the government's foreign policy, moved in the Commons a resolution which expressed regret that Her Majesty's Government had failed to maintain their avowed policy of upholding the integrity and independence of Denmark and had "lowered the just influence of this Country in the counsels of Europe, and thereby diminished the securities for peace." Mr. Kinglake's amendment was meant to check the Conservative attack. It desired in place of the above resolution "to express the satisfaction with which we have heard that . . . . Her Majesty has been advised to abstain from armed interference in the war now going on between Denmark and the German Powers." Palmerston's defence against the attack may be found in HANSARD (CLXXVI [3d Ser.], 1272-87 [July 8, 1864]).

The situation—the Schleswig-Holstein affair—which called forth Palmerston's speech is so intricate in its details that statesmen of the period found difficulty in giving brief and adequate explanations. A growing German national sentiment, thriving under the possibility of rescuing Schleswig and Holstein from the Danes, made Denmark's administrative control of the two duchies an impossible task, and England, as Denmark's patron, compelled the small state to make concessions to her neighbors' demands. The death of her King in 1863 gave opportunity for Prussia and Austria to foster plans for driving the Danes from Schleswig and Holstein; on the successful outcome of their project, these two powers would be in position to retain them jointly or to hand them over to the Duke of Augustenburg, neither of which arrangements would correspond to the terms of a treaty of 1852. Palmerston talked about intervention in behalf of Denmark, and the Danes counted on his words to their undoing—for there was no intervention though the armies of Prussia and Austria eventually marched to easy victory. English society itself was divided in its sympathies: Queen Victoria hoped for Prussian success and, after the Danish defeat, arranged for conferences in London (1864) which, however, accomplished nothing. Palmerston was averse, for England's sake, to any development of Prussia that might threaten the balance of power. He therefore backed Denmark but at the last found himself incapable either of uniting the English to his policy or of obtaining the assistance of Napoleon III (because the latter had looked in vain for more than English moral support in the contemporary Polish crisis). Under these circumstances the Lords censured and Disraeli moved his resolution in the Commons.

Sir, if any doubt could have existed when the notice of this Motion was first given as to its object and importance, that doubt must have been fully dispelled by the debate that has ensued upon it; for we are now told, fairly and plainly, that although the words

simply imply censure on one act of the Government, it is intended
as a vote of "No confidence"; and that the issue which the House
is called upon to determine is, whether Gentlemen on this side of
the House or Gentlemen on that side shall be charged with the
conduct of the affairs of the country. Now, Sir, I object to much
that has passed in this debate—but to two things mainly—first of
all, to the attempt to separate my noble Friend at the head of the
Foreign Office from the rest of his Colleagues—a most unconstitu-
tional attempt—a most unfair attempt; an attempt which ought to
have been reprobated by those who, having been in office, know
the joint responsibility of the Members of a Cabinet. Sir, I declare
on my own part and on the part of my Colleagues, that we are all
equally responsible for what the noble Lord at the head of the
Foreign Office has done; and therefore I trust that we shall not
have any more of these personal attacks upon Earl Russell, but
that whatever censure any man may wish to cast upon the conduct
of the Government may be aimed at the Government itself, and
not at any individual member of it. I also, Sir, regret deeply for
my country the pains that have been taken, by many of those who
have taken part in this debate, to villify and degrade this country.
Not content with blaming the Government, which they were
entitled to do, and endeavouring to prove that we were wrong
—which they had a right to do if they could prove it—in every
step of these transactions, they have maintained that England is
degraded, and that she has sunk in the estimation of foreign nations. And when forsooth? and since when? Why, since the
termination of the Conferences, which closed a few days ago. Sir,
I deny, on the part of the Government, the statements that have
been made. I say that England stands as high as she ever did.
And those who say she has fallen in the estimation of the world
are not the men to whom the honour and dignity of England
should be confided.

Well, Sir, but this bill of indictment was most singularly brought
in by the right honourable Gentleman who moved the Resolution;
because, in the early part of his speech, he step by step expressed
his approval of what the Government had done. He began by
admitting that the Treaty of 1852 was, when it was concluded, a
wise and good arrangement. He does not deny that all the Governments who were parties to it congratulated each other for having
made what they then thought—and there were grounds for the
opinion—a settlement that would insure the peace of Europe.
And when we are told that the Prussian Minister of that day, the
Chevalier de Bunsen, refused to put his name to a certain Protocol,

I believe I am right in saying that so eager was the Prussian Government for the treaty, that the draught was sent from Berlin to London, with a special order that he was to sign it as he received it, and was not to make any objections of his own. Well, then, whatever may have been the feelings of the Chevalier Bunsen, who was known to be a very enthusiastic champion of German unity at the time, his feelings were not shared by his Government, and it is a misrepresentation to infer, because of any objections he may have felt, that Prussia was not sincere and anxious for the conclusion of that Treaty. Saxony was equally pleased with the arrangement then made. That arrangement violated no rights. It simply was that the Danish Parliament should be invited to change the law of succession in Denmark legally, which they did—that the King should be empowered, by his prerogative, to name his successor, which he did; and that that successor should be acknowledged by the contracting Powers as heir to the Danish Crown; and that the States which were then and had been for a long time under the sway of the King of Denmark, should (as far as the object of the treaty went) remain united under the Danish sceptre. It was thought that this arrangement was secured by the change in the law of succession in Denmark, and the renunciation of the Duke of Augustenburg, who was next in succession to Holstein. Well, Sir, we know that the reason why that arrangement failed was, that the Danish Government did not give the German subjects of Schleswig the liberal administrative system to which they were entitled, and that the late King of Denmark committed the same errors which the King of Holland committed with regard to Belgium, by interfering in their languages, laws, religion, and all those things that are dear to man. That has been a constant source of expostulation on the part of the Germans, and those expostulations were not attended to as they ought to have been. The result of it was, that when the late King died these discontents, which had been smothered during his reign, burst forth as to the disputed succession to Holstein. Then came the Federal Execution in Holstein for the purpose of compelling the King Duke to revoke his Patent.

And that brings me to the point to which I have often been referred—namely, the answer I made to the honourable Member for Horsham (Mr. S. FitzGerald) at the end of last Session. It is said that we began at that time to threaten Germany. I deny that what I said implied any threat of war on the part of England, and the words which I am going to read will, I think, prove it. What I said in answer to the honourable Member was—

"I have said that we concur entirely with him, and I am satisfied with all reasonable men in Europe, including those in France and Austria, in desiring that the independence and integrity, the rights of Denmark, may be maintained. We are convinced—I am convinced, at least,—that if any violent attempt were made to overthrow those rights, and interfere with that independence, those who made the attempt would find in the result that it would not be Denmark alone with whom they would have to contend." (3 *Hansard,* clxxii, 1252).

The context shows, and it is quite plain, when I talked of every man in Europe—when I talked of France and Russia—I did not confine myself to this country. But what preceded that passage? I said just before

"It is impossible for any man who looks at the map of Europe—I did not say the map of Aldershot and Portsmouth—and who knows the great interests which the Powers of Europe feel in the independence of the Danish Monarchy, to shut his eyes to the fact that the war, begun about a petty dispute concerning the institutions of Holstein, would in all probability not end where it began, and might draw after it consequences that the parties who commenced it would be exceedingly sorry to have caused." (3 *Hansard,* clxxii, 1251).

What I was pointing to was an European war, not a war between this country and the German Powers. But, then, what was it that the honourable Gentleman, who is so much against interference, said which called forth the reply I am now quoting? Why the honourable Gentleman said, "If the Government would say"—he had said that he apprehended danger from the Execution in Holstein—that the entrance of the Federal troops into Holstein upon grounds of execution might involve consequences fatal to the integrity of Denmark, and then he went on to say,

"If the Government would say that under pretence of Federal rights the Germanic Confederation were not to interfere with the rights of the Danish Crown, and if France and Russia held similar language, the danger to which he had adverted might be obviated." (3 *Hansard,* clxxii, 1249).

The honourable Gentleman, therefore, wanted the English Government to say to the Diet, "You shall not go into Holstein for the purpose of executing your Federal law." He said, "Even if England were to say it, the danger might be avoided; but if England were to persuade France and Russia to say it also, the danger which he apprehended would be obviated." Therefore, I say, it is not for the honourable Gentleman who attacks us to say that our expostulations to Prussia and Austria against the course they were taking were not justifiable representations, since he would have had us take a still higher course, and try to prevent them doing that which by the law of Germany and the law of Europe they had a perfect right to do. We did not do that; our representations were of an entirely different character. Well, when the occupation took place, the Danish Government was recommended, not by England alone, but by England and other Powers, not to resist. They did not resist; and when the further invasion of Schleswig was threatened, we endeavoured to persuade the King of Denmark to take steps to revoke that constitution which was made the ground of the occupation of Schleswig as a guarantee for its revocation. He promised that he would do what he could, and as early as he could, for that purpose. Well, then, what was the time when, according to honourable Gentlemen opposite, who complain so much, and at the bottom of whose thoughts lies an interference by force—what was the time when, in their opinion, that interference ought to have been made? The German troops entered Schleswig about the beginning of the year—the middle of winter. That was not a time when any military or naval operations could have been undertaken by this country. Well, what did we do? From the beginning we endeavoured to persuade France and Russia to concur with us in every step which we took. Menacing language is said to have been used. Why, the menacing language was warning to the German Powers of the dangers to Europe and to themselves which might arise from an extension of the war beyond the quarter in which it had arisen.

But the right honourable Gentleman (Mr. Disraeli) in his speech approved our conduct up to September. He says it was wise and judicious, because France was with us. But he went on to say, in September a change took place, and then we disgusted France and lost her support. How, according to him, did that come to pass? It was on account of Poland and the Congress. He says, we abandoned France about Poland. But what was our course with regard to Poland? Were we not told in this House over and over again, that we ought only to interfere diplomatically in favour of Poland? Did not the honourable Member for the King's County repeatedly urge us in that direction, and was not his urging backed by honourable Gentlemen who sit near him? Even the mode of representation was pointed out. We were told not to content ourselves with simple remonstrances on the part of England, but to get France, Austria, and Prussia, and all the Powers of Europe, to concur with us in representing to Russia the expediency of dealing leniently with Poland, and acting towards the Poles in accordance with her treaty engagements. We did so; but we did not do that which we never undertook to do—make war against

Russia for that object. My noble Friend avowed that such was not his intention, and the right honourable Gentleman approved the course which we pursued; for he said a little time ago, to make war against Russia for Poland would have been an act of insanity. Therefore, it is unreasonable to allege that the course which we pursued with regard to Poland could have justly offended the Emperor of the French. It is a reflection on the French Emperor to attribute to him a feeling of that kind. Then came the Congress; and with regard to that also the right honourable Gentleman says we were quite right. No one of common understanding, I think, could imagine that a Congress under the existing circumstances could have been attended with any success. The right honourable Gentleman says that a Congress ought to follow action, and not to precede it; and a very just distinction it is, and one entirely applicable. Well, when it is alleged that the conduct of France about Denmark was influenced by what the British Government did in these two instances, it is to impute to the Government of the Emperor of the French motives and conduct unworthy a great Power which has a due regard for its own honour and dignity. France was actuated by quite different motives, and she never concealed them from us. We were certainly led in the beginning to expect that France and Russia would join us in pressing strongly upon the German Powers the impropriety and injustice of their conduct. But France very fairly told us, "A war about Denmark to you would be a naval war, to us it would be a land war. We have all Germany upon our Frontier. It would be a great undertaking, costly both in men and treasure, and one, therefore, we are not disposed to undertake for an object which is not a French object, and does not concern the dignity, the possessions, or the welfare of France." I think that was a fair argument, and we had no right to press France any further to adopt the course we had suggested. We lost, therefore, the support of France except morally and diplomatically. Russia we also applied to, and Russia gave us answers which amounted to declining any co-operation. And when one considers the bond of union which exists between Russia, Austria, and Prussia, with respect to Polish affairs, he cannot be much surprised that Russia should not be very willing to employ force against her neighbours. Well, then, step by step up to September, the right honourable Gentleman deems that our policy was wise and judicious. And I contend that after that date likewise it was wise, judicious, and honourable to the country. We laboured to persuade the contending parties to come to an agreement; we recommended just concessions to Denmark; and we remonstrated with the Germans for conduct which was unjustifiable towards Denmark. At last a Conference was proposed; the proposal came from Prussia first. We agreed to it. Some time elapsed before it could be assembled. Questions arose whether an armistice should precede it. We should have preferred that it had; but failing of that, we stipulated that it should be the first subject of discussion. We found it impossible to obtain an armistice, and therefore the first point with us was to assemble the Conference as early as possible. Well, Sir, it is said our influence is gone—we have no influence in Europe; yet, remark that we were invited by other Powers to take steps to bring about the Conference. In that Conference, as the Protocols show, step by step the neutral Powers—France, Russia, and Sweden—went in accordance with England. Nothing was done or proposed by England which was not previously agreed and concerted with those Powers—and then you say that England is degraded and lowered in the eyes of other nations, and that they have no confidence in her.[21]. . . . .

.   .   .   .

Let us examine what the Resolution is—I speak not of the first and second paragraphs, but of the last. The right honourable Gentleman in the last paragraph proposes that the House should affirm that the influence of England is lowered in the eyes of Europe, and that thereby the security for peace is diminished. That is supported by a great number of gentlemen, who maintain that we ought never to interfere in anything beyond our own shores. What, then, is the use of our influence if we are not to interfere, and how is the peace of Europe endangered by the loss of our influence, if that influence is to be confined to influence within these walls? The Resolution of the right honourable Gentleman is an admission that the doctrine of many of those who support it is unsound in the existing circumstances of the world, and that the great interests connecting a country like ours with every part of the world render it impossible for her to be passive or indifferent as to what is passing among other nations, and that circumstances requiring vigilant watching must sometimes cause her to interfere in transactions in which we are not directly concerned. Then we are told that the balance of power is an exploded doctrine belonging to ancient times. Why, it is a doctrine founded on the nature of man. It means that it is to the interest of the community of nations that no one nation should acquire such a preponderance as to endanger the security of the rest; and it is for the advantage of all that the smaller Powers should be respected in their independence

[21] Some details of the Schleswig-Holstein problem are omitted.

and not swallowed up by their more powerful neighbours. That is the doctrine of the balance of power, and it is a doctrine worthy of being acted upon. We have done our best to rescue Denmark from the danger to which she was exposed, first by counselling her to put herself right when she was wrong, and next by endeavouring to induce her aggressors to refrain from continuing their aggression; and by inducing the neutral Powers to join us in adopting the same course. And what said the right honourable Gentleman in his opening speech on this subject? He said that if England and France were agreed upon the same policy, war would be difficult; but that if England, France, and Russia were agreed, war would be impossible. Well, we tried to make war impossible. But France and Russia would not combine with us, and therefore war became possible, and took place. The right honourable Gentleman has therefore pronounced a panegyric upon our policy, and he ought to vote against his own Resolution. We adopted the best means of rendering war impossible, and the failure was not our fault.[22]

[22] The remaining portion of the speech treats of England's position before the world and her internal progress.

Chapter VI

DISRAELI

Chapter VI

DISRAELI

D ISRAELI and Gladstone are properly regarded as creators essentially of the nineteenth rather than as resultants of the eighteenth century. But Gladstone began his career among the most conservative surroundings and ideas, and Disraeli never hesitated to use the past as warrant for the pronouncement of a political faith.

Benjamin Disraeli (1804-1881) was born of a Jewish family which had migrated in the person of his grandfather from Italy. Perhaps a more ancient history of the family, which Disraeli himself outlined, owes its origin to a use of poetic license. In any case, the father, Isaac, became a well-known literary figure, and Disraeli the Younger was, as he said, brought up in a library. The son, playing at first with the idea of following the legal profession, turned eventually toward literature and produced, when he was less than twenty-three years of age, the showy, amusing, and successful novel, *Vivian Grey*.

Disraeli, in a hurry to be an important if not a great man, seemingly was on the way to his goal but, failing to catch the temper of the times and miscalculating the nature of his own abilities, became rather, during the ensuing ten years, the butt of many an English untempered smile and occasionally of an outright guffaw. In the first place he was more or less a ridiculous representative of dandyism. There is evidence, notwithstanding his own later statements to the contrary, that he appeared at social functions overbrilliantly bedecked. One quotation in the form of a note by his friend, Meredith, will suffice as illustration:

B.D. to dine with me. He came up Regent Street, when it was crowded, in his blue surtout, a pair of military light-blue trousers, black stockings with red stripes, and shoes. "The people," he said, "quite made way for me as I passed. It was like the opening of the

Red Sea, which I now perfectly believe from experience. Even well-dressed people stopped to look at me." [1]

Able as he doubtless was in conversation at dinner parties he nevertheless was attempting a path to fame hardly well-enough beaten to appeal to English conservative tastes.

In the second place his efforts in pure literature subsequent to the publication of *Vivian Grey* became more and more absurd, culminating in a story of a prince of the Captivity, entitled *The Wondrous Tale of Alroy* (1833). As a clever and appreciative contemporary wrote:

The Wondrous Tale of Alroy brought the sins of Mr. Disraeli to their climax. That work was universally hailed as a damning evidence of literary lunacy. Wild, incongruous romance, and daring tamperings with history, might have been lost sight of in the brilliancy and glare of Eastern coloring; but the infatuated attempts to reconstruct the English language—to make bad poetry do duty as rhythmical prose, till the writer seemed to be literally cantering through his work, raised an universal shout of derision. It was more than good John Bull, though apt enough to admire the unintelligible, could bear. [2]

No wonder that *Frazer's Magazine* of May 1833, in placing Disraeli in its "Gallery of Literary Characters," had depicted him as a fashionable fop and copied his own medium of expression:

O Reader dear! do pray look here, and you will spy the curly hair, and forehead fair, and nose so high, and gleaming eye, of Benjamin D'I s-ra-e-li, the wondrous boy who wrote Alroy in rhyme and prose, only to show how long ago victorious Judah's lion-banner rose. In an earlier day he wrote *Vivian Grey*—a smart-enough story, we must say . . . . .

He also was not above considering himself the poet of his epoch and published in 1834 a part of *The Revolutionary Epic*, promising, however, that in case his efforts were not well received he was prepared to "hurl his Lyre to Limbo." He kept his promise. *The Revolutionary Epic* is read nowadays for its dim references to ideas on Young England which later writings

[1] Geoffrey G. Butler, *The Tory Tradition* (London: J. Murray, 1914), p. 65.
[2] George Henry Francis, *The Right Hon. Benjamin Disraeli* (London, 1852), p. 16.

made famous rather than for its still dimmer poetic inspiration.

In the third place Disraeli's early political activities led to the impression that he was unsafe and unsound. Leaving England after the publication of *Vivian Grey* he had traveled in Italy and Switzerland and later in Spain and in the Levant.[3] His return corresponded in time with the agitation on Parliamentary reform, and Disraeli decided that political life held great possibilities for himself. His contests in 1832, 1834, and 1835, however, caused his would-be constituents to question the meaning of his political phrases, and his biographies to the present disagree as regards whether he ought to have been called Radical or Tory. One certainty was apparent before long—that he was not a Whig. Later, breaking in a startling way with the Radicals, Joseph Hume and Daniel O'Connell, and finding the type of Conservative leadership in Peel which he apparently admired, he ran in the general election of 1837 as an out-and-out Tory and was elected member from Maidstone with Mr. Wyndham Lewis as colleague. In the meantime he had written some political pamphlets of which one, *What Is He?* (1833), probably had little meaning for his readers and of which another, *Vindication of the British Constitution* (1835),[4] brought favorable comments from Peel and later much analysis from students interested in historical toryism.

He entered Parliament, then, with a reputation which had changed little from the time, four years before, when *Fraser's*, continuing its rhyming at him, had written:

He lately stood for Wycombe, but there Colonel Grey did lick him, he being parcel Tory and parcel Radical—which is what in general mad we call; and the latest affair of his we chanced to see, is *What is He?*, a question which by this time, we have somewhat answered in this our pedestrian rhyme.

Apparently he had no doubt about the possibility of his success in the House of Commons for already he had told Melbourne that he desired to be Prime Minister and he had written to his sister after hearing Macaulay's best speech: "This *entre nous*. I was never more confident of anything than that I could carry

---

[3] W. F. Monypenny, *The Life of Benjamin Disraeli* (New York: J. Murray, 1910-1920), Vol. I.

[4] *Vindication, What Is He?*, and other early political writings have been published by William Hutcheon under the title, *Whigs and Whiggism* (London: J. Murray, 1913).

everything before me in that House." [5] Alas, he had failed to discover that the House of Commons had adapted itself to a manner of address to which it demanded a degree of conformity, and Disraeli in his first speech was howled down in such way that many an auditor must have doubted the truth of his last sentence: ". . . . the time will come when you will hear me."

But the next few years witnessed a remarkable development in the man. He won the attention of members of the House even when he became the exponent of the unusual attitude as in his famous Chartist speech (cf. page 198). He produced *Coningsby* (1844) and *Sybil* (1845), the two historical novels that not only combine contemporary political and social problems with romance and advertise a philosophy which implies that monarch with nobles and church represent the natural and best leadership for the *people* but also remain unsurpassed to the present as specimens of their particular type of literature. He led a small group of Young Englanders who espoused the ideas expressed in the novels and who acted independently of the Conservative party on occasion. He had in the meantime rid himself of pressing financial difficulties by marrying in 1839 Mrs. Wyndham Lewis, twelve years his senior and widow of his former colleague. Their introduction had taken place at Bulwer-Lytton's [6] home in 1832 when Disraeli had described her as "a pretty little woman, a flirt, and a rattle; indeed, gifted with a volubility I should think unequalled and of which I can convey no idea. She told me that she liked 'silent, melancholy men.' I observed that I had no doubt of it." She had interested herself almost immediately in his political career, and after marriage she not only made for him a comfortable and cheerful home but, in spite of an education woefully lacking in historical information, seems to have given useful advice concerning his treatment of individuals and problems alike.

In the decade of the forties came the break with Peel. It may be that Disraeli had analyzed his position clearly enough in his own mind so that he realized the incompatibility existing between his own creed and the middle-class policies of his titular

[5] February 7, 1833; cf. Monypenny, *The Life of Benjamin Disraeli*, I, 223.

[6] Now best known perhaps as author of *The Last Days of Pompeii*.

leader. It is possible that he resented the omission of his name in the ministry formed by Peel. It is possible that he sincerely adjudged Peel lacking in political morality when the latter led a Parliament elected on the principle of protection toward free trade. It is conceivable that he firmly adhered to protection as a policy necessary for the welfare of the nation. His speeches in 1843 do take the question of protection out of the realm of mathematics and place it on the basis of political philosophy ("Explanation to Constituents of His Votes in Parliament," page 204).

Whatever may have been the causes for the break, Disraeli's attacks were bitterly personal and at the same time so able as to arouse the Conservative party to revolt (cf. "Agricultural Interest —Sir Robert Peel," page 210). After Peel's fall the Conservatives were divided—the Peelites remaining independent for a time and eventually gravitating toward the Liberals and the Protectionists functioning nominally under the leadership of Lord George Bentinck while Disraeli was grooming himself for the task of reviving the party. Disraeli showed political courage alike in his speech of 1847 in which amid the silence of his partisans he came out for the removal of Jewish disabilities [7] (cf. page 212), in his acceptance of the office of Chancellor of the Exchequer in the Derby ministry of 1852, and in his assent to free trade as an accomplished fact. The rejection of his budget by the House which he led for his party caused an election unfavorable to the Conservatives. The Aberdeen coalition government was formed, and on its failure Derby, by refusing to form an administration, gave the opportunity to Palmerston that Disraeli so ardently desired. Palmerston dominated politics, except for the break in 1858-1859 when Disraeli again was leader of the House and Chancellor of the Exchequer under Derby, for the rest of his life and so cut into the authority of Conservative leaders that the Conservative party seemed willing to follow the elder statesman who represented such moderate liberalism. Disraeli made many able speeches during the period: one, dealing with the subject of the gains to a country by a national church and the loss contingent upon disestablishment, is accounted by a

[7] To this period belongs the publication of *Tancred* (1847), the theme of which deals with religion.

biographer[8] as the best discussion on the subject with which he had met.

Gladstone became the heir of Palmerston but failed with the question of Parliamentary reform in 1866. Opportunity therefore again came to Disraeli, who, under Derby, introduced and passed by skillful maneuvering the Reform Bill of 1867. For his attitude on the subject, see page 216.

In the next year the goal was attained—Disraeli became Prime Minister upon the resignation of Derby. His bid for power through the enfranchisement of the working class in the boroughs brought no immediate results, and, turned out by the election of 1868, he spent a period of more than five years in opposition. But he did not allow the country to forget that he stood for "the cause of the Tory party, the English Constitution, and of the British Empire," nor did he fail to take advantage of Gladstone's growing unpopularity. For his skillful attack on the Liberals and also a defense of English institutions, see "Conservative Principles" (page 222).

On return to power in 1874 Disraeli's history becomes the history of his nation. His Tory democracy hardly produced as many essential measures for public welfare as might have been anticipated, but Gladstone had just made reforms a bit distasteful. And in affairs other than domestic he gave the nation as much drama as might be expected to come from the hero of *Vivian Grey*. Suez Canal shares were purchased (cf. Disraeli's defense, page 237), the Royal Titles Bill was passed,[9] and participation in the Balkan situation and the Berlin Congress saved Turkey from destruction, gave "peace with honor," and secured immediate popularity for himself that knew no bounds.

Inclement weather, poor crops, financial failures, and ever-increasing competition with foreign products soon led to discontent, however, so that by the election date of 1881 popular favor had turned to Gladstone. Five years before, Disraeli had gone to the House of Lords as the Earl of Beaconsfield.[10] "The Liberal

---

[8] T. E. Kebbel, *Lord Beaconsfield and Other Tory Memories* (London: Cassell and Co., Ltd., 1907), p. 29. The speech was delivered on October 30, 1862.

[9] Cf. his speech on the subject in Hansard (CCXXVII, 1719-27).

[10] The public seems to have preferred to use the name of the commoner. See, in *Punch*, "In Memoriam," April 30, 1881.

Policies" (page 245) comprises a speech dealing with foreign affairs that he gave three and a half months before his death.

Perhaps it is not unjust to Disraeli to say that he believed that a political party could better utilize a faith rather than statistical information as the basis of its action. Details and exact data were less apt to bother him than Gladstone. His attitude toward protection in the forties has already been mentioned. There is doubt regarding whether he knew how far certain principles which he accepted as guidance in passing the Reform Bill of 1867 would take him toward democracy. His lack of information on the subject of ritualism led to blunders on the Public Worship Regulation Bill of 1874. The conclusion has therefore been occasionally vouchsafed that he was superficial—the exponent of flashy theories. On the other hand, generalizations that he expressed have remained so potent that in the twentieth century leading statesmen have ascribed their policies both domestic and imperial to the genius of the remaker of Tory traditions.

Regarding his oratory, he is known less for his flights of eloquence than for his wit and sarcasm. Apt to be somewhat monotonous as a speaker, he aroused his audience when he was making his "points." And as a sympathetic biographer points out: "A brilliant repartee, a happy illustration, a choice metaphor, remain embedded in the popular memory, when longer and even higher flights of oratory are forgotten." [11]

[11] T. E. Kebbel, *Selected Speeches* (London, 1882), I, xi.

1. Chartism

Mr. Thomas Attwood, M.P. for Birmingham, moved on July 12, 1839, that "the House do resolve itself into a Committee of the whole House, for the purpose of taking into consideration the peti- *tion called the National Petition." Disraeli spoke upon the conclusion of Lord John Russell's speech (cf. HANSARD, XLIX [3d Ser.], 246-52). For data on the Chartist Movement, see page 84.*

Mr. D'Israeli [12] entirely agreed with the noble Lord as to the fallacy he had pointed out, as pervading this petition—that political rights necessarily ensured social happiness. But although they did not approve of the remedy suggested by the Chartists, it did not follow they should not attempt to cure the disease complained of. He did not think they had, up to the present moment, clearly seen what the disease really was. He could not believe, that a movement which, if not national was yet most popular, could have been produced by those common means of sedition to which the noble Lord had referred. Unquestionably, there was more or less of a leaven of sedition mixing itself up with all popular commotions; but he could not believe, that a petition signed by considerably upwards of 1,000,000 of our fellow-subjects could have been brought about by those ordinary means which were always in existence and which, five, ten, or fifteen years ago, were equally powerful in themselves, without producing any equal results.

It has been supposed, that the basis of this movement was strictly economical. He had great doubts of that, because he found, that where there were economical causes for national movements they led to tumult, but seldom to organization. He admitted also, on the other hand, that this movement was not occasioned by any desire of political rights. Political rights had so much of an abstract character, their consequences acted so slightly on the multitude, that he did not believe they could ever be the origin of any great popular movement. But there was something between an economical and a political cause, which might be the spring of this great movement, as the noble Lord must himself admit it to be. It might be mistaken, but all must confess, that it was considerable. The real cause of this, as all real popular movements, not stimulated by the aristocracy, and which, if not permanent, were still of material importance, was an

---

[12] An old spelling. The use of the third person for this report may properly lead to the observation that Disraeli wrote on July 2, 1876: "The Parliamentary reporters, who are mere machines, never discovered till too late that a considerable Parliamentary event was occurring."

apprehension on the part of the people, that their civil rights were invaded. Civil rights partook in some degree of an economical, and in some degree certainly of a political character. They conduced to the comfort, the security, and the happiness of the subject, and at the same time were invested with a degree of sentiment, which mere economical considerations did not involve. Now, he maintained, that the civil rights of the people of England had been invaded. There had been, undoubtedly, perhaps with no evil intention, perhaps from a foolish desire of following a false philosophy, and applying a system of government not suited to the character of this country, and borrowed from the experience of another—there had been, from whatever motive, an invasion of the civil rights of the English people of late years; and he believed the real cause of this movement was a sentiment on the part of the people of England, that their civil rights had been invaded. That sentiment had doubtless been taken advantage of by trading agitators, but it was participated by much more than agitators, and that discontented minority which must ever exist in all countries.

He was not one of those who ascribed the people's Charter, as it was called, to the New Poor Law; [13] but, at the same time, he believed there was an intimate connexion between the two. He ascribed the Charter and the New Poor Law to the same origin to which they owed many evils they now experienced, and many more with which they were menaced, the consequences of which, if he were not much mistaken, might yet be severely felt by persons superior to those who had signed this petition. The origin of this movement in favour of the Charter dated about the same time they had passed their Reform Bill. He was not going to entrap the House into any discussion on the merits of the constitution they had destroyed, and that which had replaced it. He had always said, that he believed its character was not understood by those who assailed it, and perhaps not fully by those who defended it. All would admit this—the old constitution had an intelligible principle, which the present had not. The former invested a small portion of the nation with political rights. Those rights were intrusted to that small class on certain conditions—that they should guard the civil rights of the great multitude. It was not even left to them as a matter of honour; society was so constituted, that they were intrusted with duties which they were obliged to fulfill. They had transferred a great part of that political power to a new class, whom they had not invested with those great public duties. Great duties

[13] It is interesting to compare Disraeli's statement with the thesis in Mark Hovell, *The Chartist Movement* (Manchester: University Press, 1918).

could alone confer great station, and the new class which had been invested with political station had not been bound up with the great mass of the people by the exercise of social duties. For instance, the administration of justice, the regulation of parishes, the building of roads and bridges, the command of the militia and police, the employment of labour, the distribution of relief to the destitute—these were great duties which, ordinarily, had been confined to that body in the nation which enjoyed and exercised political power.

But now they had a class which had attained that great object which all the opulent desired—political power without the conditions annexed to its possession, and without fulfilling the duties which it should impose. What was the consequence? Those who thus possessed power without discharging its conditions and duties were naturally anxious to put themselves to the least possible expense and trouble. Having gained that object, for which others were content to sacrifice trouble and expense, they were anxious to keep it without any appeal to their pocket, and without any cost of their time. To gain their objects, they raised the cry of cheap government—that served the first: to attain the second, they called for the constant interference of the Government. But he contended, they could not have a cheap and centralized Government, and maintain at the same time the civil rights of the people of England. He believed this was the real cause of the Charter; a large body of the people found out that their civil rights had been invaded. They had invaded their civil rights. The New Poor Law Act was an invasion of their civil rights. They could not deny, that they had based that New Poor Law upon a principle that outraged the whole social duties of the State—the mainstay, the living source of the robustness of the commonwealth. They taught the destitute not to look for relief to those who were their neighbours, but to a distant Government stipendiary. They taught the unfortunate labourer, that he had no legal claim to relief—that the relief he should receive must be an affair of charity; and he believed, that the discontent such alterations had occasioned was really the *vis inertiae* of which the active sedition of the country had availed itself—this movement for the Charter.

He knew it would be said, that Gentlemen on that (the Opposition) side of the House, were answerable for the New Poor Law as well as others. He admitted it; but the people of the country did not visit its enactment with the same acrimony upon those who assisted as upon those who originated it; and for this reason, they could not forget that they assisted the party opposite to obtain power, and the feeling of disappointment, the vindictive sentiment was excited only by the Government and its supporters, not by those who were opposed to them, although joining in passing that bill. He thought their consenting to such a bill was a very great blunder. The fact was, when the Tory party, shattered, and apparently destroyed, rose from the stupor in which they found themselves, they began to think they should have a slice of the cake and fruits of reform—that they should have some of the advantages of the cheap government system—and he believed they would yet rue the day they did so, for they had acted contrary to principle—the principle of opposing everything like central government, and favouring in every possible degree the distribution of power.

He admitted, that the prayer of the National Petition involved the great fallacy of supposing that social evils would be cured by political rights; but the fallacy was not confined to these poor Chartists. He had never passed an evening in that House that he did not hear some honourable Gentlemen say, that the people were starving, and that the only remedy was household suffrage. Was that proposition less absurd than the prayer of this petition which had been so severely criticized by the noble Lord? The petitioners demanded annual Parliaments; but whether a man called for annual or triennial Parliaments, undoubtedly the change applied for was great in either case, and he did not think the noble Lord [14] was justified in speaking in terms of derision. At least, it was futile to attempt drawing the line between the requirements of the petition and the suggestions of some of his own supporters. The fact, however, was, although the opinions of some of the supporters of the noble Lord's Government might be somewhat in advance of his own, they were still supposed to be perfectly compatible with the exercise of political powers by that class he had created, by whose influence he had obtained place, and with whose assistance he still hoped to retain power. But if the noble Lord supposed, that in this country he could establish a permanent Government on what was styled nowadays, a monarchy of the middle classes, he would be indulging a great delusion, which, if persisted in, must shake our institutions and endanger the Throne. He believed, such a system was actually foreign to the character of the people of England. He believed, that in this country, the exercise of political power must be associated with great public duties. The English nation would concede any degree of political power to a class making simultaneous advances in the exercise of the great social duties. That was the true principle to adhere to; in proportion as they departed from it, they were wrong; as they kept by it, they would approximate to that happy state of things which had been described as so desirable

[14] Lord John Russell.

by the honourable Member for Birmingham. The noble Lord had answered the speech of the honourable Member for Birmingham, but he had not answered the Chartists. The honourable Member for Birmingham had made a very dexterous speech, a skillful evolution in favour of the middle classes. But although he had attempted to dovetail the Charter on the Birmingham Union, all that had recently taken place on the appearance of the Chartists before the leaders of the union newly-created magistrates, and the speeches by members of the Convention within the last few days, led to a very different conclusion. There he found the greatest hostility to the middle classes. They complained only of the government by the middle classes. They made no attack on the aristocracy—none on the Corn laws—but upon the newly-enfranchised constituency, not on the old—upon that peculiar constituency which was the basis of the noble Lord's Government. He was aware this subject was distasteful to both of the parties in that House. He regretted it.

He was not ashamed to say, however much he disapproved of the Charter, he sympathised with the Chartists. They formed a great body of his countrymen; nobody could doubt they laboured under great grievances, and it would indeed have been a matter of surprise and little to the credit of that House, if Parliament had been prorogued without any notice being taken of what must always be considered a very remarkable social movement. They had now sat five months; their time had not been particularly well occupied, and he would just call to the attention of the House some of the circumstances which had occurred with reference to this subject. Early in the Session they had heard of lords-lieutenant of counties, noblemen and gentlemen of great influence, leaving the metropolis, travelling by railroads, putting themselves at the head of the yeomanry, capturing and relieving towns, and returning just in time to vote on some important division; and certainly he should have expected that some notice, at least, would have been taken of the occurrence by the noble Lord, the Secretary of State for the Home Department.[15] A short time afterwards, the petition called the "National Petition," was brought forward by the honourable Gentleman. He called it the National Petition by courtesy. The noble Lord had been critical upon it—he said, it was not national; the noble Lord also said, he was at the head of the reform Government, which some ventured to think was not a reform Government. They should take titles as they found them; but it had a very good title to be called "national" when it was signed by a large portion of the nation. By a sort of chilling courtesy, the honourable Member was

[15] Lord John Russell

allowed to state the contents of the petition, but the noble Lord said nothing—he gave no sign, and it was only by an accident, he believed, they had been favoured with his remarks that evening—remarks which showed great confidence in the state of the country, in the temper and virtue of the labouring classes—great confidence in himself and in his Government. He hoped the noble Lord had good and efficient reasons for the tone of confidence which he had assumed, and the air, he would not say of contumely, but of captiousness with which he had met this motion. The observations of the noble Lord would go forth to the world, and if the inference he drew from them were wrong, prompt justice would, no doubt, be done him. The noble Lord might despise the Chartists; he might despise 1,280,000 of his fellow-subjects because they were discontented; but if he were a Minister of the Crown, he should not so treat them, even if he thought them unreasonable. The noble Lord had his colonies in a condition so satisfactory—the war in the East seemed drawing to a close—his monetary system was in so healthy a state—that he could afford to treat with such nonchalance a social insurrection at his very threshold. Perhaps it was in vain to expect, whatever might be the state of the country, much attention from her Majesty's Government. Their time was so absorbed, so monopolized, in trying to make Peers, and promising to make Baronets, that but little time could now be given by them to such a subject as this; but probably in the recess, when cabinet councils would be held more frequently, they would give it some consideration. He believed that if they did not, and that if they treated it as a mere temporary ebullition, which was rather the result of a plethoric vein than of any other cause, they would be grievously mistaken; for the seeds were sown, which would grow up to the trouble and dishonour of the realm. He was convinced that if they persisted in their present system of cheap and centralized government, they would endanger not only the national character but also the national throne.

2. Explanation to Constituents of His Votes in Parliament

In the early part of his speech (cf. Kebbel's Selected Speeches [London, 1882]), Disraeli defended Sir Robert Peel against the attacks of the extreme protectionists who did not like the governmental policies of 1842. For himself, he would not pledge himself "to miserable questions of 6d. in 7s. 6d. or 8s. of duties about corn"; what he wished to secure was "the preponderance of the landed interest."

He continued:

Gentlemen, we hear a great deal in the present day upon the subject of the feudal system. I have heard from the lips of Mr. Cobden—no, I have not heard him say it, as I was not present to hear the celebrated speech he made in Drury Lane Theatre—but we have all heard how Mr. Cobden, who is a very eminent person, has said, in a very memorable speech, that England was the victim of the feudal system, and we have all heard how he has spoken of the barbarism of the feudal system, and of the barbarous relics of the feudal system. Now, if we have any relics of the feudal system, I regret that not more of it is remaining. Think one moment—and it is well you should be reminded of what this is, because there is no phrase more glibly used in the present day than "the barbarism of the feudal system." Now, what is the fundamental principle of the feudal system, gentlemen? It is that the tenure of all property shall be the performance of its duties. Why, when the Conqueror carved out parts of the land, and introduced the feudal system, he said to the recipient, "You shall have that estate, but you shall do something for it: you shall feed the poor; you shall endow the Church; you shall defend the land in case of war; and you shall execute justice and maintain truth to the poor for nothing."

It is all very well to talk of the barbarities of the feudal system, and to tell us that in those days when it flourished a great variety of gross and grotesque circumstances and great miseries occurred but these were not the result of the feudal system; they were the result of the barbarism of the age. They existed not from the feudal system, but in spite of the feudal system. The principle of the feudal system, the principle which was practically operated upon, was the noblest principle, the grandest, the most magnificent and benevolent that was ever conceived by sage, or ever practised by patriot. Why, when I hear a political economist, or an Anti-Corn-Law Leaguer, or some conceited Liberal reviewer come forward and tell us, as a grand discovery of modern science, twitting and taunting, perhaps, some unhappy squire who cannot respond to the alleged discovery—when I hear them say, as the great discovery of modern science, that "Property has its duties as well as its rights," my answer is that that is but a feeble plagiarism of the very principle of that feudal system which you are always reviling. Let me next tell those gentlemen who are so fond of telling us that property has its duties as well as its rights, that labour also has rights as well as its duties; and when I see masses of property raised in this country which do not recognize that principle; when I find men making fortunes by a method which permits them (very often in a very few years) to purchase the lands of the old territorial aristocracy of the country, I cannot help remembering that those millions are accumulated by a mode which does not recognize it as a duty "to endow the Church, to feed the poor, to guard the land, and to execute justice for nothing." And I cannot help asking myself, when I hear of all this misery, and of all this suffering; when I know that evidence exists in our Parliament of a state of demoralisation in the once happy population of this land, which is not equalled in the most barbarous countries, which we suppose the more rude and uncivilised in Asia are—I cannot help suspecting that this has arisen because property has been permitted to be created and held without the performance of its duties.

Now, I want to ask the gentlemen who are members of the Anti-Corn-Law League, the gentlemen who are pressing on the Government of the country, on the present occasion, the total repeal and abolition of the Corn Laws—I want to know whether they have soberly considered how far they are personally responsible for this degraded state of our population. And I want them to consider this most important point, which has never yet been properly brought before any deliberative assembly—how far the present law of succession and inheritance in land will survive—if that falls—if we recur to the Continental system of parcelling out landed estates—I want to know how long you can maintain the political system of the country? The estate of the Church which I mentioned; that estate of the poor to which I made allusion; those traditionary manners and associations which spring out of the land, which form the national character, which form part of the possession of the poor not to be despised, and which is one of the most important elements of political power—they will tell you "Let it go." My answer to that is, "If it goes, it is a revolution, a great, a destructive revolution." For these reasons, gentlemen, I believe in that respect, faithfully representing your sentiments, that I have always upheld that law which, I think, will uphold and maintain the preponderance of the agricultural interests of the country. I do not wish to conceal the ground upon which I wish to uphold it. I never attempted to uphold it by talking of the peculiar burthens, which, however, I believe, may be legitimately proved, or indulging in many of those arguments in favour of the Corn Laws which may or may not be sound, but which are always brought forward with a sort of hesitating consciousness which may be assumed to be connected with futility. I take the only broad and only safe line—namely, that what we ought to uphold is, the preponderance of the landed interest; that the preponderance of the landed interest has made England; that it is an immense element of political power and stability; that we should never have been able to undertake the great war in which we embarked in the memory of many present—that we could never have been able to conquer the greatest military genius the world ever saw, with the greatest means at his disposal, and to hurl him from his throne, if we had not had a territorial aristocracy to give stability to our constitution.

And I mean to say this, that if we had not done that, if we had not had that territorial power, and that preponderance of the landowner in our constitution, I do not see why Great Britain, probably very contented and very prosperous, should have been a greater power than Denmark or Sweden; but I for one am not prepared to sit under the power of a third-class if I can be a citizen of a first-class Empire. And I do not believe that any man who listens to me can differ with me upon that point. It is enough that you were born in Shropshire, that you are a portion of that ancient county, that you were born in a county full of historical recollections, a county that has taken the lead of all others in public affairs, a county where, as Lord Clarendon says, "the Cavaliers' blood lives." It is enough that you have undergone great vicissitudes; it is enough that you have lived under various dynasties; it is enough that you have sprung from a race that has done something; it is enough that you can talk of your ancestors as of a people that can be remembered—it is enough to know all this in order to feel that you do not want to be put in the catalogue of new States which may hereafter turn out something or may not—in fact, to feel that you do not want to be turned into a sort of a spinning-jenny machine kind of a nation. You want, in fact, to *be* a great people, because you *are* a great people, and because you feel that the exertions of your fathers and your own aspirations entitle you to that position: and it seems to be a reasonable ambition.

Before I sit down I do not wish to close without an observation on those who are always finding fault with the humbler classes of the community—who at the same time charitably say they are not responsible for their deterioration. I confess that, as far as I can form an opinion, the deterioration of society is not to be found only among the labourers of the country. It is not in the squalid dwellings; it is not in the miserable details of sickening poverty, that this deterioration may be found; but, in my opinion, that heroic nobility which formed this country, and that spirited gentry which has so often come forward to vindicate our rights or to defend our liberties, and which have also been the main source of our commercial greatness—for it is the nobility and gentry of the land who have founded our greatest colonies—in my opinion the present race is deficient in those qualities. There are, however, great exceptions to be made, even in the higher classes of the country; but there is a miserable philosophy of the day which ascribes everything to "the spirit of the age"—that thinks nothing is to be done by the influence of individual character, which is, after all, the only inducement to great actions, the only spur to great achievements. That opinion is much too prevalent; and there is no question that it is not merely among the lower classes that we find a lack of those great qualities which hitherto have always been associated with the noble, national character of England.

I told you when I saw you first that I should maintain, so far as my vote could maintain, the preponderance of the landed interest. I am of that opinion still. I believe the landed interest should be the basis of our political and social system. But if there be others who are of a different opinion, if it be—which I do not believe— that there are those of a different opinion in high places, and that these alterations may be brought forward, and perhaps even passed, do not let us for a moment disguise from ourselves the influence which such an event must have, I will not say upon the political power, or social condition, or financial prosperity of the country, for these are great themes, but upon the more limited but most interesting topic of the construction of parties. Rest assured, if these changes are brought forward, whoever may be the person to propose them, that we are on the eve of an age of great party convulsion—that we are on the eve of an age when we shall see no more permanent Governments, no more strong Governments, no more administrations carrying out from long and patient experience and conviction the remedies of the faults of their predecessors. Then let me tell you that, in that time, they who look for benefit from the hands of public men, or look to the favour of Courts, or the confidence of ministers, will build upon a rock of sand. No public man at that time will be in a position in which he can pursue his career who has not the power to cast his anchor deep in the rock of some great constitutional constituency. As for myself, if that happens, I shall come to you and tell you, "I am here; we are beaten; but I have done my duty. Remember what I told you when we met in the Music Hall at Shrewsbury in 1843; I told you what might happen; I told you I did not believe it would occur, but if it did occur I was prepared to act; I told you then that I had elected to support that cause which I believe upholds the power and prosperity of my country, and the social happiness of all classes. Others have thought differently; the majority, perhaps the enlightened majority, animated by that 'spirit of the age' which hitherto we have seen, have thought differently, and have had the power to act differently."

But I have still some confidence in the national character of Englishmen. I know well that before this, the country has experienced great vicissitudes. I know well that we had in England more revolutions, and upon a greater scale, than in any other country in the world. It is utterly impossible, indeed, for the French Revolution, or any other, to embrace more comprehensive objects. You have had the majesty of England brought to the block; you have had the Church, personified by Archbishop Laud, brought to the block; you have had the administration, in the person of Strafford, brought to the block—the king, the minister, and the archbishop. You have had the House of Lords voted a nuisance. You have had the House of Commons kicked out in an ignominious manner by a military officer. You have had the Church completely sequestrated. All this has happened in England. But before a quarter of a century passed over, you returned to your old laws, your old habits, your old traditions, your old convictions. In 1648 Oliver Cromwell slept at Whitehall; in 1688 [16] Charles II followed his example. And shall I tell you the reason why, after circumstances so wonderful, though no historian has noticed it; though you saw every trace of the social system uprooted by the most prejudicial, grasping, and subtle enemies that were ever invented; though the vessel became a wreck, and the king, the Church, and the constitution were swept away, the nation returned to itself? Shall I tell you how it was that the nation returned to itself, and Old England, after the deluge, was seen rising above the waters? This was the reason—because during all that fearful revolution you never changed the tenure of your landed property. That, I think, gentlemen, proves my case; and if we have baffled a wit like Oliver Cromwell, let us not be staggered even before Mr. Cobden. The acres remained; the estates remained. The generations changed: the Puritan father died, and the Cavalier son came into his place, and, backed by that power and influence,

[16] Manifestly a misstatement.

the nation reverted to the ancient principles of the realm. And this, gentlemen, is the reason why you have seen an outcry raised against your Corn Laws. Your Corn Laws are merely the out-work of a great system fixed and established upon your territorial property, and the only object the Leaguers have in making themselves masters of the outwork is that they may easily overcome the citadel.

3. Agricultural Interest—Sir Robert Peel

Disraeli, making use of a motion before the House "to take into consideration in the distribution of the surplus revenue the claims of the agricultural interest," delivered a philippic against Sir Robert Peel. Only the last section of the speech, which can be found in Hansard *(LXXVIII [3d Ser.], 1022-28 [March 17, 1845]), is given. It is inserted to show not only the unwillingness of Disraeli to change opinions along with Peel on the question of protection but also his remarkable faculty in employing biting sarcasm.*

There is no doubt a difference in the right honourable gentleman's demeanour as leader of the Opposition and as minister of the Crown. But that's the old story; you must not contrast too strongly the hours of courtship with the years of possession. 'Tis very true that the right honourable gentleman's conduct is different. I remember him, making his protection speeches. They were the best speeches I ever heard. It was a great thing to hear the right honourable gentleman say, "I would rather be the leader of the gentlemen of England than possess the confidence of sovereigns." That was a grand thing. We don't hear much of "the gentlemen of England" now. But what of that? They have the pleasures of memory—the charms of reminiscences. They were his first love, and though he may not kneel to them now as in the hour of passion, still they can recall the past; and nothing is more useless or unwise than these scenes of crimination and reproach, for we know that in all these cases, when the beloved object has ceased to charm, it is in vain to appeal to the feelings. You know that this is true. Every man almost has gone through it. My honourable friends reproach the right honourable gentleman. The right honourable gentleman does what he can to quiet them; he sometimes takes refuge in arrogant silence, and sometimes he treats them with haughty frigidity; and if they knew anything of human nature they would take the hint and shut their mouths. But they won't. And what then happens? What happens under all such circumstances? The right honourable gentleman, being compelled to interfere, sends down his valet, who says in the genteelest manner, "We can have no whining here." And that, Sir, is exactly the case of the great agricultural interest—that beauty which everybody wooed, and one deluded. There is a fatality in such charms, and we now seem to approach the same condition that Protestantism was in 1828. The country will draw its moral. For my part if we are to have free trade, I, who honour genius, prefer that such measures should be proposed by the honourable member for

Stockport; [17] than by one who, through skilful Parliamentary manoeuvres, has tampered with the generous confidence of a great people and of a great party. For myself, I care not what may be the result. Dissolve, if you please, the Parliament you have betrayed, and appeal to the people, who, I believe, mistrust you. For me there remains this at least—the opportunity of expressing thus publicly my belief that a Conservative Government is an Organised Hypocrisy.

[17] Richard Cobden.

4. Disabilities of the Jews

This speech can be found in HANSARD *(XCV [3d Ser.], 1321-30 [December 16, 1847]). It was given in support of Lord John Russell's motion, "That the House will resolve itself into a Committee on the removal of the civil and political Disabilities affecting Her Majesty's Jewish Subjects." Restrictions of 1828 were connected with the words, "true faith of a Christian," in a required oath. The Commons had passed more than* *once during the decade of the thirties a bill necessary for removing the disabilities that kept Jews out of Parliament. The Lords rejected the measures. In 1847 the city elected both Lord John Russell and Baron Rothschild to the Commons. This situation was fitted for Lord John's reforming zeal. Disraeli, the heir of Jewish traditions and a member of the Anglican Church since boyhood's day, was naturally in position to offer interesting comments.*

- - - - - - - - - - - -

What are the circumstances of the case? [18] It affects those subjects of the Queen who profess the Jewish religion. They are not many in point of number—they are a people who do not hold monster meetings; they do not form themselves into societies to act against the law; but they are a people who come and make an appeal to this House, and who ask the House whether it be prepared—as I hope it will be prepared—to admit that appeal; and among other reasons on account of the religious associations connected with the subject, I agree with the noble Lord the Member for Bath (Lord Ashley) in considering this a religious question.

For who are these persons professing the Jewish religion? They are persons who acknowledge the same God as the Christian people of this realm. They acknowledge the same divine revelation as yourselves. They are, humanly speaking, the authors of your religion. They are unquestionably those to whom you are indebted for no inconsiderable portion of your known religion, and for the whole of your divine knowledge.

Well, then, Sir, there is a prima facie reason to suppose—looking at the question upon the surface with regards to its religious associations—that the representatives of a Christian community should not look with disfavour at such an appeal made by such persons. ["Oh, Oh!"] Some Gentleman whom I do not know, and whom I cannot see, appears to express dissent. He probably is one of those who look with disfavour upon the appeal made by the Jewish people; but he appears to me to represent upon the present occasion

[18] The omitted paragraphs deal with the principle of religious liberty.

212

a small minority; because I observed that many persons who have
spoken against the proposition of the noble Lord (Lord J. Russell)
have admitted the extraordinary claims of those who profess the
Jewish religion to participate in the rights and privileges of a
Christian society, and they have felt unable to get over that difficulty. The noble Lord the Member for Bath was a signal example
of that position. I had the misfortune not to hear a portion of
that which I will call the noble speech of the noble Lord the
Member for Bath. But I had the gratification of listening to the
last and much the larger portion of his address; and if I had not
known anything about this House, I might have supposed him
to be some person rising with the inspiration of his subject, and
speaking with great authority, so irresistible was the noble Lord's
argument and so rich his illustrations, had he not ended by opposing the Motion, and acknowledging more than once that he felt
a great difficulty in assigning a distinct reason for that opposition.

The Minister, when he introduced this question to-night, felt
it necessary to glance with some obscurity to the only tangible
reason which could influence them and other Governments in
opposing the admission into Parliament of persons holding the
Jewish religion. This reason was only partly adverted to by the
Minister; but the noble Lord the Member for Bath, with the earnestness of his heart in the subject, told us that the real cause of
the prejudice against the Jews is, that they are looked upon by
the people of this country—by portions of them at least—as having
incurred a penal retribution for the crucifixion of our Lord. The
noble Lord (Lord Ashley) placed that question before the House;
and it is only because he did so that I allude to the subject. But
the strange feature in the case is, that the noble Lord stated at
the same moment, that he gave no credit to that proposition; and
that he could not bring his mind to believe that the existing Jewish
population in this or any country were, in consequence of that
mysterious and most important event in the annals of the world,
liable to any such punishment. It is well known that long before
that momentous event, the Jewish people had been dispersed
through many lands, and that the Jews of this and other European
countries may have sprung from those who had left Palestine
long before that event. The noble Lord said, then, there was no
ground for entertaining that belief. But if that is not the cause of
the opposition to the present Motion—and that is the cause out
of doors—what is the definite ground which you bring forward
in opposition to the Jewish claims? I leave the question of religious
freedom to work its own way; and I will not advert to that portion
of the subject which the noble Lord opposite (Lord J. Russell)

has touched with the ability of a master. But I look to the opposition of Gentlemen on this side of the House who object to this Motion on the ground of religious truth; and I say that it is on that ground, as well as on the ground of religious freedom, that I feel bound to give my vote for the proposition of the Minister—for if faith is valued as a sanction of conduct, with what consistency can a Christian people say that those to whom they are indebted for the doctrines of their faith—who profess the religion which every Gentleman in this House professes—for every Gentleman here does profess the Jewish religion, and believes in Moses and the Prophets? ["Oh!"] I find that there are Gentlemen who, it seems, do not believe in Moses and the Prophets, and that gives some strength to the observation made tonight about Gibbon and Hume.[19] But until I heard this scoff, I thought this was a position in the argument which might be regarded as established, and which was too clear to need refutation. Well, then I say that if religion is a security for righteous conduct, you have that security in the instance of the Jews who profess a true religion. It may not be in your more comprehensive form. I do not say it is the true religion; but although they do not profess all that we profess, all that they do profess is true.

You must admit, then, that in men who are subject to the Divine revelations that you acknowledge—whose morals are founded on the sacred oracles to which we all bow—that as far as religion can be a security for their conduct—for their public morality and justice—you have in the religion of the Jews the best sanction in the world except that of our own Christianity. You will hardly say that the religion of the Jews is not a security for their moral conduct; but then you will say, that if you admit the Jews into this House on the principle advocated by the noble Lord, you will re-christianise the country, and the professors of other religions, not like the Jews, and which have not so great an affinity to that which we profess, may enter into the House. But the best evidence in the face of Europe of our Christian sincerity is, that we admit the Jews to the highest privileges of citizenship and to the highest offices of the State, without so admitting the professors of other religions. The very reason for admitting the Jews is because they can show so near an affinity to you. Where is your Christianity, if you

[19] Sir R. H. Inglis acknowledged that Christian oaths had not excluded from office Gibbon and Hume. Gibbon, for a short time a Roman Catholic before becoming a Protestant again, is well known for his use of irony in chapters of *The Decline and Fall* which deal with the growth of the Christian church, and Hume is likewise well known for a doctrine of skepticism.

do not believe in their Judaism? Do not mix up, then, the consideration of a question which is so intimately allied to your own faith, with the different considerations that would apply to the Pagan and the Mahomedan. I am prepared to lay down the broadest principles as to the importance of maintaining a Christian character in this House and in this country; and yet it is on this very ground you will found and find the best argument for the admission of the Jews.[20]

[20] The remaining portion of the speech treats of Jewish-Christian relationships. At the end of it a restless House uttered calls of "Divide!"

5. The Reform Bill of 1867

The complete speech on the third reading of the Reform Bill of 1867 may be found in HANSARD *(CLXXXVIII [3d Ser.], 1599-1614 [July 15, 1867]). The first part of the speech traces the history of the attempts for Parliamentary reform since 1852 and tries to vindicate the bill before the House, especially against the attacks of Lord Cranborne, later Lord Salisbury, and Robert Lowe, who, with the help of forty or more followers of Whig leanings plus the voting power of the Conservative opposition, had brought defeat to Gladstone's bill of 1866. Lowe bitterly asserted that the principle of this bill was the principle of numbers as against wealth and intellect. England of necessity must turn her attention, therefore, to the education of the masses. Cranborne, a Conservative seceder from the Cabinet, declared that Disraeli had yielded to the demands of his political opponents: "If it be a Conservative triumph to have introduced a Bill guarded with precautions and securities, and to have abandoned every one of those precautions and securities at the bidding of your opponents, then in the whole course of your annals I will venture to say the Conservative Party has won no triumph so signal as this." Disraeli's defense follows.*

And, Sir, I think it cannot be said that this was a measure which bristled with securities and precautions that have been given up at the bidding of our opponents. That a great many of them have been given up I shall not deny; but they have been given up not always or in the greatest degree at the bidding of our opponents, and some of them have been given up to the general feeling of the House.[21]

Now, Sir, the noble lord [22] says that by yielding to these ten same conditions, I have virtually altered the whole character of the Bill. Now, is that true? Is the whole character of the Bill altered? I contend on the contrary, that the Bill, though adapted of course to the requirements of the year in which we are legislating, is at the same time in harmony with the general policy which we have

---

[21] It is true that Disraeli yielded to amendments on many points: a residence requirement which came to be twelve months instead of two years, inclusion of a lodger franchise, elimination of a dual-vote proposition, a lower occupation franchise in the counties, etc., but he did not yield to Gladstone's demand for a £5 rating franchise; rather he insisted on the proposition that every householder paying his own rates, if he met other qualifications, should have the right to vote. When a later amendment did away with compounding, thereby putting all occupiers of tenements upon the electoral lists, Disraeli's acceptance of the proposition really brought household suffrage to the nation's borough population.

[22] Lord Cranborne.

always maintained. [Laughter from the Opposition.] This is a question which cannot be settled by a jeer or a laugh, but by facts, and by facts and results which many of you deprecate and deplore at this moment, and in consequence of which you tell us that you mean to reopen the agitation—a thing which I defy you to do.

I begin with what the honourable gentleman [23] who smiles so serenely may regard as the most difficult question for us—namely, that of the borough franchise . . . . has there, I say, been no question, since the Government [24] of 1859, between retaining the £10 borough franchise [25] and accepting household suffrage? Have you not had the alternative offered of a multitude of schemes? Have you not heard of a franchise to be fixed at £8, £7, £6, and all sorts of pounds?

The question, therefore, for us practically to consider was—whether we were to accept this settlement of the borough franchise, we will say at £5, or whether we should adhere to the conviction at which we had arrived in 1859—namely, that if you reduced the qualification there was no safe resting-place until you came to a household rating franchise? The noble lord says that immense dangers are to arise to this country because we have departed from the £10 franchise. (Viscount Cranbourne: No.) Well, it was something like that, or because you have reduced the franchise. The noble lord is candid enough to see that if you had reduced it after what occurred in 1859, as you ought according to your pledges to have done, you would have had to reduce it again by this time. It is not likely that such a settlement of the difficulty would have been so statesmanlike that you could have allayed discontent or satisfied any great political demands by reducing the electoral qualification by 40s. or so. Then the question would arise—is there a greater danger from the number who would be admitted by a rating household franchise than from admitting the hundreds of thousands—the right honourable gentleman the member [26] for South Lancashire calculated them at 300,000—who would come in under a £5 franchise? I think that the danger would be less, that the feeling of the large number would be more national, than by only admitting what I call the Praetorian guard, a sort of class set aside, invested with peculiar privileges, looking with suspicion on their superiors, and with disdain on those beneath

[23] Robert Lowe.
[24] The Derby-Disraeli government.
[25] A qualification in the 1832 Reform Bill.
[26] Gladstone.

them, with no friendly feelings towards the institutions of their country and with great confidence in themselves. I think you would have a better chance of touching the popular heart, of evoking the national sentiment by embracing the great body of those men who occupy houses and fulfil the duties of citizenship by the payment of rates, than by the more limited and, in our opinion, more dangerous proposal.

So much for the franchise. I say that if we could not carry out our policy of 1859, the logical conclusion was that in settling the question we should make the proposition which you, after due consideration, have accepted, and which I hope you will to-night pass. Let us look at the other divisions of the subject. I will not test by little points the question of whether we have carried substantially the policy which we recommended. I say look to the distribution of seats. I am perfectly satisfied on the part of Her Majesty's Government with the distribution of seats which the House in its wisdom has sanctioned. I think it is a wise and prudent distribution of seats. I believe that upon reflection it will satisfy the country. It has been modified in one instance, to a certain degree, in favour of views which in principle we do not oppose; [27] but we have succeeded in limiting the application of that principle; and, on the whole, the policy which is embodied in the distribution of seats, which by reading this Bill a third time I hope you are going to adopt, is the policy of redistribution which on the part of the Conservative party I have now for nearly twenty years impressed on this House. And what is that policy? That you should completely disfranchise no single place; that it would be most unwise without necessity to disfranchise any centre of representation; that you should take the smaller boroughs with two members each and find the degree of representation which you wanted to supply in their surplus and superfluity of representation. You have acted upon that principle. But, above all, year after year I have endeavoured to impress on this House the absolute necessity of your doing justice to those vast, I may almost say, unrepresented millions, but certainly most inadequately represented millions, who are congregated in your counties. You may depreciate what you have agreed to, but in my opinion you have agreed to a very great measure. At any rate it is the first, and it is a very considerable, attempt to do justice in regard to the representation of the counties.

Then although I am the last person in any to under-rate the value of the assistance which Her Majesty's Government have

[27] A minority representation scheme.

received from the House in the management of this measure; although I believe there is no other example in the annals of Parliament when there has been such a fair interchange of ideas between the two sides of the House, and when, notwithstanding some bitter words and burning sentiments which we have occasionally listened to—and especially to-night—there has been, on the whole, a greater absence of party feeling and party management than has ever been exhibited in the conduct of a great measure; although personally I am deeply grateful to many honourable gentlemen opposite for the advice and aid I have received from them, yet I am bound to say that in the carrying of this measure with all that assistance, and with an unaffected desire on our part to defer to the wishes of the House wherever possible, I do think the Bill embodies the chief principles of the policy that we have professed, and which we have always advocated.

Well, but there is a right honourable gentleman who has to-night told us that he is no prophet, but who for half an hour indulged in a series of the most doleful vaticinations that were ever listened to. He says that everything is ruined, and he begins with the House of Lords.[28] Such a singular catalogue of political catastrophes, and such a programme of the injurious consequences of this legislation, were never heard of. The right honourable gentleman says, "There is the House of Lords; it is not of the slightest use now, and what do you think will happen to it when this Bill passes?" That was his argument. Well, my opinion is, if the House of Lords is at present in the position which the right honourable gentleman describes—and I am far from admitting it—then the passing of the Bill can do the House of Lords no harm, and it is very likely may do it a great deal of good. I think the increase of sympathy between the great body of the people and their natural leaders will be more likely to incite the House of Lords to action and to increased efforts to deserve and secure the gratitude and good feeling of the nation. "But," says the right honourable gentleman, "what is most terrible about the business of carrying this Bill is the treachery by which it has been accomplished." What I want to know from the right honourable gentleman is, when did the treachery begin? The right honourable gentleman thinks that a measure of Parliamentary Reform is an act of treachery, in consequence of what took place last year, when those who now bring it forward were in frequent council and co-operation with those who then and now oppose it. I can only say, for myself, that I hear of these mysterious councils for the first time. But if a compact was entered into last year, when

[28] Robert Lowe.

we were in Opposition, that no measure of Parliamentary Reform should pass, or any proposal with that object be made by us—if such a proposal is an act of treason, then the noble lord the member for Stamford [29] and his friends are as guilty of treachery as we who sit on these benches. Really I should have supposed that the right honourable gentleman would have weighed his words a little more; that when he talks of treachery he would have tried to define what he means, and that he would have drawn some hard and straight line to tell us where this treachery commenced. The right honourable gentleman, however, throws no light on the subject. He made a speech to-night which reminded me of the production of some inspired schoolboy, all about the battles of Chaeronea and of Hastings. I think he said that the people of England should be educated, but that the quality of the education was a matter of no consequence as compared with the quantity. Now, the right honourable gentleman seems to be in doubt as to what may be his lot in the new Parliament, and what I should recommend him to be —if he will permit me to give him advice—is the schoolmaster abroad. I should think that with his great power of classical and historical illustration the right honourable gentleman might soon be able to clear the minds of the new constituency of all "perilous stuff," and thus render them as soundly Conservative as he himself could desire.

I must, however, remind the right honourable gentleman when he tells us of the victims at Chaeronea, to whom he likens himself, that they died for their country, and died expressing their proud exultation that their blood should be shed in so sacred a cause. But this victim of Chaeronea takes the earliest opportunity, not of expressing his glory in his achievements and his sacrifice, but of absolutely announcing the conditions on which he is ready to join with those who have brought upon him so disgraceful a discomfiture. He has laid before us a programme to-night of all the revolutionary measures which he detests, but which in consequence of the passing of this Bill he is now prepared to adopt. The right honourable gentleman concluded his attack upon us by accusing us of treachery, and by informing us that he is going to support all those measures which he has hitherto opposed in this House—though I believe he advocated them elsewhere—and that he will recur, I suppose, to those Australian politics [30] which rendered him first so famous.

The right honourable gentleman told us that in the course we

[29] Lord Cranborne.

[30] Robert and Mrs. Lowe returned to London in 1850 after a long sojourn in Australia where he had displayed very liberal tendencies in politics.

are pursuing there is infamy. The expression is strong; but I never quarrel with that sort of thing, nor do I like on that account to disturb an honourable gentleman in his speech, particularly when he happens to be approaching his peroration. Our conduct, however, according to him, is infamous—that is his statement—because in office we are supporting measures of Parliamentary Reform which we disapprove, and to which we have hitherto been opposed. Well, if we disapprove the Bill which we are recommending the House to accept and sanction to-night, our conduct certainly would be objectionable. If we, from the bottom of our hearts do not believe that the measure which we are now requesting you to pass is on the whole the wisest and best that could be passed under the circumstances, I would even admit that our conduct was infamous. But I want to know what the right honourable gentleman thinks of his own conduct when, having assisted in turning out the Government of Lord Derby in 1859, because they would not reduce the borough franchise, he—if I am not much mistaken, having been one of the most active managers in that intrigue—the right honourable gentleman accepted office in 1860 under the Government of Lord Palmerston, who, of course, brought forward a measure of Parliamentary Reform which, it would appear, the right honourable gentleman also disapproved of, and more than disapproved, inasmuch as, although a member of the Government, he privately and successfully solicited his political opponents to defeat it. And yet this is the right honourable gentleman who talks of infamy.

Sir, the prognostications of evil uttered by the noble lord I can respect, because I know that they are sincere; the warnings and prophecies of the right honourable gentleman I treat in another spirit. For my part, I do not believe that the country is in danger. I think England is safe in the race of men who inhabit her; that she is safe in something much more precious than her accumulated capital—her accumulated experience; she is safe in her national character, in her fame, in the traditions of a thousand years, and in that glorious future which I believe awaits her.

6. Conservative Principles

This speech which contains the program of the Conservative party was given at Manchester, April 3, 1872. It may be found in Kebbel's Selected Speeches *(II, 490 et seq.). In it Disraeli not only emphasizes the place of Crown, Lords, Commons, and Church in government but he utilizes an opportunity to point out that the Liberal Party—in power since 1868—practices policies in both domestic and foreign affairs that deserve public opprobrium.*

Gentlemen, the Chairman has correctly reminded you that this is not the first time that my voice has sounded in this hall. But that was an occasion very different from that which now assembles us together—was nearly thirty years ago, when I endeavoured to support and stimulate the flagging energies of an institution in which I thought there were the germs of future refinement and intellectual advantage to the rising generation of Manchester, and since I have been here on this occasion I have learnt with much gratification that it is now counted among your most flourishing institutions. There was also another and more recent occasion when the gracious office fell to me to distribute among the members of the Mechanics' Institution those prizes which they had gained through their study in letters and in science. Gentlemen, these were pleasing offices, and if life consisted only of such offices you would not have to complain of it. But life has its masculine duties, and we are assembled here to fulfil some of the most important of these, when, as citizens of a free country, we are assembled together to declare our determination to maintain, to uphold the Constitution to which we are debtors, in our opinion, for our freedom and our welfare.

Gentlemen, there seems at first something incongruous that one should be addressing the population of so influential and intelligent a county as Lancashire who is not locally connected with them, and, gentlemen, I will frankly admit that this circumstance did for a long time make me hesitate in accepting your cordial and generous invitation. But, gentlemen, after what occurred yesterday, after receiving more than 200 addresses from every part of this great country, after the welcome which then greeted me, I feel that I should not be doing justice to your feelings, I should not do duty to myself, if I any longer considered my presence here to-night to be an act of presumption. Gentlemen, though it may not be an act of presumption, it still is, I am told, an act of great difficulty. Our opponents assure us that the Conservative party have no political programme; and, therefore, they must look with much satisfac-

tion to one whom you honour to-night by considering him the
leader and representative of your opinions when he comes forward,
at your invitation, to express to you what that programme is. The
Conservative party are accused of having no programme of policy.
If by a programme is meant a plan to despoil churches and plunder
landlords, I admit we have no programme. If by a programme is
meant a policy which assails or menaces every institution and
every interest, every class and every calling in the country, I admit
we have no programme. But if to have a policy with distinct ends,
and these such as most deeply interest the great body of the nation,
be a becoming programme for a political party, then, I contend,
we have an adequate programme, and one which, here or elsewhere, I shall always be prepared to assert and to vindicate.

Gentlemen, the programme of the Conservative party is to maintain the Constitution of the country. I have not come down to
Manchester to deliver an essay on the English Constitution; but
when the banner of Republicanism [31] is unfurled—when the fundamental principles of our institutions are controverted—I think, perhaps, it may not be inconvenient that I should make some few
practical remarks upon the character of our Constitution—upon that
monarchy, limited by the co-ordinate authority of Estates of the
realm, which, under the title of Queen, Lords and Commons, has
contributed so greatly to the prosperity of this country, and with
the maintenance of which I believe that prosperity is bound up.

Gentlemen, since the settlement of that Constitution, now nearly
two centuries ago, England has never experienced a revolution,
though there is no country in which there has been so continuous
and such considerable change. How is this? Because the wisdom
of your forefathers placed the prize of supreme power without the
sphere of human passions. Whatever the struggle of parties, whatever the strife of factions, whatever the excitement and exaltation
of the public mind, there has always been something in this country
round which all classes and parties could rally, representing the
majesty of the law, the administration of justice, and involving, at
the same time, the security for every man's rights and the fountain
of honour. Now, gentlemen, it is well clearly to comprehend
what is meant by a country not having a revolution for two centuries. It means, for that space, the unbroken exercise and enjoyment of the ingenuity of man. It means, for that space, the
continuous application of the discoveries of science to his comfort
and convenience. It means the accumulation of capital, the eleva-
tion of labour, the establishment of those admirable factories which

[31] Reference is to the activity of Sir Charles Dilke, Liberal.

cover your district; the unwearied improvement of the cultivation of the land, which has extracted from a somewhat churlish soil harvests more exuberant than those furnished by lands nearer to the sun. It means the continuous order which is the only parent of personal liberty and political right. And you owe all these, gentlemen, to the Throne.

There is another powerful and most beneficial influence which is also exercised by the Crown. Gentlemen, I am a party man. I believe that, without party, Parliamentary government is impossible. I look upon Parliamentary government as the noblest government in the world, and certainly the most suited to England. But without the discipline of political connection, animated by the principle of private honour, I feel certain that a popular Assembly would sink before the power or the corruption of a minister. Yet, gentlemen, I am not blind to the faults of party government. It has one great defect. Party has a tendency to warp the intelligence, and there is no minister, however resolved he may be in treating a great public question, who does not find some difficulty in emancipating himself from the traditionary prejudice on which he has long acted. It is, therefore, a great merit in our Constitution that before a minister introduces a measure to Parliament, he must submit it to an intelligence superior to all party, and entirely free from influences of that character.

I know it will be said, gentlemen, that, however beautiful in theory, the personal influence of the Sovereign is now absorbed in the responsibility of the minister. Gentlemen, I think you will find there is great fallacy in this view. The principles of the English Constitution do not contemplate the absence of personal influence on the part of the Sovereign; and if they did, the principles of human nature would prevent the fulfilment of such a theory. Gentlemen, I need not tell you that I am now making on this subject abstract observations of general application to our institutions and our history. But take the case of a Sovereign of England who accedes to his throne at the earliest age the law permits and who enjoys a long reign—take an instance like that of George III. From the earliest moment of his accession that Sovereign is placed in constant communication with the most able statesmen of the period, and of all parties. Even with average ability it is impossible not to perceive that such a Sovereign must soon attain a great mass of political information and political experience. Information and experience, gentlemen, whether they are possessed by a Sovereign or by the humblest of his subjects, are irresistible in life. No man with the vast responsibility that devolves upon an English minister can afford to treat with indifference a suggestion that has not occurred to him, or information with which he had not been previously supplied. But, gentlemen, pursue this view of the subject. The longer the reign, the influence of that Sovereign must proportionately increase. All the illustrious statesmen who served his youth disappear. A new generation of public servants rises up. There is a critical conjuncture in affairs—a moment of perplexity and peril. Then it is that the Sovereign can appeal to a similar state of affairs that occurred perhaps thirty years before. When all are in doubt among his servants he can quote the advice that was given by the illustrious men of his early years, and though he may maintain himself within the strictest limits of the Constitution, who can suppose when such information and such suggestions are made by the most exalted person in the country that they can be without effect? No, gentlemen; a minister who could venture to treat such influence with indifference would not be a Constitutional minister, but an arrogant idiot.

Gentlemen, the influence of the Crown is not confined merely to political affairs. England is a domestic country. Here the home is revered and the hearth is sacred. The nation is represented by a family—the Royal Family; and if that family is educated with a sense of responsibility and a sentiment of public duty, it is difficult to exaggerate the salutary influence they may exercise over a nation. It is not merely an influence upon manners; it is not merely that they are a model for refinement and for good taste—they affect the heart as well as the intelligence of the people; and in the hour of public adversity, or in the anxious conjuncture of public affairs, the nation rallies round the Family and the Throne, and its spirit is animated and sustained by the expression of public affection.

Gentlemen, there is yet one other remark that I would make upon our monarchy, though, had it not been for recent circumstances, I should have refrained from doing so. An attack has recently been made upon the Throne on account of the costliness of the institution.[32] Gentlemen, I shall not dwell upon the fact that if the people of England appreciate the monarchy, as I believe they do, it would be painful to them that their Royal and representative family should not be maintained with becoming dignity, or fill in the public eye a position inferior to some of the nobles of the land. Nor will I insist upon what is unquestionably the fact, that the revenues of the Crown estates, on which our Sovereign might live with as much right as the Duke of Bedford or the Duke of Northumberland has to his estates, are now paid into the public exchequer. All this, upon the present occasion, I am not going to

[32] By Sir Charles Dilke, Liberal.

insist upon. What I now say is this, that there is no sovereignty of any first-rate State which costs so little to the people as the sovereignty of England. I will not compare our Civil List with those of European empires, because it is known that in amount they treble and quadruple it; but I will compare it with the cost of sovereignty in a republic, and that a republic with which you are intimately acquainted—the republic of the United States of America.

Gentlemen, there is no analogy between the position of our Sovereign, Queen Victoria, and that of the President of the United States. The President of the United States is not the Sovereign of the United States. There is a very near analogy between the position of the President of the United States and that of the Prime Minister of England, and both are paid at much the same rate—the income of a second-class professional man. The Sovereign of the United States is the people; and I will now show you what the sovereignty of the United States costs. Gentlemen, you are aware of the Constitution of the United States. There are 37 independent States, each with a sovereign legislature. Besides these, there is a Confederation of States to conduct their external affairs, which consists of a House of Representatives and a Senate. There are 285 members of the House of Representatives, and there are 74 members of the Senate, making altogether 359 members of Congress. Now each member of Congress receives 1,000*l.* sterling per annum. In addition to this he receives an allowance called "mileage," which varies according to the distance which he travels, but the aggregate cost of which is about 30,000*l.* per annum. That makes 389,000*l.*, almost the exact amount of our Civil List.

But this, gentlemen, will allow you to make only a very imperfect estimate of the cost of sovereignty in the United States. Every member of every Legislature in the 37 States is also paid. There are, I believe, 5,010 members of State Legislatures who receive about $350 per annum each. As some of the returns are imperfect, the average which I have given of expenditure may be rather high, and therefore I have not counted the "mileage," which is also universally allowed. 5,010 members of State Legislatures at $350 each make $1,753,500 or 350,700*l.* sterling a year. So you see, gentlemen, that the immediate expenditure for the sovereignty of the United States is between 700,000*l.* and 800,000*l.* a year. Gentlemen, I have not time to pursue this interesting theme, otherwise I could show you that you have still but imperfectly ascertained the cost of sovereignty in a republic. But, gentlemen, I cannot resist giving you one further illustration.

The government of this country is considerably carried on by the aid of Royal Commissions. So great is the increase of public business that it would be probably impossible for a minister to carry on affairs without this assistance. The Queen of England can command for these objects the services of the most experienced statesmen, and men of the highest position of society. If necessary, she can summon to them distinguished scholars or men most celebrated in science and in art: and she receives from them services that are unpaid. They are only too proud to be described in the Commission as Her Majesty's "trusty councillors"; and if any member of these Commissions performs some transcendent services, both of thought and of labour, he is munificently rewarded by a public distinction conferred upon him by the Fountain of Honour. Gentlemen, the Government of the United States, has, I believe, not less availed itself of the services of Commissions than the Government of the United Kingdom; but, in a country where there is no Fountain of Honour, every member of these Commissions is paid.

Gentlemen, I trust I have now made some suggestions to you respecting the monarchy of England which at least may be so far serviceable that when we are separated they may not be altogether without advantage; and now, gentlemen, I would say something on the subject of the House of Lords. It is not merely the authority of the Throne that is now disputed, but the character and influence of the House of Lords that are held up by some to public disregard. Gentlemen, I shall not stop for a moment to offer you any proofs of the advantage of a Second Chamber; and for this reason. That subject has been discussed now for a century, ever since the establishment of the Government of the United States, and all great authorities, American, German, French, Italian, have agreed in this, that a Representative Government is impossible without a Second Chamber. And it has been, especially of late, maintained by great political writers in all countries that the repeated failure of what is called the French Republic is mainly to be ascribed to its not having a Second Chamber.

But, gentlemen, however anxious foreign countries have been to enjoy this advantage, that anxiety has only been equalled by the difficulty which they have found in fulfilling their object. How is a Second Chamber to be constituted? By nominees of the sovereign power? Are they to be bound by popular election? In what manner are they to be elected? If by the same constituency as the popular body, what claim have they, under such circumstances, to criticise or to control the decisions of that body? If they are to be elected by a more select body, qualified by a higher franchise, there immediately occurs the objection, why should the majority be governed by the minority? The United States of America were fortunate in finding a solution of this difficulty; but the United States of

America had elements to deal with which never occurred before, and never probably will occur again, because they formed their illustrious Senate from the materials that were offered them by the thirty-seven States. We, gentlemen, have the House of Lords, an assembly which has historically developed and periodically adapted itself to the wants and necessities of the times.

What, gentlemen, is the first quality which is required in a Second Chamber? Without doubt, independence. What is the best foundation of independence? Without doubt, property. The Prime Minister [33] of England has only recently told you, and I believe he spoke quite accurately, that the average income of the members of the House of Lords is 20,000l. per annum. Of course there are some who have more and some who have less; but the influence of a public assembly, so far as property is concerned, depends upon its aggregate property, which, in the present case, is a revenue of 9,000,000l. a year. But, gentlemen, you must look to the nature of this property. It is visible property, and therefore it is responsible property, which every ratepayer in the room knows to his cost. But, gentlemen, it is not only visible property; it is, generally speaking, territorial property; and one of the elements of territorial property is that it is representative. Now, for illustration, suppose—which God forbid—there was no House of Commons, and any Englishman —I will take him from either end of the island—a Cumberland or a Cornish man, finds himself aggrieved. The Cumbrian says, "This conduct I experience is most unjust. I know a Cumberland man in the House of Lords, the Earl of Carlisle or the Earl of Lonsdale; I will go to him; he will never see a Cumberland man ill-treated." The Cornish man will say, "I will go to the Lord of Port Eliot; his family have sacrificed themselves before this for the liberties of Englishmen, and he will get justice done me."

But, gentlemen, the charge against the House of Lords is that the dignities are hereditary, and we are told that if we have a House of Peers they should be peers for life. There are great authorities in favour of this, and even my noble friend [34] near me the other day gave in his adhesion to a limited application of this principle. Now, gentlemen, in the first place let me observe that every peer is a peer for life, as he cannot be a peer after his death; but some peers for life are succeeded in their dignities by their children. The question arises, who is most responsible—a peer for life whose dignities are not descendible, or a peer for life whose dignities are hereditary? Now, gentlemen, a peer for life is in a very strong

[33] Gladstone.
[34] Lord Derby.

position. He says, "Here I am; I have got power and I will exercise it." I have no doubt that, on the whole, a peer for life would exercise it for what he deemed was the public good. Let us hope that. But, after all, he might and could exercise it according to his own will. Nobody can call him to account; he is independent of everybody. But a peer for life whose dignities descend is in a very different position. He has every inducement to study public opinion, and, when he believes it just, to yield; because he naturally feels that if the order to which he belongs is in constant collision with public opinion, the chances are that his dignities will not descend to his posterity.

Therefore, Gentlemen, I am not prepared myself to believe that a solution of any difficulties in the public mind on this subject is to be found by creating peers for life. I know there are some philosophers who believe that the best substitute for the House of Lords would be an assembly formed of ex-Governors of Colonies. I have not sufficient experience on that subject to give a decided opinion upon it. When the Muse of Comedy threw her frolic grace over society, a retired Governor was generally one of the characters in every comedy; and the last of our great actors—who, by the by, was a great favourite at Manchester—Mr. Farren, was celebrated for his delineation of the character in question. Whether it be the recollection of that performance or not, I confess I am inclined to believe that an English gentleman—born to business, managing his own estate, administering the affairs of his county, mixing with all classes of his fellow-men, now in the hunting field, now in the Railway Direction, unaffected, unostentatious, proud of his ancestors, if they have contributed to the greatness of our common country—is, on the whole, more likely to form a senator agreeable to English opinion and English taste than any substitute that has yet been produced.

Gentlemen, let me make one observation more, on the subject of the House of Lords, before I conclude. There is some advantage in political experience. I remember the time when there was a similar outcry against the House of Lords, but much more intense and powerful; and, gentlemen, it arose from the same cause. A Liberal Government had been installed in office, with an immense Liberal majority. They proposed some violent measures. The House of Lords modified some, delayed others, and some they threw out. Instantly there was a cry to abolish or to reform the House of Lords, and the greatest popular orator [35] that probably ever existed was sent on a pilgrimage over England to excite the people in favour

[35] O'Connell.

of this opinion. What happened? That happened, gentlemen, which may happen to-morrow. There was a dissolution of Parliament. The great Liberal majority vanished. The balance of parties was restored. It was discovered that the House of Lords had behind them at least half of the English people. We heard no more cries for their abolition or their reform, and before two years more passed England was really governed by the House of Lords, under the wise influence of the Duke of Wellington and the commanding eloquence of Lyndhurst; and such was the enthusiasm of the nation in favour of the Second Chamber that at every public meeting its health was drunk, with the additional sentiment, for which we are indebted to one of the most distinguished members that ever represented the House of Commons, "Thank God, there is the House of Lords."

Gentlemen, you will perhaps not be surprised that, having made some remarks upon the Monarchy and the House of Lords, I should say something respecting that House in which I have literally passed the greater part of my life and to which I am devotedly attached. It is not likely, therefore, that I should say anything to depreciate the legitimate position and influence of the House of Commons. Gentlemen it is said that the diminished power of the Throne and the assailed authority of the House of Lords are owing to the increased power of the House of Commons, and the new position which of late years, and especially during the last forty years, it has assumed in the English Constitution. Gentlemen, the main power of the House of Commons depends upon its command over the public purse and its control of the public expenditure; and if that power is possessed by a party which has a large majority in the House of Commons, the influence of the House of Commons is proportionately increased, and, under some circumstances, becomes more predominant. But, gentlemen, this power of the House of Commons is not a power which has been created by any Reform Act, from the days of Lord Grey in 1832 to 1867. It is the power which the House of Commons has enjoyed for centuries—which it has frequently asserted and sometimes even tyrannically exercised. Gentlemen, the House of Commons represents the constituencies of England, and I am here to show you that no addition to the elements of that constituency has placed the House of Commons in a different position with regard to the Throne and the House of Lords from that it has always constitutionally occupied.

Gentlemen, we speak now on this subject with great advantage. We recently have had published authentic documents upon this matter which are highly instructive. We have, for example, just published the Census of Great Britain, and we are now in possession of the last registration of voters for the United Kingdom. Gentlemen, it appears that by the census the population at this time is about 32,000,000. It is shown by the last registration that, after making the usual deductions for deaths, removals, double entries, and so on, the constituency of the United Kingdom may be placed at 2,200,000. So, gentlemen, it at once appears that there are 30,-000,000 people in this country who are as much represented by the House of Lords as by the House of Commons, and who, for the protection of their rights, must depend upon them and the majesty of the Throne. And now, gentlemen, I will tell you what was done by the last Reform Act.

Lord Grey, in his measure of 1832, which was no doubt a statesmanlike measure, committed a great and for a time it appeared an irretrievable error. By that measure he fortified the legitimate influence of the aristocracy; but he not only made no provision for the representation of the working classes in the Constitution, but he absolutely abolished those ancient franchises which the working classes had peculiarly enjoyed and exercised from time immemorial. Gentlemen, that was the origin of Chartism, and of that electoral uneasiness which existed in this country more or less for thirty years. The Liberal party, I feel it my duty to say, had not acted fairly by this question. In their adversity they held out hopes to the working classes, but when they had a strong Government they laughed their vows to scorn. In 1848 there was a French Revolution and a Republic was established. No one can have forgotten what the effect was in this country. I remember the day when not a woman could leave her house in London, and when cannon were planted on Westminster Bridge. When Lord Derby became Prime Minister affairs had arrived at such a point that it was of the first moment that the question should be sincerely dealt with. He had to encounter great difficulties, but he accomplished his purpose with the support of a united party. And, gentlemen, what has been the result? A year ago there was another revolution in France, and a Republic was again established of the most menacing character. What happened in this country? You could not get half a dozen men to assemble in a street and grumble. Why? Because the people had got what they wanted. They were content and they were grateful.

But, gentlemen, the Constitution of England is not merely a Constitution in State, it is a Constitution in Church and State. The wisest Sovereigns and statesmen have ever been anxious to connect authority with religion—some to increase their power, some, perhaps, to mitigate its exercise. But the same difficulty has been experienced in effecting this union which has been experienced in forming a

Second Chamber—either the spiritual power has usurped upon the civil and established a sacerdotal society, or the civil power has invaded successfully the rights of the spiritual, and the ministers of religion have been degraded into stipendiaries of the State and instruments of the Government. In England we accomplish this great result by an alliance between Church and State, between two originally independent powers. I will not go into the history of that alliance, which is rather a question for those archaeological societies which occasionally amuse and instruct the people of this city. Enough for me that this union was made and has contributed for centuries to the civilisation of this country. Gentlemen, there is the same assault against the Church of England and the union between the State and the Church as there is against the Monarchy and against the House of Lords. It is said that the existence of Nonconformity proves that the Church is a failure. I draw from these premises an exactly contrary conclusion; and I maintain that to have secured a national profession of faith with the unlimited enjoyment of private judgment in matters spiritual is the solution of the most difficult problem, and one of the triumphs, of civilisation.[36]

.   .   .   .

Gentlemen,[37] I think public attention as regards these matters ought to be concentrated upon sanitary legislation. That is a wide subject, and, if properly treated, comprises almost every consideration which has just claim upon legislative interference. Pure air, pure water, the inspection of unhealthy habitations, the adulteration of food, these and many kindred matters may be legitimately dealt with by the Legislature; and I am bound to say the Legislature is not idle upon them; for we have at this time two important measures before Parliament on the subject. One—by a late colleague of mine, Sir Charles Adderley—is a large and comprehensive measure, founded upon a sure basis, for it consolidates all existing public Acts and improves them. A prejudice has been raised against that proposal, by stating that it interferes with the private Acts of the great towns. I take this opportunity of contradicting that. The Bill of Sir Charles Adderley does not touch the Acts of the great towns. It only allows them if they think fit to avail themselves of its new provisions.

The other measure, by the Government, is of a partial character.

[36] Additional material upon the church and education is omitted.
[37] The condition of the working classes leads to the following remarks.

What it comprises is good, so far as it goes, but it shrinks from that bold consolidation of existing Acts which I think one of the great merits of Sir Charles Adderley's Bill, which permits us to become acquainted with how much may be done in favour of sanitary improvement by existing provisions. Gentlemen, I cannot impress upon you too strongly my conviction of the importance of the Legislature and society uniting together in favour of these important results. A great scholar and a great wit, 300 years ago, said that, in his opinion, there was a great mistake in the Vulgate, which as you all know is the Latin translation of the Holy Scriptures, and that instead of saying "Vanity of vanities, all is vanity"—*Vanitas vanitatum, omnia vanitas*—the wise and witty King really said *Sanitas sanitatum, omnia sanitas*. Gentlemen, it is impossible to overrate the importance of the subject. After all, the first consideration of a minister should be the health of the people. A land may be covered with historic trophies, with museums of science and galleries of art, with universities and with libraries; the people may be civilised and ingenious; the country may be even famous in the annals and action of the world, but, gentlemen, if the population every ten years decreases, and the stature of the race every ten years diminishes, the history of that country will soon be the history of the past.

Gentlemen, I said I had not come here to make a party speech. I have addressed you upon subjects of grave, and I will venture to believe of general, interest; but to be here and altogether silent upon the present state of public affairs would not be respectful to you, and, perhaps, on the whole, would be thought incongruous. Gentlemen, I cannot pretend that our position either at home or abroad is in my opinion satisfactory. At home, at a period of immense prosperity, with a people contented and naturally loyal, we find to our surprise the most extravagant doctrines professed and the fundamental principles of our most valuable institutions impugned, and that too by persons of some authority. Gentlemen, this startling inconsistency is accounted for, in my mind, by the circumstances under which the present Administration was formed. It is the first instance in my knowledge of a British Administration being avowedly formed on a principle of violence. . . . . . Their specific was to despoil churches and plunder landlords, and what has been the result? Sedition rampant, treason thinly veiled, and whenever a vacancy occurs in the representation a candidate is returned pledged to the disruption of the realm. Her Majesty's new ministers proceeded in their career like a body of men under the influence of some delirious drug. Not satiated with the spoliation and anarchy of Ireland, they began to attack every institution and every interest, every class and calling in the country.

It is curious to observe their course. They took into hand the Army. What have they done? . . . . .

Let us look what they have done with the Admiralty. You remember, in this county especially, the denunciation of the profligate expenditure of the Conservative Government, and you have since had an opportunity of comparing it with the gentler burden of Liberal estimates. The Navy was not merely an instance of profligate expenditure, but of incompetent and inadequate management. A great revolution was promised in its administration. A gentleman,[38] almost unknown to English politics, was strangely preferred to one of the highest places in the councils of Her Majesty. He set to at his task with ruthless activity. The Consultative Council, under which Nelson had gained all his victories, was dissolved. The Secretaryship of the Admiralty, an office which exercised a complete supervision over every division of that great department—an office which was to the Admiralty what the Secretary of State is to the kingdom, which, in the qualities which it required and the duties which it fulfilled was rightly a stepping-stone to the Cabinet, as in the instances of Lord Halifax, Lord Herbert, and many others —was reduced to absolute insignificance. Even the office of Control, which of all others required a position of independence, and on which the safety of the Navy mainly depended, was deprived of all its important attributes. . . . . .

But, gentlemen, as time advanced it was not difficult to perceive that extravagance was being substituted for energy by the Government. The unnatural stimulus was subsiding. Their paroxysms ended in prostration. Some took refuge in melancholy, and their eminent chief alternated between a menace and a sigh. As I sat opposite the Treasury Bench the ministers reminded me of one of those marine landscapes not very unusual on the coasts of South America. You behold a range of exhausted volcanoes. Not a flame flickers on a single pallid crest. But the situation is still dangerous. There are occasional earthquakes, and ever and anon the dark rumbling of the sea.

But, gentlemen, there is one other topic on which I must touch. If the management of our domestic affairs has been founded upon a principle of violence, that certainly cannot be alleged against the management of our external relations. I know the difficulty of addressing a body of Englishmen on these topics. The very phrase "foreign affairs" makes an Englishmen convinced that I am about to treat of subjects with which he has no concern. Unhappily, the relations of England to the rest of the world, which are "foreign

[38] Mr. Childers.

affairs," are the matters which most influence his lot. Upon them depends the increase or reduction of taxation. Upon them depends the enjoyment or the embarrassment of his industry. And yet, though so momentous are the consequences of the mismanagement of our foreign relations, no one thinks of them till the mischief occurs, and then it is found how the most vital consequences have been occasioned by the mere inadvertence.

I will illustrate this point by two anecdotes. Since I have been in public life there has been for this country a great calamity and there is a great danger, and both might have been avoided. The calamity was the Crimean War. You know what were the consequences of the Crimean War—a great addition to your debt, an enormous addition to your taxation, a cost more precious than your treasure—the best blood of England. Half a million of men, I believe, perished in that great undertaking. Nor are the evil consequences of that war adequately described by what I have said. All the disorders and disturbances of Europe, those immense armaments that are an incubus on national industry and the great obstacle to progressive civilisation, may be traced and justly attributed to the Crimean War. And yet the Crimean War need never have occurred. . . . . .

The great danger is the present state of our relations with the United States. When I acceded to office I did so, so far as regarded the United States of America, with some advantage. During the whole of the Civil War in America both my noble friend near me and I had maintained a strict and fair neutrality. This was fully appreciated by the Government of the United States, and they expressed their wish that with our aid the settlement of all differences between the two Governments should be accomplished. They sent here a plenipotentiary, an honourable gentleman, very intelligent and possessing general confidence. My noble friend near me, with great ability, negotiated a treaty for the settlement of all these claims. He was the first minister who proposed to refer them to arbitration, and the treaty was signed by the American Government. It was signed, I think, on November 10th, on the eve of the dissolution of Parliament. The borough elections that first occurred proved what would be the fate of the ministry, and the moment they were known in America the American Government announced that Mr. Reverdy Johnson had mistaken his instructions, and they could not present the treaty to the Senate for its sanction—the sanction of which there had been previously no doubt.

But the fact is that, as in the case of the Crimean War, it was supposed that our successors would be favourable to Russian aggression, so it was supposed that by the accession to office of Mr. Gladstone and a gentleman you know well, Mr. Bright, the American claims would be considered in a very different spirit. How they have been considered is a subject which, no doubt, occupies deeply the minds of the people of Lancashire. Now, gentlemen, observe this—the question of the Black Sea involved in the Crimean War, the question of the American claims involved in our negotiations with Mr. Johnson, are the two questions that have again turned up, and have been the two great questions that have been under the management of his Government. . . . . .[39]

And yet, gentlemen, it is not merely our fleets and armies, our powerful artillery, our accumulated capital, and our unlimited credit on which I so much depend, as upon that unbroken spirit of her people, which I believe was never prouder of the Imperial country to which they belong. Gentlemen, it is to that spirit that I above all things trust. I look upon the people of Lancashire as a fair representative of the people of England. I think the manner in which they have invited me here, locally a stranger, to receive the expression of their cordial sympathy, and only because they recognise some effort on my part to maintain the greatness of their country, is evidence of the spirit of the land. I must express to you again my deep sense of the generous manner in which you have welcomed me, and in which you have permitted me to express to you my views upon public affairs. Proud of your confidence and encouraged by your sympathy, I now deliver to you, as my last words, the cause of the Tory Party, the English Constitution, and of the British Empire.

[39] Additional discussion on these two topics is omitted.

7. Suez Canal Shares

Sir S. H. Northcote, chancellor of the Exchequer, asked on February 14, 1876, for the vote of a sum "to pay the purchase-money for shares which belonged to the Khedive in the Suez Canal." The debate on the subject was continued on February 21, 1876. Disraeli's speech may be found in HANSARD (CCXXVII [3d Ser.], 652-61).

Owing to the bankruptcy of Ismail, the Egyptian khedive, Disraeli was able to make (November 1875) the surprise purchase of nearly half the total shares in the Suez Canal Company—not a majority interest, though a controlling interest for practical purposes. Since Parliament was not in session at the time, Disraeli borrowed £4,000,000 from the Rothschilds, thereby opening himself to much criticism from Parliamentary opponents, howbeit winning approbation from the Queen and the public. The last portion of his speech makes clear the real importance of the purchase for England.

Sir, although, according to the noble Lord,[40] we are going to give a unanimous vote, it cannot be denied that the discussion of this evening at least has proved one result. It has shown, in a manner about which neither the House of Commons nor the country can make any mistake, that had the right honourable Gentleman the Member for Greenwich [41] been the Prime Minister of this country, the shares in the Suez Canal would not have been purchased. . . . . . The right honourable Gentleman defies me to produce an instance of a Ministry negotiating with a private firm. . . . . . The right honourable Gentleman found great fault with the amount of the commission which has been charged by the Messrs. Rothschild and admitted by the Government; and, indeed, both the right honourable Gentlemen opposite took the pains to calculate what was the amount of interest which it was proposed the Messrs. Rothschild should receive on account of their advance. It is, according to both right honourable Gentlemen, 15 per cent; but I must express my surprise that two right honourable Gentlemen, both of whom have filled the office of Chancellor of the Exchequer, and one of whom has been at the head of the Treasury, should have shown by their observations such a lamentable want of acquaintance with the manner in which large amounts of capital are commanded when the Government of a country may desire to possess them under the circumstances under which we appealed to the House in question. I deny altogether that the commission

[40] Lord Hartington talking on the subject before the committee of the House.
[41] Mr. Gladstone.

charged by the Messrs. Rothschild has anything to do with the interest on the advance; nor can I suppose that two right honourable
Gentlemen so well acquainted with finance as the Member for
Greenwich and the Member for the University of London [42] can
really believe that there is in this country anyone who has £4,000,-
000 lying idle at his bankers. Yet one would suppose, from the
argument of the right honourable Gentleman the Member for
Greenwich, that such is the assumption on which he has formed
his opinion in this matter. In the present instance, I may observe,
not only the possibility, but the probability, of our having immediately to advance the whole £4,000,000 was anticipated. And how
was this £4,000,000 to be obtained? Only by the rapid conversion
of securities to the same amount. Well, I need not tell anyone
who is at all acquainted with such affairs that the rapid conversion
of securities to the amount of £4,000,000 can never be effected
without loss, and sometimes considerable loss; and it is to guard
against risk of that kind that a commission is asked for before
advances are made to a Government. In this case, too, it was more
than probable that, after paying the first £1,000,000 following the
signature of the contract, £2,000,000 further might be demanded
in gold the next day. Fortunately for the Messrs. Rothschild they
were not; but, if they had, there would in all likelihood have been
a great disturbance in the Money Market, which must have occasioned a great sacrifice, perhaps the whole of the commission. The
Committee, therefore, must not be led away by the observations of
the two right honourable Gentlemen, who, of all men in the House,
ought to be the last to make them.

But the right honourable Gentleman the Member for Greenwich
says we ought to have gone to our constitutional financiers and
advisers, the Governor and Deputy Governor of the Bank of England, and, of course, the honourable Member for Galway (Mr.
Mitchell Henry), who rose much later in the debate, and who spoke
evidently under the influence of strong feeling, also says that we
ought to have asked the Governor of the Bank of England to advance the £4,000,000. But they forget that it is against the law
of this country for the Bank to advance a sum of money to the
Ministry.

But then it may be said—"Though the Bank could not have advanced the £4,000,000, you might have asked them to purchase the
shares." But how could they have purchased the shares? They
must have first consulted their legal adviser, who probably would
have told them that they had not power to do it; but, even if that

[42] Robert Lowe.

doubtful question had been decided in the affirmative, they must have then called a public Court in order to see whether they could be authorized to purchase those shares to assist the Government. Now, I ask the Committee to consider for a moment what chance would we have had of effecting the purchase which we made under the circumstances, and with the competitors we had to en- counter, and the objects we had to attain, if we had pursued the course which the right honourable Gentleman opposite has sug- gested? "But," says the Member for the University of London— and this also has been echoed by his late right honourable Colleague —"you would have avoided all this, if you adopted the course which we indicate, and which I have just reminded the Committee is illegal, if you had only taken the illegal course we recommend, you would have got rid of this discreditable gambling, because although the Messrs. Rothschild, some of whom have been Members of this House, are men of honour, yet they have a great number of clerks who are all gambling on the Stock Exchange." Now, my belief is that the Messrs. Rothschild kept the secret as well as Her Majesty's Government, for I do not think a single human being connected with them knew anything about it. And, indeed, it was quite unnecessary for the Messrs. Rothschild to have violated the con- fidence which we reposed in them, and quite unnecessary even for the Members of Her Majesty's Government to hold their tongues, for no sooner was the proposal accepted than a telegram from Grand Cairo transmitted the news to the Stock Exchange, and it was that telegram which was the cause of all the speculation and gam- bling to which the right honourable Gentleman has referred. It is a fact that while the matter was a dead secret in England, the news was transmitted from Cairo. That was the intelligence on which the operations occurred. But I wish to say one word respect- ing the moral observations which have been made. As to gambling on the Stock Exchange, are we really to refrain from doing that which we think is proper and advantageous to the country because it may lead to speculation? Why, not a remark was made by the noble Lord, who has just addressed the House, the other night, or by me in reply, that would not affect the funds. On the one side people would say—"The Government are in great difficulty, and probably a Vote of Censure will arise out of this Suez Canal speculation," while other persons would observe—"There is evi- dently something coming about Egypt, and he is not going to let it all out." Ought we to refrain from doing what is necessary for the public welfare because it leads to stock-jobbing? Why, there is not an incident in the history of the world that led to so much stock-jobbing as the battle of Waterloo, and are we to regret that

that glorious battle was fought and won because it led to stock-jobbing? So much for the operations on the Stock Exchange. I think we have been listening all night to remarks on this transaction that have very little foundation. We have been admonished for conduct which has led to stock-jobbing and we have been admonished because we applied to a private firm when, from the state of the law, I have shown that it was absolutely necessary from the character of the circumstances we had to deal with that a private firm should be appealed to.

And now I come to the policy of the two right honourable Gentlemen, for on that portion of the subject they appear to agree very much. The right honourable Gentleman the Member for the University of London says—"You have your shares, but you have no dividends." And the right honourable Gentleman the Member for Greenwich says—"You have your shares, but you have no votes." That is the great lamentation of the two right honourable Gentlemen. Shrieking and screaming out—"You have no votes and no dividends, though you have the shares," they account for conduct on the part of the Government so totally devoid of sense and calculation as that the Government should become encumbered with all these shares, and yet possess neither the advantage of dividends nor of voting power. They say this is due to the simple circumstance that we acted in total ignorance, that we were innocent—nay, more than innocent—and that the most becoming thing for us to do would be to acknowledge and, at the same time, to regret our fault. Instead of that, they say we triumph in our ignorance, and they absolutely pretend that we were aware of the immense blunder we have committed. It is very remarkable that the two right honourable Gentlemen should have ventured to take up such a position in this case. What is this question of the Suez Canal? From the numerous Papers which have been placed before the House, the House must be tolerably aware that during the whole period of the existence of the present Parliament the question of the Suez Canal has more or less been before us. I am not sure that in the first Cabinet Council we held some decision was not come to on the subject. Then the International Commission at Constantinople had either just terminated, or was involving the Government in a painful and difficult Correspondence. We were represented at the International Commission by Colonel Stokes, who is completely master of the subject, an invaluable public servant, and a man of great intelligence, and who had completely mastered all the details of what was then a very complicated question. From that time until we made the purchase in October last Colonel Stokes has been in almost constant attendance at the Foreign Office.

The question of the Suez Canal was constantly before us, and therefore I need not go further to show to the Committee that, although it happened to be a subject upon which we were called in the present instance to decide hastily, we had the advantage of much previous knowledge. Why, my right honourable Friend the Chancellor of the Exchequer was intimately acquainted with the subject, and was himself present at the opening of the Suez Canal. Nothing, in short, can be more unfounded than the assumption of the two right honourable Gentlemen, who wished to convey to the House that Her Majesty's Government had entered into their agreement in perfect ignorance of all the circumstances of the case. This, in fact, was the style of the whole speech of the right honourable Gentleman (Mr. Lowe). Take this away; convince the right honourable Gentleman—or convince, what is easier and more satisfactory, the Committee—that we were aware of these circumstances, and the right honourable Gentleman himself confesses that he might as well have made no speech at all.

Then the right honourable Gentleman the Member for Greenwich (Mr. Gladstone) proceeds in his attack in his own way, and makes a great many objections, but takes up two great positions as grounds of condemnation. "First of all," he says, "I object to this purchase, because it will give you no influence." That is the assertion of the right honourable Gentleman. I might meet it with a counter assertion. I might offer many arguments to show that it will give us a great deal of influence. I might refer to that which has already occurred, and which, though not in its results very considerable, shows some advantage from what has been done, while before a year has elapsed it will possibly show much more. I might refer to the general conviction and the common sense of society that such an investment cannot be treated as absolutely idle and nugatory, as the right honourable Gentleman wishes to treat it. The right honourable Gentleman takes a position from which it is certainly difficult to dislodge him, because it is perfectly arbitrary. He says—"You have no votes." He views the question abstractedly. He says—"Here is a company, and you have a great many shares in it, but you are not allowed to vote, and therefore it follows you can have no influence." But everybody knows that in the world things are not managed in that way, and that if you have a large amount of capital in any concern, whatever may be the restrictions under which it is invested, the capitalist does exercise influence.

Then the right honourable Gentleman says—"You have no real control over the purchase you have made; and yet that purchase will lead to great complications." Sir, I have no doubt that complications will occur. They always have occurred, and I should

like to know the state of affairs and of society in which complications do not and will not occur. We are here to guard the country
against complications, and to guide it in the event of complications;
and the argument that we are to do nothing—never dare to move,
never try to increase our strength and improve our position, because
we are afraid of complications is certainly a new view of English
policy, and one which I believe the House of Commons will never
sanction. I think under these two heads all the criticisms of the
right honourable Gentleman are contained. But the noble Lord [43]
who has just addressed us says many points were made by the right
honourable Gentleman which the Chancellor of the Exchequer
did not answer. There is no precedent of a British Ministry treating with a private firm; my right honourable Friend did not answer that. [Mr. Gladstone: I did not say so.] The right honourable Gentleman, however, says he made no observation of the kind.
Then the noble Lord says my right honourable Friend never answered the charge about speculations in Egyptian Stock. Well,
I have answered that charge. The noble Lord says my right honourable Friend never touched upon the amount of the commission.
I have touched upon it. He says that we never thoroughly cleared
ourselves from the charge of not buying the 15 per cent shares.
I am here to vindicate our conduct on that point. In purchasing
the shares we did, we purchased what we wanted, we gained the
end we wished, and why we should involve the country in another
purchase, when we should thereby only have repeated the result
we had already achieved I cannot understand. The noble Lord
says my right honourable Friend never expressed what expectations
we had of receiving the £200,000 a-year from the Khedive, but
we do not suppose that interest which is at the rate of 5 per cent
is quite as secure as it would be if it were at the rate of 3¼ per
cent. Then the noble Lord says that my right honourable Friend
never met the charge of the right honourable Gentleman that our
policy would lead to complications with other nations. We believe,
on the contrary, that, instead of leading to complications with other
nations, the step which we have taken is one which will avert
complications. These are matters which to a great degree must
be matters of opinion; but the most remarkable feature of the long
harangue of the right honourable Gentleman the Member for
Greenwich is that it was in a great degree a series of assumptions,
abstract reasonings, and arbitrary conclusions, after which he sat
down quite surprised that the Vote should be passed unanimously,
and requesting his allies to attack us for not answering that which

[43] The Marquess of Hartington.

we have felt not to be substantial, but to consist of assumptions which we believe experience will prove to be entirely false.

The right honourable Gentleman charged us, lastly, with not having answered a charge of having abandoned a strong position. The right honourable Gentleman pictured us as having been in a good position before this—a position which he charged us with having abandoned for one of a more doubtful character. Here again, what proof does he bring of the charge he makes? We found ourselves in a position which has been called a strong position, but we could not for a moment think that our position with regard to the Canal was satisfactory. The International Commission sat, as honourable Members know, before the Conservatives acceded to power, and the work it did was greatly assisted by our Predecessors, and by a number of other able and eminent men; but, as I have said, no one who remembers all the circumstances of the case and what has occurred since, can for a moment pretend that our position with regard to the Canal was then satisfactory. At the moment Turkey was in a very different position from that which she occupies at present, as far as authority is concerned. The Khedive himself was in a very good position; and yet those who are familiar with what occurred at that time know the great difficulties which the Government experienced, and the very doubtful manner in which, for a considerable time, affairs looked with regard to the whole business.[44] Therefore I do not agree with the right honourable Gentleman. I feel that at this moment our position is much stronger, and for the reason that we are possessors of a great portion of the capital invested in the Canal.

The noble Lord himself has expressed great dissatisfaction, because I have not told him what the conduct of the Government would be with regard to the Canal in a time of war. I must say that on this subject I wish to retain my reserve. I cannot conceive anything more imprudent than a discussion in this House at the present time as to the conduct of England with regard to the Suez Canal in time of war, and I shall therefore decline to enter upon any discussion on the subject. . . . . . What we have to do tonight is to agree to the Vote for the purchase of these shares. I have never recommended, and I do not now recommend this purchase as a financial investment. If it gave us 10 per cent of interest and

[44] As Disraeli implies, Turkey had recently gone bankrupt and the Khedive was in financial difficulties so that safeguards in dealing with De Lesseps, the projector of the canal, who was anxious for French domination had disappeared for England. Yet four fifths of the shipping that used the canal was British.

a security as good as the Consols, I do not think an English Minister would be justified in making such an investment; still less if he is obliged to borrow the money for the occasion. I do not recommend it either as a commercial speculation, although I believe that many of those who have looked upon it with little favour will probably be surprised with the pecuniary results of the purchase. I have always, and do now recommend it to the country as a political transaction, and one which I believe is calculated to strengthen the Empire. That is the spirit in which it has been accepted by the country, which understands it though the two right honourable critics may not. They are really seasick of the "Silver Streak." [45] They want the Empire to be maintained, to be strengthened; they will not be alarmed even it be increased. Because they think we are obtaining a great hold and interest in this important portion of Africa—because they believe that it secures to us a highway to our Indian Empire and our other dependencies, the people of England have from the first recognized the propriety and the wisdom of the step which we shall sanction tonight.

[Question put, and agreed to.

Resolution to be reported this day;
Committee to sit again upon Wednesday.]

[45] The English Channel.

8. The Liberal Policies

This speech, dealing with Gladstone's new government, was delivered on January 6, 1881. It may be found in HANSARD *(CCLVII [3d Ser.], 15-25).*

Its pessimistic tone typifies Disraeli's last utterances on foreign affairs (cf. Bernard, Lord Coleridge, This for Remembrance [London: T. F. Unwin, Ltd., 1925], pp. 144-46). Its full significance becomes more nearly comprehensible if it be related to the material in Gladstone's speech, "The British Empire — Foreign Affairs" (page 283). Gladstone had attacked Conservative policies with fervor in his famous Midlothian campaign of 1879—everything from the confusion in finance to the restlessness of Europe, the misadventures in Africa, and the violence to the sanctity of life in the hills of Afghanistan. The Liberals won the general election of 1880, and there was, perchance, little that Disraeli could do in 1881 save complain.*

The Earl of Beaconsfield, who was cheered on rising, said,—My lords, I wish I could feel it my duty to treat the matters before us to-night in as pleasant a manner as the two noble lords [46] who have just addressed us have done. I agree with my noble friend [47] and neighbour who moved the address that the times are critical, and, although I am sure that your lordships are not pessimists, and although, whatever my errors are, pessimism is not generally among the imputations made against me, I confess I have never addressed Parliament with a more deep sense of anxiety and gloom than that which the present state of affairs brings me to feel. There have been occasions in which our foreign affairs have filled us with anxiety, occasions on which our colonial position has been very critical. There have been occasions before this on which our domestic interests, influenced by Ireland, filled the nation with alarm. There have been occasions also in which events have occurred which have demanded the serious attention of Parliament, and which cannot, perhaps, be ranged under the heads I have noticed. But, my lords, I do not recollect a time in which, not only our position in important colonies, not only the almost unparalleled state of our relations with Ireland, but the many other troubles which may require your attention this session, all at the same time have occurred and have demanded the deepest consideration, the deepest sense of responsibility, on the part of your lordships. And, my lords, I am bound to say that I cannot help feeling that much of the disaster with which we have to grapple at present, is to be

[46] Lord Carrington and the Earl of Yarborough.
[47] Lord Carrington.

attributed in a great degree to the spirit in which Her Majesty's present ministers acceded to office.

My lords, in old days, in times within our experience, when there was a change of administration, it was always considered the duty of both parties to effect no more alteration in the general conduct of our affairs than was absolutely necessary. On former occasions it was generally understood that though there ought to be, and, of course, there was, a due assertion of differences of party principles, still, so far as it was possible, unnecessary changes were to be discouraged in the general conduct of our affairs, so that there should be some continuity of policy; and though there were imputations made, I fear sometimes with justice, but often very unjustly, against our parliamentary government, of the inconsistency in which it involved our affairs, very frequently parliamentary government could not justly be open to that imputation. Well, my lords, it must be admitted that this action to which I have referred introduced some feeling of magnanimity into public life, and its absence is very much regretted. No doubt it added greatly to the strength of our functions. But when the new administration was formed nothing of the kind was done. On the contrary, in every manner and on every occasion it was announced that the change of Government meant a change in every part and portion of the Government; that everything which had been concluded was to be repudiated; that everything consummated was to be reversed, and upon the most important questions, either of our foreign relations, our colonial situation, or our domestic policy with regard to Ireland, upon all these questions the utmost change must immediately and rapidly be accomplished. Perpetual and complete reversal of all that had occurred was the order that was given and the profession that was announced.

See, my lords, how this has worked. Take the case which the noble lord who has just addressed you adduced—take the case of our foreign relations. The system of repudiating everything that was approved, promoted, or carried into effect by their predecessors, this system may be tried very well upon the very subject to which the noble lord has referred. Everything was to be altered. Well, though you might denounce and abuse the Treaty of Berlin, you could not repudiate that treaty, and you could not reverse it. The Treaty of Berlin, being so completely disapproved of by the new Government, it was proposed, most ingeniously, that, as there had been a Congress at Berlin, there should also be a Conference at Berlin; and it was generally understood and felt by everyone that that meant that the regulations of the Congress of Berlin were in fact to be modified, changed, and superseded by the determinations of the Conference.[48] Now, how has that been accomplished? In my observations to-night I will avoid arguing on matters of policy, for which there will be other occasions; but all sensible men will agree that, whatever may have been the defects of the Treaty of Berlin—though I admit none—or the points that may have been neglected or left unsettled, one thing was quite clear and was generally admitted, that at last the peace of Europe was secured. I believe that the Conference of Berlin had the contrary effect, and I think I am not using an unauthorised expression when I say that the result of that Conference was, that the war in the East of Europe and in the West of Asia was on the point of being revived, and England was near being a belligerent, and a belligerent, too, against our old ally. No one can say now that the peace of Europe is certain, or that we are perfectly secure. We have very little information on this subject, though I presume that more will be afforded, but from what we see there is no doubt that even in the space of twenty-four hours events may occur which might shake that peace. What is the cause of all this? It is because Her Majesty's Government, directly they took office, got into this system of superseding and disturbing everything their predecessors had settled.

Now let me advert to another question—that, namely, of Afghanistan. That is a question that must come before the House and I believe my noble friend the late Governor-General of India [49] will take an opportunity of bringing it before your lordships' notice. Whatever may be our opinion as to the policy or impolicy of the military occupation of Afghanistan, in this, I think, all will agree —that it was an event of great political moment, and that it was undertaken in consequence of information, part of which only has as yet been revealed to the country, but which is adequate to enable them to learn that it was preceded by startling incidents of conduct on the part of another great Power,[50] which demanded serious consideration. Her Majesty's Government may be perfectly right in the views they take on the subject of Afghanistan. The occupation of that country may have been a most impolitic act, and it may be their duty to counteract its effect, and to terminate the policy that we attempted to establish. All this may be perfectly true, but all impartial persons will feel that such a step should be taken with great prudence, that it should be taken gradually, and that ministers ought not to have gone to the housetops to proclaim their peril to the world—their peril; I may rather say their

---

[48] Neither Disraeli nor his chief biographer has more to say on this point.
[49] The Earl of Lytton.
[50] Russia.

perplexity. We must remember also that the military feat of the invasion and occupation of Afghanistan was no mean one. Rarely have the discipline and valour of our troops, both British and native, been more distinguished, and, above all, we have produced a General equal to any conjuncture of the war. These were all circumstances that won respect in Asia and Europe; but the ministers, as I say, go to the housetops to proclaim to every bazaar in the East that they do not know what to do, and that, after all this anxiety, they are going to scuttle out of the country as fast as they can.

What I want your lordships chiefly to observe is the consequence of such conduct, which is of the most destructive and deleterious kind. It may have been our policy to quit Afghanistan, but if we quit it in this spirit and after such declarations every military adventurer feels, "This is my opportunity: the British are going to leave this country, and I will succeed them as far as I can." Clearly, you have produced a state of anarchy, and at last you say that you will consummate your confession of impotence and blundering by giving up the city of Candahar. But why has all this taken place? Because there have been declarations made on the subject, declarations of the most unmeasured kind; because the country has been agitated to believe that the change of Government would instantly terminate the dangerous occupation of Afghanistan; and because pledges made in total ignorance of the circumstances of the case have now to be redeemed at the cost of the credit of the country. Both in foreign affairs and in Afghanistan—in the one because the peace of Europe is no longer assured but menaced, and in the other because Central Asia is in a state of anarchy—you have now to pay the cost of declarations made in a polemical and not in a political sense to the people of the country.

I must now touch on that subject which, after all, absorbs all our thoughts at the present moment, and that is the subject of Ireland. When the late Government were responsible for the administration of affairs, the state of Ireland undoubtedly caused much anxiety. In ordinary circumstances I believe the skilful administration of my noble friend near me would in no way have been disturbed; but we had a terrible visitation, and have at the same time to deal with a body of men who will take advantage of distress to render the work of government more difficult. Fortunately the famine was not as fatal as we once feared, and the measures taken by the Government and supported by private charity almost unprecedented, which, under the direction of a noble lady,[51]

---

[51] The Duchess of Marlborough.

touched the hearts of the Irish for the time, gave us every hope that we might proceed without further disaster. The Peace Preservation Act certainly had a beneficial effect, and greatly assisted the Government; and our opinion was, although we had before us information which is, no doubt, well known to the present ministers, that it would be possible to carry affairs safely through with the law that then existed, and that, with the mitigation of the calamity that then prevailed, we might grapple with the conspirators, who seek not merely separation from this country, but the establishment of an independent foreign Power.

Just before the general election I felt it my duty, occupying the position I then did, to place before the country issues which I thought were of vast importance, and which demanded at that critical time the consideration of the country. Not sitting in the other House of Parliament, and therefore not having the privilege of addressing my old constituents, as in old days, I thought it becoming to address to the Lord-Lieutenant of Ireland a letter, in which I called the attention of the country to the state of Ireland. I placed before the country only two points. I warned it to be most careful not to meddle thoughtlessly with foreign affairs, because I foresaw that if it did, there would be a chance, and more than a chance, of a European war. What has occurred has, I think, quite justified that warning; but we can at least hope that, a war not having occurred, Her Majesty's ministers may have been successful in preventing it. But as regards Ireland, in my letter to the Lord-Lieutenant—on March 8, I think it was—I warned the country that if the Government did not show a becoming vigilance, something would happen which would be almost as bad as famine and pestilence. . . . . .[52]

I think it utter mockery to discuss any questions connected with Ireland now, except the restoration of peace and order, the re-establishment of the sovereignty of the Queen, and a policy that will announce to Europe that the spirit of England has not ceased, and that, great as are the dangers that now environ ministers, the Parliament of England will be equal to the occasion.

[52] There is omitted further details on the Irish situation.

Chapter VII

GLADSTONE

Chapter VII

GLADSTONE

G LADSTONE acknowledged, in a speech of 1866 on Parliamentary reform,[1] the sources of his early political philosophy:

"I was bred under the shadow of the great name of Canning; every influence connected with that name governed the first political impressions of my childhood and my youth; with Mr. Canning I rejoiced in the removal of religious disabilities from the Roman Catholic body, and in the free and truly British tone which he gave to our policy abroad; with Mr. Canning I rejoiced in the opening he made towards the establishment of free commercial interchanges between nations; with Mr. Canning and under the shadow of that great name, and under the shadow of the yet more venerable name of Burke, I grant my youthful mind and imagination were impressed . . . . ."

He was, indeed, more conservative than his words suggest and thus came to represent for a considerable period, as Macaulay has said, the rising hope of stern and unbending Tories.

William Ewart Gladstone (1809-1898) was a member of a wealthy commercial family of Liverpool which held large sugar plantations in the West Indies. He went to Eton and then Oxford, where as a student he won highest honors and, as a debater, the presidency of the Oxford Union. Religious by nature, he thought of entering the church but was eventually persuaded by his father that politics held vast possibilities for good. His conservative tendencies and his abilities came to the attention of the Duke of Newcastle, by whom he was asked to stand for the borough of Newark in 1832. He declared himself under obligation to watch and resist "uninquiring and undiscriminating desire for change" in his hustings address, won the election, and took his seat for the session of 1833.

The year 1833, therefore, saw the beginning of a Parliamen-

---

[1] Hansard, CLXXXIII (3d Ser.), 129 (April 27, 1866).

tary career which, lasting sixty-three years, was destined to be the longest active career of any English statesman of first rank. He was "opposed in 1833 to men who might have been his grandfathers; he was opposed in 1893 to men who might have been his grand-children." [2] His speeches during those years covered the whole range of politics; they are to be found here and there in 366 volumes of the *Parliamentary Debates* and utilize 15,000 columns. A mere list of all addresses delivered both within and beyond the House of Commons fills 85 pages. In addition, [3] there came from his pen numerous books and articles chiefly on religious subjects and on the Homeric question. Besides, his personal papers, correspondence, memoranda, etc., known as the Hawarden Papers, "comprise between 200,000 and 300,000 documents over all of which is impressed by the annotation or otherwise the individuality of Mr. Gladstone." [4] He may be said, indeed, to have been the embodiment of energy.

Gladstone took official position in Peel's government of 1834-1835 as junior Lord of the Treasury and later as Under Secretary of State for the colonies. Again in 1841 he served under the same leader as Vice-President of the Board of Trade. Winning promotion by 1843, he accepted the presidency of the Board of Trade with Cabinet rank. In this position he became involved in a question of Parliamentary control of railways. The speech (page 261) he made suggests that he was early opposed to *laissez faire* in a case where the public needed governmental protection. He had already shown much ability as an able and frequent speaker but disagreed with the Cabinet on a religious question concerning Ireland and withdrew from its membership. A short time later, however, he assumed the secretaryship of state for the colonies, and, since this appointment obliged him to vacate his seat and since he was no longer willing to defend the Corn Laws as a patron of Newark might desire him to do, he did not offer himself for re-election. Strange to say, he was therefore in the Cabinet but not in the House at the very time that Peel sorely needed his assistance in debates.

[2] James Bryce, *William Ewart Gladstone* (New York: Century Company, 1898), p. 19.

[3] Cf. Arthur Tilney Bassett, *Gladstone's Speeches, Descriptive Index and Bibliography* (London: Methuen and Company, Ltd., 1916), pp. 6-91.

[4] *The Gladstone Papers* (London: Cassell and Company, Ltd., 1930), p. 5.

The fall of Peel's last administration may be said to have ended the early career of Gladstone. During the period he is seemingly in contrast to Disraeli in the lack of interest in the distressing problems of the workingman.[5] It is true that in his election speech in 1832 he had declared that labor should receive adequate pay but the generalities so smoothly and sympathetically stated by Disraeli on the subject of the oppressed poor are more or less lacking from Gladstone's expressions. On the other hand judgment can hardly be passed rightly upon the latter's contribution without consideration of his budgetary accomplishments in the fifties and sixties. If, as he believed, the social and economic condition of the masses can best be ameliorated by a reduction in the pressing burden of taxation, by fiscal freedom, by extended trade, by more abundant employment and higher real wages,[6] then, perhaps, may his budget speeches of 1853 and 1860 be placed side by side with Disraeli's novels as factors influential in producing a happier environment for the working classes.

In any case his budgets brought fame—whether or no they made practicable for England, as has been claimed, the change from high protection to a full measure of free trade. The speech of 1853 took over four hours to deliver, was received with considerable enthusiasm, and is readable even today though another, "International Monetary Conference" (page 299), gives more interesting data from the view of present discussions at the same time that it typifies Gladstone's abilities to think and speak logically on financial matters. The budget of 1853 simplified and reduced the custom duties and recouped these losses by increasing the income tax and by introducing a succession duty on real property; it thus placed, it may be affirmed, the burden of taxation upon the section of society best able to bear it. Subsequent budgets had to be prepared with the idea of meeting the outlay of the Crimean War, but the budget of 1860 is particularly noteworthy for being bound up with the problems of a commercial treaty with France and the abolition of the paper duty at home.

[5] Cf. Walter P. Hall, *Mr. Gladstone* (New York: W. W. Norton and Company, Inc., 1931), pp. 42-43.

[6] Cf. Francis W. Hirsh, *Gladstone as Financier and Economist* (London: Ernest Benn, Ltd., 1931), p. xxii.

By the accomplishment of the latter object in 1861 freedom of the press and the extension of intelligence were furthered.

Gladstone hardly knew, however, though he had served as Chancellor of the Exchequer under the Liberals, with which party his political future lay. But a trip to Naples where he saw at firsthand degrading prison conditions and a total disregard of justice caused him to challenge that part of a Conservative program which was linked to repression. His interest in Italian liberty placed him at Palmerston's side even if he was unable to accept the latter's chauvinism as represented in the Don Pacifico incident. He probably was questioning whether or no Disraeli could ever become a compatible colleague. He felt reactions from his constitutency of Oxford University which, if it was conservative, nevertheless was in advance of the pocket borough of Newark. As Gladstone himself was wont to sum up the situation, the slow and relentless forces of conviction were carrying him away from his early affiliations. He remained as Palmerston's Chancellor of the Exchequer during the early sixties albeit he was not Palmerstonian in his attitude toward questions of military expenditure or Parliamentary reform. Indeed his famous speech in 1864 (cf. "Parliamentary Reform," page 264) on the question of further enfranchisement may be said to be precursory to the activity in 1866 and 1884. In the early sixties, too, he already showed that tendency in his non-Parliamentary speeches, more noticeable, perhaps, in his later career, to talk to the galleries. His speech at Newcastle, for example, in which he forcefully declared that Jefferson Davis and other leaders of the South had made a nation was unfortunate in its effect as he later acknowledged.[7] Incidentally he was so far from retaining rancor against the American assailants of those words that he later faced unpopularity at home to settle the Alabama claims under the Treaty of Washington (1871) and gave to the world the principle of international arbitration in a most serious and important problem.

The election of 1865 brought defeat to Gladstone at Oxford. He was returned from South Lancashire, however, and announced to his new constitutents that he was now "unmuzzled." In the future he was to be no mere upholder of tradition but

[7] John Morley, *The Life of William Ewart Gladstone* (New York: The Macmillan Company, 1903), II, 81.

the reformer and pioneer. The opportunity in fact was at hand. Three months to the day from the South Lancashire statement Palmerston lay dead. Earl Russell formed a ministry in which Gladstone was not only Chancellor of the Exchequer and leader of the House but also the *primum movens* in the administration. Unfortunately he soon discovered that the forces of conviction had not leavened equally the minds of all members of his party. A section led by Robert Lowe still adhered to Whig ideas on Parliamentary reform, the Radicals following John Bright were crusaders of democracy, the majority waited upon Gladstone's guidance. He chose Parliamentary reform, brought in the bill of 1866, pleased the Radicals, alienated the Whigs, met defeat with his measure, and caused the resignation of the government. Disraeli had better luck with Parliamentary reform but in turn met with defeat not only in the House but in the election of 1868, largely on the question of disestablishment of the Anglican Church in Ireland.

Gladstone became Prime Minister in 1868. He had reached what Disraeli called the top of the greasy pole. His history, for the period 1868-1874, like the history of Disraeli in the subsequent administration, is the history of England. Good woodman that he was, he attacked three branches of Ireland's upas tree and lopped off two: in spite of the Lords' opposition he carried disestablishment; he also passed a land act which gave Irish tenants compensation for unexhausted improvements, but he failed in his Irish education schemes. Among domestic reforms Gladstone's administration accomplished an extension of the principle of competition for civil service, an end of university tests which excluded Nonconformists from academic privileges, an experiment in the use of the ballot, a scheme of national education, and changes in the organization of the Army. For Gladstone's statement of his attainments to the year 1871, see "Accomplishments of the Administration" (page 270). Unfortunately, reforms were apt to disturb vested rights; the Education Act made the Dissenters in his own party rebellious because of terms which they considered too advantageous to the Established Church; and trade-unions, more important in politics since the passage of the 1867 Reform Act, were fretful over their inability to force legislation that would work effectively for their interests. The election of 1874 was lost.

By 1875 Gladstone determined to give up the leadership of his party and to devote his energy to writing. However sincere he may have been in intentions, he soon found developments in the Balkans and Disraeli's foreign policy arousing his passions. His pamphlet, *Bulgarian Horrors and the Question of the East,* which was published in September 1876, was sold at a rate of more than 10,000 copies a day; in it he demanded that the Turks relieve the countries which they had desolated by carrying off themselves: "Their Zaptiehs and their Mudirs, their Bimbashis and their Yuzbashis, their Kaimakams and their Pashas, one and all, bag and baggage."

He attacked, within a few months, the pro-Turkish administration of Disraeli from railway platforms. Much as political motives and policies may have influenced him, still more did his religious enthusiasm force him to demand protection for the Eastern Christians. But, even so, numerous speeches in a Midlothian campaign of 1879 (cf. "The British Empire—Foreign Affairs," page 283) afford evidence of his anxiety for a Liberal victory in the next general election.

Gladstone won the election of 1880 but it can hardly be truthfully said that his new administration was as successful as the previous one from 1868 to 1874. At the beginning, the question of whether Bradlaugh could affirm or take the oath of office tended to undermine his control of the House. Ireland was a constant source of trouble; Irish Nationalists carried on a campaign of obstruction in Parliament to such a degree that the introduction of the principle of closure was deemed necessary. Conduct of foreign affairs and especially the death of Gordon at Khartoum suggested that Gladstone's abilities were hardly comprehensive enough for an adequate treatment on his part of problems of the empire or even of the Union. On the other hand he passed the Reform Bills of 1884-1885, which extended the working of the Act of 1867 to the counties and accomplished some needed redistribution, the Corrupt Practices Act of 1883 which dealt fairly effectively with the problems of bribery at elections, and, most important perhaps of all his legislative achievements, the Irish Land Bill of 1881. This measure permitted governmental interference with private property by purporting to give the Irish the three F's—in the tongue of the Liberals, fair rent, fixity of tenure, free sale; in the tongue of the

Conservatives, fraud, force, folly. Perhaps any act was destined to fail that attempted to give fair rent in a decade of rapidly changing economic conditions, but in any case this particular measure was not to the universal liking of the Irish, whose factious opposition caused the Liberals once again to turn to coercion.

By the time a new election was held the Irish problem had become a specter to both major political parties. The Conservatives who had taken office a few months earlier upon the defeat of the Liberal budget bill, contained, among leading members, personages who were not averse to trying some form of Home Rule. Gladstone's position was, for a time, unknown except that he expressed hope of a Liberal majority sufficiently large that his party without the aid of Irish Nationalists might be able to pass appropriate legislation. His hope was not fulfilled. The election returns showed that Conservatives and Irish Nationalists equaled numerically the Liberals, and Gladstone determined to introduce a Home Rule Bill.

The Liberal leader has frequently been blamed for attacking the Irish problem before he had consolidated his position politically by passing legislation for the rural laborers who had stood by him in the election of 1885. But, in opposition to this criticism, it may be said that Ireland was a problem pressing for solution and that Gladstone, by reason of his own advanced age, needed to be "in a hurry." Whether or no he was influenced by considerations of future fame, it is a fact that he had already won great renown for domestic legislation, but the leader who solved the Irish problem would be not only the Grand Old Man to his own party but the greatest European statesman of the nineteenth century. But the feat was too great even for the energy and ability of a Gladstone. Assailed alike by political opponents and by members of his own party, 93 of whom voted against him, his measure lost on the second reading by 343 to 313. But before the division had taken place Gladstone gave one of his most interesting speeches (cf. "Government of Ireland Bill," page 288). The appeal to the nation which he now demanded (1886) was unsuccessful. A new opportunity was not presented until 1892 when at eighty-two years of age he formed his last administration. A Home Rule Bill which he then sponsored was passed by the Commons but defeated by the Lords.

His last words in the House of Commons in March 1894 referred to a problem upon which a new century has acted by the Parliament Bill of 1911.

Resigning at last from further official services to a sovereign whose reign he had helped to make famous, he received from the Queen "not one syllable . . . . either as to the future or the past." English financiers, more grateful than Her Majesty, were wont to praise the last administration in so far as it had stated with finality through its leader an adherence to the gold standard ("International Monetary Conference," page 299).

As an orator Gladstone probably outranked all his contemporaries save John Bright. The expressive modulation of his voice, the grace and variety of his gestures, the force of his delivery, the lively imagery coming from his illustrations and quotations, the skillful use of sarcasm, the flash of his eye, the impression which he conveyed of his own conviction—all are famous. Likewise was he remarkable for the range of his interests which, save for certain aspects of scientific and historical research, was comprehensive (cf. "Training in the University," page 307). So great was his oratorical fame, indeed, that the speeches themselves need vindication. They are sometimes spoken of as unreadable though at the time of delivery their effectiveness was such as to change the course of history. In reality, a careful perusal of them will not leave even the reader of today untouched, especially in those passages where the orator's indignation is expressed or where, on the other hand, his ideas are supported by appropriate quotations from the classics.

Gladstone in his last years remained actively engaged in literary work and, to some extent, interested in current European problems. He died in May 1898, carried off by the same disease, probably, of which his early political hero, Canning, had died.

1. Railways

Gladstone asked the House, on February 5, 1844, to appoint a committee to inquire into many points connected with railways. The request was granted, and on March 4 a report was called to the attention of the Commons (HANSARD, LXXIII [3d Ser.], 516). Out of the committee's activity came a bill dealing largely with Parliamentary rights to purchase future railways and with matters involving passenger service. Gladstone's speech, which ended by moving a second reading, began with a discussion of the composition and opinions of the committee. It then dealt with the opponents of the measure (cf. HANSARD, LXXVI [3d Ser.], 480-509 [July 8, 1844]). Only a small portion of it is presented.

Those powerful Companies that were now somewhat strong in impeding the legislative power of Parliament, would become stronger by delay. If they were now strong in their opposition to this Bill, they would increase in strength in a future Parliament. He therefore warned the House how they let slip the present opportunity for adopting a proposition which he thought would be effectual for the execution of those powers it was deemed wise and salutary to establish. If this were done, it should not be his fault. If the House allowed this opportunity to pass by, on them be the responsibility. Did the House think that when they should have to confront twice the power they now had to contend with, increased as that power would be by the success of their efforts now, over a Committee of the House of Commons, and over the Executive Government—did they think that their opponents would be more moderate then than now? Considering that, even now, they would not allow Parliament to reserve a legislative power over future railways, how much greater would be their opposition after they had shown their strength, and the House had shown its weakness by truckling to that power. To the postponement of this measure, therefore, as truckling to that power, he would be no party.

This was a curious and instructive part of the case. One portion of the opponents of this Bill were Directors and officers, and parties connected with railways, who adopted the very high line against the interference of Parliament altogether. The Chairman [8] of the Great Western Railway Company, the honourable Member for Reading, was the chieftain among that class. He, with others, adopted what was called the high line; that honourable Gentleman was opposed to proceedings to legislate upon any general principles,

[8] Charles Russell.

and he seemed to think that he was supported by all the Railway Proprietors in the doctrines which he endeavoured to enforce; but that was a great mistake. He (Mr. Gladstone) knew several very large Proprietors of railway shares, who did not join in that opposition to Parliamentary interference. There were no public meetings held on the subject. He would undertake to say that of the Grand Junction Railway Company, there would be no public meeting to oppose the present Bill. A majority of the Directors might petition Parliament, but there would be no public meeting of the Company called. No doubt some of the Directors might say, as some of the Directors of other Companies did, that all Parliamentary interference was inexpedient; that things ought to be left as they were; that the Legislature ought to trust to the effects of competition; that the system which now existed, had given the country a great many very fine railways; that the public were now carried faster and at a cheaper rate than they had ever been. It was said, let matters, therefore, be allowed to go on as at present, and let the country trust to the effects of competition. Now, for his part, he would rather give his confidence to a Gracchus, when speaking on the subject of sedition, than give his confidence to a Railway Director, when speaking to the public of the effects of competition. Those who took the high line, as he said, told the world, that the effect of the proposed plan would be to chill all competition, and if honourable Members did not shut their eyes, they must see sufficient of competition to form a sound judgment on the present measure.

But now he came to the notable quarrel which had subsisted for a time between the London and Birmingham Company on the one hand, and the Grand Junction on the other, and in which those two Companies were at deadly odds; and so far as Railway Companies could be said to be capable of ferocity, they might be described as ferocious. It was said, that one result of this quarrel would be most flourishing prospects for the public; there were to be several new lines of railways; the Chester and Birmingham was to be carried on to Birkenstead, then there was to be one from Shrewsbury to Chester, and thence to Liverpool. For the public advantage all this was to be done. But the Grand Junction Company were determined to show as much public spirit, and so they projected a line from Stafford to Bedford, completing the line the whole way to London, independently of the London and Birmingham line. This was the nature of the dispute between the two Companies. But these Railway Companies were singularly philanthropic among themselves. Their quarrels were like lovers' quarrels, and they reminded him of a quotation once felicitously made use of by Mr. Fox—

"Breves inimicitiae, amicitiae sempiturnae"

The two Companies met together and made up their quarrel; but the line from Birmingham to Chester, and from Stafford to Bedford, were gone to the land where all things were forgotten. He would show to what extent the doctrine of this high school of non-interference on the subject of railways went, by referring to the evidence of Mr. Saunders who belonged to that school. That gentleman was asked:—

"Do you not think that as matters now stand, if another Railway Company is ready to come forward, and offers to carry the public at a lower rate than the London and Birmingham now carry them, that is a reason for Parliament to say, we will have the public carried cheaper, and therefore will sanction the line?" The answer was—"Most unquestionably not." "The London and Birmingham charging 30s. for a first-class, and 20s. for a second-class passenger, I understand you to say that if a body of persons, competent in point of capital, were to come forward and say, 'We are ready to make a Railway, and to give all the accommodation the existing Railway gives, and to carry at 20s. and 15s.' Parliament ought not to sanction those parties going forward with their project?"—Answer: "Most undoubtedly I do say that."

The fear which Mr. Saunders and others entertained was that the effect of the proposed interference by Parliament would be, that a panic would prevail amongst all Railway Proprietors, and no one would again apply his capital to such purposes; and this he (Mr. Gladstone) would say, that if the present Bill were defeated, that defeat would be mainly owing to Mr. Saunders. . . . . .

2. Parliamentary Reform

Mr. Gladstone expressed the following opinions on May 11, 1864, during the debate on the second reading of Mr. E. Baines's Borough Franchise Bill. The first part of the speech, which may be found in HANSARD *(CLXXV [3d Ser.], 312-27), deals largely with the desirability of discussing Parliamentary reform in its various aspects.*

Again, Sir, let us look for a few moments at the altered, the happily altered, relations of the working classes to the Government, the laws, the institutions, and, above all, to the throne of this country. Let us go back—it is no long period in the history of a nation—to an epoch not very many years before the passing of the Reform Bill, and consider what was the state of things at a time when many of us were unborn, and when most of us were children—I mean, to the years which immediately succeeded the peace of 1815. We all know the history of those times; most of us recollect the atmosphere and the ideas, under the influence of which we were brought up. They were not ideas which belonged to the old current of English history; nor were they in conformity with the liberal sentiments which pervaded, at its best periods, the politics of the country, and which harmonized with the spirit of the old British Constitution. They were, on the contrary, ideas referable to those lamentable excesses of the first French Revolution, which produced here a terrible re-action, and went far to establish the doctrine that the masses of every community were in permanent antagonism with the laws under which they lived, and were disposed to regard those laws, and the persons by whom the laws were made and administered, as their natural enemies. Unhappily, there are but too many indications to prove that this is no vague or imaginary description. The time to which I now refer, was a time when deficiences in the harvests were followed by riots, and when rioters did not hold sacred even the person of Majesty itself. In 1817, when the Prince Regent came down to open Parliament, his carriage was assailed by the populace of London; and what was the remedy provided for this state of things? Why, the remedy was sought in the suspension of the *Habeas Corpus* Act; or in the limitation of the action of the press, already restricted; [9] or in the employment of spies and the deliberate defence of their employment, who, for the supposed security of the Government, were sent throughout the country to dog the course of private life, and

[9] See Canning's speech, "Vindication of Governmental Policies," page 21.

to arrest persons, or to check them, in the formation of conspiracies real or supposed.

And what, let me ask, is the state of things now? With truth, Sir, it may be said that the epoch I have named, removed from us, in mere chronological reckoning, by less than half a century, is in the political sphere separated from us by a distance almost immeasurable. For now it may be fearlessly asserted that the fixed traditional sentiment of the working man has begun to be confidence in the law, in Parliament, and even in the executive Government. Of this gratifying state of things it fell to my lot to receive a single, indeed, but a significant proof no later than yesterday. [Cries of "No, no!" and laughter.] The quick-witted character of honourable Gentlemen opposite outstrips, I am afraid, the tardy movement of my observations. Let them only have a very little patience, and they will, I believe, see cause for listening to what I shall say. I was about to proceed to say, in illustration of my argument, that only yesterday I had the satisfaction of receiving a deputation of working men from the Society of Amalgamated Engineers. That Society consists of very large numbers of highly-skilled workmen, and has two hundred and sixty branches; it is a society representing the very class in which we should most be inclined to look for a spirit of even jealous independence of all direct relations with the Government. But the deputation came to state to me that the society had large balances of money open for investment, and that many of its members could not feel satisfied unless they were allowed to place their funds in the hands of the Government, by means of a modification in the rules of the Post Office savings banks. Now that, I think, I may say, without being liable to any expression of adverse feeling on the part of honourable Gentlemen opposite, was a very small but yet significant indication, among thousands of others, of the altered temper to which I have referred.

Instead, however, of uttering on the point my own opinions, I should like to use the words of the working classes themselves. In an address which, in company with my right honourable Friend the Member for Staffordshire,[10] I heard read at a meeting which was held in the Potteries last autumn, they say, of their own spontaneous Motion, uninfluenced by the action of their employers, in relation to the legislation of late years—

"The great measures that have been passed during the last twenty years by the British Legislature have conferred incalculable blessings on

[10] Gladstone's personal friend, C. B. Adderley, onetime follower of Peel.

the whole community, and particularly on the working classes, by unfettering the trade and commerce of the country, cheapening the essentials of our daily sustenance, placing a large proportion of the comforts and luxuries of life within our reach, and rendering the obtainment of knowledge comparatively easy among the great mass of the sons of toil."

And this is the mode in which they then proceed to describe their view of the conduct of the upper classes towards them—

"Pardon us for alluding to the kindly conduct now so commonly evinced by the wealthier portions of the community to assist in the physical and moral improvement of the working classes. The well-being of the toiling mass is now generally admitted to be an essential to the national weal. This forms a pleasing contrast to the opinions cherished half a century ago. The humbler classes also are duly mindful of the happy change, and, without any abatement of manly independence, fully appreciate the benefits resulting therefrom, contentedly fostering a hopeful expectation of the future. May heaven favour and promote this happy mutuality! as we feel confident that all such kindly interchange materially contributes to the general good."

Now, such language does, in my opinion, the greatest credit to the parties from whom it proceeds. This is a point on which no difference of opinion can prevail. I think I may go a step further, and consider these statements as indicating not only the sentiments of a particular body at the particular place from which they proceeded, but the general sentiments of the best-conducted and most enlightened working men of the country. It may, however, be said, that such statements prove the existing state of things to be satisfactory.

But surely this is no sufficient answer. Is it right, I ask, that in the face of such dispositions, the present law of almost entire exclusion should continue to prevail? Again, I call upon the adversary to show cause. And I venture to say that every man who is not presumably incapacitated by some consideration of personal unfitness or of political danger is morally entitled to come within the pale of the Constitution. Of course, in giving utterance to such a proposition, I do not recede from the protest I have previously made against sudden, or violent, or excessive, or intoxicating change; but I apply it with confidence to this effect, that fitness for the franchise, when it is shown to exist—as I say it is shown to exist in the case of a select portion of the working class—is not repelled on sufficient grounds from the portals of the Constitution by the allegation that things are well as they are. I contend, moreover, that persons who have prompted the expression of such sentiments as those to which I have referred, and whom I know to have been Members of the working class, are to be presumed worthy and fit to discharge the duties of citizenship, and that to admission to the discharge of those duties they are well and justly entitled.

The present franchise, I may add, on the whole—subject, of course, to some exceptions—draws the line between the lower middle class and the upper order of the working class. As a general rule, the lower stratum of the middle class is admitted to the exercise of the franchise, while the upper stratum of the working class is excluded. That I believe to be a fair general description of the present formation of the constituencies in boroughs and towns. Is it a state of things, I would ask, recommended by clear principles of reason? Is the upper portion of the working classes inferior to the lowest portion of the middle? That is a question I should wish to be considered on both sides of the House. For my own part, it appears to me that the negative of the proposition may be held with the greatest confidence. Whenever this Question comes to be discussed, with the view to an immediate issue, the conduct of the general body of the operatives of Lancashire cannot be forgotten. What are the qualities which fit a man for the exercise of a privilege such as the franchise? Self-command, self-control, respect for order, patience under suffering, confidence in the law, regard for superiors; and when, I should like to ask, were all these great qualities exhibited in a manner more signal, I would even say more illustrious, than under the profound affliction of the winter of 1862? [11] I admit the danger of dealing with enormous masses of men; but I am now speaking only of a limited portion of the working class, and I, for one, cannot admit that there is that special virtue in the nature of the middle class which ought to lead to our drawing a marked distinction, a distinction almost purporting to be one of principle, between them and a select portion of the working classes, so far as relates to the exercise of the franchise.

But, Sir, this Question has received a very remarkable illustration from the experience of the last few years. So far as Lancashire is concerned, we have the most extraordinary evidence—evidence amounting almost to mathematical demonstration—of the competency of the working man to discharge those duties of retail trade and the distribution of commodities, which are commonly intrusted to the lower part of the middle class. I allude to the evidence afforded by the marvellous success in that particular county (and I hope the example of that county may not be too eagerly followed elsewhere) of the cooperative system. For my own part,

---

[11] Reference to the cotton famine of the American Civil War period.

I am not ashamed to say that, if twenty or ten years ago anybody had prophesied to me the success of that system, as it has recently been exhibited in Rochdale and other towns in the north—if I had been told that labouring men would so associate together with mutual advantage, to the exclusion of the retail dealer who comes between the producer and the consumer of commodities, I should have regarded the prediction as absurd. There is, in my opinion, no greater social marvel at the present day than the manner in which these societies flourish in Lancashire, combined with a consideration of the apparent soundness of the financial basis on which they are built; for the bodies of men who have had recourse to the co-operative system have been, as it would appear, those who have stood out with the most manly resolution against the storms of adversity, who have been the last to throw themselves on the charity of their neighbours, and who have proved themselves to be best qualified for the discharge of the duties of independent citizens. And when we have before us considerable numbers of men answering to this description, it is, I think, well worth our while to consider what is the title which they advance to the generous notice of Parliament in regard to their appeal to be admitted in such measure as may upon consideration seem fit, to the exercise of the franchise. I, for myself, confess that I think the investigation will be far better conducted if we approach the question at an early date, in a calm frame of mind, and without having our doors besieged by crowds, or our table loaded with petitions; rather than if we postpone entering upon it until a great agitation has arisen.

And now, Sir, one word in conclusion. I believe that it has been given to us of this generation to witness, advancing as it were under our very eyes from day to day, the most blessed of all social processes; I mean the process which unites together not the interests only but the feelings of all the several classes of the community, and which throws back into the shadows of oblivion those discords by which they were kept apart from one another. I know of nothing which can contribute, in any degree comparable to that union, to the welfare of the commonwealth. It is well, Sir, that we should be suitably provided with armies, and fleets, and fortifications; it is well too that all these should rest upon and be sustained, as they ought to be, by a sound system of finance, and out of a revenue not wasted by a careless Parliament, or by a profligate Administration. But that which is better and more weighty still is that hearts should be bound together by a reasonable extension, at fitting times, and among selected portions of the people, of every benefit and every privilege that can justly be conferred upon them; and, for one, I am prepared to give my support to the Motion now made by my honourable Friend (Mr. Baines), because I believe, and am persuaded, that it will powerfully tend to that binding and blending and knitting of hearts together, and thus to the infusion of new vigour into the old, but in the best sense still young, and flourishing, and undecaying British Constitution.

3. Accomplishments of the Administration

Gladstone gave this speech to his constituents at Greenwich on October 28, 1871. The first part of it treats especially with the ministerial economy that was causing discontent among the dockyard work- ers. *It may be found conveniently in toto in Bassett's* Gladstone's Speeches, Descriptive Index and Bibliography *and with slight variations in phraseology in* The Times *(London) of October 30, 1871.*

I now pass on from the subject of the promises that I made to you in 1868; because I am not aware that there was any other question of very great consequence upon which, at that time, it was my duty materially to dilate. But we have gone on from these to other subjects; and what have they been? They have been three—three, I mean, which I place in the first order of magnitude. One of them is the abolition of purchase in the army, one of them is the education of the people—and one of them is the protection of the voter by the ballot. Well, now, first in attacking purchase in the army, we were perfectly well aware that we were assailing class interest in its favourite and most formidable stronghold, and I rejoice to think that in a single session we have been able to achieve a work so formidable. It is indeed achieved at a great cost; because, when the people of England set about political reforms they never accomplish them in a niggardly spirit, but their practice is to make generous compensations to those who may have suffered, aye sometimes even to those who only may imagine themselves to suffer, by them; and in every doubtful case to adopt the liberal course of action. But what is the real case of the British army? The public has been practised upon by writers who seem to find a kind of luxury in panic and alarm; and who endeavour to propagate these feelings throughout the country without success; although, for my part, I regard them with rather less of charity—I do not mean the people, but the endeavours—with rather less of goodwill and sympathy, than I should regard the propagation of the small-pox or the cattle plague. You have always had in this country, both as to officers and as to men, an army of the noblest and the very best material. Allow me to give you a short anecdote, to vary the wearisomeness of my discourse. I daresay many of you have heard the name of Bewick, who was a famous woodcutter—an artist of great celebrity, a northern man. He lived, I think, in the time of the American War. Besides his woodcutting, he determined that. as it was a time of danger, and he had an English heart in his bosom, he would learn a little soldiering. So he and two or three of his friends sent for the drill sergeant, and the drill sergeant put them through their exercise, but he only troubled them with one precept, and it was this, "Now mind, my lads, what you have to do is this: When you go into action, you must stand like a brick wall." And that has been the great quality of the British soldier— that under all circumstances he has been ready to stand, and has stood, "like a brick wall." And there was a time when standing "like a brick wall" was almost enough to win a battle. It will not do now. War, instead of being a rude test of strength, has become one of the most highly developed of all the arts practised by mankind. I know not whether to regret it or to rejoice at it; I simply state the fact that, instead of trusting simply to the native and sterling qualities of the people, we must now endeavour to add to these qualities every advantage that can be imparted by the most skilful and effectual training.

With a view to this training—not merely of the men, where it is comparatively simple, but of the officers, who, even more than the men, are the strength of the army, and the essential condition of its efficiency—we have asked the country to pay a large sum of money. The country has met the call with cheerfulness, and has witnessed with satisfaction the downfall of a great monopoly. And, gentlemen, with respect to our alarmists, what have we lately seen? For the first time, at least the first upon such a scale and under such conditions, we have made a very great step in advance, by endeavouring to put a portion of our forces into mimic action upon the open lands of Hampshire. The performances of those troops have been witnessed by most enlightened and distinguished foreign officers from every great country in Europe. We were told at the end of the session, and told by an ex-Minister, whose words would naturally carry force with his countrymen, that we had an army that could not march; and a gallant colonel rose in the house (A Voice: "One of your own party.")—if so, all the better for the purpose, but he was an opponent—a gallant colonel told the House of Commons, that he felt obliged to break through the rules of its procedure in order to raise a discussion upon the question of the manoeuvres, for he said such was the course of the Government, that it was a question not merely of the well-being, but of the very existence of the British army. This was the condition to which we were reduced. Well, now, gentlemen, we have had time to receive back from foreign courts the most interesting reports made to their respective Governments by those distinguished officers; and I am rejoiced to inform you that their character is of the most encouraging description. Not only in every case do they declare a warm admiration—I will not say an unbounded admiration, in order that I may avoid anything like hyperbole—for the material of both our officers and our men; but of the various branches of the service, as to their efficiency, they speak in terms of the highest honour; and while as friendly critics they point out, and as we knew they would point out, and as we hoped they would point out many matters upon which we need and may endeavour to improve, they show that the condition of the army, so far from justifying the ridiculous apprehensions that have gone abroad, is one that ought to fill all Englishmen with hope and satisfaction, and to prove to us that never were our establishments more efficient; never were we more able, if it should please Providence to bring upon us the necessity, to entrust its defence to troops and to officers worthy of their country, and qualified to make the defence effectual. And now let me say one word with respect to the War Minister. It has been the fashion during the present year to scoff at Mr. Cardwell. I can only say that when he is condemned I, for my part, am glad to share the condemnation. But I venture to affirm that no man, who has held the seals of office since the Secretaryship of War was established, has done so much for the reform and efficiency of the army; and I am quite sure that when he retires from that office, he will leave behind him a name entitled to the approval and the gratitude of the country. There, gentlemen, is our justification, summarily stated, for dealing with the question of purchase. I press on to other matters.

Were we wrong in dealing with the question of education? ("No, no.") Very well. Has there ever been, I would next venture to say to the most jealous critic of the Education Act—has there ever been achieved in this country so great a step in advance towards the attainment of an object which we believe to be vital to the welfare of the nation? It is not all done at once—it cannot be all done at once. A measure so great and comprehensive, and at the same time so novel, cannot be perfect. The differences of opinion that prevail in this free country make it quite impossible to meet the views of all. Indulgence, equity, the sacrifice of extreme opinions, must be asked for in every quarter. But I ask those who are least satisfied with the Education Act this one and simple question—Whether it is not a great step, nay, a great stride, achieved upon the path of real progress? The objects of that measure shall be very shortly stated. The great object of all was to make education universal and effective. This was to be done, and in doing it we sought, and I think reason and common sense required us to seek, to turn to account for that purpose the vast machinery of education already existing in the country, which had been devised and mainly provided by the Christian philanthropy and the voluntary action of the people. That was the second condition under which the Act was framed. The third was, and I think it was not less wise than the two former, that we should endeavour to separate the action of the State in the matter of education, and the application of State funds, in which I include funds raised by rate, from all subjects on which, unhappily, religious differences prevail. Those, I may say, were three of the principles of the measure; and the fourth principle, not less important than the others, was this: that we should trust for the attainment of these great objects, as little as possible to the central Government, and as much as possible to the local authorities and the self-governing power of the people. And let me say in passing, that in my opinion if there be one portion of our institutions more precious in my view than another, it is that portion in which the people are locally organized for the purposes of acquiring the habits and instincts of political action, and applying their own free consciences and free understandings to dealing with the affairs of the community. A most valuable Act was passed by Mr. Stansfeld in the last Session of Parliament which, I trust, will be the beginning of immense good in that respect, and I refer to it here because it touches upon the principle of the Education Act, which I have just mentioned, viz., that as far as possible the application of the Act should be left in the hands of the local authorities. I am not surprised nor disappointed, and I hope that you are neither the one nor the other, if we find that some difficulties have arisen in working out the detail of the Act. (Mr. Gladstone paused here to refresh his voice from a small bottle of restoratives. As he did so, a voice in the crowd was heard exclaiming, "Give us some," to which the right honourable gentleman rejoined, amidst much laughter, "Yes, you would want some if you had to do what I have.") The right honourable gentleman continued:—

Great interest has been excited, both in this and in other constituencies, with respect to the payment of fees to denominational schools for the teaching of those children whose parents are found to be unable to bear the charge of their education. Now, perhaps, it will be a comfort to you to know that at least there is some hope that the extent of this particular grievance and difficulty may not be very wide. In the town of Stockport the Education Board has lately resolved to introduce the principle of compulsion, which, as I have stated, or as I have implied, was one of the principles of the Education Act. They have, by issuing their notices to that effect, added 25 per cent. to the number of children attending schools. In 400 cases they have had to admonish parents, and to warn them that they would be punished unless they complied with the Act; but the whole amount of money—although there are as yet no rate-schools in action, and they have been obliged to allow all children to be sent to denominational schools—which they have as yet paid to these schools in aid of poor parents comes only to £47. But, gentlemen, I have no doubt that this question is a grave and serious question, and I will not attempt to say more upon it than this: On the one hand we shall endeavour to adhere to the principle of the Act which aims at severance between the application of State funds and controverted matters in religion. On the other hand I must pause for my own part, and I believe my colleagues would feel themselves obliged to pause before they could resolve to say to the parent who desires to send his child to a school of his own persuasion, but is unable to pay the charge, and who is compelled by public authority to send it to some school, "If you attempt to send your child to a school of your own persuasion, if you will not send it to a school of the principles of which you disapprove—namely, to a rate-school, —we will send you to prison." I do not believe public opinion would sustain us in such a course as that.

Well, gentlemen, with regard to the remaining one of these great subjects—namely, the Ballot,[12]—I will only say we believe it to be your opinion that we have made a good and wise choice in pressing that important question on the attention of Parliament. The enfranchisement, the wide enfranchisement of the working classes, was intended to give the boon of political power not only to the class, but to every individual in the class. We have, therefore, to secure in the case of these persons, many of them to a considerable extent from their temporal circumstances dependent upon others, that the vote which we invite them to give shall be given freely— freely as respects landlord, freely as respects customer, freely as respects employer, freely as respects combination of the working-class itself; and I rejoice to think, gentlemen, that, although the Royal Assent has not yet been given to a bill for secret voting, yet for every practical purpose, after the proceedings of last Session, the question has very nearly reached the stage of final triumph.

I will now, gentlemen, for the present assume that, as regards the class of greater subjects, on which I had the honour of addressing you at the time of my election, and as regards those greater questions to which we have invited Parliament principally to apply itself, you may be disposed to think we have not made the unreasonable or injudicious selection, although we had to choose from among many matters of deep interest and importance.[13]. . . . .

[12] *I.e.*, the secret ballot.
[13] A short discussion on the need of future legislation relating to health is omitted.

There is a question of the future on which we have heard much said of late—I mean the question of the constitution of the House of Lords. (A Voice: "You had better leave that alone.") My friend there says, "Leave the constitution of the House of Lords alone." I am not prepared quite to agree with my friend, because the constitution of the House of Lords has often been a subject of consideration among the wisest and the most sober-minded men; as, for example, when a proposal—of which my friend disapproves apparently—was made, a few years ago, to make a moderate addition to the House of Lords, of peers holding peerages for life. I am not going to discuss that particular measure; but I will only say, without entering into details that would be highly interesting, but which the vast range of those subjects makes impossible on the present occasion—I will only say that I believe there are various particulars in which the constitution of the House of Lords might, under favourable circumstances, be improved. And I am bound to say that, though I believe there are some politicians, bearing the name of "Liberal," who approve of the proceedings of the House of Lords with respect to the Ballot Bill at the close of the last Session—I see a gentleman disposed to differ from me, and I have no doubt that his opinion is entitled to the greatest weight: if he likes to address this assemblage, I daresay they will be delighted to hear him, but, if I do not stand in his way, perhaps he will allow me to go on—I must own that I deeply lament that proceeding on the part of the House of Lords. It seems to me to have been a great error. After the House of Commons, which had been engaged in other and most serious labours for four or five months, had given some six weeks of the Session—six weeks of very arduous labour —mainly to maturing the Ballot Bill, it appears to me to have been a great and grievous error, I cannot call it anything less, on the part of the House of Lords, in the second week in the month of August, to say that really such was the time at which they had arrived as to render it impossible for them to afford to that measure the number of days—not a very large number of days, according to all precedent and likelihood—that it would have required from them. In the year 1835, the House of Lords, which had a Conservative majority in the face of a Whig Government, not only devoted the month of August, but carried into September the labour necessary for a subject not more important than the Ballot, and at that epoch a subject which had come prominently before the public for the first time—I mean the subject of municipal corporations. But the House of Lords at that juncture was led by a great man. The Conservative majority was guided by the Duke of Wellington; and, although, for my own part, I am not able, in

all its parts, to admire the statesmanship of the Duke of Wellington, I shall always profoundly admire the tact, and the skill, and
the sound constitutional judgment with which he managed the
House of Lords, so as to prevent that particular branch of the
Legislature from being placed in dangerous conflict with the popular
branch or with the sentiment of the country. But the reform of
the House of Lords, which has been recommended in many quarters, is briefly this,—and here I think I am coming to a point of
probable agreement with my honourable friend, if he will allow
me so to call him. The reform recommended is this—that we should
eject and expel from the House of Lords what is termed the
hereditary principle. Now, gentlemen, I hope I am at least earnest
and sincere in my intentions as to being what passes for a Liberal
politician; but before I agree, and before I commit myself to expel-
ling from the House of Lords, the hereditary principle, I will
think once, I will think twice—nay, I will think even thrice. It
is not on account of this or that particular error committed by a
public assembly that we are vitally or profoundly to change the
established and accustomed usages and principles of the Constitution. Mark what has since happened. Lord Shaftesbury, whom
I mention with a profound respect on account of his earnest and
devoted philanthropy, went the other day down to Glasgow, and
he received a most warm welcome on the part of the vast population of that city—the working population of that city. In consequence of that incident, some politicians threw up their hats, and
exclaimed that the people of Glasgow approved of Lord Shaftesbury's motion with regard to the Ballot Bill. I think that was a
precipitate conclusion. But this I conceive was shown by his reception—that the people of Glasgow, being a sagacious people, were
not disposed, on account of that particular error, to draw rapid
and precipitate conclusions, either against a man or against a body
which had performed distinguished services. I will ask you two
things; this is a question of so much interest to all, that even
after the length to which I have necessarily been drawn, I beg your
attention to two points on this portion of our subject. Before you
determine to expel the hereditary principle from the House of
Lords, I first ask you, what you will substitute for the hereditary
principle? (A Voice—"Five years' election.") That is a fruitful
hint, but yet I have another point to suggest, and it is this: I have
a shrewd suspicion in my mind that a very large proportion of
the people of England have a sneaking kindness for this hereditary
principle.

I do not mean, gentlemen, by these words that a large proportion of the people of England either desire, or intend, or would

permit that which I hope that they never will desire, or intend, or permit—namely, that the House of Lords should exercise a paramount control over the legislation of the country. That is quite another matter. But this I do say—that the people of England are not, like the people of France, lovers of naked political equality. England is a great lover of liberty; but of equality she never has been so much enamoured. Gentlemen, in judging of this question, I must say that possibly the observation of the manner in which, for such long periods, and under so many varieties of form, the love of equality in France has proved insufficient to save our generous and distinguished neighbours from the loss of liberty—the observation of these facts may tend to confirm the people of the three kingdoms in the feelings that I think they entertain; but I want to put this to you as a practical question. The only mode of judging whether an Englishman—and I use the word "Englishman" for the people of the three kingdoms—is not unfriendly to social inequalities is by watching the working of our institutions in detail. My observation has not been of a very brief term—I wish it had been, for then I should have been younger than I am now—and it is this: that whenever there is anything to be done, or to be given, and there are two candidates for it who are exactly alike—alike in opinions, alike in characters, alike in possessions,— and one is a commoner and the other a lord, the Englishman is very apt indeed to prefer the lord. . . . . . This I do say, as my own conviction, that the general sentiment most prevailing in this country is that those who compose the House of Lords are men, or are the descendants of men, of whom a very large proportion are, or were in other times, put into that house for public services, and people are disposed to look with considerable favour upon such men, and likewise upon the descendants of such, until they have proved themselves unworthy. And they know that in effect, not by compulsion, but by the free will of the people, this body of gentlemen in the House of Lords exercise throughout the country a vast social and political influence; and lastly, that many of them— although the good ones have to carry, as it were, on their backs the dead weight and the responsibility of the bad—many of them perform their duties in an admirable and exemplary manner. Under these circumstances, gentlemen, though I hope I shall, while I remain in public life, be able to act zealously and cheerfully with you for the promotion of Liberal opinions, I, for one, have never understood by Liberal opinions either precipitate conclusions or subversive opinions. And I hope we shall well consider, before we commit ourselves to vast changes, to the introduction of new and far-reaching principles, what the results are likely to be.

Now, gentlemen, I am drawing very near to my close; but I must still detain you while I refer to a sentiment, which undoubtedly has been more perceptible in the country during the present year, than I have noticed it in a good many former years. I mean a suspicion on the part of many members of the working class, that they are not governed as they ought to be, and that their interests are not properly considered. I will not enter upon the particular causes, connected with the uneasy state of Europe, which may go far to account for this sentiment; but I will venture to say this, that I think the working man will do well briefly and calmly to review the history, with regard to himself, of the last eighteen years. I take that period.—I might take a longer one—but I take that period because it enables me to present results in a tolerably simple form, and because it is a period within which I have been most intimately conversant with a multitude of questions, in which the welfare of the mass of the community is deeply and directly concerned. Within these eighteen years, what has taken place affecting all classes of the community, but especially, and more than all others, affecting the working classes of the people? In the first place, perfectly free access has been given for the entry into our ports of everything that they can want from every quarter of the world— I mean perfectly free, whether as regards prohibitions or as regards protective duties. In the second place, we have seen remitted during those eighteen years an amount of taxation which I will not undertake—and which it is not necessary for me at this moment—to state minutely; but I will venture to assert that the taxation upon commodities, which he has seen remitted within that period, is something between £15,000,000 and £20,000,000 sterling per annum. That remission of taxation, in which the working man is so especially interested, has not been purchased by an augmentation of the burdens upon other classes; because the Income-tax, though it is higher now than I should like to see it—namely, at 6d. in the pound—is still one penny lower than it was eighteen years ago, before those fifteen millions of taxes were remitted. Within these eighteen years, his class has been invested largely with the Parliamentary franchise, and he now sees himself at the point where he may reasonably hope that, before he is six or eight months older, he will be protected in the free exercise of that franchise by means of the Ballot. The Parliament has passed an Act which aims at securing for all his children, under all circumstances, a good primary education, and which provides that, if unhappily he is unable himself to meet the cost, it shall be defrayed for him by the State and by his wealthier neighbours. Whilst this provision has been made for primary education, endeavours have been made, through reforming the Universities, through the entire abolition of tests, and through an extensive dealing with the public and the grammar schools of the country, to establish the whole of our schools in a hierarchy of degrees—the several orders of education rising one above the other—so that, whenever there is in a child a capacity to rise, he may, with facility, pass on from point to point, and may find open to him the road through knowledge to distinction. But education would not be of great use to the people unless the materials of study were accessible; and therefore, at no small cost of political effort, the material of paper has been set free of duty, and every restriction, in stamp or otherwise, upon the press has been removed. The consequence has been the creation of a popular press which, for the lowness of its price, for the general ability—aye, for the general wisdom and moderation with which it is written, and for the vast extent of its circulation, I might almost venture to call, not only an honour to the nation, but the wonder of the world. And in order that the public service might indeed be a public service—in order that we might not have among the civil offices of the State that which we had complained of in the army—namely, that the service was not the property of the nation, but of the officers, we have now been enabled to remove from the entry into the Civil Service the barriers of nomination, patronage, jobbing, favouritism in whatever form; and every man belonging to the people of England—if he is able to fit his children for the purpose of competing for public employment—may do it entirely irrespective of the question of what is his condition in life, or the amount of means with which he may happen to be, or not to be endowed. I say confidently, in the face of those of the working community who may hear me, and to the minds of all those who may pay the least attention to these words through any other medium, that when, within such a period as I have described, measures like these have been achieved, while there may remain much to be done—I am the last to deny it, I am the first to assert it—there is reason to look with patience and indulgence upon a system under which such results have been accomplished; some reason for that loyalty to the Throne, and that attachment to the law, which are the happy characteristics of the people of this country.

But while I would exhort you to impose upon the Government and the Legislature every burden that they are, in their own nature, capable of bearing, in my mind they are not your friends, but in fact, though not in intention, your enemies, who teach you to look to the Legislature, or to the Government, for the radical removal of the evils which afflict human life. I read but a few days

ago, in a questionable book, verses which I think contain much
good sense, and which I will read to you:—

> "People throughout the land
> Join in one social band,
>   And save yourselves.
> If you would happy be,
> Free from all slavery,
> Bannish all knavery,
>   And save yourselves."

It is the individual mind, the individual conscience; it is the individual character, on which mainly human happiness or human misery
depends. The social problems which confront us are many and
formidable. Let the Government labour to its uttermost, let the
Legislature spend days and nights in your service; but, after the
very best has been achieved, the question whether the English
father is to be the father of a happy family and the centre of a
united home, is a question which must depend mainly upon himself. Those who propose to you schemes like those Seven Points
of which I spoke [14]—who·promise to dwellers in towns that every
one of them shall have a house and garden in the country—those
who tell you that there shall be markets for selling, at wholesale
price, retail quantities—I will not say, gentlemen, that these are
impostors, because I have no doubt that they are sincere; but I
will say that they are quacks—they are misled and beguiled by a
spurious philanthropy, and when they ought to give you substantial, even if humble and modest, boons, they are endeavouring,
perhaps, without their own consciousness, to delude you with
phantasms, and to offer you glowing fruit which, when you attempt
to taste it, will prove to be but ashes in your mouth. No, gentlemen, what we have to ask ourselves are questions which depend
upon ourselves individually in the main to answer. How are the
ravages of strong drink to be checked? In an age when, from
year to year, more and more women are becoming self-dependent
members of the community, how, without tampering with the
cardinal laws that determine providentially their position in the
world, how are we to remove the serious social inequalities under
which I, for one, hold that they labour? How, in a country where
wealth accumulates with such vast rapidity, are we to check the
growth of luxury and selfishness by sound and healthy opinion?
How are we to secure to labour its due honour?—and I mean not

---

[14] An illustration from an omitted part of the text.

only the labour of the hands, but the labour of the man, with any and with all the faculties that God has given him? How are we to make ourselves believe, and how are we to bring the country to believe, that in the sight of God and man labour in this world is honourable, and idleness is of all things most contemptible? Depend upon it I do but speak the serious and solemn truth when I say that, within and beneath the political questions that are found upon the surface, lie the deeper and more searching questions that enter into the breast, and that strike home to the conscience and the mind of every man; and it is upon the solution of these questions, and other questions such as these, that the well-being of England must depend.

Gentlemen, I use the words of a popular poet when I give vent to the sentiments of hope with which, for one, I venture to look forward to the future of the country. He says—

> "The ancient virtue is not dead,
> And long may it endure
> May wealth in England . . . ."

(and I am sure he means by wealth the higher sense of it—prosperity alone, but healthful and sound prosperity)—

> "May wealth in England never fail,
> Nor pity for the poor."

May strength and the means of material prosperity never be wanting to us. But it is far more important that there shall not be wanting the disposition to use those means aright. And now, gentlemen, I shall go home from this meeting, after having given you the best account in my feeble power, within the time and under the circumstances of the day, strengthened by the comfort of your kindness and your indulgence, to resume my share in public labours. And no motive will more operate upon me as an incentive to the discharge of duty than the gratitude with which I look back upon the, I believe, unexampled circumstances under which you chose me for your representative. But I shall endeavour and shall make it my special aim to show that gratitude less by words of sounding compliment or hollow flattery than by a manful struggle, according to the measure of my gifts, humble as they may be, to render service to a Queen who lives in the hearts of the people— and to a nation, with respect to which I will say that through all posterity, whether it be praised or whether it be blamed, whether it be acquitted or whether it be condemned, it will be acquitted or condemned upon this issue—of having made a good or bad use of the most splendid opportunities; of having turned to account, or having failed to turn to account, the powers, the energies, the faculties which mark the people of this little island as among the small and select company of great nations that have stamped their name on the page of history as gifted with the qualities that mark the leaders of mankind.

4. The British Empire—Foreign Affairs

The following short selection is taken from the opening speech of the Midlothian campaign as delivered at Edinburgh on November 25, 1879. Gladstone was attempting to arouse public opinion against Beaconsfield's foreign policy. The complete speech may be found conveniently in The Times (London) *of November 26, 1879, or in Bassett's* Gladstone's Speeches, Descriptive Index and Bibliography.

Well, gentlemen, you know—I need not enter into details—what was the general state of our foreign relations. The topic of our foreign relations can be disposed of in one minute. It is constantly said, indeed, by the scribes of the Government, and it was intimated by Lord Salisbury—to whom I will return in greater detail at a future time,—that the foreign policy of the late Government was discreditable. Well, but here I have got a witness on the other side. I have got the witness of Lord Beaconsfield's Foreign Secretary at the time when he took office. At the time when he took office in the House of Lords, Lord Derby, then enjoying the full undivided confidence of the Conservative party, used these words on the 19th March, 1874: "At the present moment the condition of the country in regard to our foreign relations is most satisfactory. There is no State whatever with which our relations are not most cordial." Now, our unfortunate friends and fellow-citizens, the Tories, are constantly called upon to believe that at the time they took office the state of the country, in regard to foreign relations, was most unsatisfactory, and that with no State were our relations most cordial, because by every State we were undervalued and despised. Gentlemen, there was not a cloud upon the horizon at the time when the charge of foreign affairs was handed over to Her Majesty's present Government. Does that imply that there was nothing serious to be done? Oh no, gentlemen, depend upon it, and you will find it to your cost before you are five years older, you will know it better than you do to-day; depend upon it that this Empire is an Empire, the daily calls of whose immense responsibilities, the daily inevitable calls of whose responsibilities, task and overtask the energies of the best and ablest of her sons. Why, gentlemen, there is not a country in the history of the world that has undertaken what we have undertaken; and when I say "what we have undertaken," I don't mean what the present Government have undertaken—that I will come to by and by—but what England in its traditional established policy and position has undertaken.

There is no precedent in human history for a formation like the

British Empire. A small island at one extremity of the globe peoples the whole earth with its colonies. Not satisfied with that, it goes among the ancient races of Asia and subjects two hundred and forty millions of men to its rule. Along with all this it disseminates over the world a commerce such as no imagination ever conceived in former times, and such as no poet ever painted. And all this has to do with the strength that lies within the narrow limits of these shores. Not a strength that I disparage; on the contrary, I wish to dissipate, if I can, the idle dreams of those who are always telling you that the strength of England depends, sometimes they say upon its prestige, sometimes they say upon its extending its Empire, or upon what it possesses beyond these shores. Rely upon it the strength of Great Britain and Ireland is within the United Kingdom. Whatever is to be done in defending and governing these vast colonies with their teeming millions; in protecting that unmeasured commerce; in relation to the enormous responsibilities of India—whatever is to be done, must be done by the force derived from you and from your children, and derived from you and your fellow-electors, and from you and from the citizens and people of this country. And who are they? They are, perhaps, some three-and-thirty millions of persons,—a population less than the population of France; less than the population of Austria; less than the population of Germany; and much less than the population of Russia. But the populations of Austria, of Russia, of Germany, and of France find it quite hard enough to settle their own matters within their own limits. We have undertaken to settle the affairs of about a fourth of the entire human race scattered over all the world. Is not that enough for the ambition of Lord Beaconsfield? It satisfied the Duke of Wellington and Mr. Canning, Lord Grey and Sir Robert Peel; it satisfied Lord Palmerston and Lord Russell, aye, and the late Lord Derby. And why cannot it satisfy—I do not want to draw any invidious distinction between Lord Beaconsfield and his colleagues; it seems to me that they are all now very much of one mind, that they all move with harmony amongst themselves; but I say, why is it not to satisfy the ambition of the members of the present Government? I affirm that, on the contrary, strive and labour as you will in office—I speak after the experience of a lifetime, of which a fair portion has been spent in office—I say that strive and labour as you will in Parliament and in office, human strength and human thought are not equal to the ordinary discharge of the calls and duties appertaining to Government in this great, wonderful and world-wide Empire. And therefore, gentlemen, I say it is indeed deplorable that in addition to these calls, of which we have evidence in a thousand forms, and of our insufficiency to meet which we have evidence in a thousand forms—when, in addition to these calls, all manner of gratuitous, dangerous, ambiguous, impracticable, and impossible engagements are contracted for us in all parts of the world.

And that is what has lately been happening. I am not now going to discuss this question upon the highest grounds. I assail the policy of the Government on the highest grounds of principle. But I am now for a few moments only about to test it on the grounds of prudence. I appeal to you as practical men, I appeal to you as agriculturists, I appeal to you as tradesmen—I appeal to you in whatever class or profession you may be, and ask whether it is not wise to have some regard to the relation between means and ends, some regard to the relation between the work to be done and the strength you possess in order to perform it. I point to the state of our legislation, our accumulated and accumulating arrears constantly growing upon us; I point to the multitude of unsolved problems connected with the administration of our Indian Empire—enough, God knows, to call forth the deepest and most anxious reflection of the most sober-minded; and even the most sanguine man, I say, might be satisfied with those tasks.

But what has been the course of things for the last three years? I will run them over almost in as many words. We have got an annexation of territory—I put it down merely that I might not be incomplete—an annexation of territory in the Fiji Islands, of which I won't speak, because I don't consider the Government is censurable for that act, whether it were a wise act or not. Nobody could say that that was their spontaneous act. But now let us look at what have been their spontaneous acts. They have annexed in Africa the Transvaal territory, inhabited by a free European, Christian, republican community, which they have thought proper to bring within the limits of a monarchy, although out of 8,000 persons in that republic qualified to vote upon the subject, we are told, and I have never seen the statement officially contradicted, that 6,500 protested against it. These are the circumstances under which we undertake to transform republicans into subjects of a monarchy. We have made war upon the Zulus. We have thereby become responsible for their territory; and not only this, but we are now, as it appears from the latest advices, about to make war upon a chief lying to the northward of the Zulus; and Sir Bartle Frere, who was the great authority for the proceedings of the Government in Afghanistan, has announced in South Africa that it will be necessary for us to extend our dominions until we reach the Portuguese frontier to the north. So much for Africa.

I come to Europe. In Europe we have annexed the island of Cyprus, of which I will say more at another time. We have assumed jointly with France the virtual government of Egypt; and possibly, as we are to extend, says Sir Bartle Frere, our southern dominions in Africa till we meet the southern frontier of the Portuguese—possibly one of these days we may extend our northern dominions in Africa till we meet the northern frontier of the Portuguese. We then, gentlemen, have undertaken to make ourselves responsible for the good government of Turkey in Asia—not of Asia Minor, as you are sometimes told exclusively, but of the whole of that great space upon the map, including the principal part of Arabia, which is known geographically as Turkey in Asia. Besides governing it well, we have undertaken to defend the Armenian frontier of Turkey against Russia, a country which we cannot possibly get at except either by travelling over several hundreds of miles by land, including mountain-chains never adapted to be traversed by armies, or else some thousands of miles of sea, ending at the extremity of the Black Sea, and then, having to effect a landing. That is another of our engagements.

Well, and as if all that were not enough, we have by the most wanton invasion of Afghanistan, broken that country into pieces, made it a miserable ruin, destroyed whatever there was in it of peace and order, caused it to be added to the anarchies of the Eastern world, and we have become responsible for the management of the millions of warlike but very partially civilized people whom it contains, under circumstances where the application of military power, and we have nothing but military power to go by, is attended at every foot with enormous difficulties.

Now, gentlemen, these are proceedings which I present to you at the present moment in the view of political prudence only. I really have but one great anxiety. This is a self-governing country. Let us bring home to the minds of the people the state of the facts they have to deal with, and in Heaven's name let them determine whether or not this is the way in which they like to be governed. Do not let us suppose this is like the old question between Whig and Tory. It is nothing of the kind. It is not now as if we were disputing about some secondary matter—it is not even as if we were disputing about the Irish Church, which no doubt was a very important affair. What we are disputing about is a whole system of Government, and to make good that proposition that it is a whole system of Government will be my great object in any addresses that I may deliver in this country. If it is acceptable, if it is liked by the people—they are the masters—it is for them to have it. It is not particularly pleasant for any man, I suppose, to spend the closing years of his life in vain and unavailing protest; but as long as he thinks his protest may avail, as long as he feels that the people have not yet had their fair chance and opportunity, it is his duty to protest, and it is to perform that duty, gentlemen, that I come here.

5. Government of Ireland Bill

Mr. Gladstone's speech may be found in HANSARD (CCCVI [3d Ser.], 1215-40 [June 7, 1886]). The first few pages, which are omitted, deal largely with questions of amendments and procedure such as might follow the acceptance of the principle of the measure by a second reading. In the speech Gladstone refers to the Grattan (Independent Irish) Parliament, 1782-1800, the legislative union of England and Ireland (1801), and various acts to redress Irish grievances (Disestablishment Act, 1869, Land Act of 1881) in which he had participated prominently. Recently he had come to accept Irish Home Rule, led, perhaps, by "the slow and relentless forces of conviction" plus—his political opponents asserted—the pressure of Charles Stewart Parnell and his Irish Home Rule party. More than ninety of his followers broke with him on the issue. Perhaps the writer may be permitted to divulge the sentiment that after reading hundreds of Parliamentary speeches he feels the peroration of this speech to be the most affecting one in Hansard.

. . . .

I wish now to refer to another matter. I hear constantly used the terms Unionists and Separatists. But what I want to know is, who are the Unionists? I want to know who are the Separatists? I see this Bill described in newspapers of great circulation, and elsewhere, as a Separation Bill. Several Gentlemen opposite adopt and make that style of description their own. Speaking of that description, I say that it is the merest slang of vulgar controversy. Do you think this Bill will tend to separation? ["Hear, hear!"] Well, your arguments, and even your prejudices, are worthy of all consideration and respect; but is it a fair and rational mode of conducting a controversy to attach these hard names to measures on which you wish to argue, and on which, I suppose, you desire to convince by argument? Let me illustrate. I go back to the Reform Act of Lord Grey.[15] When that Reform Bill was introduced, it was conscientiously and honestly believed by great masses of men, and intelligent men, too, that the Bill absolutely involved the destruction of the Monarchy. The Duke of Wellington propounded a doctrine very much to this effect; but I do not think that any of those Gentlemen, nor the newspapers that supported them, ever descended so low in their choice of weapons as to call the measure "the Monarchy Destruction Bill." Such language is a mere begging of the question. Now, I must make a large demand on your patience and your indulgence—we conscientiously believe that there

[15] Passed in 1832.

are Unionists and Disunionists; but that it is our policy that leads
to union and yours to separation. This involves a very large and
deep historical question. Let us try, for a few moments, to look at
it historically.

The arguments used on the other side of the House appear to
me to rest in principle and in the main upon one of two suppositions.
One of them, which I will not now discuss, is the profound in-
competency of the Irish people; but there is another, and it is this.
It is, I believe, the conscientious conviction of honourable Gentlemen opposite that when two or more countries, associated but not
incorporated together, are in disturbed relations with each other,
the remedy is to create an absolute legislative incorporation. On
the other hand, they believe that the dissolution of such an incorporation is clearly the mode to bring about the dissolution of
the political relations of those countries. I do not deny that there
may be cases in which legislative incorporation may have been
the means of constituting a great country, as in the case of France.
But we believe, as proved by history, that where there are those
disturbed relations between countries associated, but not incorporated, the true principle is to make ample provision for local independence, subject to Imperial unity. These are propositions of the
greatest interest and importance. Gentlemen speak of tightening
the ties between England and Ireland as if tightening the tie were
always the means to be adopted. Tightening the tie is frequently
the means of making it burst, whilst relaxing the tie is very frequently the way to provide for its durability, and to enable it to
stand a stronger strain; so that it is true, as was said by the honourable Member for Newcastle (Mr. Joseph Cowen), that the
separation of Legislatures is often the union of countries, and
the union of Legislatures is often the severance of countries. Can
you give me a single instance from all your historical inquiries
where the acknowledgment of local independence has been followed by the severance of countries? [Cries of "Turkey!" "Servia!"]
I was just going to refer to those countries, and to make this admission—that what I have said does not apply where a third
Power has intervened, and has given liberty in defiance of the
Sovereign Power to the subject State. But do you purpose to wait
until some third Power shall intervene in the case of Ireland, as
it intervened in the case of America? [An honourable Member:
We are not afraid.] I never asked the honourable Gentleman
whether he was afraid. It does not matter much whether he is
afraid or not; but I would inculcate in him that early and provident
fear which, in the language of Mr. Burke, is the mother of safety.
I admit that where some third Power interferes, as France inter-

fered in the case of America, you can expect nothing to result but severance with hostile feeling on both sides. But I am not speaking of such cases. That is not the case before us. But I ask you to give me a single instance where, apart from the intervention of a third Power, the independence of the Legislatures was followed by the severance of the nations? I can give several instances where total severance of countries has been the consequence of an attempt to tighten the bond—in the case of England and America, in the case of Belgium and Holland. The attempt to make Belgians conform to the ways and ideas and institutions of Holland led to the severance of the two countries.[16]

.   .   .   .

I can understand, then, the disinclination which honourable Gentlemen opposite have to go into history as to these cases; but it will be unfolded more and more as these debates proceed, if the controversy be prolonged—it will more and more appear how strong is the foundation upon which we stand now, and upon which Mr. Grattan stood over 86 years ago, when he contended that a union of the Legislatures was the way to a moral and a real separation between the two countries.

It has been asked in this debate, why have we put aside all the other Business of Parliament, and why have we thrown the country into all this agitation for the sake of the Irish Question? ["Hear, hear!"] That cheer is the echo that I wanted. Well, Sir, the first reason is this—because in Ireland the primary purposes of Government are not attained. What said the honourable Member for Newcastle (Mr. J. Cowen) in his eloquent speech? That in a considerable part of Ireland distress was chronic, disaffection was perpetual, and insurrection was smouldering. What is implied by those who speak of the dreadful murder that lately took place in Kerry? [17] And I must quote the Belfast outrage along with it; not as being precisely of the same character, but as a significant proof of the weakness of the tie which binds the people to the law. Sir, it is that you have not got that respect for the law, that sympathy with the law on the part of the people without which real civilization cannot exist. That is our first reason. I will not go back at this time on the dreadful story of the Union; but that, too, must be unfolded in all its hideous features if this controversy is to be prolonged—that Union of which I ought to say that, with-

[16] Mr. Gladstone then gave examples of the efficacy of home rule in preventing separation.

[17] Cf. Herbert Paul, *A History of Modern England* (New York: The Macmillan Company, 1906), V, 25, 30. See also, for disturbances in Ireland, the *Annual Register* from 1882 on.

out qualifying in the least any epithet I have used, I do not believe that that Union can or ought to be repealed, for it has made marks upon history that cannot be effaced. But I go on to another pious belief which prevails on the other side of the House, or which is often professed in controversies on the Irish Question. It is supposed that all the abuses of English power in Ireland relate to a remote period of history, and that from the year 1800 onwards from the time of the Union there has been a period of steady redress of grievances. Sir, I am sorry to say that there has been nothing of the kind. There has been a period when grievances have been redressed under compulsion, as in 1829, when Catholic Emancipation was granted to avoid civil war. There have been grievances mixed up with the most terrible evidence of the general failure of Government, as was exhibited by the Devon Commission in the year 1843. On a former night I made a quotation from the Report which spoke of the labourer. Now I have a corresponding quotation which is more important, and which speaks of the cottier. What was the proportion of the population which more than 40 years after the Union was described by the Devon Report as being in a condition worse and more disgraceful than any population in Europe? Mr. O'Connell has estimated it in this House at 5,000,000 out of 7,000,000; and Sir James Graham, in debate with him, declined to admit that it was 5,000,000, but did admit that it was 3,500,000. Well, Sir, in 1815 Parliament passed an Act of Irish legislation. What was the purpose of that Act? The Act declared that, from the state of the law in Ireland, the old intertangled usages and provisions containing effectual protection for the tenant against the landlord could not avail. These intertangled usages, which had replaced in an imperfect manner the tribal usages on which the tenure of land in Ireland was founded—Parliament swept them away and did everything to expose the tenant to the action of the landlord, but nothing to relieve or to deal with, by any amendment of the law, the terrible distress which was finally disclosed by the Devon Commission.

Again, what was the state of Ireland with regard to freedom? In the year 1820 the Sheriff of Dublin and the gentry of that county and capital determined to have a county meeting to make compliments to George IV.—the trial of Queen Caroline being just over. They held their county meeting; the people went to the county meeting, and a counter-address was moved, warm in professions of loyalty, but setting out the grievances of the country and condemning the trial and proceedings against the Queen. The Sheriff refused to hear it. He put his own motion, but refused to put the other motion; he left the meeting, which continued the debate, and he sent in the military to the meeting, which was broken up by force. That was the state of Ireland as to freedom of Petition and remonstrance 20 years after the Union. Do you suppose that would have been the case if Ireland had retained her own Parliament? No, Sir. Other cases I will not dwell upon at this late hour, simply on account of the lateness of the hour. From 1857, when we passed an Act which enabled the landlords of Ireland to sell improvements on their tenants' holdings over their heads, down to 1880, when a most limited and carefully framed Bill, the product of Mr. Forster's benevolence, was passed by this House and rejected by an enormous majority in the House of Lords, thereby precipitating the Land Act of 1881, it is impossible to stand by the legislation of this House as a whole since the Union. I have sometimes heard it said, You have had all kinds of remedial legislation. The two chief items are the Disestablishment of the Church and the reform of the Land Laws? But what did you say of these? Why, you said the change in the Land Laws was confiscation and the Disestablishment of the Church was sacrilege. You cannot at one and the same time condemn these measures as confiscation and sacrilege, and at the same time quote them as proofs of the justice with which you have acted to Ireland.

I must further say that we have proposed this measure because Ireland wants to make her own laws. It is not enough to say that you are prepared to make good laws. You were prepared to make good laws for the Colonies. You did make good laws for the Colonies according to the best of your light. The Colonists were totally dissatisfied with them. You accepted their claim to make their own laws. Ireland, in our opinion, has a claim not less urgent.

Now, Sir, what is before us? What is before us in the event of the rejection of this Bill? What alternatives have been proposed? Here I must for a moment comment on the fertile imagination of my right honourable Friend the Member for West Birmingham.[18] He has proposed alternatives, and plenty of them. My right honourable Friend says that a Dissolution has no terrors for him. I do not wonder at it. I do not see how a Dissolution can have any terrors for him. He has trimmed his vessel and he has touched his rudder in such a masterly way that in whichever direction the winds of Heaven may blow they must fill his sails. Let me illustrate my meaning. I will suppose different cases. Supposing at the Election—I mean that an Election is a thing like Christmas, it is always coming—supposing that at an Election public opinion should be very strong in favour of the Bill. My right honourable Friend

---

[18] Joseph Chamberlain did much to wreck Irish Home Rule.

would then be perfectly prepared to meet that public opinion, and tell it—"I declared strongly that I adopted the principle of the Bill." On the other hand, if public opinion was very adverse to the Bill, my right honourable Friend, again, is in complete armour, because he says—"Yes, I voted against the Bill." Supposing, again, public opinion is in favour of a very large plan for Ireland. My right honourable Friend is perfectly provided for that case also. The Government plan was not large enough for him, and he proposed in his speech on the introduction of the Bill that we should have a measure on the basis of federation, which goes beyond this Bill. Lastly—and now I have very nearly boxed the compass—supposing that public opinion should take quite a different turn, and instead of wanting very large measures for Ireland should demand very small measures for Ireland, still the resources of my right honourable Friend are not exhausted, because then he is able to point out that the last of his plans was four Provincial Councils controlled from London. Under other circumstances I should, perhaps, have been tempted to ask the secret of my right honourable Friend's recipe; as it is, I am afraid I am too old to learn it. But I do not wonder that a Dissolution has no terrors for him, because he is prepared in such a way and with such a series of expedients to meet all the possible contingencies of the case. Well, Sir, when I come to look at these practical alternatives and provisions, I find that they are visibly creations of the vivid imagination born of the hour and perishing with the hour, totally and absolutely unavailable for the solution of a great and difficult problem, the weight of which, and the urgency of which, my right honourable Friend himself in other days has seemed to feel.

But I should not say now that our plan has possession of the field without a rival. Lord Salisbury has given us a rival plan. My first remark is that Lord Salisbury's policy has not been disavowed. It is, therefore, adopted. What is it? [A laugh.] Another laugh? It has been disavowed; what is it? Great complaints are made because it has been called a policy of coercion; and Lord Salisbury is stated to have explained in "another place" that he is not favourable to coercion, but only to legislative provisions for preventing interference by one man with the liberty of another, and for insuring the regular execution of the law. And that, you say, is not coercion? Was that your view six months ago? What did the Liberal Government propose when they went out of Office? They proposed to enact clauses against the—[Cries of "No, no!" from the Opposition.]

Lord Randolph Churchill (Paddington, S.): They never made any proposal.

Mr. W. E. Gladstone: Perhaps not; but it was publicly stated. It was stated by me in a letter to the right honourable Gentleman.

Sir Michael Hicks-Beach: In October.

Mr. W. E. Gladstone: Certainly; but it was stated in order to correct a rather gross error of the right honourable Gentleman. It was stated as what we had intended when we were going out of Office—unless I am greatly mistaken, it was publicly stated in this House long before. However, it is not very important. What were the proposals that we were about to make, or that we were supposed to be about to make? Well, a proposal about "Boycotting"—to prevent one man interfering with the liberty of another; and a proposal about a change of venue to insure the execution of the ordinary law. And how were these proposals viewed? Did not the Tories go to the Elections putting upon their placards— "Vote for the Tories and no Coercion?"

Sir Walter B. Barttelot (Sussex, North-West): No, no!

Mr. W. E. Gladstone: I do not say that every Tory did it. The honourable and gallant Baronet cries "No." No doubt he did not do it; but he had no Irish voters.

Sir Walter B. Barttelot: If I had I would have done it.

Mr. W. E. Gladstone: Then it means this—that these proposals which we were about to make were defined as coercion by the Tories at the Election, and Lord Salisbury now denies them to be coercion; and it is resented with the loudest manifestations of displeasure when anyone on this side of the House states that Lord Salisbury has recommended 20 years of coercion. Lord Salisbury recommended, as he says himself, 20 years of those measures which last year were denounced by the Tories. But what did Lord Salisbury call them himself? What were his own words? His words were—

"My alternative policy is that Parliament should enable the Government of England to govern Ireland."

What is the meaning of those words? Their meaning, in the first instance, is this—The Government does not want the aid of Parliament to exercise their Executive power; it wants the aid of Parliament for fresh legislation. The demand that the Parliament should enable the Government of England to govern Ireland is a demand for fresh legislative power. This fresh legislative power, how are they to use?

"Apply that recipe honestly, consistently, and resolutely for 20 years, and at the end of that time you will find Ireland will be fit to accept any gift in the way of local government or repeal of Coercion Laws that you may wish to give."

And yet objections and complaints of misrepresentation teem from that side of the House when anyone on this side says that Lord Salisbury recommended coercion, when he himself applies that same term in his own words. A question was put to me by my honourable Friend the Member for Bermondsey (Mr. Thorold Rogers), in the course of his most instructive speech. My honourable Friend had a serious misgiving as to the point of time. Were we right in introducing this measure now? He did not object to the principle; he intimated a doubt as to the moment. I may ask my honourable Friend to consider what would have happened had we hesitated as to the duty before us, had we used the constant efforts that would have been necessary to keep the late Government in Office, and allowed them to persevere in their intentions. On the 26th of January they proposed what we termed a measure of coercion, and I think we were justified in so terming it, because anything attempting to put down a political association can hardly have another name. Can it be denied that that legislation must have been accompanied by legislation against the Press, legislation against public meetings, and other legislation without which it would have been totally ineffective? Would it have been better if a great controversy cannot be avoided—and I am sensible of the evil of this great controversy—I say it is better that Parties should be matched in conflict upon a question of giving a great boon to Ireland, rather than—as we should have been if the policy of January 26 had proceeded—that we should have been matched and brought into conflict, and the whole country torn with dispute and discussion upon the policy of a great measure of coercion. That is my first reason.

My second reason is this. Let my honourable Friend recollect that this is the earliest moment in our Parliamentary history when we have the voice of Ireland authentically expressed in our hearing. Majorities of Home Rulers there may have been upon other occasions; a practical majority of Irish Members never has been brought together for such a purpose. Now, first, we can understand her; now, first, we are able to deal with her; we are able to learn authentically what she wants and wishes, what she offers and will do; and as we ourselves enter into the strongest moral and honourable obligations by the steps which we take in this House, so we have before us practically an Ireland under the representative system able to give us equally authentic information, able morally to convey to us an assurance the breach and rupture of which would cover Ireland with disgrace.

There is another reason, but not a very important one. It is this. I feel that any attempt to palter with the demands of Ireland, so conveyed in forms known to the Constitution, and any rejection of the conciliatory policy, might have an effect that none of us could wish in strengthening that Party of disorder which is behind the back of the Irish Representatives, which skulks in America, which skulks in Ireland, which I trust is losing ground and is losing force, and will lose ground and will lose force in proportion as our policy is carried out, and which I cannot altogether dismiss from consideration when I take into view the consequences that might follow upon its rejection.

What is the case of Ireland at this moment? Have honourable Gentlemen considered that they are coming into conflict with a nation? Can anything stop a nation's demand, except its being proved to be immoderate and unsafe? But here are multitudes, and, I believe, millions upon millions, out-of-doors, who feel this demand to be neither immoderate nor unsafe. In our opinion, there is but one question before us about this demand. It is as to the time and circumstance of granting it. There is no question in our minds that it will be granted. We wish it to be granted in the mode prescribed by Mr. Burke. Mr. Burke said, in his first speech at Bristol—

"I was true to my old-standing invariable principles, that all things which came from Great Britain should issue as a gift of her bounty and beneficence rather than as claims recovered against struggling litigants, or at least, if your beneficence obtained no credit in your concessions, yet that they should appear the salutary provisions of your wisdom and foresight—not as things wrung from you with your blood by the cruel gripe of a rigid necessity."

The difference between giving with freedom and dignity on the one side, with acknowledgment and gratitude on the other, and giving under compulsion—giving with disgrace, giving with resentment dogging you at every step of your path—this difference is, in our eyes, fundamental, and this is the main reason not only why we have acted, but why we have acted now. This, if I understand it, is one of the golden moments of our history—one of those opportunities which may come and may go, but which rarely return, or, if they return, return at long intervals, and under circumstances which no man can forecast. There have been such golden moments even in the tragic history of Ireland, as her poet says—

"One time the harp of Innisfail
Was tuned to notes of gladness."

And then he goes on to say—

> "But yet did oftener tell a tale
> Of more prevailing sadness."

But there was such a golden moment—it was in 1795—it was on the mission of Lord Fitzwilliam. At that moment it is historically clear that the Parliament of Grattan was on the point of solving the Irish problem. The two great knots of that problem were—in the first place, Roman Catholic Emancipation; and, in the second place, the Reform of Parliament. The cup was at her lips, and she was ready to drink it, when the hand of England rudely and ruthlessly dashed it to the ground in obedience to the wild and dangerous intimations of an Irish faction.

> "Ex illo fluere ac retro sublapsa referri,
> Spes Danaum."

There has been no great day of hope for Ireland, no day when you might hope completely and definitely to end the controversy till now—more than 90 years. The long periodic time has at last run out, and the star has again mounted into the heavens. What Ireland was doing for herself in 1795 we at length have done. The Roman Catholics have been emancipated—emancipated after a woeful disregard of solemn promises through 29 years, emancipated slowly, sullenly, not from goodwill, but from abject terror, with all the fruits and consequences which will always follow that method of legislation. The second problem has been also solved, and the representation of Ireland has been thoroughly reformed; and I am thankful to say that the franchise was given to Ireland on the re-adjustment of last year with a free heart, with an open hand, and the gift of that franchise was the last act required to make the success of Ireland in her final effort absolutely sure. We have given Ireland a voice: we must all listen for a moment to what she says. We must all listen—both sides, both Parties, I mean as they are, divided on this question—divided, I am afraid, by an almost immeasurable gap. We do not undervalue or despise the forces opposed to us. I have described them as the forces of class and its dependents; and that as a general description—as a slight and rude outline of a description—is, I believe, perfectly true. I do not deny that many are against us whom we should have expected to be for us. I do not deny that some whom we see against us have caused us by their conscientious action the bitterest disappointment. You have power, you have wealth, you have rank, you have station, you have organization. What have we? We think that we have the people's heart; we believe and we know we have the promise of the harvest of the future. As to the people's heart, you may dispute it, and dispute it with perfect sincerity. Let that matter make its own proof. As to the harvest of the future, I doubt if you have so much confidence, and I believe that there is in the breast of many a man who means to vote against us to-night a profound misgiving, approaching even to a deep conviction, that the end will be as we foresee, and not as you do—that the ebbing tide is with you and the flowing tide is with us. Ireland stands at your bar expectant, hopeful, almost suppliant. Her words are the words of truth and soberness. She asks a blessed oblivion of the past, and in that oblivion our interest is deeper than even hers. My right honourable Friend the Member for East Edinburgh (Mr. Goschen) asks us to-night to abide by the traditions of which we are the heirs. What traditions? By the Irish traditions? Go into the length and breadth of the world, ransack the literature of all countries, find, if you can, a single voice, a single book, find, I would almost say, as much as a single newspaper article, unless the product of the day, in which the conduct of England towards Ireland is anywhere treated except with profound and bitter condemnation. Are these the traditions by which we are exhorted to stand? No; they are a sad exception to the glory of our country. They are a broad and black blot upon the pages of its history; and what we want to do is to stand by the traditions of which we are the heirs in all matters except our relations with Ireland, and to make our relations with Ireland to conform to the other traditions of our country. So we treat our traditions—so we hail the demand of Ireland for what I call a blessed oblivion of the past. She asks also a boon for the future; and that boon for the future, unless we are much mistaken, will be a boon to us in respect of honour, no less than a boon to her in respect of happiness, prosperity, and peace. Such, Sir, is her prayer. Think, I beseech you, think well, think wisely, think, not for the moment, but for the years that are to come, before you reject this Bill.

6. International Monetary Conference

Sir H. Meysey-Thompson, concluding that scarcity of gold and demonetization of silver were the chief causes of an existing depression, moved that the government procure the reassembly of the monetary conference, recently held at Brussels, with the idea "of finding some effective remedy in concert with other nations." Mr. Gladstone's reply is contained in HANSARD (IX [4th Ser.], 606-19 [February 28, 1893]).

In his reply, Gladstone pointed out that the Brussels conference was assembled on the direct invitation of the United States and that it would be discourteous for England to supersede that nation by reassembling a conference to define a world policy on bimetallism—a procedure which the mover of the motion apparently hoped for. Gladstone believed that the Powers had been divided at Brussels into two moieties, one of which wished for no change, the other of which was not disinclined to discuss with England any change that she might indicate to be desirable. But the English Government, being "in an unhappy state of mental destitution," had no plans for change in the reconstruction of currency. Gladstone then proceeded to the consideration of the standard of value.

. . . .

I will not go into all the points raised by the Mover and Seconder of the Motion, but I will come to the consideration of what is the standard of value and what are the qualities which give to that standard of value those merits which have led mankind to seek it through a long and painful process, and to find their way step by step towards it, and having got it, to retain it. It seemed to me strange that no notice was taken by the honourable Mover of this Motion of a question of the most practical and vital importance which has been raised by Mr. Giffen,[19] and which evidently lies at the very threshold of the subject, when we view it as a subject which has attained acceptance by Parliament, and which is now to assume a legislative form. The point is this: What is to take place in this country with respect to the enormous sums of money that are held at call? Now, I do not wish to impute anything, except that which is accepted by the promoters of the Motion. What are the facts? The complaint is a complaint of low prices. The desired condition which it is sought to bring about is a state of rising prices; the means to be adopted are to supply the people, who require money for the payment of debts or purchase of commodities, with a currency to which they will have access on easier terms. They are to get that currency cheaper. Very well. The consequence of that

[19] An expert on statistics.

will be, if that currency is to be obtained cheaper, that any given nominal amount will be worth less in that currency than it is in the present currency. It is unquestionably easy to lower the currency a little by a very mild and genial process, like some of those medicines which are administered to the system and work without violence or pain. Now, I ask any honourable Gentleman in this House to put himself in the position of a man who has money at call. I trust all those whom I am addressing are in that happy position. He has money at call, and that money must be paid to him under the law, every farthing of it, in sovereigns. But suppose the honourable Gentleman by his eloquence, and the aid of those who support him, should have induced this House to pass a Bill, under influences prevailing elsewhere, by which after a particular day the money out at call, and now repayable in sovereigns to him, and in nothing worse, would become repayable in either sovereigns or silver in a ratio arbitrarily fixed by the State, what would be the effect? After that particular date they would get for the money out at call rather less in real value than they would get before that date. The consequence would be that monometallists, bimetallists, silver men and gold men—every one of you—would call in every farthing you have out at call. You are not going to be content with £90 or £95 after a given date if you can get £100 by calling in your money before that given date. By-the-bye, I think Mr. Giffen, the highest living authority—though there are many living authorities well acquainted with this subject—estimates that the sum so out at call is about £600,000,000; and I want to know what is to be the effect of saying to the owners of that £600,000,000, "Allow your money to remain where it is and you will have to take £90 or £95 for every £100, but before a given date you could get £100." I want to know whether they would not call in their money when they could get £100; and I want to know, too, what would be the effect of that on the credit of the country, and on the stability and firmness of many of the best and most stable banking and commercial houses in the land?

There is another point that I would just refer to for a moment in the speech of the honourable Mover of this Motion, as it deserves some notice. Does he anticipate the re-entry of the human race into the Garden of Eden? For he seems to think that unless we adopt his plan we shall fall below our present mediocre and mixed condition, and very likely go down lower into some other region which it would not be prudent, becoming, or politic to name. That appeared to me to be the tendency of it, and the purport of it when developed into its full meaning. He spoke of the condition of our manufactures pining in a miserable manner for the last 20 years under the operation of monometallism, and he said that the cotton districts in particular were to go down to prairie value. That is the expression he used—prairie value. Such are the eyes with which the honourable Baronet reads the facts of our condition. He says that till 1873, when the Bank of France coined silver freely for every one who took it there, we did wonders; we were in a state of continual advancement; but that since 1873, we have been pining regularly away, until we are now little better than skin and bone, and the prairie value is all that will be left to us in place of the vast manufactures and the vast invested capital in the cotton trade of the country. Is that a fair representation of the course of the cotton trade of this country during the last 20 years? I am informed, from no secret sources, that during less than that time the cotton trade has changed enormously. I take the year 1877 and compare it with 1891—this period of decline, of depression, of divergency between gold and silver, and of all the horrors that will naturally be expected to follow. What was the state of the cotton trade in 1877? I believe I am correct in saying that it was then represented by 1,100,-000,000 lbs.; while, in 1891, that miserable, perishing industry presented to us only the small figure of 1,800,000,000 lbs. I am speaking of imported raw cotton, which is the measure and extent of the industry. Is it not singular that gentlemen should come down here primed with facts, and that the facts should be so acted upon, through the warmth of their philanthropic affections burning to attain a happier state of things for mankind, that they should not be able to take cognizance of figures like those, which show within the past 14 years an increase of something like 60 per cent. in the aggregate extent of the cotton trade of this country?

What I have endeavoured to bring to my own mind, and what I should like to bring to the minds of others, is the consideration of this question—What is the standard of value? We know perfectly well that gold is our standard of value. But what is meant by a standard of value?—for till we know this I do not see how we are to attain to a right position for judging of the qualities which ought to recommend to us this or that form of legislation, including the estimation of our own standard of value. I understand by a standard of value a common measure of commodities. It is a commodity itself. I admit that ought to be fully recognised. But when you seek for a good standard of value you seek for that by the terms of which you may express the real value—that is, the real purchasing power and force of every other commodity whatsoever. What is important to the owners of or the persons interested in those other commodities? To supply them with a good standard of value. We have passed beyond the stage of barter. Barter and exchange are

the primary necessity of mankind in their first efforts towards civilisation. Barter may be the first form of that exchange, but barter is
so inconvenient and so hampered by the conditions under which it
acts, that no large extension of human intercourse or commerce
can take place under that system, and, consequently from the very
first stages of the history of mankind there are efforts, sometimes of
barbarous tribes, more energetic and more forcible as they attain
more strongly towards civilisation, to get at something like a standard of value. The object of it is this—that the man who has goods
to sell, and is going to accept for those goods a certain portion of
the standard of value, should know the real compensation he receives for the thing he is going to give up, and what he can make
of the money which is to be given to him as representing the value
of the object he is parting with. In the same way, with regard to
the man who buys, he also wants a standard of value which will
represent to him as exactly as possible the power that will be in his
hands when he has bought the commodity with its value measured
by the amount of circulating medium that he is willing to give for
it. It is exactly like the case of a standard of height, by which you
can compare with the utmost exactitude the man of 5 feet with the
man of 6 feet. What you want in this standard of value to make it
do its work properly is fixity, steadiness, stability, and continuity.
You want its properties to be such that what it is to-day it shall be
to-morrow, and what it is to-morrow it shall be the next day.

Mr. A. J. Balfour (Manchester, E.): Hear, hear!

Mr. W. E. Gladstone: I am very glad to hear the right honourable
Gentleman opposite assent to that. Fixity and invariability are the
first elements of a standard value. It should be valuable, uniform,
and portable, and these are qualities which gold possesses. But the
grand thing is, if it is to be a good standard of value, it should
possess fixity and invariability. That fixity and invariability cannot
be absolute. If you find any commodity whatever, which should
always maintain exactly one and the same relation to the sum total
of all the exchanges to be effected in the world, then you will have
an absolutely perfect standard; but that you cannot do. We do not
pretend that gold is an absolutely unchangeable standard of value;
but the belief is, at any rate, held by a large portion of civilised
mankind—it is a belief growing and gaining ground from year to
year—that gold is the best standard of value, because, above all, it
is the least variable standard of all. The Commission which sat
some time ago did not admit that the supposed scarcity of gold had
been proved, and the honourable Baronet the Mover of the Resolution did not supply that proof. There are no proofs. There are
some great commodities which are very low. It is not for me to

dogmatise about it; but this I can say, that no proof of a gold famine has been supplied. But then, Sir, it is obvious and just to observe that the fall in some commodities—in wheat most conspicuously—is the natural result of the combined action of certain causes, the existence of which is well known, one of them being the long continuance of peace, and therefore the larger and the more free application of human industry to the business of production, and the enormous cheapening of the means of communication.

Is it true that every great commodity has fallen in value? Quite the contrary. Let us look at another very great commodity—at what is, perhaps, the greatest commodity in the world, greater even than gold—that of human labour. I want to know whether that is not rising all over the world, and whether it has not risen enormously in this country, in almost every branch that can be named. Compare the wages of domestic servants with what they were 30 or 40 years ago, in the blessed period, according to the honourable Baronet. Take also the limited class about whom I happened to hear the other day—the theatrical profession. I have it on unquestionable authority that the ordinary payments received by actors and actresses have risen largely. No one is unaware of the increase of fees in the medical profession, and I am bound to say that there are none more nobly earned in the world than by that description of labour. I do not know whether there are any in this House who are personally cognisant of all the circumstances connected with the gold discoveries. They were extremely curious and of the greatest interest; and I make this concession—that at the period of the gold discoveries, if, had it not been for those discoveries, we must have had a gold famine in the world; but owing, as some would say, to a happy accident, or, as others would say, under the influence of an old-fashioned belief, to the wise, providential adaptations which are constantly at work, the gold discoveries in California, and afterwards in Australasia, corresponded with the most astonishing development of industrial power ever known in the history of the world. It was at that very time when the railway system began, when the ocean steamer system was transformed, when the telegraph came into existence, and a multitude of material changes, all operating in the same direction; and at that very time came what is probably more powerful than all—Free Trade legislation. The result was an enormous extension of human industry, and a vast enlargement of the exchanges which had to be effected in the world. The gold discoveries appeared to meet the great want thus created, and certainly no gold famine was experienced in England at that time; but these gold discoveries became exceedingly large, especially when the Australian discoveries were rapidly accumulated on the

Californian supply. The effect was that there went abroad an opinion, entertained just as strongly and as conscientiously as the present opinion about a gold famine, that there was a plethora. I am not exaggerating when I say that not only the ignorant herd, but many men of sense, and practical men who were high and solid authorities on questions of economy, believed firmly about 40 or 45 years ago that gold was depreciated 20 or 30 per cent. I might mention a few names. There was the late Viscount Cardwell, as good an economist as I have ever known among purely political men; there was Mr. Cobden, who, in addition to his other great gifts and powers, undoubtedly stood very high as a political economist; and there was the distinguished friend of Mr. Cobden, M. Chevalier, who published a book, the main proposition of which was that gold had undergone a real depreciation of 20 per cent. All that has blown over now, and nobody believes at present in any such depreciation.

I believe it so happened, too, that at that period silver was in a state of considerable steadiness, and afforded a very fair test of values in the market. I think I should be right in saying that silver then rose from 5s. to 5s.2d. per ounce, and that gold fell about 3 per cent. That was a most severe trial, and there is no epoch in history, not even in the 16th century—when such remarkable changes were produced by the discovery of America—when so vast and enormous an addition had been made, almost at a moment's notice, to the monetary transactions of the world, and to the necessity thereby created for an enlargement of the circulating medium. That test gold has stood, and has not varied more than about 3 per cent. I should say that is a very respectable case to make out for gold as a circulating medium. If, under such pressure and such an agony of trial I might almost call it, the fluctuation of gold amounted to only a trifle, the position of gold as a standard of value is splendidly demonstrated.

Now, Sir, it is proposed to give silver a share in the supply as a circulating medium, but what has been the case with regard to silver? The supply of silver appears to be subjected to more extraordinary variations than any ever known in the case of gold. The variation in the value of silver within the last 20 or 30 years is not less than 40 per cent., and not only that, but the honourable Baronet who made the Motion told us that we are not at the end of the variation, for he said that the rupee, which was once worth 2s., and which is now worth 1s. 2½d., will probably go down further, to 1s. or even to 9d. That means, therefore, that unless you step in and give the artificial assistance of the law this great commodity of silver, which it is proposed to bring into partnership with gold as supplying a standard of value for the conduct of all exchanges, will, under the operation of actual facts, aided a little by the prophecies of the honourable Baronet, fall between 60 per cent. and 70 per cent.

Am I right in contending that fixity is the proper requirement of a standard of value? If it is, I want to know how you can improve that standard of value which, under the severest circumstances, has never varied more in this country than 3 per cent. or 4 per cent., how you can prove that by associating with it a commodity which has actually varied to the extent of 40 per cent., and with respect to which those who regard it with the largest amount of favour anticipate a further variation of 25 per cent. or 30 per cent. Do you suppose this is all to be set right by fixing a ratio? On what day will you fix a ratio? And if you fix your ratio, what will be the state on the next day of the markets with reference to the commodities for which you are fixing a ratio? Do you think a man who has money to receive will be content to take less because, stepping out of your province, you have told him that he ought to be satisfied with a less valuable commodity than that which he expects? I do not believe it. I believe the opinion of those who look to fixing a ratio is that it must be a mutable ratio. I do not enter into the question whether a double standard is conceivable under certain circumstances. I believe it is. I look at the actual facts which are before me, and I ask, Is there any period during the last 30 years when you could have fixed a ratio between gold and silver by law on a given day, and when you would not have been compelled to change it again and again? If so, what is our standard of value to be? I do not mean what is the idea of the standard of value to be. Are we to choose it for its fixity, or are we to choose it for its liability to indefinite and eternal change?

The honourable Member spoke rather with ridicule upon the position of this country as the great creditor of the countries of the world. Well, Sir, it is the great creditor of the countries of the world; of that there can be no doubt whatever; and it is increasingly the great creditor of the countries of the world. I suppose there is not a year which passes over our heads which does not largely add to the mass of British investments abroad. I am almost afraid to estimate the total amount of the property which the United Kingdom holds beyond the limits of the United Kingdom, but of this I am well convinced, that it is not to be counted by tens or hundreds of millions. One thousand millions probably would be an extremely low and inadequate estimate. Two thousand millions or something even more than that is very likely to be nearer the mark. I think under these circumstances it is rather a serious matter to ask this country to consider whether we are going to perform this su-preme act of self-sacrifice. I have a profound admiration for cos-mopolitan principles. I can go a great length in moderation in recommending their recognition and establishment; but if there are these £2,000,000,000 or £1,500,000,000 which we have got abroad, it is a very serious matter as between this country and other coun-tries. We have nothing to pay them; we are not debtors at all; we should get no comfort, no consolation out of the substitution of an inferior material, of a cheaper money, which we could obtain for less and part with for more. We should get no consolation, but the consolation throughout the world would be great. This splendid spirit of philanthropy, which we cannot too highly praise—because I have no doubt all this is foreseen—would result in our making a present of £50,000,000 or £100,000,000 to the world. It would be thankfully accepted, but I think that the gratitude for your benevo-lence would be mixed with very grave misgivings and doubts as to your wisdom. I have shown why we should pause and consider for ourselves once, twice, and thrice before departing from the solid ground on which you have within the last half-century erected a commercial fabric unknown in the whole history of the world—be-fore departing from that solid ground you should well consult and well consider and take no step except such as you can well justify to your own understanding, to your fellow-countrymen, and to those who come after us.

7. Training in the University

Gladstone gave the lord rector's address to the students at Glasgow on December 5, 1879. He spoke on the three great professions— medicine, law, and the ministry— and what he called the new profession of the teacher. Passing from the subject of professions, he made a few remarks upon studies. Only that portion that treats of history is given in the following extract. The complete speech can be found in Gladstone's Political Speeches in Scotland *(Edinburgh, 1880). This portion is presented partly for the light which it throws upon Gladstone's attitude of mind and partly for the vindication which it seemingly gives to a collection of speeches such as this volume contains.*

There is one among the pursuits of what I have termed humanity upon which, before I close, I would particularly remark, because it is a branch which is only now beginning in England to assume its proper place in education and in letters, and as to which I am under the impression that Scotland also may have been backward, notwithstanding its loyal care for all the records of its own olden time. Excuse me, then gentlemen, if I return for a few moments to the subject of historical studies. These studies do not, it is true, directly subserve the purpose of any particular profession. To be a good historian does not make a man a good lawyer, or a good physician, or a good divine. They must, therefore, when they are put upon their trial, or when the question lies between them and some other study, be judged not according to their immediate effect in enlarging the apparatus of professional knowledge, but by their immediate effect upon the man himself in his general aptitudes, and by their mediate effect through these upon his professional competency. They can only then be recommended, gentlemen, subject to conditions. The law of necessity, the limitation of time, may not allow us to widen our course of application so far as to include them. Again, they can only be recommended in the sense of a large, not of a narrow utility. But in so far as a happy lot may give you liberty of choice, I would urge and entreat you, gentlemen, to give a place, and that no mean place, in the scheme of your pursuits, to the study of human history. The several kinds of knowledge need to be balanced one with another, somewhat as the several limbs of the body need a proportioned exercise in order to secure a healthy and equable development. The knowledge of the heavenly bodies, the knowledge of the planet on which we live, of the qualities of its material elements, and of all its living orders, valuable, nay, invaluable as it may be shown to be, is nevertheless knowledge wholly inferior in rank to the knowledge of the one living order that beyond measure transcends all the rest, and that has, for perhaps its most distinctive characteristic, this, that it possesses a history.

This history is among the most potent and effective of all the instruments of human education. It introduces us to forms of thought and action which are infinitely diversified. It gives us far larger materials of judgment upon human conduct, and upon the very springs of action, than any present experience can confer. Allow me to observe to you, gentlemen, that judgment upon human conduct is perhaps the most arduous among all the tasks to which the mind of man can be addressed. It is a work the perfect performance of which, I apprehend, surpasses all our powers. To some it may sound like a paradox, but I believe it to be the simple truth, that no man, and no combination of men, is capable of weighing action in the scales of absolute justice, any more than the greatest artists that ever lived in Greece were competent to express absolute beauty by the force of their imaginations and the labour of their hands. But as in the case of the artist the constant effort to reach an unattainable perfection availed to produce approximations at least to ideal excellence, so in the case of the historian the steady and loyal endeavour to be absolutely just and true in the lofty task of passing judgment will keep the head steady and the foot sure in many a dangerous path by bog and precipice, and will give mighty aid in raising the mind of man to its best capacity for the noblest of all its operations, the search and discernment of the truth. But there is one peculiar note of the consummate historic student, nay the historic reader, which deserves beyond all others to be pressed upon your attention, and in which he partakes of the highest quality of the historian himself. Let us ask ourselves what is that highest quality? Of him who betakes himself to the writing of history, to the telling us what man and the world have been in other times, much indeed is required. He must, for example, be learned, upright, exact, methodical, and clear. This is much, but it is not enough. The question remains behind—By what standard is the child of the present to judge the children of the past? Our mental habits are shaped according to the age in which we live, our thought is saturated with its colour. But, in like manner, those who went before us in the long procession of our race, took the form and pressure of their own time. Therefore, they must not be judged according to the form and pressure of ours. Those who in other days denounced death against idolators, or those who inflicted it upon heretics, must not be sentenced without taking into view the enormous difference in mental habits produced by two opposed religious atmospheres,—the one, in which dogma was never questioned; the other, in which doubt, denial, and diverse apprehension

so prevail as greatly to bewilder and unsettle the ordinary mind.
Charles the First must not be tried by the rules of a constitutional
monarchy, now so familiar to our thoughts and language. Queen
Elizabeth, working under the terrible conditions of her epoch and
her position, must not be judged by the standards which will be
applicable to Queen Victoria. The great Popes of the Middle Ages,
especially the two greatest of them all, Gregory the Seventh and
Innocent the Third, must not be denounced as aggressors upon
civil authority, without bearing in mind that in those days the
guardians of law and right were oftentimes the glaring examples of
violence, lawlessness, and fraud. The historian, and in his measure
the reader of the historian, must lift himself out of what is now
called his own environment, and by effort of mind assume the point
of view and think under the entire conditions which belonged to
the person he is calling to account. In so far as he fails to do this, he
perverts judgment by taking his seat on the tribunal loaded with
irrelevant and with misleading matter. But in so far as he succeeds,
he not only discharges a duty of equity, but he acquires by degrees a
suppleness and elasticity of mental discernment which enable him
to separate, even in complicated subject-matter, between the wine
and lees, between the grain and the chaff, between the relevant
matter in a controversy—which, when once ascertained and set in
order, easily leads up to a right judgment—and the bypaths of prejudice, ignorance, and passion, which lead away from it. The historical mind is the judicial mind in the exactness of its balance; it
is the philosophic mind in the comprehensiveness and refinement
of its view. Nor is there any toiler in the wide field of thought who
more than the historian requires to eschew what is known in trade
by the homely but expressive phrase of "scamping" his work. He
must, if only for his own sake, and to give himself a chance of
holding a place in the kindly memory of men, bestow upon his work
that ample expenditure of labour of which Macaulay, independently
of all his other brilliant gifts, has given to this age a superlative and
rare example. In him we have an illustration of a vital truth; in
mental work the substance and the form are so allied that they
cannot be severed. The form is the vehicle through which the
work of the substance is to pass; if the point of the arrow be too
blunt, the strength of the arm is vain; and every student, in whatever branch, should carry with him the simple specific of recollect-
ing the well-known saying of Dr. Johnson, who, when he was asked
how he had attained to his extraordinary excellence in conversation,
replied that, whatever he had had to say, he had constantly taken
pains to say it in the best manner that he could.

Chapter VIII

SALISBURY

Chapter VIII

SALISBURY

LORD SALISBURY (1830-1903), Disraeli's successor as leader of the Conservative party, was much more nearly attuned to the early nineteenth-century toryism than to Tory democracy. He believed that questions should be considered in their historic connections and that existing institutions should be changed only so far as to remedy practical evils. As disdainful as Burke himself was he of the type of legislation and government which upon the basis of a priori reasoning would attempt to plan for the future. "Large conceptions" in lawmaking, he would have maintained, were characterized "by their disregard of justice and individual liberty, or their sacrifice of realities to the symmetry of cherished theories." [1]

Lord Robert Cecil, as he was known by courtesy title, was the second son of the second Marquis of Salisbury and representative of a family famous in Elizabeth's day. He was trained at Eton and at Oxford where, as Secretary and Treasurer of the Oxford Union Society, he showed enough promise to call forth from some of his colleagues the prediction that he might become Prime Minister. Neither he himself nor his father, however, apparently thought very highly of his abilities. In his reaction to the politics of the day he showed himself, as a schoolboy, an uncompromising Tory, and supported protection; in his reaction to the past he displayed a like attitude and made Strafford his hero. His training had been hindered by poor health; upon leaving school he therefore attempted recovery by going to the Cape in a sailing vessel. Before his return almost two years had elapsed and he had visited Australia and New Zealand.

At twenty-two he was uncertain of the future. Happily for him, an opportunity soon arose to represent the pocket borough

[1] Lady Gwendolen Cecil, *Life of Robert, Marquis of Salisbury* (London: Hodder and Stoughton, 1921-1932), III, 167.

of Stamford; he was elected to the House of Commons in 1853
and continued to represent the same constituency until he became a peer. His maiden speech, in opposition to Lord John
Russell's proposals for university reform and in defense of
ancient endowments, showed that he still possessed the same
conservative feelings he had displayed in his school days, but
in reality he may be classified as almost an independent in his
speeches and activities while a member of the lower house. He
distrusted Disraeli and disagreed with him on the question of
admission of Jews to Parliament as well as on the question of
Parliamentary reform. He criticized many of the policies of the
Liberals such as repeal of the paper duties and competitive or,
rather, qualifying examinations for civil service. But, on the
other hand, when he deemed a practical reform necessary, he
spoke out with sharpness as in his denunciation of the harshness
of the London Boards of Guardians to the destitute poor. His
opinions during the decade of the sixties can best be obtained
from his writings in the *Quarterly Review*. Concomitantly with
the development of his abilities as an essayist grew his aptitude
for Parliamentary conflict, but, whether writing or speaking, he
was the constant defender of property and the legislature as it
was then constituted.

Lord Robert became Lord Cranborne upon the death of his
brother in 1865 and shortly afterward was asked to join the
Derby-Disraeli ministry as Secretary of State for India. But he
resigned in March 1867 rather than agree to Disraeli's proposal
for extensive Parliamentary reform and thereafter denounced
his former leader in such way as to recall to mind the aspersions
cast by that leader himself upon Peel's change of front in the
matter of protection. For Cranborne's attitude on democracy as
expressed even prior to his acceptance of office, see "Representation of the People" (page 319).

Lord Cranborne remained a rebel for no great length of time
for Gladstone's Irish policy was destined to reunite the Conservatives. His own opinions of that policy were to be heard in the
House of Lords, however, since the death of his father in 1868
led to his transference to the Upper House. "The Lords and the
Established Church in Ireland" (page 327) gives his views on
the functions of the House of Lords and also his defense of the
Established Church in Ireland.

During a large part of the period 1868-1874, when his party was in opposition, Lord Salisbury acted as chairman of the Great Eastern Railway and upon the Conservative return to power accepted again the India office even though he still distrusted Disraeli. In the embroilment of the Eastern question, however, he rather suddenly veered to the latter's support. Explanation of the situation is perhaps best taken from the official biographer: "Lord Salisbury was compelled by circumstances to trust his chief,—and found in fact that he could do so with impunity. Collaboration was the cause and not the result of the change of sentiment." [2]

He was given the Foreign Office in 1878. The new duties appealed to him and brought him fame. He acted as second plenipotentiary at the Congress of Berlin and when, after Disraeli's death, he became leader of the party and was returned to power he took the Foreign Office himself. Perhaps his antipathy to democratic movements caused him to look with favor upon an office where secrecy could, to a degree, be justified. In any case, as Prime Minister he was not responsible himself for the enactment of social legislation, though, influenced by Reaney's *Bitter Cry of Outcast London,* he spoke for better dwellings [3] (cf. "Housing of the Working Classes," page 336) and his administration passed certain practical measures, such as the Local Government Act of 1888 which gave the conduct of local affairs to the popularly elected county councils. But the union and the empire was his theme. Supported by the Liberal Unionists he opposed Gladstone's plan for Irish Home Rule. That he had ever thought to "dish the Whigs," as Disraeli was reputed to have attempted with Parliamentary reform, by meeting the demands of the Irish Nationalists does not seem possible to the official biographer. In any case when Gladstone came out for Home Rule, a Conservative leader would be inclined to reject it. The speech, delivered at Liverpool in 1888, deals with the Irish question and also touches on free trade (cf. page 343).

Of the dates of his prime ministership, 1885-1886, 1886-1892, and 1895-1902, the middle period saw him attaining his greatest achievements. Guiding the imperial spirit which was represented

[2] Cecil, *Life,* II, 202.
[3] He had been interested in the subject earlier. Cf. Cecil, *Life,* II, 4.

in Professor Seeley's *Expansion of England* (1883), he gave a degree of dignity to the scramble for Africa, managing at the same time to keep from war with France and to get an understanding with Germany on the subjects of Heligoland and Zanzibar (cf. page 348). He provided by the Naval Defense Act of 1889 for the completed construction of ten new battleships and sixty cruisers within four and a half years. His was the administration in charge of the Golden Jubilee of 1887 and the first imperial conference. And as for territorial increase Lord Rosebery estimated in 1896 that two and a half million square miles had been added to the British Empire within twelve years. Here was an empire builder whose emphasis on colonial development contrasted brilliantly in its seeming achievements with the imperialism of Disraeli! Even so the jingoes were far from satisfied. His moderation, especially in his later prime ministership, compared unfavorably in their eyes with the enthusiasm of Joseph Chamberlain and Cecil Rhodes. Almost guilty of flouting was he in declaring that if military advisers were allowed full scope they would insist on the importance of garrisoning the moon in order to protect the country from Mars. Certainly he seemed restrained in his attitude toward the German Emperor's attempted meddling with the Transvaal question and toward President Cleveland's fulminations on the Venezuela boundary. He was friendly to the United States during the Spanish-American War even though Canning in 1822 had warned, "What cannot and must not be is that any great maritime Power should get possession of Cuba," and, in abandoning the Clayton-Bulwer Treaty, he left the United States free to construct and defend a transisthmian canal practically on her own terms.[4] But though he had cordial relations with America and kept together the concert of Europe, he finally reaped in the Boer War a bitter fruitage from imperalism. His lack of vigor[5] in the conduct of the war was caustically attacked by such a periodical as *Punch* just as his lack of insight in using a favorable opportunity for reforming and strengthening the House of Lords has been the

---

[4] Cf. *Quarterly Review,* October 1912.

[5] He is depicted in the *Westminster Gazette,* November 29, 1901, as the dormouse. Cf. "Saki" [Hector H. Munro], *The Westminster Alice* (New York: The Viking Press, n.d.).

cause of chagrin to Conservative adherents.[6] But he doubtless gloried—notwithstanding a growing inactivity—in the pride of the London *Times* of the Diamond Jubilee Year:

The position of the colonies as they stand to-day and the attitude which they now assume towards each other and towards the mother country are not the least of the witnesses to the innate statesmanship of the British race. It is the race which has created the colonies. It is the race which yearly is knitting them closer and closer to each other and to their common home.[7]

There was wanting in him, however, the keen vision for practical means of accomplishing imperial association (cf. "The Empire," page 357) and also that lesser faculty, the prescience that days of social legislation (1906-1914) must, from the very disclosures of the Boer War, be at hand. Rather, he was willing to apply himself to the defense of the administration—upon occasions of attack at the opening of the new century—by utilizing, at least in part, the thesis of the inability of the British constitution to function with immediate success during a crisis (cf. page 360). Finally in 1900, in ill health and sorrowing over the loss of a wife who had been responsible at least in part for his attainments, he gave up the Foreign Office, though the premiership was his until the end of the war in South Africa.

Lord Salisbury had other interests besides politics: In early life he studied botany and in the decade of the sixties began experimentations in chemistry. He also was a student of the factual data of history but cared little for the philosophic aspects of the subject. An example of his attitude is to be found in his presidential address at the British Association for the Advancement of Science at Oxford in 1894 in which his theme was the history of scientific progress. He was so far from being insensible to the practical that, taking advantage of a stream which flowed through his estate at Hatfield, he contrived to have his home one of the first two houses in England to use the incandescent light of Edison, and, playing with the telephone in its early stages of development, he often startled his guests by unexpectedly voicing from the shrubbery, "Hey, diddle, diddle, the cat and the fiddle;

[6] Cf. Herbert Maxwell, *A Century of Empire* (London: E. Arnold. 1911), III, 230.

[7] Editorial, *The Times* (London), June 11, 1897.

the cow jumped over the moon." [8] He was also under obligation to learn much about agriculture in handling his estate.

As a young speaker in the House of Commons he showed much natural ability at epigrammatic expression and frequently caused an adversary to writhe. His dignified presence gave effectiveness to his speeches in the House of Lords, where he spoke without notes and with little display of rhetoric and declamation. Aroused by Gladstone's campaign, he felt obliged to take the stump and between 1880 and 1886 spoke on more than seventy public platforms to audiences that often could be counted by thousands. But as a public speaker he lacked passion in his eloquence and, to a large degree, personal magnetism. Perhaps his nearsightedness caused him to react to an unseen audience as if it were lifeless.

In any case he was and is noteworthy not as a popular orator but as the exponent of colonial and foreign affairs. Popular emotions he deemed a pernicious influence upon foreign policy and secrecy in the foreign office a necessity even in a democratic age. To the student, therefore, the difficulties, if not the impossibility, of broad generalizations in history may become apparent when consideration is given to the fact that a century noteworthy in English history for the growth of political democracy should have produced on its ending in Salisbury a statesman much more conservative than the representative of its inception, Canning.

[8] Cecil, *Life,* III, 8.

1. Representation of the People

The following speech is taken from Hansard *(CLXXXIII [3d Ser.], 6-24 [April 27, 1866]). The omitted first two colums of "Rep-resentation of the People" attack Gladstone's interpretations of Con-omitted first two columns of "Rep-ing class.*

.   .   .   .

For myself, I will venture to make my confession of faith on the subject of the working classes. I feel there are two tendencies to avoid. I have heard much on the subject of the working classes in this House which I confess has filled me with feelings of some apprehension. It is the belief of many honourable Gentlemen op-posite that the working classes are to be our future Sovereign, that they are to be the great power in the State, against which no other power will be able to stand; and it is with feelings of no small horror and disgust that I have heard from many honourable Gentle-men phrases which sound, I hope unduly, like adulation of the Sovereign they expect to rule over them.

Now, if there is one claim which the House of Commons has on the respect of the people of this country, it is the great historic fame it enjoys—if it has done anything to establish the present balance of power among all classes of the community, and prevent any single element of the Constitution from overpowering the rest, it is that in presence of all powers, however great and terrible they may have been, the House of Commons has always been free and independent in its language. It never in past times, when Kings were powerful, fawned upon them. It has always resisted their unjust pretences. It always refused to allow any courtierly instincts to suppress in it that solicitude for the freedom of the people of this country which it was instituted to cherish. I should deeply regret, if at a time when it is said we are practically about to change our Sovereign, and when some may think that new powers are about to rule over the country, a different spirit were to influence and inspire the House of Commons. Nothing could be more dangerous to the reputation of the House, nothing more fatal to its authority, than that it should be suspected of sycophancy to any power, either from below or above, that is likely to become predominant in the State.

My own feeling with respect to the working men is simply this —we have heard a great deal too much of them, as if they were different from other Englishmen. I do not understand why the nature of the poor or working men in this country should be differ-

319

ent from that of any other Englishman. They spring from the same race. They live under the same climate. They are brought up under the same laws. They aspire after the same historical model which we admire ourselves; and I cannot understand why their nature is to be thought better or worse than that of other classes. I say their nature, but I say nothing about their temptations. If you apply to any class of the community special temptations, you will find that class addicted to special vices. And that is what I fear you are doing now. You are not recognizing the fact that, dealing with the working classes, you are dealing with men who are Englishmen in their nature, and who have every English virtue and vice: you are applying to them a special training, and yet refuse to look forward to the special result, which all who know human nature must inevitably expect.

Those Members who have sat on Election Committees will, I think, agree with me, that the franchise is a convertible commodity. It has a value, indeed, in two ways. The franchise has a direct money value to those who do not care much about public affairs in the way of bribery. It has an indirect value to those who do care about public affairs in the way of encouraging unjust and special class legislation. If you give the franchise to those who may naturally be tempted to misuse it, you must expect that the larger proportion who are not deeply interested in public affairs will be liable to the temptation—I do not say they will always yield to it—of treating it as a saleable commodity. The minority, more influential, more deeply interested in public affairs, will be liable to the temptation of treating it not as a saleable commodity, but as something to get for them laws with respect to taxation and property, specially favourable to them as a class, and, therefore, dangerous to all other classes of the community. That is the temptation to which you are exposing the working man by giving him the franchise. I say further that you are exposing him to it more than other classes of the community for this simple reason, that he is poorer. It is perfectly true that the poor have their virtues as well as the rich, and that the rich have their vices as well as the poor. But the vices of the poor have, unfortunately, a special bearing on their fitness for the exercise of political rights. The poor are liable more than the rich to be tempted if you place in their hands anything that is pecuniarily convertible. A great deal of odium has been cast on some Members of this House because they have stated that the working classes are more venal than the rich. That is not true as to their nature, but it is true as to the temptations to which they are exposed. It is ridiculous to say that £50 will not tempt a man more of whose income it forms a third or a fourth than one of whose income it forms only the thirtieth or fortieth part; and therefore all bribes whether in the direct form of money value, or in the indirect form of class legislation, must be expected to operate more on the working classes than on any other class of the community. It is not a paradox, but a simple truism, that a man who is hungry will care more for a good dinner than one who has already dined. But, Sir, that seems to me to be the simple truth about—I will not say the working classes, for I dislike to treat any particular vocation as distinct and separate in this community—but as to those who have less property in the country. In proportion as the property is small, the danger of misusing the franchise will be great. You may cover that by senti-ment, you may attempt to thrust it away by vague declamation, but as a matter of fact and as a matter of truth it will remain all the same.[9]. . . . .

I now come to the speech of the honourable Member for West-minster [10]—certainly the most able and most convincing speech that has been made in the course of the debate. The honourable Gentle-man argued in favour of the concentration of the franchise. He said it was true that the working classes were represented up to a certain point, but that their representation was valueless, because it was not sufficiently concentrated. Now, I entirely agree with the honourable Member to this extent, that the concentration of the franchise of the working classes would in many cases be highly desirable. I concur with him that the presence of a certain number of working men in this House would be no derogation to the dignity of this Assembly, but would be a positive addition to its power and its value in the estimation of the community. In fact, if I might go as far as to make a definite proposition, I should say that I would readily sacrifice twenty or thirty seats of what the right honourable Gentleman the Chancellor of the Exchequer calls the "Mountain," with a very apt recollection of their political associa-tions, and I would substitute in their place working men. I believe that the natural leaders of the working classes—the prominent men among them—would make better representatives than some persons of a higher class, who, for reasons best known to themselves, desire to identify themselves with those classes.

But the whole argument of the honourable Member appears to be supported by this fallacy. He admitted distinctly that the preponderance of the working classes in this House was a thing to be avoided; he admitted that if the working classes returned a

[9] There is omitted a discussion of party maneuvering.
[10] John Stuart Mill.

majority of the Members, that the possibility or the probability was that they would endeavour to place upon the statute book theories which he more than any other man objected to. Up to this point I began to think that the honourable Gentleman's speech was in favour of the Amendment.[11] But, surely the honourable Member will require, before he votes in favour of the Bill, proof that what he fears will not result from it. I, at least, expected from him proof that the policy of the Government, as explained by their Bill, was not that the working classes should obtain a majority. But did he prove that? No, he never attempted to do so—he stopped short of the question altogether. He passed over to the cattle plague and to other general topics, and he never attempted to prove that the working classes would not have a preponderance of power under this Bill. That is the point I want to see proved; that is the point that this Amendment requires to be proved. The test by which a good Reform Bill may be distinguished from a bad one is, that under it the working classes shall not now, or at any proximate period, command a majority in this House. If the honourable Gentleman does not prove that, the keystone of his argument is wanting. It is not difficult to show danger or ruin in this direction. The honourable Member for Birmingham, in his speech the other night, pointed out to us that, as we arrange the re-distribution of seats so do we arrange the re-distribution of power.

Mr. Bright: I said, that in that way you might destroy popular representation.

Viscount Cranbourne: Exactly so; and you would do the other thing. You might produce Re-publicanism on the one hand and absolute despotism on the other. I think the honourable Gentleman was good enough to say that if the right honourable Member for Calne [12] and myself had the re-distribution of seats the popular power would be destroyed; but I rather think that if he and the honourable Member for Leicester had to re-distribute them we should have a precisely opposite result, and the popular, or, rather, the democratic party would be the only one left in the country.[13] . . . .

Who are they who support the present Bill? Are its supporters the moderate Liberals, or do they come from the ranks of those who have loudly announced their intention of destroying the House

---

[11] *I.e.*, to have placed before the House a redistribution plan as well as the franchise qualifications. He would have been acting, in that case, against the Russell-Gladstone ministry, which brought in the Reform Bill of 1866.

[12] Robert Lowe.

[13] Details on the question of redistribution and on the past history of Parliamentary reform are omitted.

of Peers and the Established Church? Are they not those who delight in rendering homage to American institutions, and whose desire it is to see those institutions adopted as a pattern for this country? We have heard a great deal about certain meetings which have been held in various portions of the country in support of this measure, and we have been informed that the sentiments of its advocates, as expressed at these meetings, have been distinguished by their moderation. I should like the House to listen for a minute or two to some of those opinions, and to judge for themselves how far they accord with the description furnished by the honourable Member for Birmingham and by the right honourable Gentleman the Chancellor of the Exchequer. Now, Sir, in many parts of the country these meetings were evidently carefully kept in order. They rather misconducted themselves last year, and those who took part in some of them gave expression to opinions which created alarm in the minds of some honourable Members in this House. Accordingly, the most watchful control has of late been, as far as possible, exercised over them. But still in some places they have escaped from this control, and in some portions of London, especially where those who have taken part in them have not been entirely under the power of the wire-pullers, no concealment of the objects desired has been attempted. Now, Sir, we heard the opinions of the honourable Gentleman [14] the Member for Finsbury upon this subject, and I should like to call attention to what was said at an open-air meeting held at Clerkenwell, in this borough. That meeting was presided over by a Mr. Lucraft, a cabinet-maker, who said—

"For 800 years the Lordlings had ruled them, and had ruled them with a rod of iron. They had accumulated millions. The Marquess of Westminster and Lord Stanley had thousands of acres, while those who worked for their living could not get a foot of ground. Under the laws of Master and Servant,[15] whilst they had doubled the income of the country the working men had not benefited in any fair proportion. Well, they were afraid that by this Bill the working men would get in, which he believed would be the case. Mr. Bligh seconded the resolution, maintaining that capital was the overplus of labour, and that as the working men had produced it they ought to have it shared amongst them; that they had created £800,000,000 in one year, and only got £200,000,000 for their share."

[14] McCullagh Torrens.
[15] Under existing conditions a workingman could be arrested on warrant and imprisoned for breach of contract while the employer could be attacked only by civil action.

Those gentlemen were all very enthusiastic in favour of the Reform Bill. That meeting was adjourned, and on its re-assembling some more opinions of the same kind were delivered—

"Mr. Finlen trusted they would never cease to insist on having a Reform Bill from the House of Commons which would enable every man unconvicted of crime to have a vote in the election of a Member of Parliament. He believed the Government could not have done a better thing than bring in a Bill pure and simple as they had done. It was true it did not go far, but it went as far as the House of Commons seemed likely to let it, for he believed the House of Commons would have gone stark staring mad if any clause had been introduced into that Bill for the re-distribution of seats. Mr. Bradlaugh, in seconding the resolution, said that was the second of a series of meetings which would have to be held in order to show the Houses of Parliament that the working classes of England, although they knew that that Bill by itself would be of very little good to them, were ready to support any Bill which would advance that Reform for which they were striving. He was of opinion that every man had a right to enjoy the franchise in the country where he was born. This Bill was only one step in the scale, and there would be very few Sessions allowed to pass without another Bill being introduced which would go a great deal further. Let them firmly make up their minds that the smaller measures contained in the present Bill should only be the stepping-stones to the grand staircase, and they would succeed."

In the same way, at a gathering of the National Reform League, which, I believe, has held meetings throughout the country, the following Motion was submitted by a gentleman now well known to the House—Mr. Odger [16]—

"That the council, while strictly adhering to the principle of manhood suffrage as the only just, sound, permanent, and satisfactory basis of representation for this country, deems it its duty to give its cordial support to the measure of Reform now before Government as tending to the object the League has in view."

These expressions of opinion are important in my eyes as casting light upon the sentiments which have been enunciated by the honourable Member for Westminster during this debate. The honourable Gentleman had been asked what reforms he would introduce to the legislation of the country. He was told that it was illogical to ask for a change in the House of Commons unless he could point to a change in our legislation as likely to ensue on that Reform. The honourable Member for Westminster made a very pregnant reply. He said it would not be a practical proceed-

[16] A member of the union of makers of ladies' shoes.

ing to tell the present House of Commons what legislation would result from the adoption of this measure. Now, Sir, knowing the opinions entertained by the honourable Gentleman the Member for Westminster, as expressed in his writings, upon the subject of property and land—knowing that he regards the landowners as servants of the State, and as men who may be discarded at any moment, I confess that I regard with the greatest apprehension the concealment of the objects with which the new Parliament is to deal. But on whatever side you regard this measure, you find it beset with concealment. The right honourable Gentleman the Chancellor of the Exchequer will not tell us of what constituencies this new Parliament is to be composed, and the honourable Member for Westminster will not tell us what measures this new Parliament is to pass. No, nor will he even tell us what measures he desires it should pass. There appears to be something extremely ingenious in the legerdemain of modern statesmanship which, with a singular want of concealment and reticence, exposes the very machinery by which we are to be deceived. The Government asks us simply to vote for this Bill, and transfer our power to persons of whom it tells us nothing; and the honourable Member for Westminster tells us to transfer our power to a body which will pass measures of which he will tell us nothing. I feel certain that whenever there is this concealment there is something to conceal. I am quite sure that if the Chancellor of the Exchequer could tell us of schedules which would recommend his Bill to the House, he would have told us of them long ago; and I am quite sure that if the honourable Member for Westminster could have named any measures to be passed in a Reformed Parliament which would have recommended this Bill to the House, he would have named them long ago. But the very fact that they have found it necessary to preserve silence as regards the particulars of those things which they look forward to with so much complaisance convinces me that, so far from being pleased, the majority of the House would recoil from what they anticipate.

So far as my vote is concerned, I will not vote for this kind of legislation; I will not speculate in the dark; I will not follow a guide who tells me that he is going into an unexplored country, but declines to inform me at least as to its nature or the probable results of the expedition, and who will give me no other information than that he has destroyed bridges behind him and burnt his boats. We have been threatened alike by the right honourable Gentleman the Chancellor of the Exchequer and by the honourable Member for Birmingham. We have been told that if we resist this Bill we shall discredit our party permanently, and the working classes will never vote for those who refused to give them the suffrage. I disdain to look upon such considerations at a juncture of this constitutional importance. We have been told to be wise, and wise in time. I know of only one thing that is truly wise at such a time as this, and that is to have courage to vote honestly. Whatever may happen to our party, it is clear that the Government is offering an indignity to the House of Commons by the course they are pursuing; it is attempting to break and bind down our independence; it is attempting to force us to vote for a Bill of the nature and effect of which we have no knowledge upon which we can depend, and therefore it seems to me that whatever the consequences may be, our first duty to our country and to ourselves is clear, and that is to resist the Bill to the utmost.

2. The Lords and the Established Church in Ireland

Mr. Gladstone, the opposition leader, moved in May 1868 that leave be granted to bring in a bill which should provide for the stoppage both of any new appointments in the Church of Ireland and of all serious outlay of money by the ecclesiastical commissioners in Ireland. This action was taken in preparation for the anticipated disestablishment of the Anglican Church in Ireland. The bill was read the third time in the House of Commons on June 16 and sent to the Lords. Salisbury's speech was made during the debate on the second reading in the House of Lords (HANSARD, CXCIII [3d Ser.], 79-96 [June 26, 1868]). It may be pointed out that Lord Salisbury did accept—as he implied he would do in this speech—the verdict of the electorate which brought Gladstone to power by the election of 1868; he worked against the more reactionary Lords in passing with amendments the Irish Church Disestablishment Bill of 1869.

This Bill is founded on certain Resolutions which state in the most distinct and absolute way that disestablishment is the object of Mr. Gladstone, who has stated as much in his speeches. In language which can leave nothing to desire from its completeness, he has asserted that every vestige of property, except, I think, Sir Benjamin Guinness's endowment, is to be taken from the Church of Ireland. Now, my noble Friend (the Earl of Carnarvon) made many observations this evening in which I entirely concur, if I understood him rightly, as to the unwisdom under present circumstances of what is called a pure no-surrender policy. Personally, if I consulted my own disposition, I should have no objection to fight à outrance; but I confess, from the experience I have had, my inclination is to say, "How can you expect to hold the fortress; it's no use holding out, for the troops won't stand to their guns?" Therefore, my Lords, if there were any intermediate proposal before the House, I should doubt whether I should assent to it or not—of course, everything depends upon its provisions. I should esteem any Minister who voted against his convictions in support of such a proposal wanting in self-respect, but I should not say that any Member of your Lordships' House, who cannot escape from responsibility by resigning, was debarred from modifying his convictions in deference to a great public exigency.

But these questions do not arise upon the present occasion. None of that very eloquent diatribe which my noble Friend [17] delivered

[17] Cf. the speech of the Duke of Somerset.

against those who stand out for a no-surrender policy applies in this instance. Nothing in the nature of a compromise—nothing which the most flattering critic would describe as a compromise—has been offered to the acceptance of either House of Parliament. My Lords, we are told that to agree in time is to prevent a demand for something more. But I have no doubt that those who brought forward this proposal would have already demanded something more if they had been able to find it. I do not doubt their possible power so far as political action is concerned; but there is this limit in the nature of things, that when you have abolished a thing you can do nothing more with it; and it is an absolute and complete spoliation that Mr. Gladstone has offered to the Irish Church. The noble Duke who has just sat down (the Duke of Somerset), told us that two-thirds of its property were to be left to the Irish Church. Two-thirds of the property! Why, I heard Mr. Gladstone make his calculations, and I think it was three-fifths of the property that were to be left to the clergymen of the Church. These are very estimable gentlemen: I am glad that some provision is to be made for them; it would be a great breach of the rights of private property if some were not made. But as a promise of consolation to the Church of Ireland it is absolutely worthless. It is a matter of perfect indifference to the Church of Ireland whether the present holders of livings are compensated or not. Therefore, my Lords, I want to make this point very clear. We are dealing with a Bill which, in the first place its own advocates will not defend; in the second place, with a proposition as large, as extreme, and as sweeping as it is possible for human or radical ingenuity to devise.

Now, my Lords, on what grounds is this great change recommended? We are told that they are two—that one of them is justice, the other rests upon considerations of expediency. Now, whenever we argue that this thing is dangerous to some other interests—dangerous to the Union and to the Church—we are met with the assertion, "It is just"; and because it is just, we are told we must do it, come what may.

Well, let us examine this plea of justice. Let me, in the first instance, take exception to a species of testimony with which I may say we have been inundated. I think it may be called the "foreign-friend argument." Several noble Lords on the opposite Bench, having a large foreign acquaintance, have given us the views of their friends in abundance—as if that were the proper argument to offer to an English Parliament; that they told us the opinions held in society that they have been accustomed to frequent; and they say so and so is held to be what the House of

Lords should do. Well, my Lords, I listened to the opinion of these foreign friends, and I found that the late Foreign Secretary (the Earl of Clarendon) was much smitten by the article of an illustrious writer in the *Revue des Deux Mondes*. None would be wanting in respect for that illustrious writer; but among his claims for our respect we must remember that he can boast of this characteristic, that he is a most earnest believer in the Church in which he was brought up, and that Church is the Roman Catholic. I must say that if England were judged on the "foreign-friend" ground—on the principles put forward by this critic in the *Revue des Deux Mondes*, there are many actions in our history that would be very severely condemned. I even doubt whether my noble Friend's critic in the *Revue des Deux Mondes* could entirely approve the English Reformation.

Now, my Lords, when you come to talk of justice in holding property, it is a question of title. If my right to my land is good, it is absurd to say there would be justice in taking it from me and giving it to somebody else. Therefore the question of justice resolves itself into an examination of the title by which the property is held. No one says, as I understand, that this title is bad. If it be bad, the property vests in some one else. But we have no second claimant for this property with which it is proposed to deal. One of the greatest difficulties lying before you in this case is the way in which this property shall be applied if it be taken. I do not understand that anyone has disputed that in a Court of Law the Church's title to this property is good; but there appears to be some idea in the minds of noble Lords, either that the Church is different from other corporations, or that there is something weak in the title of corporations which exposes them to peculiar operations of this kind. I am fully aware of the power of phrases judiciously used. The noble Earl who introduced this Bill (Earl Granville) told us that the existing state of things was the paying of the clergy of a minority out of a public fund. I have heard again that fund called public property. These are very significant phrases. Whenever anybody wants to rob his neighbour of anything he always says the thing he covets is national property. I speak for a moment as a Railway Chairman when I say I have heard somebody lately assert that railways are national property: and I have heard the assertion with alarm. Where is the title of this national property? Will you find it in any deed, in any charter, in any statute book, or in any treatises of law? No. You will not find it in any of these things. It has simply been evolved from the innermost depths of the Liberal consciousness. There is not the slightest vestige of external proof in favour of this claim on the part of the nation to dispose of this property. There is, indeed, only one claim advanced, and that is that in past times violent Sovereigns and unscrupulous Parliaments have dealt with Church property in the manner that best pleased their violent passions or inclinations, and you conclude that because it has once been subjected to violence you have the right to resort to violence again. But, beyond the fact that this property may have been violently dealt with at different portions of our history, you have no argument which you can urge in favour of what you call its peculiarly national character.

Well, there were some noble Lords who apparently felt the weakness of these arguments, and were alive to the absolute impossibility of proving that the title by which the Church of Ireland holds its property is different from that by which the property of any other corporation is held, and, boldly supplying the link which is missing, they told us that the property of corporations was at the pleasure of Parliament. The noble Earl opposite (the Earl of Kimberley) told us that the State was the heir of corporations such as the Irish Church. Unfortunately the State appears to have a power which many heirs may envy—that of killing off the possessors of the property which it desires to inherit. Now, my Lords, I can only say with regard to such statements as these that they are based upon a code of law which is totally new in this country. Do not imagine that you can perpetrate this illogical violence, and then go no further than you originally intended. I can quite believe that you intend to go no further; but others will take up the principles which you have started, and drive in the wedge which you were the first to insert, and the result will be that you will be led into consequences from which you, I believe, would be the first to shrink with alarm. But there is one peculiarity in this position to which I think the corporations of this country should have their attention called. It is bad enough that the supposed perpetuity of corporations should be entirely abolished; it is bad enough that it should be laid down that the State is the heir to the property of a corporation which it may destroy at any moment, or as any party exigency may arise. But observe the peculiarity of this case. It is not because the property has been abused—it is not because its trusts have not been fulfilled—it is not because in some cases its trusts have become impossible of fulfilment; that might be remedied by a much more moderate measure—it is not because its means are required by other classes; but it is because a certain body of men grudge and envy those now in possession of this property that you are prepared to take it away by force. But how far do you intend to carry this right of dispossession and to yield to demands dictated by feelings of grudge and envy? Now, my

Lords, I do not wish to push too far the analogy between corporate and private property. I am willing to acknowledge the very great difference, the existence of which every one must see; but I feel convinced that if you familiarize the minds of the people of this country with the idea of yielding to the mere display of discontent, and the mere ostentation of envy, you will cause injury to property otherwise secure, and it is not with corporate property that this principle will end. So much, then, for the question of justice.

The other question is one of expediency. We are told that this Church is unpopular, and that the Irish will not be pacified until it is destroyed. But there are other matters which it is equally important to consider. You have been informed to-night by a most rev. Primate who is fully qualified to judge (the Archbishop of Armagh) that the abolition of this Church will be followed by great discontent in the North of Ireland; that it will be followed by a large emigration; that Ireland will lose a large proportion of that already too scanty class—the resident landlords within her border. But you cannot stop here. You talk of the immovable loyalty of the Orange population. Now, my Lords, I do not believe in such a thing as immovable loyalty. I believe that if you commit a deep and glaring injustice upon any portion of the population, however loyal, they will nourish in their breasts feelings of re-sentment which will not, perhaps, break out into open disturbances, but which will still be in the highest degree disastrous to the coun-try, which will find their support wanting in the hour of its need. I would ask your Lordships to put yourselves in the place of some Protestant congregation in Dublin or the North. Hitherto the Protestants have paid willingly to the Protestant clergyman the tithes to which he has had a right from time immemorial. Without asking for any change, they suddenly find the clergyman taken away, the money hitherto devoted to his support bestowed upon the erection of a lighthouse or some other similar work, while they themselves are called upon to contribute towards the support of a minister who ought to have been supported out of the money already contributed by them. It would not be in human nature to bear this contentedly. I have spoken of Ireland and the Church of Ireland to-night, but these are mere expressions, having no ethnological and scarcely any historical value. The Ireland which you assume for the purposes of the present argument is not the Ireland of the Union; because, if you take all the country together, and take it as one nation, your alarming statistics will at once disappear, because the Church of England will still be the majority. On the other hand, if you regard the country in its true ethnological aspect, you will make out no case whatever in that part of the country where the Protestants prevail. In fact, it is simply by lumping the Protestant and Roman Catholic portions of Ireland together, and by cutting off England altogether, that you contrive to make up these formidable statistics. But if you so disregard the connection between the two countries, and embody that feeling in an Act of Parliament, you will find persons perfectly willing to follow your principle to the logical result of severing all connection between the two countries; and in the hour of your trial you will find the Orangemen, who have hitherto been so strong a support, very little inclined to exert themselves in defence or in promotion of an arrangement which has been attended by such bitter fruits to them. Then come the arguments about the Church of England. I agree with my noble Friend that the cry of "the Church in danger" is a cry of too serious a character to be lightly raised. I do not want to press that point, but I wish to know what you will do in the case of Wales and Cornwall, for instance, where the Church of England is in a great minority? It may not be a case of 12 per cent—but I suppose legislation does not depend upon fractions—but it is a case of great minorities. If you once acknowledge the principle that the Church is to be disestablished whenever it is in a minority, how can you resist the application of the argument to Wales and Cornwall?

You may say that this Bill will have no effect upon the Church of England: but has it not had an effect already? In every part of the country the people are beginning to feel that the Church Establishment is not so safe as it was. This is alike the feeling of the clergy and of the people, and both are beginning to prepare against the issue. And in what way do they prepare themselves? How does a Church suddenly turned into the wilderness prepare to protect itself? Why, its first instinct is to protect itself by a strong development of sacerdotal organization—by a strong and powerful clerical organization. This, perhaps, may not be a great evil in a spiritual point of view; but I know there are many among your Lordships who will regret it. That will infallibly become more and more characteristic of the members of the Church of England when they begin to feel that their connection with the State is a mere question of time, and that, therefore, they must prepare themselves for the evil day. This danger has not been much alluded to, and I feel the way in which this attack is organizing the clergy, is one of the most formidable difficulties of the present time.

Well, but then comes the policy of conciliating the Irish. Your proposal seems to be to still the waters of this agitating time, as the ancient Greeks were wont to do, by offering up a victim to the avenging Deities; but are you quite sure that the avenging Deities are prepared to accept your offering? I have heard many elaborate attempts to prove that Fenianism [18] is the true necessity that has caused this movement. But is it not an extraordinary phenomenon that for the first time in the history of rebellions you have rebels who do not know the real motive which is the cause of their rebellion? This is the age of rebellions—we have seen them in all countries—but I have never before heard of one where they were at a loss to state the grievances they desired to see removed. You tell us that though the Fenians never raised a cry against the Established Church, it is the Established Church which is really at the bottom of their agitation. It is impossible to conceal from ourselves that something very different is at the bottom of the Fenian movement; and I suspect that the Irish people hear that many Liberal landlords have joined in this attack on the Irish Church, they will say the reason is that they think they will save themselves by making the parson their Jonah, and throwing him overboard. My Lords, it is against the land, and not against the Church, that this Fenian agitation is really directed. You offer them that they do not ask for; you offer them that which will not pacify them. Talk of the monuments of conquest—the landlord is a much more complete monument of conquest than the clergyman. The clergyman does not hurt the peasant; if the clergyman be taken away, the peasant would be no richer, but rather poorer; but the landlord holds the property which the peasant, in his traditions, well remembers once to have belonged to his sept. If you seek to appease the danger by mere concession—if you yield to the mere demands of anger—or, to use the euphemistic language we have heard—if Fenian outrages are to make you reason calmly and dispassionately—it is to the landlord, and not to the clergyman, that you should really turn your attention.

My Lords, I have only one word more to say, and it is with respect to the position of this House. We have heard from the opposite Bench several very animated appeals to this House, and several constitutional lectures as to our duties. The noble Earl the late Foreign Secretary (the Earl of Clarendon) went so far, as I understood him, as to tell us that we must watch public opinion more closely, and pay greater attention to the majorities in the other House of Parliament. My Lords, it occurs to me to ask the noble Earl whether he has considered for what purpose this House exists, and whether he would be willing to go through

[18] The word Fenian is derived from an old Irish word meaning "champion of Ireland." The aim of the Fenians was to throw off English rule.

the humiliation of being a mere echo and supple tool of the other House in order to secure for himself the luxury of mock legislation? I agree with my noble Friend the noble Earl (the Earl of Derby) below me that it were better not to be than submit to such a slavery. I have heard many prophecies as to the conduct of this House. I am not blind to the difficulties of its position in this peculiar age—I am not blind to the peculiar obligations which lie on the Members of this House in consequence of the fixed and unalterable constitution of this House. I quite admit—every one must admit—that when the opinion of your countrymen has declared itself, and you see that their convictions—their firm, deliberate, sustained convictions—are in favour of any course, I do not for a moment deny that it is your duty to yield. It may not be a pleasant process—it may even make some of you wish that some other arrangement were existing; but it is quite clear that whereas a Member of a Government, when asked to do that which is contrary to his convictions, may resign, and a Member of the Commons, when asked to support any measure contrary to his convictions, may abandon his seat, no such course as this is open to your Lordships; and therefore, on these rare and great occasions, on which the national mind has fully declared itself, I do not doubt your Lordships would yield to the opinion of the country— otherwise the machinery of Government could not be carried on. But there is an enormous step between that and being the mere echo of the House of Commons. My Lords, I quite admit that the difficulty of ascertaining the opinion of the country may be great. Perhaps no more striking instance of that ever occurred than in reference to this very question thirty years ago. The tide then ran very strongly against the Irish Church. Popular opinion appeared to be pronounced. The House of Commons acted upon it, and sent up Bills to this House which your Lordships systematically objected. And in course of time it turned out that you were right— that you knew the opinion of the nation better than the House of Commons. The nation became apathetic, the question slept, and for a whole generation we have heard no more of the Irish Church. That is a proof at once of the difficulty of deciding what is the opinion of the nation, and of the duty incumbent on your Lordships of taking your course not less with firmness than with prudence. I have no fear of the conduct of the House of Lords in this respect. I am quite sure—whatever judgment may be passed on us, whatever predictions may be made, be your term of existence long or short—you will never consent to act except as a free, independent House of the Legislature, and that you will consider any other more timid or subservient course as at once unworthy of your traditions, unworthy of your honour, and, most of all, unworthy of the nation you serve. I admit that the future is full of difficulty, and that on many questions of doubt and perplexity which may be submitted to the House your prudence and judgment may be sorely taxed; but I am quite clear that with respect to this Bill, so vague, unmeaning, ill-constructed, and having behind it projects of change so vast, so crude, so sweeping, your Lordships can have but one duty, and that is to reject it.

3. Housing of the Working Classes

This speech may be found in HANSARD (CCLXXXIV [3d Ser.], 1679-1700 [February 22, 1884]). Favorable action was taken on the motion for the appointment of a royal commission to look into the housing of the working classes, but a bill, based on the report of the commission, contained provisions that are not very important.

The Marquess of SALISBURY, who rose to move an humble Address to Her Majesty, for the appointment of a Royal Commission to inquire into the housing of the working classes in populous places, said: My Lords, I rise to call your Lordships' attention to a subject exceeding in importance and gravity even the terrible and deplorable tidings which have just been laid before the House.[19] The matters to which I have to draw your attention do not affect current politics; they do not concern the struggles of Parties, or the praise or blame of Ministries; and yet they touch more closely the springs of national well-being and prosperity than even the deep and grave questions with which Parliament has been recently occupied. My Lords, the matter which I have to bring before your Lordships, and upon which I have to ask your Lordships to address the Crown, is the question of the housing of the working classes. It is a question that has, of late, excited very much interest, and has elicited so large a mass of testimony, that I am relieved from the necessity of proving my case for the consideration of Parliament. I have received numberless pamphlets and writings during the past Recess on the subject; the attention of persons of every class, of every creed and school of politics, has been turned to this question of the housing of the poor; and I have met no one who does not admit that there is a great problem to be solved, and a great evil to be remedied.

I know, however, that there are some who think that what has already been done, both in the way of inquiry and legislation, is sufficient to justify us in holding our hand, or, rather, sufficient to make it important that we should hold our hand, in order that we may not seem to interfere with the goodwill of those who have already taken this matter up. There is a letter from a Member of the House of Commons in the newspapers to-day which raises the question directly. I refer to Mr. Brodrick's letter, in which he states his opinion that such a Royal Commission as that which I am moving for might have the effect rather of diminishing and slackening the effort of the local authorities, and those upon

[19] Telegrams concerning the Sudan.

whom the duty of dealing with this matter rests, instead of stimulating and aiding them. I attach great importance to the advice that is given in that communication; but I think that hardly sufficient consideration is paid in it to the manifold and complex character of the particular evil with which we are concerned, and with which we have to deal. That evil is not, as it is generally treated, of a simple character. It is of a very complicated character.

There are four different evils from which the working classes in our great towns and populous places are suffering, into which inquiry is very necessary, and to which Parliament should be invited to apply such remedies as it may decide. I observe that most of those who have given their minds to the discussion—and, as far as I can gather, that includes Her Majesty's Government themselves—treat this question as if it were purely a sanitary question in its most restricted sense. The impression seems to exist that if the sanitary legislation which is already on the Statute Book were carried out, the whole of the evil would be met. Now, a consideration of the character of the evil with which we have to deal would, I think, dispel that impression. It is, in the first place, and undoubtedly in a most important sense, a sanitary question. The neglect, or the imperfect fulfilment, of the requirements of public health, more especially in regard to the statutory provisions in the matter of sewage, is certainly a matter of primary interest in connection with this subject. The accounts that have been laid before us, in great abundance, with reference to the condition of the dwellings of the working classes in this Metropolis, undoubtedly show that in this primary requirement as regards health those dwellings are lamentably deficient. The sewage arrangements are in a state fit enough, not only to excite loathing on the part of those who have visited those places, but to convince us that a satisfactory condition of the public health is impossible so long as the present state of things continues.

But the sewage question is not everything, nor is it the only one we must consider. If it were simply a question of proper arrangements with respect to sewage matters, the legislation that is already on the Statute Book certainly would seem to be adequate. It is a question to which the attention of Parliament has been constantly directed, and the legislation upon it is abundant and very drastic. The local authority has a right to require that proper communications with the sewers, proper arrangements as to privies, water-closets, &c., and a proper and sufficient water supply, shall be carried out in every dwelling-house. If they are not carried out, any two inhabitants have the right of forcing the attention of the local authority to the matter. And the decision of a justice is sufficient to impose upon the owner the necessity of making the proper arrangements, and, in default of his so doing, the local authority is authorized to make them at his expense. It is impossible to imagine provisions, which, if adequately carried out, could be more resolute and determined than those which Parliament has already adopted. But we know that, for some reasons or other, these beneficent provisions have not had their full effect, and that is one of the grounds on which I ask Parliament to make an inquiry. It is impossible to produce enactments, so far as mere enactments go, which could more completely effect the object we have in view. Therefore, it is impossible not to see, in that case, that there must be something wrong. Either there must be some insuperable obstacle, which it requires other measures to remove, against the carrying out of those provisions, or the authorities upon whom the duty of carrying them out devolves have been lamentably wanting in regard to the obligations and duties that are cast upon them. This is, at all events, a matter which Parliament should inquire into.

I will say, with respect to this particular point of sewage, that it is intimately connected with the question of water supply. You cannot expect sewage arrangements to be perfect so long as the water supply is imperfect; and that question of water supply is intimately linked on to the question of the Water Companies which has already baffled and affected more than one Administration. How far it is the fault of the legislation that affects the Water Companies that the water supply is insufficient, how far the local authorities are inefficient, how far obstacles which we do not at present sufficiently recognize interfere with the law—these are matters which we cannot ascertain by discussion in this House, or in the newspapers, and which require a careful and accurate investigation by a Commission. We must not be too impatient in this matter. It is not a great many years ago—I dare say a great many of those now present remember how, some years ago, it was brought forcibly to the mind and senses of Parliament that the drainage of the Metropolis was in an unsatisfactory condition, owing to the state of the Thames, which absolutely prevented legislation during a considerable period of the Session. But the Parliament of that time, by the hands of Lord John Manners, who was then First Commissioner of Works, made the necessary provisions to enable the Metropolitan Board of Works to carry out a scheme for the drainage arrangements of the Metropolis; and it is only since the completion of that scheme 15 years ago that it has been possible to place the sewage arrangements of this great city in a satisfactory condition. It may be that, although progress is going on, it is not

sufficiently rapid. Still, a more full employment of the appliances
which we now have would solve that part of the difficulty.

But when we speak of the bad condition of the houses of the
poor, we may mean, besides bad drainage, that the houses are in
bad repair. There, again, the Statute Book contains, as far as the
law goes, an adequate remedy. The Metropolitan Board of Works
has abundant and perfect power to cause the repair of a building
to be carried out, and, in default of the repairs being carried out,
to cause the removal of any building which is in a condition dangerous to those who inhabit it. If that power has not been sufficiently exercised, and if dangerous structures have not been removed,
again, it is a matter for careful and impartial inquiry what is the
obstacle which has prevented the Metropolitan Board from carrying out the intentions of Parliament in this respect.

But the difficulties with respect to the housing of the poor are
not confined to the actual structure of the dwellings in which they
live. Some of them have arisen, not only from the construction
of particular houses, but from the position of houses with respect
to each other. They are built too closely, or built in courts and
alleys where ventilation cannot penetrate, where the sun cannot
operate, and where, consequently, all influences that minister to
disease are unusually powerful, and do not receive their natural
checks. This is a matter, also, which has engaged the attention
of Parliament. It was in reference to, and to get rid of, these
"unhealthy areas," as they are called, that the measure associated
with the name of my right honourable Friend (Sir R. Assheton
Cross) was passed in 1875. It is, undoubtedly a measure which has
already effected great good; but its further progress seems to be
barred by some serious obstacles. A Committee of the House of
Commons was appointed to inquire into this particular point, and
sat for two Sessions, and collected very valuable evidence. I do not
think that it solved at all the question why this Act has not been
more fully applied. But it, at all events, brought to light this fact
—that the application of the Act was accompanied by extreme
expense. It was impossible to destroy these insanitary areas and
courts without sufficiently compensating all those who had any
existing interest in them—ground landlords and leaseholders, and
the actual tenants—and those compensations, largely increased, and
often doubled by the cost of legal, surveying, and other expenses,
have raised the cost of the operations to a point which even, for so
wealthy a body as the Metropolitan Board of Works, is almost
prohibitory. At all events, a very heavy burden was laid upon the
ratepayers of the Metropolis. I think it was calculated with regard
to a considerable number of these areas, that whereas the price

which was obtained for them did not exceed 5s. a foot, the Board had to pay as much as a guinea a foot in order to obtain possession of them, and the balance between the two prices was so much additional burden to the already heavily-weighted ratepayers of the Metropolis. This is undoubtedly a very serious evil, and I do not think that, although the Committee opened up the ground, they investigated thoroughly the particular cause to which this vast expense is due, and it is very desirable that the cause should be ascertained.

In respect to this point, suggestions have been made by many persons of authority—some, I am sorry to say, of official authority, which are hardly consistent with the principles Parliament has observed in dealing with property. It has been proposed that the ground landlords and the leaseholders should be deprived of a portion of their compensation, in order to make it more easy for Parliament to destroy these unhealthy areas, and to substitute for them more wholesome dwellings. I do not think that that is a matter which ought to be submitted to the Commission. I think these are questions of principle—large questions, on which Parliament itself ought to, and will have exclusively to decide. The question how far, and what kind of compensation should be given, and how far any abuses that have arisen will require to be limited, is a matter which Parliament itself must settle. With respect to this matter of compensation, I would venture to say to those politicians, whoever they may be, who desire to put a portion of the cost of those sanitary reforms upon the ground landlord, or the leaseholder, or any other person having an interest in the locality, if they intend to go upon the principle of taking away compensation, let them have the courage of their opinions. I would address them with the words employed by Martin Luther—"Pecca fortiter." If they mean to meet this great evil by any kind of confiscation; let them get all advantage out of confiscation that they can by taking the property with the unceremonious facility which would befit a Turkish Pasha or a Burmese officer. To confiscate, to take off something to which the owner has a right, and only by that to gain 6d. or 1s. in the price per foot—that seems to me a most improvident proceeding. If they wish to get the whole advantage, they must confiscate more largely—they must confiscate the whole. There is no use in incurring all those penalties, which an unfailing Nemesis inflicts upon the authors of public plunder, unless they get a sufficient amount of booty to indemnify them for the operation. These three elements of the bad housing of the poor are those to which attention has been principally directed, and I think it has been unduly directed to the exclusion of one other.

It has not been noticed sufficiently that the great and peculiar evil is the overcrowding of the poor, and that all the remedies which are proposed for these other evils, instead of diminishing over-crowding, only tend to exaggerate it. What is your remedy for dealing with all these bad houses, bad localities, and unhealthy areas? Your remedy is, knock down and turn out—to knock down unhealthy houses and clear unhealthy areas. But the immediate effect of all these operations is to increase the overcrowding on the spaces that remain. The people who are turned out of these un-healthy dwellings must find places somewhere, and all the remedies which have hitherto been proposed seem to me to fail in this point— that they absolutely increase the principal evil instead of diminish-ing it. They absolutely increase the overcrowding instead of doing anything to mitigate it. The idea seems to be that if you are sufficiently severe on unhealthy houses—if you clear away unhealthy areas with a sufficiently relentless hand—you will, somehow or other force somebody else to build healthy houses in healthy local-ities—that you will inflict upon the poor who are turned out such an intolerable amount of evil that somebody else will come forward and assist them. Even if that were true, it would be a most cruel method of proceeding. Even if it were true that you could, by the mere process of destroying every unhealthy house, ultimately force the building of healthy houses, still it would be a very gradual operation, and there would be an intermediate period during which the suffering would be intense. But the truth is, in this country at least, you cannot proceed by those violent methods. If you pass an Act of Parliament, of which the practical result will be the in-fliction of great misery upon a considerable number of people, you may be quite certain that the Act of Parliament will be mere waste paper. It will not be carried out by the authorities. No provision, however drastic, no administrative arrangement, however perfect, will prevent that inevitable result. The consequence is, that as long as you confine your attention to purely sanitary legislation, and do not bear in mind this difficulty of overcrowding, which is really the dominant one, your sanitary legislation will be in vain. People will not be turned out of unhealthy houses if there is nowhere else to go. The local authorities, press them as you may, transform them as you will, will not carry out your enactments. That is really the most important matter on which, it seems to me, the Commission should inquire. If we have this overcrowding, unless you can meet it, it will neutralize all your efforts; and you can do nothing to meet it, unless you possess sufficient knowledge of the precise character of the evil.

What is wanted is to know where and what are the localities

in which the overcrowding exists, and how many of those who are thus crowded together are forced to dwell in that locality? As everybody knows who has followed this discussion at all, the great thing in London is that, with respect to a certain class of the population at least, you cannot move them to a distance from their industry, or they will cease to be able to pursue it. The result is that the obvious remedy of taking these people into the country only applies to a limited portion of those whose difficulties you have to meet. And, therefore, we want to know what is that portion, what is the number of persons who could not pursue their industry, living at a distance from London, where they might obtain some reasonable accommodation, and in what particular localities do they congregate? If you once had that information fully obtained and laid before Parliament and the country, I believe it would be possible, in the first instance, to apply, with greater clearness and effect, the remedy which would carry away those who can live out of London, to see how far cheap trains carrying people out of London might be employed, and what building operations are requisite, where they are required, and to what extent they must be carried out. That is really the gist and kernel of the whole matter. That is the difficulty we have to meet.

Are large building operations requisite; and, if requisite, where are they to be carried on; and at whose cost? I do not affect to answer these questions now. If I could answer them, I should not ask your Lordships to seek for a Royal Commission. It is because enormous difficulties attach to all these questions that I think investigation, and speedy investigation, is necessary.

My Lords, I have carefully avoided any words indicating that I think any man or class of men are to blame for the existing state of things. Of course, I do not and will not say that there are not persons who are to blame; but I say that any attempt to escape from the urgency of the problem by throwing the blame on any class of men is futile wholly. It is absurd to say the ground landlord is to blame. If he has got houses which come within the operation of the law, the law is strong enough to assert itself, and to force him to do his duty. But if he is not within the grasp of the law, he is not exposed to any blame. The ground landlord, or the mere temporary and intermediate owner of a house, like everyone else, has to sell the goods he possesses in the open market for the price he can obtain for them, and it is ridiculous to blame him for obtaining the best price he can.[20]. . . . .

---

[20] Lord Salisbury continues to discuss the evils of overcrowding.

4. Irish Home Rule—Free Trade

The following speech, which in its complete form took one hour and five minutes to deliver, was given at Liverpool. It may be found in The Times (London) of January 12, 1888. In it Lord Salisbury took up two very perplexing problems of the day: Ireland and free trade. After Gladstone's defeat on the Home Rule Bill a general election was held that gave power to Salisbury for six years (1886-1892). He was able to rely upon the support of the Liberal Unionists, who had left Gladstone, so long as he opposed Home Rule and in fact soon ap- *pointed one of their members, Goschen, as Chancellor of the Exchequer. As he himself explains he meant to put down criminal activities in Ireland but at the same time to give relief from an unmerited distress that had been ubiquitous since his assumption of office. As for free trade, Salisbury and many other Conservatives had been suspected during this decade of economic disabilities of flirting with "fair" traders—theorists and businessmen who wished for some modification of free trade. He answers the challenge in his own way.*

Mr. Forwood,[21] Ladies, and Gentlemen,—I have to thank you most heartily for the kindness of your reception, and for that address, so indulgent in substance and so beautiful in form, which you have kindly placed in my hands. Mr. Forwood was good enough to say that I was in the forefront of the present battle. (Hear, hear.) It occurred to me, when he said it, that that would be more truly said of the audience representing the town I have the honour to address. (Hear, hear.) It is Liverpool that is in the forefront of this battle (cheers)—Liverpool, which has a deeper interest than any other city in the connexion between England and Ireland; which knows better than any other city the character of those by whom Ireland is inhabited ("hear, hear," and laughter), their good points and their bad, their weak points and their strong; and should be a judge, if any city by opportunities could be, of the policy that it is our wisdom to pursue towards them. (Hear, hear.) It seems to me that there is some propriety in the fact that I have the honour to address you just one year after the formation of the present Government. I mean after the formation of the Government which marked our close combination with the Unionist party in including among its members our Chancellor of the Exchequer, Mr. Goschen. (Cheers.) It is just a year ago since he received the seals of office from Her Majesty's hands and since I received them as Foreign

[21] The chair was filled by Mr. A. B. Forwood, the chairman of the Liverpool Constitutional Association.

Secretary, and there is a propriety, as it were, in my presenting to you our first report of our year's proceedings on this tremendous enterprise in which we are engaged. (Hear, hear.) On the whole I think you will agree with me that it ought to be favorable. (Cheers.) If you will look back to the state of opinion with respect to our prospects and our difficulties 12 months ago, and compare them with the view which I think all spectators now entertain, there will not be wanting circumstances and occasions for congratulations. (Cheers.) But we have had a difficult task to perform, a difficult battle to fight. We have not had simply to fight a battle, as Mr. Forwood has said, for the unity of the Empire, not simply to contend with the arguments of those who desired to assail it. No; those who desired to assail it thought it better to hold their tongues on the matter nearest to their hearts (cheers, and a voice, "Old Billy Gladstone's a traitor"). Their main object was undoubtedly to prepare the way for Home Rule, but they saw that it was not acceptable to the English people, and the judgment given at the polls was decidedly against them. Therefore they adopted another policy. They relied upon their conviction that Ireland could not be governed unless we gave to the Irish agitators all that they demanded. They based on that imagination all their hopes, and they directed all their policy to secure that their imagination should be fulfilled. The one thing to secure was that Ireland should not be governable. They did not say much about the Home Rule Bill, when originally they found that to mention it only was to scatter their party into a thousand atoms. (Laughter and cheers.) When the Bill was introduced Mr. Gladstone hoped that he would induce his party (groans, and a voice, "Judas") to accept the clauses of it, but he found very soon that that was a mistake. Then he earnestly entreated his party to throw the clauses over, but to accept the second reading. They would not even do that, and now he has buried it deep—its substance and its provisions. He does not tell us the text of the significance of the measure that he proposes. He has abandoned the clauses; he has abandoned the second reading. He is satisfied if only anybody will agree to accept the title of the Bill. (Laughter and cheers.) But naturally it is not much use trying to prove the title to a Bill, and the way they have tried to prove that Home Rule must be granted is, as I have said, by showing that Parliament is ungovernable without it. (Cheers.)

We set ourselves at once to work to provide those legislative enactments both in the way of punishment of crime (hear) and in the way of relief of unmerited distress, which seemed to us most likely to bring about the peace and that readiness to be governed which are essential to every civilized and progressive community.

(Cheers.) Every effort was made to resist the progress of these meas-ures. I do not say that every line in them is that which, if we had no Parliament to deal with, is precisely that which we should have chosen. But we kept before us this one consideration, that above all things we must provide the machinery by which crime should be punished in Ireland; that unless we could govern Ireland the Union would be condemned in the popular estimation, and that almost any sacrifice that might be made would be pardoned if it should have the result of securing this great object on which our eyes are set. (Cheers.) Well, we passed our Bill; we were pursued to the end with every species of travesty and misrepresentation. It is said, in spite of the highest legal authority, that we had placed new crimes on the Statute-book. ("Shame.") We have the best authority for stating that that allegation is absolutely false. (Cheers.) We introduced new machinery for punishing the crimes which the law had already denounced. (Hear, hear.) But our opponents well knew that this was a critical matter, and that if our new legislation succeeded their argument as to Home Rule would make small im-pression even upon the most indifferent part of the English people. (Cheers.) Therefore, from the first, they have strained every nerve that the law should not be obeyed in Ireland; they have sent over English agitators to urge the Irish to break the law ("Shame"); and I am glad to say that some at least of these English agitators have been punished. (Prolonged cheering, and cries of "Gladstone.") In England, names of the highest authority such as I have just heard whispered from the gallery were used for the purpose of hounding the people against the police, of bringing the law into disrepute, and of encouraging, by every effort that is not in itself amenable to punishment, men to trample the law of their country under foot. ("Shame.") I do not think the enterprise has succeeded.[23] . . . . .

Mr. Shaw-Lefevre writes to the papers to say that there was reason to believe that in the autumn of 1885—that was when a Con-servative Government was in office—there were eminent members of Lord Salisbury's Government, including Lord Carnarvon, who were favorable to some form of Home Rule for Ireland, but that the policy had been rejected by a majority of the Cabinet.

Mr. Shaw-Lefevre went on—"I continue in this belief, in spite of the recent very guarded denials of Lord Salisbury." I do not know what he calls a guarded denial. It appears to me that unless one is exceedingly peremptory in one's language, unless one's phrases

---

[23] There is omitted a discussion on the statements of Gladstone and his followers, such as Mr. Shaw-Lefevre, that Conservatives really were perceiv-ing the necessity of giving some kind of Home Rule to Ireland.

are seasoned with a certain amount of imprecation (laughter) and unless one's English is absolutely monosyllabic, Mr. Shaw-Lefevre does not consider it otherwise than a guarded statement. (Laughter.) I do not wish to say anything, I do not wish to use any language that would be at all offensive to his feelings, but in language as peremptory and as distinct as it is possible to use I beg to say that the assertion that there were other members of the Cabinet of 1885 besides Lord Carnarvon who had expressed feelings in favor of Home Rule is an utter, complete, and absolute falsehood. (Cheers.) I hope that he will not think that a guarded term. (Laughter.) I shall be prepared to reinforce it if he does. (Cheers.)

But what I wish to ask is, What right have our opponents to use poisoned weapons of this kind? (Hear, hear.) When Mr. Gladstone speaks of what is ordinarily said by the Conservatives in private, when Mr. Shaw-Lefevre speaks of the opinions expressed by the Cabinet of 1885, they are speaking of things which must have been outside their own personal knowledge. Now, supposing there was a bank against which certain persons had feelings of great antipathy, and those persons were to go about and say "It is all very well for that bank to say that it has got money; we know that it is insolvent, and that it does not intend to pay its bills"—I will not ask you what opinion you would form of such a statement; but what opinion do you think a jury of your countrymen would form? I do not see why that which would be dishonesty of the most extreme character in private affairs should be absolute innocence in politics. (Cheers.)

Another point on which the policy of creating division in the solid phalanx opposed to him commended itself to Mr. Gladstone was the question of free trade. He spoke about it at Dover, and he not only said all kinds of things about me, but he said that Lord Hartington and Mr. Goschen were not to be trusted in the matter of free trade. That did seem to me the most grotesque misstatement which it was possible for a man to make, and to show the poverty of resources which were still at his disposal for the purpose of his party. (Cheers.) Mr. Gladstone was pleased to say that my statements were very unclear and difficult to understand, and he coupled with that a compliment to my intellect which implied that I was very insincere. Mr. Gladstone's compliments usually have a back-handed blow of that kind. (Laughter.) I am afraid that on the question of clearness of explanation my ideas are not exactly similar to Mr. Gladstone's (a voice, "I hope not"); but at least I know that when he clearly explains his future policy in respect to Ireland it costs me several hours of hard study, and I end with a bad headache. (Laughter.) I wish to say a word to illustrate and to enforce the statement to which he took exception. The statement was that I objected to protection, but that I did not on that account approve of all the fiscal arrangements and all the fiscal doctrines to which Mr. Gladstone had given his sanction. I believe that many fiscal doctrines injurious in their character and not only not consonant with free trade, but absolutely opposed to it, are sheltered under its broad mantle, and you are required to believe it. (Cheers.) Let me give one or two illustrations. Mr. Forwood alluded in terms of just praise to the efforts of my friend Baron de Worms in favor of abolishing bounty upon sugar. (Cheers.) Now, that is one very good case in point. What does bounty on sugar do? It favors the consumer, undoubtedly it does; and what I may call your freetrader presumes that everything that favors the consumer, whether it be legitimate or whether it be not, must be sanctioned by the doctrine of free trade; and so you see people writing in the newspapers that because it is good for the consumer it ought to be encouraged. They do not see that advantages to the consumer secured by illegitimate means are only transitory in their character, and that when they have served the purpose of destroying the industry against which they have been levelled the advantage to the consumer will cease. (Cheers.) Let me take another matter, the duties upon articles of luxury, articles such as silks and laces and wine, and so on. (Hear, hear.) It is, of course, very desirable to admit them free, but the question is, which bears heaviest upon the springs of industry—a tax which affects the man who consumes laces and silk and wine, or a tax which affects the ordinary income-tax payer? (Hear, hear.) Why, it is obvious that you might stop the whole consumption of laces and silks and wine without inflicting a very deep wound on the well-being of the country, but the weight which the income-tax places on the springs of prosperity and of industry is very serious indeed. (Hear, hear.) I must correct this by saying that I am discussing now an abstract point. Do not imagine that I am giving you what is called an advance of Mr. Goschen's Budget. (Laughter and cheers.) [23]

[23] The speech gives a little additional data on economic questions and then continues for a half hour's duration on the Irish question.

5. Anglo-German Agreement on Heligoland and Zanzibar

The following speech was delivered on July 10, 1890. It may be found in HANSARD *(CCCXLVI [3d Ser.], 1258-71). It is interesting for its expression of Salisbury's sentiments toward Germany and toward the partition of Africa as well as for its references to the slave trade and to navalism, the public enthusiasm for which had been stimulated by the ministry's recent formulation of a standard, i.e., an equality with the two strongest navies of the Continent.*

My Lords, I rise to move the Second Reading of a Bill for the purpose of confirming a portion of the Agreement which was signed at Berlin on Tuesday week—that portion of it which provides for the cession of the Island of Heligoland to the German Empire, and, as the Bill is exclusively concerned with that island, I will make some remarks with reference to it; but I hope your Lordships will not consider me out of order if I go afterwards for a few moments into the general provisions of the Agreement in regard to other places than Heligoland. Perhaps, in strict order, I ought not to do so, but in this House we are indulgent in that respect.

The island of Heligoland, as your Lordships are aware, is about three-quarters of a mile in extent, in the bay formed by Germany and the peninsula which ends in Denmark. It was taken in the year 1807, at a time when we were at war with Denmark, to whom it then belonged. Denmark was then the owner of the Frisian territory of Schleswig, to which this island naturally and by population belonged. It was of value to us in that great war for a reason that would not occur at first sight. The year when it was taken was the year following the issue of the Berlin Decrees by Napoleon, of which the aim was to ruin England by the exclusion of her manufactures and commodities from the Continental markets. It was natural that this strange and unprecedented policy should be met by efforts to break through the line which he had set up, and Napoleon's policy was, to a great extent, fought by the smuggler. Heligoland was of great use, lying within 20 miles of the nearest German coast. It was of great use as a store for goods afterwards to be in that manner introduced into the Continental markets in spite of Napoleon's Decrees. Towards the end of the war, but before it had concluded, and while Napoleon was still fighting gallantly in the Eastern Provinces of France, in January, 1814, a Treaty was concluded at Kiel, of which the main object was to provide that Norway, which had previously belonged to Denmark, should thenceforth belong to Sweden. In that great contest Denmark had the misfortune to take the wrong side, and Sweden had the good fortune to take the right side, and the transfer of Norway from Denmark to Sweden was the expression of that fact. Heligoland, which also had been taken from Denmark, was by the same Instrument transferred to the British Crown. I do not think there were any further stipulations with respect to it. It remained part of the territory of this country by virtue of the Treaty of Kiel. No doubt the motive for retaining it was partly the natural wish to retain territory, and partly that, as our contest was not then concluded, the value of the island was still considerable.

It was held as a military post for some years. Up to the year 1821 there was a military establishment in the island; but in that year—not a year when peace theories were in vogue, but when the military spirit was very strong in this country—it was determined to withdraw the military establishment, and since that time the island has remained unoccupied by any considerable force, unfortified and practically unarmed. It has remained entirely undefended, and I believe there has been no attempt to defend it. Certainly there has been no indication of any intention on the part of Parliament or the Executive Government of the country to undertake the arming or defending of it; and I believe there is no doubt that the recommendation of the Colonial Defence Commission was expressed strongly against any such course. In truth, the value of the island is generally recognised for any strategic purposes as very small. It has no harbour. It has an open roadstead, which is untenable in a northwest wind, which is the prevailing wind.

The commercial value of the island, again, as far as this country is concerned, may be expressed by very minute figures. I believe the import of British goods into the island in the course of the year amounts to £50 in value, or not quite that. The population are, as I have said, Frisian. They speak Low German, the language of the coast opposite. I believe there are only 5 per cent. that are not of that nationality, and they have not materially altered—they have increased in numbers, not much during the intervening period.

Now, the point that we have to consider on the present occasion is, Is this island of any strategic value to this country? I have shown that commercial value, from the want of a harbour and for want of a market, it has none. Has it any strategic value? In time of peace, of course, the question of strategic value does not come up, but it may just be mentioned that even in time of peace it is apt to be a slightly inconvenient possession, because I think it was found during the late Franco-German War that its proximity to the German coast was sufficient to invite attempted breaches of neutrality, which are very convenient to belligerents, but which we know to our cost are apt to be exceedingly onerous to neutrals. But I will not dwell upon a consideration of that kind, which is not of paramount importance; I will ask, what would be the value of the island to us strategically in case of war? There are two cases—one a great deal more probable than the other, or rather less improbable than the other. One is the case of our being at war with Germany. Well, as I have said, the island is entirely unfortified. It lies within a few hours' steam of the great arsenal of Germany. If I am to suppose what I imagine is so utterly improbable a case as a war with Germany, I presume that if this island remained in our possession, the very day of the declaration of war a sufficient force, with all necessary materials and guns, would be despatched to it, and would arrive at the island probably considerably before any relieving fleet could arrive from our side. Experts differ a good deal as to its value in the case of war with Germany. Some think it of no value at all, while others think that it might be useful as a coal depot to a blockading fleet; but a coal depot, when England is so near, though it may be a convenience, can hardly be called a great advantage. The case, therefore, in respect to a war with Germany would be that it would expose us to a blow which would be a considerable humiliation, and it would not confer upon us any great advantage, if any advantage, in the conduct of the war on our side.

But let us take the much less improbable supposition of our being at war with somebody else. This island is undefended, and can be defended only by a sufficient Naval force. If we were at war with any other Power it would be, therefore, necessary for us to lock up a Naval force for the purpose of defending this island, unless we intended to expose ourselves to the humiliation of having it taken. My Lords, our fleet is a large one, and I am happy to say it has recently been augmented, but it is none too large for the work it has to do, with our extensive and extending Empire, stretching into every corner of the globe, and meeting with new rivalries at every turn. I think all who have studied the subject will say that in defending our dependencies, and in defending our line of trade, our fleet, great and powerful as it is, would be taxed up to its fullest energies. I think we should labour under a distinct disadvantage if we have a position contributing in no degree to the defence of the Empire without commercial or other value, and which yet, in order to avoid a humiliating blow, would require a certain Naval force to be locked up and kept useless for every other purpose. On these grounds, my Lords, we have come to a conclusion, which I imagine is the conclusion held by many persons, and has been held for a long time, that this island, unfortified and undefended, is not an advantageous possession, but that it is one which for a proper consideration it would be well for the Empire to be divested.

But the consideration has been raised by noble Lords opposite and others who deal with the question from a different point of view. It is said that the inhabitants of the island are opposed to the cession, and that their veto ought to be conclusive. My Lords, I do not think that the inhabitants of the island are opposed to the cession. There is no reason that they should be. They have not a long descended ancestral connection with the British Crown. There may be men there, living now, who were alive when the island was originally taken. They are related by the closest bonds of language, of race, of religion, with those who live almost within site of their shores. Their pecuniary interests, to come down to motives which are less noble to dwell upon, though they are often powerful in these cases—their pecuniary profit in no way is increased by the connexion of the island with this country, nor can they look with any advantage to the continuance of that connexion. On the contrary, their whole prospect of gain depends on the large number of German bathing excursionists who go there in the summer, and that source of wealth would not diminish, but would, if anything, increase, if the island formed part of the German Empire. And it is probable, though the island is worthless to us from a strategic point of view, it will not be thought to be worthless to those near whose coasts it lies, and the military expenditure which would be the result of any determination to fortify it will form a large addition to the resources of the islanders, and I have no doubt has already been discounted by them. I am informed, and your Lordships, I think, have been generally informed, that a very enterprising nationality have already purchased up most of the land in the island. But while I say this, I cannot admit the doctrine that the decision of a population of a position that has been occupied for military and belligerent purposes is conclusive with respect to the uses to which that position should be put or the destiny which shall attend it.

You must draw a line between two sorts of possessions—those possessions which you rule for the benefit of the population that is in them, and those possessions which you hold in order to contribute to the defence of the Empire as a whole; and that latter class of positions, of which we have several, cannot complain of any injustice if it is said that Imperial considerations must occupy a place of paramount importance in the mind of the Government of this country with respect to them, just as local considerations would occupy a place of paramount importance with respect to positions of another kind. My Lords, cession is a very uncommon event, and it is not very likely to be repeated; but this doctrine, which has been rather insinuated on the present occasion, may stretch much further than cession. A hint was given that we ought to have taken the opinion of the people in some form or other, and we could only take it by way of plebiscite. Well, if people are asked to vote by plebiscite on a question of Imperial policy like this, they may also claim to vote on the question whether their country shall not be ceded; if their opinion is to weigh so heavily on the question whether they are to be ceded, it ought to weigh equally heavily in the other direction. But there is another case—a case which might become practical and important, having nothing to do with cessions—I mean the case where it is necessary to get rid of, or to induce the inhabitants to depart when the danger of war is imminent, and the possibility of actual siege arrives. My Lords, most of you who have paid any attention to these subjects know that a problem of a very serious kind attaches to one of our most important positions in that respect, and you would be very unwise to admit that posts which are occupied, or have been occupied, for belligerent purposes, Imperial purposes—that the paramount disposition of them can be affected because the population which has grown up upon the position has interests in a different direction. My Lords, I said we have come to the conclusion that this island is one which it would be not only no disadvantage, but an advantage to this country to transfer, if we could obtain for it a satisfactory consideration.

The consideration for which we look lies on the East Coast of Africa. There we have obtained, as will have been seen from the Treaty which has been laid on the Table, an undertaking from Germany that she will not oppose our assumption of the protectorate of Zanzibar, and likewise a similar engagement with respect to the Sultanate of Witu, and the long line of coast dependent on Witu to the north. The objects of these stipulations are, of course, to make our influence predominant in these countries. With Witu we have had no ancient connection, but it has become a position of considerable value in consequence of the large tract of country which has been acquired by the British East Africa Company, reaching up from the coast to the Victoria Nyanza Lake. As long as the Sultanate of Witu was in the hands of another Power, there was a possibility of annexations and expeditions to the north of us, which would have cut off British influence and British dominion from the sources of the Nile, from the Lake Albert Nyanza and the valley which lies at the base of the mountains of Abyssinia. The advantage of the acquisition of Witu is that it cuts off any rivalry in this respect, and that, save for the Italian dominion over Abyssinia and its dependencies, we have no rivalry to fear from any European civilised Power until we reach the confines of Egypt. I do not, by any means, say that is an advantage of which all the results will appear immediately, for, as we know, the valley of the Nile is occupied by another Power which is not European and which just at present is not very much inclined to make room for us. But the advantage of limiting our rivalry to an Asiatic or African tribe is one which those who are engaged in these enterprises appreciate very highly.

But, in addition to this, we have obtained the promise that Germany will not resist our assumption of the protectorate of Zanzibar, including the Island of Pemba. Zanzibar has 300,000 of a population which has very close commercial connection with our fellow-subjects in India, and the more closely it is brought under our influence the more that commerce is likely to flourish. It lies in the pathway from the Red Sea to Southern Africa; it must always be a commercial place of the first importance; it maintains an enterprising population and has a fertile soil; and there is no spot in all those waters more valuable to a maritime and commercial nation than Zanzibar and Pemba.

But it has also to us a very special interest—that, with the exception of what goes on in the Red Sea, I think all the living slave trade, all the slave trade which is now actually in operation, goes upon that sea and is fed by the Arab traders from Pemba and Zanzibar, and the closer our influence over the Government of the Sultan becomes, the more we may hope we shall succeed in that great effort for which this country has sacrificed so much—the effort to destroy the slave trade and gradually to extirpate domestic slavery. I believe that in that effort we shall have a thorough support from the present enlightened Sultan of Zanzibar. We have every ground to believe that he sympathises with us in this respect, and the relations in which we will now stand under the new arrangement to that ruler will very much facilitate our task.

But what it is important your Lordships should observe is that the only impediment to our complete influence in Zanzibar was the counter influence of Germany. Germany had a power in the Court of Zanzibar owing to the settlements it occupied on the mainland and the rights it had acquired over the Zanzibar coast; and however friendly the relations of the two Governments have always been, it nevertheless must inevitably be the case where two nationalities are struggling for the mastery that the struggle is not entirely destitute of the elements either of irritation or of danger. It has been said that in taking back our influence at Zanzibar we have only undone what we ourselves had previously done—that we gave to Germany her power over Zanzibar and are taking it back again, and I think that in the observations of Lord Rosebery the other night there was a considerable trace of that impression. [The Earl of Rosebery: Hear, hear!] That is not the case. I think it is well that anybody, in considering the recent history of Africa, should take notice of the enormous change which has taken place in the attitude of this and other countries towards it during the last 10 years.

Up to 10 years ago we remained masters of Africa practically, or the greater part of it, without being put to inconvenience by protectorates, or anything of that sort, by the simple fact that we were masters of the sea, and that we have had considerable experience in dealing with the native races. So much was that the case that we left enormous stretches of coast to the native rulers in the full confidence that they would go on under native rulers, and in the hope that they would gradually acquire their own proper civilisation without any interference on our part. Then suddenly we found out that that position, however convenient, had no foundation whatever in international law. We had no rights over all these vast stretches of coast both on the West and East Coast of Africa. We had no power of preventing any other nation from coming in and seizing a portion of them, and the noble Lord opposite, Lord Granville, was suddenly confronted with a demand on the part of Germany, first on one part of the African coast and then on another part of the African coast, to be allowed to occupy enormous stretches of territory which, up to that time, had been looked upon as practically under the protection of England. I do not mention this as complaining of the noble Lord for the decision he took. On the contrary, I think it was a necessary decision. It was impossible that England should have the right to lock up the whole of Africa, and say that nobody should be there except herself; and I think that the noble Lord opposite arrived at a correct solution of the difficulty when he frankly allowed that Germany as well as England should take part in the task of developing the vast untrodden fields of Africa, making them into new outlets for colonisation by the excessive population at home, and new fields of industry and trade. But I only demur to the statement made that I did it. It was entirely settled before we came into office.[24] . . . .

I think that the constant study of maps is apt to disturb men's reasoning powers. Certainly the enthusiasm which has been evoked for this desolate corner of Africa has surprised me more than anything else in this controversy. We have had a fierce conflict over the possession of a lake whose name I am afraid I cannot pronounce correctly—I think it is Lake Ngami—our only difficulty being that

[24] Further details on Zanzibar and inland territories are omitted.

we do not know where it is. We cannot determine its position within 100 miles, certainly not within 60 miles, and there are great doubts whether it is a lake at all, or only a bed of rushes. I am very anxious that full scope should be given to the enterprise of men who have undertaken concessions in that country from a well-affected chief named Moremi; and I think that the whole country of Moremi has been retained within the British sphere. But when I hear the language that is used, the hopes that are entertained, and the extraordinary reasoning as to the future which is based upon them, I cannot help thinking of similar language and similar dreams entertained by our ancestors some 300 years ago connected with the well-known projects for reaching the land of El Dorado. I hope and believe that this is only language, and that the practical sense of our countrymen will not lead them to take for absolute gospel all that has been said on the subject of these countries for the last few months.

I will not trouble your Lordships now with one or two other arrangements in other portions of that part of Africa or the de-limitations of territory which have been made there. If I were to do so I believe my noble Friend opposite, Lord Aberdare, would be the only person who would understand me, and I think I may there-fore venture to pass them by. But I will say that during these nego-tiations it occurred to me more than once that it might be wiser to break them off altogether and to allow the years to pass over us until the natural progress of emigration and civilisation and the struggle for existence should have determined in a far more effective way than can be done by Protocols and Treaties who are to be supreme, and in what part of that vast continent each nation is to rule. But, on reflection, we could not convince ourselves that that, though far the most comfortable course, would be our duty, because in the front of this advancing tide of colonisation there are numbers of men of both nationalities—men of energy and strong will, but prob-ably not distinguished by any great restraint over their feelings—who would be urging, in every part where rivalry existed and the two Powers touched, the claims of each nation to supremacy in each particular bit of territory, pressing them upon the natives, getting from native chiefs Treaty after Treaty, each Treaty conflicting with the other, and trying to establish by means which must constantly degenerate into violence the supremacy of that nation for which they were passionately contending. In such circumstances, whatever the friendliness of the Government at home, some friction and col-lisions could not be averted. The Governments of Germany and England have been on the most friendly terms, and I think have been able to impart at least a considerable portion of their own friendliness and moderation to those who served under them, but it is impossible to impart it to those not under their control, though they share our nationality, and are keen for the object which we also desire. It is impossible to restrain them. It is impossible to prevent the danger of collisions, which might be murderous and bloody; and then when those collisions took place, the echo of them would be heard here, they would be recounted and magnified in newspapers in both countries, they would be pressed upon popular passion until even the Governments themselves might not be able to resist the contagion of the feeling evoked. The happy sympathy and agreement which exist between the two Governments, and which I trust may long exist, would naturally be exposed in no limited time to very serious risks if we had allowed to remain undecided the many causes of conflict and the many questions of territory and right which had arisen in various parts of the continent between the two countries, and especially in the island of Zanzibar, where we should have been brought to close quarters, and where many questions of difficulty would have arisen. I fear that if the existing state of things had gone on the harmony of the two countries might not be long maintained.

My Lords, I commend this Agreement to your approval, not as pretending that we have gained or that Germany has gained any great advantage. I believe we have gained on both sides advantages, because each has obtained what suited its own purposes, and of which it could make the most valuable use. I think we have each obtained what is most advantageous to us, but I do not pretend that either country has gained any advantage over the other. What I believe is that we have come to a common agreement which will remove all danger of disunion and conflict between us, and which will cement, I hope for a long time, the good feeling of those who by sympathy, by interest, and by descent, ought always to be friends.

MOVED, "THAT THE BILL BE NOW READ 2ᵃ."
—(THE MARQUESS OF SALISBURY.)

6. The Empire

This speech, given at the banquet to the colonial premiers during the Diamond Jubilee, may be found in The Times (London), *June 19, 1897.*

The Earl of Rosebery had just expressed the hope that the premiers would not separate without making an effort to draw the bonds of empire closer.

Lord Salisbury, who was received with loud cheers, said: Your Royal Highness, my lords, and gentlemen,—As in duty bound, on behalf of the Legislatures, home and colonial, I beg to tender you our hearty thanks for the earnestness and cordiality with which you have received this toast. I have observed, however, that in the brilliant speech of the noble lord [25] who gave this toast, as in other parts, we have been thinking less of the Legislatures of these colonies than of that Royal figure whose memory and the thought of whom dominates all our reflexions and proceedings, and those of that brilliant company of rulers from distant lands who have brought the symbol of empire as a homage to her people. (Cheers.) I am, therefore, rather departing from that which has been the custom in our speeches in addressing myself to the subject of colonial Legislatures. I heartily concur in that apophthegm which has been cited more frequently than any other on the present occasion —that brevity is the soul of wit. I have been selected as one—I am glad only one among them, for it might have been alone too burdensome a task for my shoulders—to respond for the Legislatures at home and abroad. At home I am connected with one particular branch of the Legislature to which the noble lord himself is equally and as indissolubly attached as myself (Laughter), and from whose praises I have no doubt he restrained himself by a tremendous effort. Of that assembly I will only say that it is the oldest among all these Houses or Legislatures whose health you have drunk. It is the oldest and some have thought that it was marked by a feebleness indicating decadence and decay. But those who have thought so, whoever they were, have had occasion to revise their opinions. (Laughter). I will only speak of what I know—viz., the Legislature in which I sit—and I am told that there are other Legislatures in which men talk more than they should, and I heard that their proceedings are unreasonably prolonged by the natural passions which each individual has to listen to his own voice. But if such things exist, which I do not know, at all events they do not exist in the

[25] The Earl of Rosebery.

House of Lords. If brevity is the soul of wit, the House of Lords
streams with wit at every pore. (Loud laughter.)

But I am not underrating the importance or the dignity of
younger Assemblies who are associated in this toast. I can remember considerable misgivings when they were set up, and I am bound
as a Tory to confess that I was not entirely free from those misgivings. But I am also bound to confess that they were entirely
without foundation and mistaken; and without going into particular
allusions which might be painful, I think that the dignity and
character with which the deliberations of our colonial Assemblies
are conducted have nothing to learn from the proceedings of Parliaments even in the most ancient cities of this continent.

Sir, I will not detain you longer, but I will remind you that this
toast really does include within itself all the aspirations and hopes
with which we have associated ourselves together this evening.
(Cheers.) We are representing here the growing Empire of Great
Britain. We do not know precisely what future is before us. We
are aware that we are the instruments of a great experiment. There
have been many emigrations, many colonies, before our time. The
relation between mother country and dependency has often been set
up, but those empires have never lasted, for either the colonies have
been swept away by some superior force, or the mother country, by
unjust and imprudent government, has driven the colonies to sever
the bond which bound them. The fact has been that such empires
have never lasted. We are undertaking the great experiment of trying to sustain such an empire entirely upon the basis of mutual goodwill, sympathy, and affection. (Cheers.) There is talk of fiscal
union, there is talk of military union. Both of them to a certain extent may be good things. Perhaps we may not be able to carry them
as far as some of us think, but in any case they will not be the basis
on which our Empire will rest. Our Empire will rest on the great
growth of sympathy, common thought, and feeling between those
who are in the main the children of a common race, and who have
a common history to look back upon and a common future to look
forward to. (Cheers.) It is the triumph of a moral idea in the construction of a great political organization which is the object and
the effort in which we have all joined, and of which our meeting
together is the symbol and seal; but the success of this effort will
depend upon the conduct of these various Legislatures, great and
small, because with them at last the government must lie. It depends upon their character and their self-restraint, whether this experiment shall succeed. The high ideal of a Legislature is to be the
arbiter among conflicting interests and classes. The danger to which
in our time all Legislatures are exposed is that they will make

themselves the instrument of one class to the loss and peril of the rest. Whether our great experiment of a colonial empire succeeds depends upon whether these Legislatures—to which we wish all success and a brilliant future—are able to exercise self-control and fulfil their high ideal. If they are they will produce an empire which the world has not yet seen, and which will make a powerful advance in the progress of humanity.

7. Address in Answer to the Queen's Speech. South Africa and the Empire—The English Constitution

This speech was given in the House of Lords during the debate on the Queen's speech. It represents Salisbury's reply to a question concerning the blame that might be attached to the government for the condition in which the ultimatum of the South African Republic found them (cf. HANSARD, LXXVIII [4th Ser.], 26-34 [January 30, 1900]).

Salisbury had reason for uttering pessimistic words since the crises of the Boer War had not been well handled either by the generals in the field or by the Cabinet at home. His observation about the defects of the English constitution as an instrument of war—and the remarks apply to similar constitutions elsewhere in force—is an observation men have frequently repeated in the twen-

tieth century as a result of experiences in the two World Wars. The historian may, perhaps, feel not pessimism but rather a sense of optimism in that Salisbury, by speaking to his generation on the subject, acknowledged, like his eminent predecessors in office and like the political philosophers, Burke and his critics, that change in the functioning of government is to some degree a necessity and a desirability. Indeed, only because of such a process of growth could the constitution respond to national needs and continue to stand. Conservative though Salisbury may have been, he faced what he thought to be a reality and was in a position on the basis of his assumption to give warning, even if in the vaguest manner, to the future.

. . . . . But when the noble Earl [26] says that we must have known, that it was impossible we should not have known—he got into a fervour of enthusiasm over the certainty of the knowledge that we must have possessed—about the artillery and munitions of war that the Republics were introducing—I ask, How on earth were we to know it? I believe, as a matter of fact—though I do not give this as official—that the guns were generally introduced in boilers and locomotives, and the munitions of war were introduced in pianos. It was not our territory, we had no power of search, we had no power of knowing what munitions of war were sent in, and we certainly had no power of supervising their importation into the Republics.

The Earl of Kimberley: Do you know nothing of the armaments of other nations?

The Marquess of Salisbury: Not so much as we ought to. It is a very remarkable peculiarity of public opinion in this country that

[26] The Earl of Kimberley.

people always desire to eat their cake and have it. They rejoice very much in the spiritual complacency which is afforded them by the reflection that they have a very small Secret Service Fund. Information, however, is a mere matter of money and nothing else. If you want much information, you must give much money; if you give little money, you will have little information. And, considering the enormous sums which are spent by other Powers, not least by the Transvaal Republic, which I was told on high diplomatic authority has spent £800,000 in one year in secret service, and comparing these with the ridiculously small sums that have for a great number of years been habitually spent by English Governments, it is impossible to have the omniscience which the noble Earl seems to regard as the necessary attribute of Her Majesty's Government. . . . . .

. . . . . I do not believe in the perfection of the British Constitution as an instrument of war. As an instrument of peace it has not yet met its match, but for purposes of war there is more to be said. If you look back over the present century you will see there have been four occasions on which the British Government has engaged in war. On each occasion the opening of these wars was not prosperous, and on each occasion the Government of the day and the officers in command were assailed with the utmost virulence of popular abuse. These were the Walcheren expedition, the Peninsular War, the Crimean War, and now the South African War. . . . . .

. . . . . But the moral I wish to draw from this uniformity of experience is that it is not the extraordinary folly or feebleness of particular Ministers or generals with which you have to deal, which is the sole cause of your reverses. There must be something else. We cannot have been so unlucky as to have fought four times and to have lighted upon the most incompetent and worthless Ministers that the world has ever produced. It is evident there is something in your machinery that is wrong, and that leads me to accept with a very doubting mind the glowing eulogism which the noble Earl passed upon the fighting qualities of the British Constitution. I am inclined to doubt these qualities, and I will recommend to the meditation of the noble Lord these considerations. The art of war has been studied on the continent of Europe with a thoroughness and self-devotion that no other science has commanded, and at the end we find ourselves surrounded by five great military Powers, and yet on matters of vital importance we pursue a policy wholly different from those military Powers. Do not understand for a moment that I am guilty of such profanity as to blame the British Constitution. I am not. I am pointing out that in this matter we enjoy splendid isolation. Of course, first and foremost stands conscription, and no one imagines, even among the youngest of us, that he will ever live to see conscription adopted in this country. Then comes the employment as experts of persons sitting in Parliament exercising power over the military administration, who are named by the Government, but who have not to obtain the approval of the electors and the constituencies. It is an important and very difficult question. Then there is the big question of promotion by seniority, a delicate subject; but I doubt if you will find that promotion by seniority prevails in any of the great armies of Europe to the extent it prevails here. Then there is that matter of secret service to which I have already referred. There is no other country which is content to protect itself with so slight a supply of funds as our own; and last of all I feel I am laying my hand on the sacred feature of the Constitution when I say there is the Treasury. At the present time I feel assured that the powers of the Treasury have been administered with the greatest judgment, and the greatest consideration, and do not imagine for a moment that I support the idiotic attacks which have been made on the present Chancellor of the Exchequer.[27] He is a Minister who has filled the office with the greatest consideration to the powers of the Treasury; but I say that the exercise of its powers in governing every department of the Government is not for the public benefit. The Treasury has obtained a position in regard to the rest of the departments of the Government that the House of Commons obtained in the time of the Stuart dynasty. It has the power of the purse, and by exercising the power of the purse it claims a voice in all decisions of administrative authority and policy. I think that much delay and many doubtful resolutions have been the result of the peculiar position which, through many generations, the Treasury has occupied. Do not imagine for a moment that I say it is in any way due to those with whom I have had the honour of sitting in the Cabinet. Now I notice these things because I was stimulated to it by the enthusiasm—what I call the 1688 enthusiasm—which has animated the mind of the noble Lord. I do not think that the British Constitution as at present worked is a good fighting machine. I have stated that it is unequalled for producing happiness, prosperity, and liberty in time of peace; but now, in time of war, when great Powers with enormous forces are looking at us with no gentle or kindly eye on every side, it becomes us to think whether we must not in some degree modify our arrangements in order to enable ourselves to meet the dangers that at any moment may arise......

. . . . . I do not say that the danger may not be easily exaggerated. Many a country has begun a great war with difficulties of the kind.

[27] Sir Michael Hicks Beach.

We have only to look at what the Northern States of America went through at the beginning of the Civil War, to see how easy it would be to draw a mistaken inference from the reverses with which we have been met at the opening of this war. We have every ground to think that if we set ourselves heartily to work, and exert all the undoubted instruments of power we possess, we shall bring this war to a satisfactory conclusion. I think we must defer the pleasing task of quarrelling among ourselves until that result has been obtained. We have a work that now appeals to us as subjects of the Queen—as Englishmen; and it must throw into shadow the ancient claim, the well-known and acknowledged claim, which party expedience has upon the action of all our statesmen. The noble lord has spoken of what men have said in the other House. I confess I saw with some regret that a noble lord of great position is about to bring this great issue into a party conflict. It is much to be regretted. The only place where he will create sympathy, where he will arouse enthusiasm, is at Pretoria. Our object must be to retrieve ourselves as rapidly as possible from the situation into which we have got. We are in this position. It is worse than many we have gone through before, for we are repelling men who have invaded our territory, and the reverses we have suffered are in consequence of our inability to drive them back. That is a position which cannot last. Remember that this Empire which we sustain is a valuable, splendid, but also a very responsible possession to support. If anything happens to tear asunder the great continental countries, by the mere force of their geographical juxtaposition, they must come together again, and the evil will be repaired. There is not in our Empire any coercing or retaining force which will answer the same end; and unless we can sink all lesser issues, unless we take all smaller passions into the one great duty of sustaining our country in this crisis, we shall run the danger of convulsions which will certainly tarnish its lustre, and perhaps menace its integrity.

INDEX

Index

Aberdare, Lord, 355
Aberdeen, Lord, 139, 195
Adams, John Quincy, 12
Adderley, Sir C., 232, 265
Afghanistan, 131, 245, 247, 248, 285, 286
Africa, 131, 166, 169, 173, 244, 245, 285, 286, 316, 317, 348, 352, 353, 354, 355; slave trade in, 131, 166, 169, 173; way to India, 244; political misadventures in, 245; annexation in, 285, 286; war in, 316, 317; partition of, 348, 352, 353, 354, 355
Alroy, 192
America (United States), 17, 51, 105, 123, 141, 148, 149, 167, 168, 173, 175n, 226, 227, 228, 235, 236, 256, 267, 270, 289, 290, 296, 299, 304, 316, 323, 363; government in the United States, 17; export of gold to United States, 105; help to British seamen, 141; problem with states, 148; Negroes in, 167, 168, 173, 175n; Constitution of the United States, 226, 227, 228, 323; Civil War in, 363; Civil War claims, 235, 236, 256; cotton famine from, 267; war period, 270; intervention in, 289, 290; disorder in, 296; invitation to monetary conference from, 299; gold discovery in, 304; potato blight in, 123; Spanish-American difficulties, 51; Spanish-American War, 316
American colonies, 4, 292
American Revolution, 5, 18, 145
Anne, Queen, 24, 35, 36

Anti-Corn Law League, 93, 204, 205, 209
Army, 52, 65, 131, 234, 257, 270-72, 279, 362; Wellington in, 52; oaths, 65; Indian, 131; as institution, 234, 257; reform of, 270-72, 279; conscription, 362
Ashley, Lord, 212, 213
Asia, 205, 247, 248, 284, 286, 353; lack of civilization in, 205; effect of liberal policy upon, 247, 248; British rule in, 284, 286; rivalry in, 353
Association for the Advancement of Science, 317
Attwood, T., 198, 202
Augher, 59
Augustenburg, Duke of, 180, 182
Australia, 220, 303, 304, 313
Austria, 35, 157, 180, 183, 184, 185, 284

Baines, E., 264, 269
Balfour, A. J., 302
Balkans, 196, 258
Ballot (secret), 85, 179, 257, 270, 274, 275, 276, 278
Bank (of England), 79, 80, 93, 105-16, 238
Bankes, H., 30, 31
Barbadoes, 72
Baring, A., 34
Barttelot, Sir W., 294
Beach, Sir M. Hicks, 294, 362
Belgium, 138, 182, 290
Belfast, 290
Bentham, J., 95
Bentinck, Lord G., 195
Berlin, 182, 196, 246, 247, 315, 348
Bexley, Lord, 80

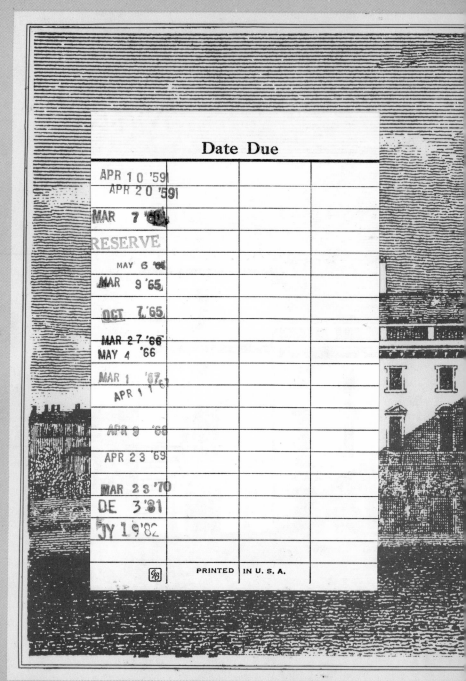

The Houses of